Latin American Law

M.C. Mirow

Latin American Law

A HISTORY OF

PRIVATE LAW AND INSTITUTIONS

IN SPANISH AMERICA

UNIVERSITY OF TEXAS PRESS

AUSTIN

Requests for permission to reproduce material from this work should be sent to Permissions, University of Texas Press, P.O. Box 7819, Austin, TX 78713-7819.

∞ The paper used in this book meets the minimum requirements of ANSI/NISO Z39.48-1992 (R1997) (Permanence of Paper).

Library of Congress Cataloging-in-Publication Data

Mirow, Matthew C. (Matthew Campbell), 1962–
Latin American law : a history of private law and institutions in Spanish America / M. C. Mirow.— 1st ed.
        p.   cm.
Includes bibliographical references and index.
ISBN 0-292-70232-9 (cloth : alk. paper)
1. Civil law—Latin America—History.   2. Justice, Administration of—Latin America—History.   I. Title.
KG125.M57   2004
346.8'009—dc22   2003020986

TO ANGELA, CAMILA, AND ANDREA

CONTENTS

LIST OF ILLUSTRATIONS

No other person has guided my approach to legal history as much as John Baker, and I thank him for his support and guidance. I am especially indebted to William Nelson, the NYU Colloquium on Legal History, and the NYU School of Law, which supported my research there. Alain Wijffels has constantly encouraged my work. I thank him for his friendship and his willingness to share his expertise in the history of the *ius commune*. Bernard Rudden gave wise advice at several crucial moments of this project, and I shall always remember his kind words of encouragement.

Numerous others, of course, have provided help in many ways. I delight in thanking Juan Aguirre, Richard Amelung, Tom Baker, Lauren Benton, William Hamilton Bryson, Charles Bouchard, Jonathan Bush, Jorge Esquirol, Phil Gavitt, Alejandro Guzmán, Richard Helmholz, Michael Hoeflich, Clive Holmes, Iván Jaksić, Mark Lambert; Abelardo Levaggi, Mon Yin Lung, Ian Magedera, Monica Ortale, Ken Parker, Jonathan Pratter, Janet Reinke, Francisco Reyes, Carlos Rosenkrantz, John Frederick Schwaller, Paul Shore, Victor Uribe-Uran, Richard Valantasis, Consuelo Varela, Dan Wade, and Mike Widener. Jonathan Miller and another reader for the University of Texas Press made excellent comments for improving the text. Lauren Benton corrected numerous errors of substance and style with skill and wisdom. Jack Rummel superbly edited the manuscript, and Theresa May, Rachel Chance, Lynne Chapman, Allison Faust, Laura Young Bost, and Nancy Bryan of the Press made publishing this book a pleasure. I thank these readers for their expertise, thoughtfulness, and care. Errors, whether from rejecting some of their suggestions or from other sources, are mine.

I have been privileged to be associated with several institutions that have valued and fostered my work on many levels. My dean, Leonard Strickman, has provided the utmost support, encouragement, and friendly advice for which I am grateful. In like manner, David Abulafia, John Attanasio, Manuel José Cepeda Espinosa, Mary Doyle, Peter Gray, Russell Osgood, John Sexton, Tom Read, and Sir William Wade are owed my thanks.

The following institutions have provided essential sources for this work: Archivo General de la Nación, Bogotá; Biblioteca Nacional, Bogotá; Cambridge University Library; Florida International University; Newberry Library, Chicago; NYU Law Library; Rice University Library; St. Louis University; Spencer Library, University of Kansas; Tarlton Law Library, University of Texas; Universidad de los Andes; Universidad Pontificia Bolivariana; University of Miami; and Yale Law Library. I express thanks to the following for funding aspects of my work related to this book: the National Endowment for the Humanities, St. Louis University Law School, the Beaumont Fund of St. Louis University, and South Texas College of Law. I thank Fr. Boniface Ramsey, Bro. Damian McCarthy, and the Friars of St. Vincent Ferrer Priory, New York, for their generous hospitality.

My family, near and far, deserves the most thanks. The Mesa Francos of Medellín, the Pages of Cambridge, the Unraus of Los Angeles, and the Mirows of Denver have unquestioningly bolstered me throughout this undertaking. I thank my parents, Gregory and Shirley Mirow. My father also directly contributed to this work by drawing the handsome illustrations and maps. This book would not have been possible without the unfailing encouragement and support of my family, to whom I dedicate this work.

This book aims to provide a brief introduction to the history of private law and legal institutions in Spanish-speaking Latin America from the colonial period to the twenty-first century. The need for this work can be seen in the scant attention law is given in standard treatments of Latin American history. Latin Americanists, however, are increasingly turning to court records and legal documents as sources, and it is hoped that this work will provide needed legal background as social, political, economic, and environmental historians explore these vastly underused and extremely important sources. Lawyers, law students, and law professors will also find this survey useful for understanding the place of law in contemporary Latin American society. The historical foundations of legal practices, viewpoints, and attitudes will become increasingly important as the United States develops ever-growing economic, educational, social, and cultural ties to Latin America. This book is also written for legal historians. The time has not yet come to write a synthetic social history of Latin American law, but this work provides an essential platform of institutional and mostly autonomous legal history on which more critical histories may be constructed. The wide gap between law as written and law as practiced in Latin America dates back at least to the early colonial period, and perhaps this work's greatest weakness is that it necessarily relies on and depicts so much of the former. Some would even question the usefulness of such a one-sided legal history. But it is from the springboard of law-as-written, the "bookish law," presented here that others will be able to dive more gracefully and more effectively into the parchments, papers, archives, and records of lawyers, judges, courts, families, businesses, and governmental entities.

As a general and first exploration of relatively uncharted waters, this work sets out a framework for further investigation and criticism; it seeks to be a first step rather than the last word. On many topics this work raises more questions than it solves, but this reflects the general state of scholarship in the area. By revealing areas in the history of Latin American private law that have not been addressed by scholars, this work seeks to lead others to answer even the most basic questions concerning legal change and development in Latin America. Thus portions of this work simply show how little is known about certain topics and areas of Latin American law, such as the system of civil liability and tort law or the development of legal structure of business organizations.

In this light, I recognize that problems abound. Cross-country generalizations and regional studies are problematic, as is the exclusion of non-

Spanish-speaking countries and the uneven present literature on which this study draws. For example, the legal history of the Spanish colonial period, *derecho indiano*, is reasonably well documented, and generalizations are more readily made when one central authority governed the entire region.[1] The historiography of law in Latin America is itself a fascinating and wide-open field that is not addressed here, and yet I have tried to be aware of the political environment in which my secondary sources were produced. Painting with a broad brush is dangerous, and in this work I have felt the painful uneasiness that accompanies simplification and compression. Where possible I have translated words and terms into English where there seems to be no loss of meaning or legal significance. For some terms I have retained the Spanish, and definitions may be found in the glossary.

This book uses a classical chronological method of presenting the materials. After a brief prologue describing indigenous law, the work breaks into a tripartite structure based on the following periods: colonial, independence and early republic, and the twentieth century. Within each part, several similar topics are addressed, including courts, legal profession, sources of law, personal status, land and inheritance, and commercial law. Each part also contains chapters that do not carry forward these general topics but instead select a few important developments or institutions from each period. For example, the colonial part contains a chapter on slavery, the independence part contains a chapter on codification, and the twentieth-century part contains a chapter on land reform.

In attempting to set out more than five hundred years of legal development, the work does not adopt one thesis or theory about legal change. If it were to do so, much of the introductory and general nature of the work would be lost in favor of rallying support for a particular viewpoint that could be consistently argued for such a large period. Surely, this is the type of work this book hopes to inspire, perhaps through the exasperation of those who want a unified theory of legal development and change. The work, however, has been guided by several themes within each part and also some overarching themes, and these may be helpful to readers approaching the text. One theme is the way private law expresses political and social power; rules of private law and their supporting institutions respond to changing social needs, external influences, and internal pressures. Thus, throughout this work, we see that foreign influences, inequality, institutions such as the church, and the demands of economic power shape private law. These themes all come into play in the course of the development of private law in Latin America.

The brief prologue is here to remind us that law was present before European contact, and that such systems of law both informed and affected colonial and even present-day law. For the colonial period, private law facilitated economic extraction from the colonies and sought to replicate Spanish society in a new setting while accommodating new legal objects. In the independence period, private law responded to new republican values and nationalism through substantive changes in rules and through codification based on European models. For the twentieth century, private law responded to the increasing demands of national commerce and social advances. An important shift noted during this work is a decrease in the importance of imported private law from Europe as a source and an increase in domestic developments, although still often informed by North American and international private law.

Some themes reach across all parts of this work. First, written law matters. Even in countries where there is a wide gap between written law and practiced law, written law is a starting place, a mark of aspirations, and an organizing structure. To note shifts, influences, and transplants in law and its sources is not the final aim of legal history; it is but a necessary step toward more exacting studies.

Second, private law matters. Even the very term *private law* may be problematic for some readers. In this work, I use the term to group those areas of the law that concern relationships among individuals and legal entities and to exclude the relationship of individuals to the state or the structure of the state. Although the term lacks precision and may be inaccurate and at times almost anachronistic as applied to precolonial and colonial law, it remains, at its core, a useful term and distinction. Even in the colonial period, the law governing disputes between individuals and structuring private property and business was a defined body of law. Certainly, aspects of the state and "public law" impacted these activities, but that does not mean that the distinction crumbles.

Private law and the mechanisms for enforcing it touch the daily lives of people. Private law constructs and reflects political power, economic power, and social structures. With proper enthusiasm, lawyers and scholars have recently been exploring other important aspects of Latin American law, especially constitutional law, criminal tribunals, and international human rights and humanitarian law. Nonetheless, private law has been a somewhat neglected subject. Land, inheritance, ownership, contracts, and business dealings are important facets as well. This study should contribute some ideas about these topics to the larger discussion.

Latin American Law

Texcocan supreme legal tribunal.

| | | | | | | | | | | | | | | | | | | | | | | | | | | | | | | | | | | | | | | | | | | | | | | |

Prologue

INDIGENOUS LAW

L AW, in one form or another, preceded the landing of the Spanish. These indigenous legal systems present a vast and relatively unexplored topic. Rather than attempt to synthesize a description of these systems, in this Prologue I want to remind the reader that the Spanish colonial system was both erected alongside and often constructed over existing indigenous legal structures of varying sophistication and abilities. Although usually obscuring indigenous law completely, some colonial Spanish institutions adopted or coexisted with indigenous legal developments.

Serving only as an example of the possible complexity of indigenous law at the time of Spanish contact, Aztec law has been sufficiently studied to provide at least a general sketch of its principal contours.[1] The legal system of the Aztec state of Texcoco in the fifty years before the Spanish arrival provides a good example because this was an area of early Spanish contact and conquest. It is, however, atypical in its complexity and level of development.

In the fifteenth and early sixteenth centuries, the Triple Alliance of Texcoco, Tenochtitlán, and Tlacopan formed an Aztec Empire that shared and combined the governmental functions we think of today as political, administrative, and judicial. These functions were carried out through a hierarchical monarchy, supported by the pillars of tribute, war, and land.[2] The alliance covered areas in the modern Mexican states of Hidalgo, Puebla, Veracruz, Guerrero, and Oaxaca and used various military, social, and familial methods to maintain and to expand its power and influence. The area under Texcocan control had about half a million inhabitants of several ethnic groups at the time of Spanish contact.[3]

At the highest level of Texcocan legal authority was the ruler and his council of fourteen advisers. Below this, four councils dealt with important aspects of government organized by subject; they were the Council of Music, Arts, and Sciences (associated with the priesthood); the War Council; the

Treasury Council; and the Supreme Legal Council.[4] The existence of this separate supreme legal tribunal, along with an appellate court structure and a trained judiciary, indicates the prominence of law in Aztec society.[5] Indeed, the Aztecs had appellate tribunals with judges, litigants, and courtrooms, and even a calendar requiring the speedy resolution of cases. Jerome Offner summarized these aspects from several early and conflicting sources and has found the following elements of the Texcocan legal system in place during the last decades of Aztec independence:

1. A Supreme Legal Council existed in Texcoco, made up of at least twelve judges with territorial jurisdiction whose decisions could be appealed to at least two higher judges, who sentenced only with the approval of the ruler.
2. A close kinsman of the Texcocan ruler was president of the legal council.
3. At least half of the judges were drawn from the nobility.
4. The jurisdictional units of the judges were six and/or fifteen in number.
5. The legal council occupied two large rooms or one large room divided into two parts.
6. General councils were held every ten to twelve days, and every eighty days; all cases pending were settled at these latter councils.[6]

The Supreme Judicial Council had a comprehensive civil and criminal jurisdiction. "Crimes and disputes involving homosexuality, treason, sumptuary regulations, adultery, theft, drunkenness, slaves, property, lands, and the statuses of and differences between offices all came under the jurisdiction of this council."[7] Although the Council on Music, Art, and Sciences had some jurisdiction over crafts and thus over defective products, and although merchants exercised some limited jurisdiction over trade, the Supreme Judicial Council was the central tribunal with jurisdiction not only over commoners and nobles, but also over merchants, craftsmen, soldiers, and priests.[8]

There were other legal forums below the Supreme Judicial Council. For example, local lords of the empire exercised a jurisdiction over their nonnoble subjects, and separate legal institutions existed for nobles and commoners, even to the extent that certain lower courts for the two classes were located in different cities, whose decisions were then reviewable in the legal center Texcoco.[9] Individual towns also had courts, which were subordinate to regional judicial districts. Below the town level each ward, *calpulli*, had a level on which legal matters were addressed.[10] Although evidence is lacking for Texcoco, at least in neighboring Tenochtitlán the head of the ward had a jurisdiction over "marital disputes and could even order a divorce and divisions of property," but the overall nature of the legal institutions of the *calpullis* are unknown.[11]

The procedure of Aztec law was solemn and oral with witnesses swearing to tell the truth "upon the earth goddess by placing a finger in the earth and then putting it to their tongue. The verb 'to swear' in Nahuatl, accordingly, is *tla-qua* (to eat earth)."[12] Accused persons were not permitted to defend themselves, but generally "judges used confrontation between litigants to learn more about the case."[13] Decisions were reached speedily, and an eighty-day limit was the maximum allotted time for any case.[14] Scientific or at least empirical fact-finding seems to have been a part of legal procedure. "Indeed, religious beliefs entered into court procedure only to help ensure that witnesses told the truth and to provide ex post facto divine approval for the passing of sentences in serious cases."[15]

There is little evidence to establish the existence of a group of individuals trained to serve exclusively as advocates in the courts.[16] But considering the complexity of the legal rules, institutions, and a trained judiciary, "advocates of some kind might well have existed in the pre-Conquest Texcocan legal system."[17] There was, however, clearly a special place in society for the judiciary. A separate school was dedicated to the training of judges. Thus, the judicial office, in society and government, was well defined and subject to rules ensuring its impartiality, honesty, and public performance. Judges were punished for hearing cases privately or for accepting gifts or bribes. Special lands were set aside to ensure judicial compensation by the state. Judges were assisted in their duties by bailiffs and scribes or painters.[18]

Grounded in assertions of its antiquity, Texcocan law was rigidly applied in a legalistic manner. Indeed, the earliest recorded Aztec legal code addressed the concerns of a hunter and gatherer society, and by the time of first Spanish contact, substantial rules were provided by a code of eighty laws divided into four parts, one for each council. These were recorded in pictorial glyphs.[19]

This system of courts and laws served a hierarchy of Aztec society that included an hereditary nobility, priests, merchants, and artisans. The divide between nobles and commoners was of great legal importance because one's status would determine not only what tribunal had jurisdiction but also, in certain areas of law, the applicable substantive rule of law.[20] Below wealthier commoners in society, the ordinary agricultural workers lived as members of communal landholding groups or wards, *capullis*. These workers also paid tribute and provided military service.

Women in Aztec society owned property, and some women merchants were reportedly quite wealthy. An accounting of property each spouse brought to a marriage for division on divorce also indicates that women were viewed as property owners. Daughters of nobility were given lands for their support, and despite a lack of direct evidence, it appears that women also inherited property and made effective transfers of property on death.[21] Thus, women possessed certain rights over property, but these rights might have been mediated through the oldest male among siblings acting as a guardian.[22]

Below nobles and commoners were serflike agricultural workers tied to the land, and slaves.[23] In comparison to its European counterpart, Aztec slavery appears to have been more fluid. Slavery might result from capture in battle, being sold by one's parents, selling oneself, or as punishment for crime. A family might contract to supply a slave to a noble and fulfill the obligation through rotation. Children of slaves were free and manumission was possible through a legal act of the owner, marrying one's owner, purchasing one's freedom, escaping, or obtaining royal asylum.[24] Owners had to treat slaves well, but after a number of warnings, an owner could punish a slave by putting a wooden collar around his neck, selling him to another, and even selling him for eventual human sacrifice.[25] Slavery encompassed a wide range of social and property relationships under Aztec law; the status of some slaves was based on contractual agreement, but other slaves were considered property. Some slaves "could also have families, property, and even other slaves. . . . Slaves who had been enslaved as a legal punishment and who thus had no contractual relationship with their owners, and collared slaves, who had violated the terms of their contract, were undoubtedly the personal private property of their owners, and so certainly suffered under the most severe and restrictive forms of slavery."[26]

Aztec law regulated marriage. Attempted marriages with close relatives were prohibited and punished as offenses, although in some areas it was a permitted practice to take the wife of a deceased father, excepting one's mother, or of a deceased brother. Adultery was highly regulated, with numerous levels of offence depending on such factors as the class and sex of the offender. Polygamous marriages were possible, especially among nobles, and one of the wives was identified as legitimate for the purposes of inheritance so that the son of this wife would inherit the father's property.[27] A brother customarily married his sibling's widow. Divorce for cause existed, and the one found to have blame lost half his or her goods. On divorce, sons remained with the father and daughters with the mother. Widows and divorced wives were required to wait before remarriage.[28]

The ruler of Texcoco distributed land claimed through an established ritual of possession as conquest bounty.[29] The law regarding land tenure was complex and included elements of both communal and private ownership.[30] The type of holding available to an individual depended on the status of the owner. For commoners, "on the lower legal levels of the empire, land might have been bought, sold, rented, and passed on to heirs within and between wards with little more than perfunctory review—or with no review at all—by political officials."[31] Even though these lands were treated as private property, the ward theoretically also owned them communally. Lands held by nobles could be either held individually and freely alienable or only for their benefit and inalienable. Certain lands were attached to particular political offices, such as lands used to support a lesser ruler, or institution, such as palace lands, or held for a particular purpose, such as war lands. A system of allocating both tribute and serf or commoner labor on lands made some property more profitable than other.[32] Offner's work on land tenure destroys a common misperception of preconquest universal communal ownership; "Monolithic views of a simplistic individual usufruct, communal tenure of land by all commoners in Central Mexico, need no longer be taken seriously."[33]

Even landholding by commoners was not uniform or simple. "The landholding patterns indicate individual tenancy of land, land inheritance and concomitant fractionation, along with the acquisition of extra land, perhaps via rental or purchase agreements, by individuals and households."[34] Scattered and fractionated landholding was not unique to commoners. Dispersed landholding by rulers on an individual basis increased political stability by tying their wealth to the interests and stability of regions other than their own.[35]

In addition to land, houses and personalty were recognized as property. In some areas of the empire, groups of related individuals, rather than nuclear families, had various interests in houses. In other areas, however, nuclear families predominated. Both men and women owned personal property and often passed the property on according to gendered activities associated with particular types of property.[36] For commoners, who often lived communally in residential structures, inheritance patterns were relatively simple: "The common people divided their property equally (in principle) among the offspring of the deceased."[37] It is unclear, but likely, that "offspring" included daughters.[38] For nobles, the nature of inheritance was more complex and apparently followed political succession patterns favoring passage of property from father to son. Other sources indicate that brothers each took their father's property in succession in order of birth. If there were no person to take the property, it escheated to the local ruler or town who then distributed the property to others.[39]

Although Aztec society did not have money, a complex system of barter was in place, and commercial disputes were sometimes subject to specialized tribunals.[40] Trade covered substantial distances and the need for specialized tribunals reflects both the complexity of issues that could arise as well as the frequency of disputes. Aztec women played an active part in sedentary trade, such as the production and trade of cloth.[41] Numerous methods led to effective debt collection, with imprisonment and slavery as possible punishments, the latter being used to offset the debt due. Debts were inherited, but never to the extent that the surviving spouse and children faced slavery. The existence of laws regarding interest is uncertain.[42]

The Aztec Empire was not the only pre-Columbian civilization to have a legal system with significant attributes; the Incas of Peru also had a complex legal system. At the time of Spanish contact, the Inca Empire governed from 4 to 8 million inhabitants from its imperial center Cuzco.[43] Although a hierarchical structure of government existed, there is little to indicate that separate courts, judges, or legally trained representatives existed apart from the regular combined governmental duties of Inca officials.[44] The application of substantive rules of law varied according to the social position of those involved in the crime or dispute.[45] Agricultural workers were required to supply services to the Inca in a system of rotational work called the *mita,* and some workers, *yanacona,* were tied to the Inca or the nobility and lacked freedom.[46] Women had a much lower status than men in Inca society, and in some circumstances were treated as inheritable property.[47] Indeed, the Inca owned some women and distributed them for religious purposes or as personal rewards. Others remained the property of the Inca.[48] Marriage and upper class polygamy were regulated and adultery punished by law.[49]

Landholding and inheritance were important aspects of the Inca legal system. Land was held for the Inca (government), the Sun (religion), and the people to be worked by collective units, called *ayllus.* Land was also held by individual grantees who received the land as favor from the Inca.[50] Furthermore, land might be attached to particular government offices, which because of the hereditary nature of the office, kept these lands in a particular family.[51] Personal property was inheritable, and land was inherited depending on the type of land, the status of the owner, and local variation. Male heirs such as sons, brothers, and nephews were favored.[52]

Immediately after the conquest, law had an important function in mediating between Indian and Spanish culture and cultural differences were expressed through disputes concerning property or family structure.[53] Certain aspects of Spanish legal culture matched closely with preconquest customary law, including tribute payments, jointly held lands, slavery and other forms of forced labor, and special courts for particular classes of litigants. For example, the Spanish colonial *ejido,* in which lands were used in common, would have been similar to the preconquest forms of communal ownership. Spanish tribute and forced labor systems had preconquest elements or parallels, such as the Incan *mita.*[54] Nonetheless, causation is difficult to determine.[55] Furthermore, Spanish legislation did not set out to destroy all indigenous legal customs, but specifically stated that such customs would govern to the extent they were compatible with the crown and the church.[56]

Thus, some Latin American societies had substantial legal structures in place at the time of Spanish conquest. There may be questions about whether the Aztec system was an exception among the cultures and civilizations present before the arrival of the Spanish, but recent anthropological scholarship has done much to expand our appreciation of the subtleties and complexities of legal systems based on oral, customary traditions, let alone those incorporating established legal institutions, personnel, courtrooms, and documentary evidence. Spaniards landed on a continent with significant indigenous legal traditions.

Part I

Colonial Period

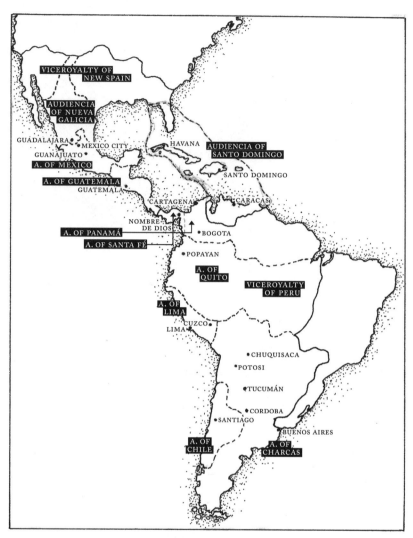

Colonial Latin America. The Audiencias of Spanish America.

Conquest and Colonization

Despite its fundamental role in shaping and defining society,
Spanish colonial law has remained something of a
mystery to modern scholars.

CHARLES R. CUTTER

The Legal Culture of Northern New Spain, 1700–1810

L AW and legal institutions served the crown's needs of conquest and colonization.[1] This appears self-evident to those working in Latin American colonial history, and yet few have set out to demonstrate how or why this is true. Recent scholarship, however, has begun to tackle the function of law as a mechanism of political and cultural hegemony in Latin America.[2] Private law served numerous purposes in colonial society, and noting several important aspects here may help to characterize the sources, rules, and institutions discussed in this work.

First, law was an essential tool of royal economic and social control over distant possessions. A massive bureaucracy sought, and in part succeeded, to extend and replicate Spanish royal structures and Spanish society that supported the law. Law and the administration of justice were not just important functions of government, they served as its center.[3] Thus colonial Spanish law attempted to manage in detail vast territories, which, in practice, because of their distance from the peninsula, were able to exercise substantial autonomy.[4]

Second, law facilitated the extraction of wealth from the colonies by Spain. Law regulated trade between the colonies and the peninsula and between the colonies themselves. The extraction of precious metals and the allocation of forced labor by Indians and slaves for mining and agriculture were the subject of extensive legislation. All aspects of personal property, inheritance, landholding, and commercial activities were carefully controlled by peninsular law or laws crafted specifically for the colonies.

Third, law, legal institutions, and litigation were common elements in a shared Castilian mindset and were deeply embedded in daily affairs and activities. Although the precise nature of substantive laws or procedural and jurisdictional rules were not commonly understood, litigation in Castile was not limited to a few wealthy property holders, but rather extended as a social practice far into the middling and even lower classes. The Castilians were quite litigious.[5] Indeed, litigation was so common that one historian of Spain of this period suggested that the very first step in researching any contemporary individual is to search the records of the courts because everyone was involved in a lawsuit at one point or another. "An educated Castilian was one who, if not expert in, was at least well acquainted with law, procedure, and legal reasoning."[6]

Fourth, Spanish colonial law had to accommodate and address new segments of society that did not exist or were extremely small in peninsular Spain. These included Indians, a substantial slave population, Creoles, peninsular Spaniards in the colonies, and people of all the racial and class strata resulting from the inevitable sexual unions across these often shifting or indefinite lines.

The colonial law responded to these political, economic, and societal demands. The basis of colonial private law was Spanish law, which must be briefly presented to understand its colonial manifestations.

Law in American Conquest

Law provided the very basis on which Spain claimed the ability to possess the new territories and to rule them. Spaniards asserted legal rights in the land from the very beginning, and Columbus used European legalistic means to assert the claim of his monarchs.[7] The origin of Spain's claim to the Indies was a series of papal bulls.[8] These set a territorial line between Spanish and Portuguese possessions and defined the broad grant of powers given to Spain. They provided the starting point leading to the Treaty of Tordesillas (June 7, 1494) in which Spain and Portugal agreed to a line dividing territories at 370 leagues west of Cape Verde.[9]

Because the crown evangelized for the church, it took over many rights and privileges cautiously guarded by the church elsewhere. Building on the Crusades, the "reconquest" of the peninsula, and the significant rights the church ceded in Portugal's colonization of Africa, the Spanish crown's royal patronage (*Patronato Real*) of the church meant that it collected the church's revenues, controlled appointments to ecclesiastical positions, and filtered information between its colonies and Rome.[10] In 1501, Castile received the right to the church's tithes for its evangelizing the Indies by Pope Alexander VI. In 1508, Spain was granted the universal patronage of the church in the Indies and the right to present bishops and other benefices. In 1543, it was given the right to reorganize and change ecclesiastical jurisdiction.[11] The crown cautiously guarded these valuable economic and political powers. For example, in 1574 the *Ordenanzas del Patronazgo* mediated the claims of regular and secular clergy, dramatically increasing the power of the latter in settled areas and removing the orders' control from many others.[12] The evangelical justification was reflected in the language used to describe Spanish activities in Latin America. Contemporary sources speak of "pacification" and "population" of lands rather than "conquest." And in theory, the Indies were not "colonies" but carried the name "provinces" or other similar political subdivision.[13]

The theological gymnastics brought about by conquest and colonization, particularly as Spaniards subdued Indians with religious conversion as justification, have been discussed elsewhere. While the positions of church officials and theologians like Sepúlveda, Las Casas, Vitoria, and Suárez are an important part of the intellectual history of the conquest and treatment of Indians, they tell us little about the function of private law in conquest and colonization.[14] Those involved with private law did not necessarily remove themselves from the fray; Gregorio López, who produced a gloss of the extremely influential collection of private law, the *Siete Partidas,* found the papal donation valid but condemned the war stemming from it. His gloss contributed to the crown's ordinances governing discovery.[15]

The *Requerimiento* (requirement) drafted by the Spanish jurist Juan López de Palacios Rubios, provides an interesting insight into the legal (legalistic) mind of the sixteenth-century Spaniard, a mentality that certainly surfaced in the application of private law.[16] The *Requerimiento* was a brief statement of the Spaniards' claim to the new lands read to Indians before battle. It required their submission to the authority of the church and Spanish crown. The results for disagreeing with the statement were spelled out in great detail:

But if you do not do this or if you maliciously delay in doing it, I certify to you that with the help of God we shall forcefully enter into your country and shall make war against you in all ways and manners that we can, and shall subject you to the yoke and obedience of the Church and of their highnesses; we shall take you and your wives and your children and shall make slaves of them, and as such shall sell and dispose of them as their highnesses command; and we shall take away your goods and shall do to you all the harm and damage that we can, as to vassals who do not obey and refuse to receive their lord and resist and contradict him; and we protest that the deaths and losses which shall accrue from this are your fault, and not that of their highnesses, or ours, or of these soldiers who come with us. And that we have said this to you and made this Requerimiento we request the notary here present to give us his testimony in writing, and we ask the rest who are present that they should be witnesses of this Requerimiento.[17]

Although it most likely usually fell on ears that did not understand Spanish, when it reached those who did understand through translation by those who had earlier contact with Spanish, it was sometimes met by disbelief and laughter which all too soon turned tragic. Some Indian responses unwittingly echoed contemporary Spanish theologians, who argued that the world was not the pope's to give.[18]

The very nature of exploration and conquest were defined in terms of private law rather than public rights and responsibilities. Explorers wishing to undertake conquest had to enter into a private contract with the crown called a *capitulación*, and these contracts were sometimes even prepared and executed after the fact. These carefully negotiated contracts provided for the political power a conquistador would have, how extensive his jurisdiction would be, and what rights he would have to Indian labor and precious metals. The three parts of the *capitulación* were a license to explore, an enumeration of the rights and obligations of the discoverer, and the conditional nature of these rights based on the discoverer's success. Success usually depended on founding a required number of cities in which the discoverer would distribute lands and houses, undertaking this without prejudicing the Indians, and maintain a residence there for usually between four and eight years. Various graduated titles, such as *adelantado, alcalde mayor,* or *corregidor,* were granted according to the number and size of municipalities established.[19] These titles were usually granted for life and might pass to a second or further generation.[20] For example, Columbus's *capitulación,* granting him the titles of admiral, viceroy, and governor, gave him one tenth of the precious products of his discoveries.[21] Because these titles were sometimes hereditary, a woman "accidentally" served as viceroy twice during the colonial period.[22]

Structuring exploration and colonization through private law and contractual obligations was an advantage to the crown because it did not have enough money to fund such activities on its own. Even if it were sufficiently wealthy to fund such expeditions, these undertakings were very risky, and the crown shifted the risk of failure to private hands. Similarly, if success was attained, the compensation for such success could be carved out of the newly discovered wealth and lands. It was easy to grant generous privileges out of property and territory whose value and quality were unknown. Once the potential for extracting tremendous wealth from the colonies was fully understood by the crown, it began to reconsider its earlier generosity.

After the first wave of explorers, the Board of Trade in Spain usually served as the representative of the crown, which by the mid sixteenth century was starting to question if it had ceded away too many important rights to this first group of adventurers. Addressing this growing royal concern, the Board of Trade began to renegotiate its position with the powerful colonial landholder rulers. Subject to royal confirmation, colonial authorities later could grant *capitulaciones* for further exploration and settlement. Similarly, as discussed later, such motives informed the attempts of the crown to limit the inheritability of the *encomiendas,* grants of forced labor by native populations.

Certain of its right to colonize under the church and having cleverly used contractual relationships to further its colonial ambitions, Spain set about standardizing its political and legal empire in the colonies. The importance of legal institutions and legal sources was clear to the crown in this endeavor.

Spanish Private Law on the Eve of Conquest

In the colonial period, the laws of the kingdom of Castile, as the kingdom claiming dominion over newly discovered territories, governed private law in Latin America. Only royal legislation specifically drafted for the Indies would provide controlling rules of law supplementing Castilian law. Thus the laws concerning family, successions, property, and contract, indeed all private law without supplemental legislation in colonial Latin America, were the laws of Castile.[23] It would be very tempting to dismiss the Castilian law of this period as a confused, overlapping mass of royal decrees, compilations, and other legislation. These royal legal materials were further subjected to continuous modification by special privileges held by, most notably, the church and religious bodies, but also by certain cities and regions, and the military. Merchants might also settle disputes using their own system of rules and institutions. Furthermore, forensic practices, highly influenced by the *ius commune* and natural law traditions of contemporary Spanish universities, make even the task of determining the law as written a substantial undertaking. Thus, Castilian law on the eve of the conquest was no simple matter. Nonetheless, a brief outline of its most important sources will inform the development of private law in the Spanish colonies.

Castilian private law, and thus colonial private law, was periodically compiled into various collections of legal materials.[24] These collections of Castilian law were the product of Iberian history and an increasing Castilian control of the peninsula. Because of the number of sources to be presented in this chapter, any treatment of their substantive rules of law will be taken up in the following chapters so that the general sweep of the various sources is not obscured by a discussion of the doctrinal changes any particular collection may have introduced.

After Roman forces left the Iberian Peninsula, the territory experienced several waves of invasions, until the Visigoths established themselves. They brought the collection of laws known as the Breviary of Alaric or the *Lex Romana Visigothorum* (506), substantially based on the Roman law found in the Theodosian Code.[25] In the mid seventh century, Visigoth rulers applied another collection of laws, called the *Lex Visigothorum, Fuero Juzgo,* or *Liber Judiciorum,* in the peninsula.[26] Islamic forces pushed the Visigothic leaders into isolated and mountainous areas where they developed some distinct legal institutions. In the southern coastal zones, the Franks invaded and applied their laws alongside the *Fuero Juzgo* for the Visigoths. It is likely such laws exerted a personal, rather than geographic, jurisdiction over those people belonging to a particular group. For the next three hundred years, the main cultural force on the peninsula was Islam, and although permanent influences can be seen in Spanish language, agriculture, commerce, and political organization, it appears little was shared concerning legal development.²⁷ This was in part due to the Muslim leaders' policy of maintaining the applicability of extant legal rules in place for the non-Muslim population.²⁸ From the mid eleventh century until the end of the fifteenth century, Christian military forces and agricultural settlers would slowly push Islam from the peninsula. Along with this "reconquest" came new sources of law, new ideas about political structure based in local autonomy, and new perceptions about how to reward those involved in military enterprises. Because the end of the reconquest period touches the beginning of exploration and colonization of Latin America, many reconquest notions about law and local power were put into play in the Indies.

To understand the new collections of laws arising from the reconquest, the system of *fueros,* local autonomous power and special privileges granted by a grateful crown, must be explained.²⁹ As groups of people and territories shifted from Islamic to Christian control through their cooperation with the crown, many were in a good position to request special privileges such as exemption from customary payments to the crown or the power to establish their own local laws. Sometimes these laws did not diverge greatly from Islamic law, maintaining certain societal expectations in private law matters. These grants of special privileges became known as *fueros,* and in time the term was expanded to mean a collection of laws. The *Fuero Viejo de Castilla* (c. 1248, final version 1356) is an important example of these laws, which favored the military interests fighting at the crown's behest. As local *fueros* developed and borrowed from each other, the crown also created its own collections called the *Fuero Real* (1250s), which was extended to various important cities probably as a means to unify and control the laws of regional power centers. Where a local or the royal *fuero* did not control, one of two regional *fueros* would provide a rule of law: in Castile, the *Fuero Viejo de Castilla;* in the rest of the area, the *Fuero Juzgo.*³⁰

With the rebirth of Roman law in Europe, Alfonso X (Alfonso the Wise) and his advisers, some of whom had studied in the center of thirteenth-century legal education, Bologna, drafted a new collection of laws. Indeed until the sixteenth century many Spanish lawyers received their legal training at this university, and a Spanish College was established there in 1369.³¹ Under the spell of Justinian's *Digest* and numerous commentaries on it, Alfonso's advisers produced a foundational text that would govern much of Spanish and Latin American private law for more than five hundred years, the *Siete Partidas* (1265).[32] Although the *Siete Partidas* was apparently drafted first as a model set of laws to be copied, and although it was later given status as a supplementary law, it was quickly appropriated as a source of first reference.[33] The *Siete Partidas* not only served royal interests by undermining the power of the *fueros,* but also provided substantial advantages to the interests of commerce and landed estates. It gave much more precise rules concerning commercial contracts and commercial law than the *fueros* and also provided for the entailing of landed estates into a primogeniture inheritance scheme.[34] In the sixteenth century, Gregorio López wrote glosses to the *Siete Partidas,* and this version was widely circulated in Latin America.[35]

With so many possible sources of law, rules were established to guide lawyers and judges on how to rank sources to determine the particular provision to apply in a given dispute. For example, in the first of a number of laws ranking authorities, the *Ordenamiento de Alcalá de Henares* (1348) provided that lawyers and judges should look first to the *Ordenamiento* itself, then the local and royal *fueros,* then the *Siete Partidas.*[36] This method of setting out the order of precedence of various sources through a separate law would remain a feature in Latin American law until codes replaced the Castilian sources in the mid nineteenth century.

This method also aided university-trained lawyers, who naturally gravitated toward the Roman and canon law as taught in the universities, to determine governing rules. With the consolidation of the kingdoms in 1479 brought by the earlier marriage of Isabel of Castile and Ferdinand of Aragon, the movement to central royal power led to various legislative reforms, which tried to replace and limit the use of the traditional sources of the *corpus iuris civilis,* its glosses and commentaries. The *Ordenanzas Reales de Castilla* (1480) and the *Leyes de Toro* (1505) are examples of this legislative activity.[37] The *Leyes de Toro,* later glossed by Antonio Gómez, resolved various doubts resulting from the multiplicity of sources available to provide rules of private law. Attempting to bolster the legal independence and control of the kingdom, the *Leyes de Toro* provided new laws concerning testaments by representatives, and the regulation of bequests and *mayorazgos* (entailed estates). It also attempted to prohibit the use of Roman law, which had been limited earlier in 1427 and 1499. The 1499 rule of citation permitted advocates to present only the biggest names in Roman and canon law—Bartolus, Baldus, Juan Andrés, and Panormitanus—as commentary sources. University training and the forensic usefulness of the full panoply of Roman and canon law sources made such attempts ineffective, and again in 1713 the Council of Castile stated that Roman law should be merely supplemental.[38] In 1741 the crown required that royal law be taught alongside Roman and canon law in the universities, and compliance was eventually accomplished by supplementing Roman law with royal law comparisons.

Numerous groups and activities were granted or created their own systems to provide rules and resolve disputes outside the general structure of the royal legislation. For example, commercial and maritime activities were regulated by specialized commercial tribunals (*consulados de comerciantes*), which often looked to maritime collections such as the *Roles de Olerón*, also known in Spanish as the *Fuero* or *Leyes de Layrón*, and the *Consulado del Mar* for resolving disputes. Merchants also operated under their own sets of commercial guidelines, such as the *Ordenanzas de Burgos*, a collection of rules mostly from the sixteenth century regulating trade and maritime insurance.[39] Agricultural disputes and interests might be mediated though a strong grangelike organization, the *Mesta*, and an organization with administrative and judicial control over the means of communication and transportation, the *Santa Hermandad*, also had an important jurisdiction. These special jurisdictions were also later adapted to Latin America.[40] Perhaps the most important source of private law not yet mentioned was the church and its system of canon law.[41]

Several compilations of laws were constructed in Spain during the colonial period and these often served as sources for private law in Latin America. Most important is the *Nueva Recopilación de Castilla* of 1567, containing more than four thousand laws in twelve volumes.[42] Building on the *Ordenanzas Reales de Castilla* (1480), a succession of lawyers worked toward this new *Recopilación;* they included López de Alcocer, Escudero, and López de Arrieta y Atienza.[43] The work was republished several times in the sixteenth century, expanded in the seventeenth and again in the eighteenth. Supplements to this work in the 1770s were separately compiled and are called *Autos acordados*. A new collection in 1805, the *Novísima Recopilación*, came so late in the colonial period that its use in and application to Latin America were minimal.[44]

As discussed in later chapters as they relate specifically to colonial law, these sources supplied the general rules governing property, land, inheritance, contracts, debts, obligations, and procedures for both Castile and its colonies. For these areas of law, little new legislation was enacted to govern problems or situations unique to the colonies. In other areas of the law, there were substantial changes. The sources of private law remained surprisingly stable throughout the conquest period, but new structures and institutions were needed to govern the colonies, and new courts were established to handle a mainstay of Castilian society, litigation, which was brought with the Spaniards to the soil of America.

Structures and Courts

THE political and social landscape of the colonies was covered with competing interest groups and factions. In fact, there was greater complexity in the colonies than in Spain. The colonies contained European-born Spaniards, Creoles, regular clerics, secular clerics, viceroys, archbishops, local ruling landholders, colonizers, Indians, city government officials, local royal authorities, soldiers, foreigners, slaves, merchants, miners, pirates, bandits, and smugglers. Different classes and races mixed and overlapped. All these inhabitants contributed to a complex whirl of social, economic, legal, and jurisdictional interaction.[1] The legal structures available to these individuals followed the general political structure of the empire, and perhaps some even larger regional structures.[2]

Slow transportation and communication between Spain and the colonies resulted from the great geographical distance between the two. Spanish institutions effectively bridged this vast space and governed a multitude of aspects of daily life with jealous, watchful specificity. The economic interests in Latin America were too great to neglect. The crown, usually through its delegated institutions, had to be informed of "virtually everything" that occurred in the colonies.[3] Not only was it kept informed, but it or its institutions made most of the decisions, almost always including the appointment of lower officials.[4] With the system's obsession with precision, attention to detail, and massive bureaucratic structures, some scholars have concluded that this administrative machinery of the Spanish colonies left a legacy of "bureaucratic confusion, administrative delay, mistrust of government officials, and disrespect for law."[5] Other scholars have concluded that the church and colonial royal institutions mostly provided stability, and their reduction in power or removal at independence caused governmental crises.[6] Some scholars have seen the presence of overlapping institutions and multiple conflicting standards in colonial administration as positive aspects of the colonial system. These institutions and rules provided both lower-level colonial flexibility through selective application and royal central authority through selective enforcement.[7]

Close royal supervision of the colonies has also been seen as one of the reasons why the Spanish colonies, upon independence, were unable quickly to create their own institutions of self-governance.[8] Furthermore, despite the appearance of centralized royal control, in regional centers there was often more than one tribunal in which litigants could bring suit. Jurisdictions frequently overlapped, and there were numerous specialized courts. The hierarchy and structure of these courts were complex, and yet they reflected the ability of the crown to govern and dispense justice to favored interests from afar.

The two most important colonial institutions were the Council of the Indies and the Board of Trade (Casa de Contratación), both in Spain. Both of these institutions functioned according to sets of rules, or ordinances, that were occasionally revised during the colonial period.[9] Originally part of the Council of Castile, the Council of the Indies gained separate status in 1524. The council at first had almost complete governmental control over the colonies. Its power was not limited to economic and secular affairs, but included the substantial authority to control the church by viewing, approving, or suppressing papal bulls and writs for the colonies under the crown's royal patronage.[10] Thus, in addition to its secular governmental functions, it had significant ecclesiastical authority in the colonies.[11] It had an appellate civil jurisdiction over *audiencia* cases exceeding a certain value and decisions of the Board of Trade.[12]

The council had three important sets of ordinances dating from 1542, 1571, and 1636. Functioning autonomously in judicial matters and grants of property in the Indies since the 1520s, the council established its judicial procedures in the 1542 ordinances, which required it to meet daily to determine cases. Cases of over five hundred pesos required three votes; under the limit, two votes. Its jurisdiction covered visitations of colonial officials, *repartimientos* of Indians, cases of *segunda suplicación,* and important civil cases.[13] The second set of ordinances was the result of royal scrutiny and reform. In 1569, the crown appointed a member of the General Council of the Inquisition, Juan de Ovando, to visit and inspect the council. As a result, he drafted a new set of ordinances for the council addressing not only its administration of spiritual affairs and the royal patronage, but also how the council should promulgate laws generally. These ordinances were approved in 1571.[14] The ordinances of 1636 increased personnel and salaries.[15]

Composed of high-level university-trained lawyers and clergy, the council had from six members in its early days to nineteen members by the mid seventeenth century.[16] Its membership and staff consisted of a president, a grand councilor, other councilors (including eight university-trained lawyer-councilors, according to the *Recopilación* of 1680), a legal advisor (*fiscal*), two secretaries, an assistant to the grand councilor, three *relatores*, a scribe of the court, four *contadores*, a general treasurer, two solicitor-fiscals, a *cronista mayor*, a *cosmógrafo*, a chair of mathematics, a *tasador de los procesos*, a lawyer, a *procurador de pobres*, a chaplain, four porters, and an *alguacil*.[17] The personnel of the council included a number of well-known lawyers and legal authors, including Gregorio López, the best-known commentator of the *Siete Partidas*, Juan de Solórzano Pereira, who wrote an important five-volume work on the status of Indians and colonial institutions called the *Política indiana*, and Antonio Rodríguez de León Pinelo, whose work was a precursor to the important collection of colonial laws known as the *Recopilación de las Indias*.[18] Solórzano Pereira and León Pinelo also served in colonial governing bodies, *audiencias*.[19] The council created a separate treasury committee (Junta de Hacienda de Indias) in 1575.[20] This only met a few times and was obsolete by 1604.[21] The council was reformed substantially under the Bourbons who governed Spain during the eighteenth century. With the creation of the universal secretary of the Indies in 1714, the council became a consultative body and judicial tribunal.[22] This new official often served as president to the council. A second minister of the Indies was added in 1787 to supervise justice matters. In the late 1770s, the council itself was divided into two chambers, one dealing with government and another with justice. After a short abolition by the Cortes of Cádiz in 1812, the council was restored in 1814, only to be finally abolished in 1834.[23]

A second important institution, the Board of Trade in Seville, ran all aspects of trade with the Latin American colonies, including taxation, legal disputes, import and export, gold imports, licenses of passage, and the administration of estates of decedents in the colonies. The board was established in 1503 and its first set of ordinances was prepared in 1510.[24] New ordinances for the board were put in place frequently; for example, in the sixteenth century, there were five sets of ordinances.[25] The board had a substantial judicial function and in 1510 a *juez letrado* (university-trained judge) was appointed to give legal advice to the board, which from 1511 assumed jurisdiction in civil and criminal matters associated with trade and navigation.[26] Its jurisdiction was expanded and defined again in 1539 to include all violations of its ordinances, local civil disputes touching on crown revenues, and crimes committed en route to America. Some of its decisions could be appealed to the Council of the Indies.[27] In 1772, the crown moved the board from Seville to Cádiz and, in light of dwindling trade and royal control of trade, the board was abolished in 1790.[28]

Within the colonies, the largest political subdivision was the viceroyalty, led by a viceroy, who represented the king in the territory. Viceroys were first appointed for Nueva España (area of Mexico) and Peru; two more were added in the eighteenth century for Nueva Granada (area of Colombia) and Río de la Plata (area of Argentina). Although the terms of viceroys varied considerably throughout the colonial period, five years was considered usual.[29] A viceroy was assisted by a personal secretariat; in earlier times consisting of a few secretaries and clerks, but by the late eighteenth century this had swelled in some instances to a staff of more than thirty members in five departments.[30]

Three institutions checked the viceroy's power: his *audiencia,* random royal inspections sent from the crown, and a routine accounting (*residencia*) at the end of his term.[31] Documents related to a viceroyalty included the instructions (*instrucciones*), a chronicle of his rule to instruct others (*memorias*), and a statement of who should serve on his death until a new viceroy was appointed (*pliego de mortaja*).[32] Some viceroys, such as Francisco de Toledo of Peru from 1569 to 1581, demonstrated exceptional legislative ability and left behind a record of substantial legal drafting. His ordinances addressing land tenure, Indian status, judicial procedure, and mining earned him the appellation of the "Peruvian Solon."[33]

Because the viceroy's legal activities as judge and legislator are emphasized here, it is noteworthy that in the later colonial period, the new legal office of the regent reasserted royal control. The *Instrucción de Regentes* (1776) limited substantially the independent judicial power of viceroys by reaffirming their political, rather than judicial, function.[34] After this date, the regent sat in judicial proceedings when the viceroy was absent.[35]

Underneath the viceregal centers, the colonies were divided into further administrative areas. These were typically regional *audiencias,* and smaller subdivisions, such as *alcaldías mayores* and *corregimientos.*[36]

The key institution that worked in tandem with the royal official was the *audiencia,* a governing body with a fixed territorial jurisdiction. The term *audiencia* is used to refer to different elements of colonial government. Depending on context, an *audiencia* may be a political subdivision subject to the power of a group of men under a royal representative, or the group of men itself. More than one *audiencia* might be under the jurisdiction of a viceroy. For example, the *audiencias* of Mexico, Guadalajara, and Santo Domingo were all under the supervision of the viceroy of New Spain.[37] *Audiencias* had combined powers of government that today we may think of as including legislative, executive, and administrative functions. Nonetheless, *audiencias* also exercised an increasingly important judicial function, and from the early sixteenth century, the *audiencias* of the viceroyalties of New Spain (Mexico) and Peru (Lima) were almost entirely judicial bodies.[38] The first *audiencia* serving as a court was created in Santo Domingo in 1508 and was staffed with three judges.[39] *Audiencias* had both a civil and criminal jurisdiction, carried out by, at first, a handful of judges, *oidores,* who were the most important *audiencia* officials. As the number of *oidores* was increased to handle more and more disputes, these judges might be grouped according to jurisdiction. For example, in Mexico City during the seventeenth century, the *audiencia* was composed of eight *oidores* with civil jurisdiction and four *alcaldes de crimen* with criminal jurisdiction.[40] *Oidores* often had other ancillary duties that included collecting the tax called the *cruzada,* serving as a probate judge, inspecting the fleets, and serving as a judge for commercial appeals from commercial tribunals, *consulados.*[41] Legislation set out the ideal structure and staff of these *audiencias,* but in practice, many were understaffed.[42] It is likely that the colonial *audiencias* were modeled on the most powerful Castilian tribunal of the day, the Audiencia y Real Chancilleria de Valladolid.[43]

The *audiencia* had a general appellate jurisdiction over lesser courts within its borders, and an original jurisdiction for criminal and civil cases within a certain radius of the court.[44] It might also have a limited personal jurisdiction over civil disputes involving Indians within a certain radius of the court.[45] *Audiencias* were to hear cases for three hours in the morning and give their decisions in the afternoon every day except Sundays and holidays.[46]

During the sixteenth and seventeenth centuries, the geographical areas defined by the *audiencias* were divided between the two viceroyalties of New Spain and Peru. Although there were slight variations in alignment, name, the degree of control the viceroyalty exercised over them, and precise date of founding, the general structure remained the same during the period. The viceroyalty of New Spain included the *audiencias* of Santo Domingo (1526), Mexico (1527), Guatemala (1542), and Guadalajara (1560). The viceroyalty of Peru included the *audiencias* of Panama (1535), Lima (1542), Santa Fe de Bogotá (1549), Charcas (1559), Quito (1563), Chile (1609), and Buenos Aires (1661).[47] By the eighteenth century, the viceroyalty of New Spain included the *audiencias* of Santo Domingo, Mexico, Guatemala, and Guadalajara. Peru included the *audiencias* of Lima, Chile, and Cuzco. Nueva Granada included the *audiencias* of Santa Fe de Bogotá, Panama, Quito, and Venezuela. Río de la Plata included Buenos Aires and Charcas.[48]

Responding to regional events and developing in sometimes ad hoc ways, the functions and powers of *audiencias* fluctuated during the colonial period.[49] All *audiencias* were not equal; the viceroyal *audiencias* of Lima and Mexico were at the top of the pyramid. Judicial officials carefully calculated their career paths and might even refuse promotions or lateral moves based on location, climate, the prestige of the position offered, and the *audiencia* concerned.[50] Attempts at harmonizing the structure, activities, and procedures of the *audiencias,* especially those underneath the viceroyalty level, were made; the ordinances of the *Audiencias,* also called the Ordinances of Monzón, from 1562 is an example of such reform.[51]

In addition to the *oidores,* larger *audiencias* had numerous other officials. The duties of these officials reveal the multifaceted activities of *audiencias.* *Alcaldes de crimen* heard criminal cases. *Fiscales* guarded royal financial interests. *Alguaciles mayores* carried out the court's orders. The *chanciller* guarded the royal seal. *Relatores* prepared summaries for the court, and *escribanos de cámara* handled the heavy load of writing documents. *Receptores de penas de cámara* handled fines levied by the court for court infractions. *Receptores ordinarios* relieved the filing burdens placed on other officials. Interpreters aided with native languages and porters ensured that the domestic aspects of the tribunal were running well. There were so many officials that other officials served the function of dividing work between them. The *tasador repartidor* decided whether a certain task was to go to a *relator* or scribe.[52] Because the *audiencias* were charged with the administration of the property of decedents in the colonies, in 1550, the post of *juzgado de bienes de difuntos* (probate judge) was created. An *oidor* of the *audiencia* was chosen to fill this function for two years. This official handled the administration of decedents' estates, including the payment of debts and the renting and sale of decedents' property. Decisions of this probate judge could be appealed to the *audiencia.*[53]

The introduction of the regent in 1776 not only affected the judicial functions of the viceroy, but also those of the *audiencia.* The regent, who served under and alongside the viceroy or president, became responsible for the *audiencia's* legal and economic work. With notice to the viceroy or president, the regent could establish additional tribunals such as the *sala extraordinaria de justicia civil o criminal,* or an *acuerdo de justicia.*[54] The regent had the duty of assuring that cases were moving smoothly through the court, voted on cases where he sat, summarily decided small disputes, personally accepted filings with the court, and determined jurisdictional conflicts between the civil and criminal *salas* of the *audiencia.*[55] Thus, by carrying out the judicial function, the institution of the regents marks a movement toward judicial independence from the *audiencia* in the late eighteenth century.[56]

Although *audiencias* handled much of the colonies' high-level governmental functions, numerous other separate or lower institutions also contributed to government. Just as fifteenth-century Spain contained many regions, groups, or interests that had effectively carved themselves away from the general application of laws and general jurisdiction of the courts, so too, through a *capitulación,* a discoverer might receive wide grants of power that would exempt him and his territories from viceroy and *audiencia* supervision. Likewise, the crown could also carve out special jurisdictional pockets with broader autonomous powers for smaller-scale viceroylike officials called *capitanes generales, presidentes,* or *comandantes generales.*[57] Thus, the viceroyalty and *audiencia* structure may be characterized as the usual form of political and legal ordering, but not all areas fell under the jurisdiction of an *audiencia* and its legal autonomy could be a matter of contention.

Continuing with the usual structures, from the mid sixteenth century forward, Courts of the Province (*juzgados de provincia*) met on Tuesdays, Thursdays, and Saturdays in the plazas of some cities where *audiencias* sat.[58] These courts were presided over by *oidores* of the *audiencia* on a rotation basis, each serving for three months of the year. They had a full civil jurisdiction, and their judgments could be appealed to the *audiencia,* but the *oidor* of the first judgment would not have a vote on appeal.[59] It appears that in Lima and Mexico, a court of four *alcaldes de crimen* (confusingly with both criminal and civil jurisdiction) replaced the *juzgados de provincia.*[60] As a general rule, these tribunals would not hear cases that had already begun on the local level of the *alcaldes ordinarios.*[61] Special judicial apparatuses might be constructed to handle serious or complicated legal cases apart from the regular *juzgados de provincia,* and *audiencias* commissioned judges (*jueces de comisión*) specially designated for these matters.[62] When regents were appointed in the eighteenth century, they took over the *juzgados de provincia.*[63]

On the next level, depending on the size, importance, and history of the territorial subdivision, officials known as governors, *corregidores,* or *alcaldes mayores* held the administrative and judicial power.[64] For example, the *audiencia* of Mexico contained about ten *corregimientos* and about ninety *alcaldías mayores.*[65] If a governor was not legally trained, the record of the case was sent to a university-trained *abogado* for a legal opinion to be approved by the governor. In more remote areas, assembling the paper record by qualified people, such as the scarce notaries, and transporting it to an *abogado* made for slow process.[66] Officials on this level were closely tied to the local governing bodies, *cabildos,* and often guided their decisions.[67]

By 1790, the intendancy system did away with this level of royal official. For example, in New Spain, the extant two hundred officials on the level of *corregidores* and *alcaldes mayores,* who were usually Creoles, were replaced by twelve intendants.[68] Similarly, in the 1780s, the viceroyalty of Río de la Plata was partitioned into eight intendancies.[69] Intendants assumed much of the contentious jurisdiction of the officials they replaced and became sole instance judges for disputes concerning many royal interests, notably disputes over the sale and distribution of royal lands.[70] The intendancy system also attempted to consolidate and unify the colonial court system by limiting the special jurisdictional tribunals outside of the general courts to those addressing tax, church, mining, and commercial matters. Although the general reforms advanced the restoration of the central authority of the crown, these legal reforms, however, have not been seen as particularly successful.[71]

Below this level were the local authorities. Various officials addressed a panoply of administrative and bureaucratic concerns. Town councils (*cabildos*) were composed of *regidores* who appointed officials with local judicial functions (*alcaldes* or *alcaldes ordinarios,* usually two), local policelike functions (*alguaciles*), and record-keeping duties (*secretarios* and *notarios*). Other officials looked after finances, represented local interests (*procuradores*), and maintained prices and the quality of goods and livestock.[72] Municipalities could be a city, a town, or a place, each with a corresponding bureaucratic structure. The larger the municipality, the more officials. Founding towns or cities was itself a highly legislated activity, spelled out in minute precision in works such as the *Ordenanzas de Poblaciones* of 1573, the most important example of this Spanish supervision.[73] Numerous city officials served the municipality, some with seats on the *cabildo* and others not included in the *cabildo.*[74] For example, metropolitan cities had a judge (*adelantado, alcalde mayor, corregidor,* or *alcalde ordinario*), two or three treasury officials, twelve *regidores,* two *fieles ejecutores,* a *procurador general,* and numerous other officials. If it was a diocesan or sufragan city, it had eight *regidores;* towns and places usually had four *regidores* and *alcaldes ordinarios.*[75] In the late colonial period, *cabildos* struggled for funds and personnel; their strength waxed and waned depending on the support and duties they received from the intendants. Nonetheless, the judicial function of *cabildo* officials continued to be important in dispensing municipal justice.[76]

In typical colonial fashion, the *cabildos* had a mixture of governmental functions, and those of the most powerful cities, such as Mexico City or Lima, could go face to face with royal *audiencias* in political and jurisdictional battles. In fact, the local authority of these *cabildos* even expressed itself during the independence period when, for example, the *cabildo* of Buenos Aires took a leading role in the independence of Argentina.[77]

Cabildo membership varied throughout the colonial period. At first, the founders of cities selected *cabildo* members, and later, the *cabildo* itself had the power to select replacements by vote. Nonetheless, in an effort to raise revenue, *cabildo* positions were sold.[78] Some *cabildo* positions also became perpetual and hereditary.[79] Others, like the *regidor perpetuo,* were royal appointments.[80] *Cabildo* members needed to be citizens of the city (*vecinos*) and maintain a household there.[81] As positions on the *cabildo* became alienable and proprietary, the local elite controlled these institutions.[82] Nonetheless, the position of local judge, *alcalde ordinario,* was usually elected and somewhat free from such control.[83]

The judicial members of the *cabildo* were to meet daily and, as a court, had a wide jurisdiction. If an *alcalde ordinario* could not serve, the *alférez real* or the most senior *regidor* sat in his place. Each year one of the *alcaldes ordinarios* was elected to serve as a judge of minors (*juez de menores*) who protected the interests of children. The positions were not paid, but the *alcaldes* collected the court fees, which are reported to have been modest.[84] When *alcaldes* were illiterate, a witness signed their judgments.[85] As demands on the courts increased, auxiliaries might be appointed to the *alcaldes ordinarios,* and *alcaldes* could appoint their own *tenientes.*[86] For example, in 1786, the *cabildo* of Buenos Aires had to define the jurisdiction of these lesser judges by limiting their civil jurisdiction to matters under a certain sum.[87] The functions and judicial nature of the *cabildo* were subject to various legislative acts or *ordenanzas* that might delineate these activities beyond the standard provisions in the general collections of applicable laws such as the *Recopilación* of 1680.[88]

As described by the *Siete Partidas,* procedure in civil cases on all levels was mostly written.[89] A formal complaint led to summoning the defendant who answered by denial or counterclaim (*reconvención*). Evidence was presented through documents and testimony reduced to writing (*prueba*).[90] Interrogatories were read to and answered by witnesses and these, along with supporting documents, were often summarized for the court by *relatores* who presented the case to the judge.[91] Substantive responses in the interrogatories were limited to agreement, disagreement, or lack of knowledge, with each response coupled with the manner in which the witness obtained the information.[92] Procedural motions could be presented throughout the process; these included motions based on the failure of a party to respond (*rebeldía*), on misconduct of court personnel (*recusación*), on requests to adjust procedural deadlines, and on a challenge to the veracity of the evidence offered.[93] Substantive legal opinions of the *abogados* (jurisconsults) might be presented in *informaciones.*[94]

It was a time-consuming, slow process.[95] After a hearing where the *abogados* were permitted to present their case orally, the court might render a final decision (*sentencia*).[96] These decisions were not required to state reasons for giving judgment to one party or the other, and often merely stated that one party had proved his case or not.[97] Thus, no tradition of judicial decisions as sources of law developed. Each step was not only associated with various fees, but also additional gratuities, bribes, were often needed to move the case forward at each juncture.[98] Fees were usually set as a multiple of the fees then assessed in Castile, such as three times the rate then in effect.[99] Writing of litigation in colonial Mexico, Woodrow Borah has stated that it "was a hazardous process characterized by cost and corruption."[100] Graft, in part resulting from inadequate compensation of officials, was a persistent problem in the colonial administration of justice.[101]

The most common work on procedure was Juan de Hevia Bolaños's *Curia*

Philipica, reportedly first published in 1603.[102] Local works on procedure were uncommon, perhaps with the exception of present-day Bolivia, where Francisco Gutiérrez wrote a book touching on court procedure. Likewise, in Venezuela in the 1780s one royal official promulgated a set of instructions that included orders to number the pages of the court filings, to have no blank space between lines, to accept papers only from lawyers approved by the *audiencia,* and other general rules regarding filings.[103] Even on the local level of the *alcalde ordinario,* procedure was written, but conducted summarily to provide a quicker decision.[104]

A system of ecclesiastical courts was also present in the Indies. Ecclesiastical procedures had the public perception of also being very slow; a common saying was, "if you want to become immortal, start an ecclesiastical suit."[105] Apart from its broad jurisdiction over purely spiritual matters, the church had an important jurisdiction touching the civil status of most people in colonial society. Its jurisdiction included espousals, marriages, and their annulment or dissolution.[106] Many rights to take property, based on a valid marriage or legitimacy, hinged on such determinations. Procedure here was also based on written documents submitted to the court. The ecclesiastical jurisdiction in the colonies was greatly limited by the royal patronage, so that, for example, royal courts took up the testamentary jurisdiction of ecclesiastical courts.[107] With the powers of the royal patronage, the crown limited appeals to Rome by having ecclesiastical judgments reviewed by other metropolitans in the Indies.[108] A decision by two metropolitans in the Indies was final and no appeal could be brought to the papal courts in Rome.[109]

The Inquisition was present in the colonies, but had no private law jurisdictions.[110] Nonetheless, its jurisdiction over the importation of prohibited books and materials made it a frequent presence at ports. Tribunals of the Inquisition were established for Mexico City and Lima in 1569 and for Cartagena in 1610.[111] Furthermore, the Inquisition might assert its privileges to disrupt royal structures and to hinder royal civil proceedings.[112]

Just as the church and its tribunals had a monopoly in spiritual matters, councils of trade (*consulados*) significantly monopolized commerce and disputes related to commerce. Thus, another important exception to the general jurisdiction of the courts and officials was commerce.[113] Matters concerning commerce were found in a pocket of jurisdiction controlled by councils of trade (*consulados*) established under royal authority in both Spain and the colonies. Meeting in the Board of Trade in Seville, a council of trade for the Indies (*consulado* or Universidad de Mercadores) was established in 1543 to handle all manner of trade disputes arising from the colonial markets. This removed much of the demanding caseload from the Board of Trade, which retained an appellate jurisdiction over these cases.[114] Modeled after their peninsular counterparts in Seville, Burgos, and later Bilbao, the colonial cities Mexico and Lima had the earliest councils of trade composed of a prior and two consuls. Reflecting their monopolistic control of trade and commerce, these councils handled all manner of commercial disputes: purchases and sales, contracts, partnerships (particularly for navigation and trade), insurance, accounts, and labor disputes between sailors and ship owners.[115] One way of ensuring that disputes were brought before the *consulado* was to prohibit members from suing other members elsewhere.[116] Later *consulados* in New Spain were established in Veracruz, Guadalajara, and Puebla.[117] The *consulado* of Cartagena was established in 1725 with a jurisdiction for the port, but extended in 1795 to the viceroyalty, excluding Quito and Popayán.[118] Buenos Aires did not receive a *consulado* until 1794.[119] *Consulados* in Santiago and Havana were also established in the late 1790s.[120]

The procedure for the late colonial council of Buenos Aires is typical. In contrast to the written procedure of most courts, the plaintiff and defendant in these commercial tribunals presented their cases orally by themselves and through witness and documentary evidence before the council.[121] If the parties did not agree to settle or place the case in arbitration, documents outlining the dispute would be signed by the parties, and the judges would decide the matter in the parties' absence.[122] Procedural rules excluded the parties' use of documents prepared by university-trained lawyers, although such lawyers might serve as *asesores* to the judges of the council.[123] Decisions in matters over a thousand pesos could be appealed to a special tribunal (*tribunal de alzadas*) composed of the dean and two others of the *audiencia*. The council's jurisdiction extended over the entire viceroyalty and deputies sitting with others could hear cases in ports and commercial centers.[124]

Another jurisdiction with its own related legal structure was tax and revenue. At first, royal revenue officials (*oficiales reales*) brought their claims in the *audiencia*, but they were later given an original jurisdiction in taxation with appeal to the *audiencia*.[125] Revenue officials were subject to account, originally before the Council of the Indies, but after 1605 three regional tribunals of last resort were established for this purpose in Mexico City, Lima, and Santa Fe de Bogotá.[126]

Numerous other separate tribunals existed for fiscal disputes, and in addition to ecclesiastical and commercial tribunals, there were also separate courts for mining (from 1777) and military cases.[127] Thus one may find references to the varied jurisdictional situation of the colonies, including "Juzgados de Bienes de difuntos, Tribunales de Cuentas, Tribunales Indígenas, Tribunales de Comercio y de Minas, de Aguas, Jueces de Pesquidores y Residenciadores, [and] Jueces Hacedores de diezmos."[128] Some of these courts had their original basis in the *fueros*, such as "Tribunales Militares, Eclesiásticos, Universitarios, de Protomedicato, de Comedia y Administrativo."[129] Other courts kept the means of transportation free from banditry and took action against violent crime and prohibited liquors (Santa Hermandad [1631]; Tribunal de la Acordada [1722]).[130] In addition to their criminal jurisdiction, these judges of the Santa Hermandad (*alcaldes de Hermandad* or *jueces cuadrilleros*) had a summary, oral, civil jurisdiction in matters up to thirty pesos.[131] Other tribunals handled small, but important, slices of jurisdiction, such as the judges of the Mesta (*alcaldes de Mesta*) who heard disputes concerning cattle or the Court of Mail (Juzgado de Correos), which from 1776 heard cases concerning the post.[132]

Indian structures existed as well. Recent scholarship has demonstrated that indigenous tribunals continued to function after the conquest. These courts can be viewed as a layer of forums underneath the royal courts.[133] Indian barrios in Mexico had *gobernadores* and *jueces gobernadores,* and Kellogg has found that in the records of the *audiencia,* "Indian alcaldes, *regidores,* alguaciles, scribes and interpreters were also mentioned frequently."[134]

There was also a layer of royal authorities charged with protecting the interests of Indians. In New Spain, a separate royal court was established for Indian causes and from 1592 this Juzgado General de Indios de la Nueva España, General Indian Court of New Spain, served as an administrative clearinghouse for such disputes, by directing them to various other courts or deciding their merits. Due to the volume of business the court received, it was necessary to place substantial minimum jurisdictional amounts to limit the number of cases it heard.[135] The jurisdiction of such specialized courts was not, however, exclusive, and many Indians chose to bring their actions in the ordinary courts of the *corregidores* or *alcaldes mayores.*[136]

The variety of these available tribunals indicates that legal disputes were often subject to numerous and overlapping jurisdictions. Nonetheless, some general patterns can be discerned.[137] Small disputes were handled by the local *alcaldes,* with appeal to the *cabildo.* Small disputes between Indians were likewise handled within the Indian structures. Larger disputes and often those between Indians and Spaniards were heard before a royal *alcalde mayor* or *corregidor,* sometimes with appeal to the *audiencia.* The *audiencias* themselves had an original jurisdiction over certain matters of great importance, such as those touching the royal patronage of the church. The *audiencia* also had a means to determine if ecclesiastical jurisdiction was warranted in a particular dispute through a procedure known as the *recurso de fuerza.* From the 1590s, each *audiencia* had a protector of Indians to monitor dealings with the indigenous population.

From the various institutions just described it might appear that judicial forums densely populated the Spanish colonies. In fact, there were many areas that were not served or underserved, and in this regard, this study, with its focus on central institutions, personnel, and legal sources, may offer a skewed vision of the general condition. As Charles Cutter has noted, "The centers, not the peripheries, were the exceptions,"[138] and "the empire failed to incorporate the peripheries in a meaningful way into its judicial superstructure."[139] "In fact, *most* provinces of New Spain made do without a fully staffed judiciary."[140] Until further studies of peripheral communities are available, generalizations from the exceptions are all that can be offered.

To what extent informal mechanisms were used to settle disputes outside the courts is difficult to determine. Settlement was, of course, a viable means of resolution before the bringing of a legal action, and many societal forces encouraged parties to settle. These included the extended familial relations established though, for example, godparents (*compadrazgo*), the pressure that might be exerted by guild or trade associations, the desire to maintain harmony within various lay religious groups (*cofradías* and *hermandades*), and informal intervention by parish priests.[141] The *Siete Partidas* sets out procedures for informally settling disputes by arbitrators (*arbitratores, amigables componedores,* or *arbitri*) or mediators (*alvedriadores*). Arbitrators were expected to decide in accordance with the law, while mediators might proceed without being subject to technical legal rules.[142] Indian communities were also subject to significant pressure to settle disputes.[143] The mere filing of a legal action must have often led the way to a settlement apart from judicial action, and it appears that judges brought pressure to have the parties settle.[144] Nonetheless, in the late colonial period, numerous forms of more institutionalized dispute resolution existed apart from civil trials. Judicially supervised or mandatory conciliation and arbitration (which might cast aside laws and *fueros*) were known in this period.[145]

Courts, like the other structures of colonial government, were funded through various taxes. Most important, the crown taxed the principal function of the colonies, mining silver. The crown usually received between 16 and 20 percent of mined precious metals declared to its inspectors and also ran a system of monopolies for certain goods such as playing cards, gunpowder, spices, and tobacco. It took treasure trove, administered its own lands, and collected both payments to buy offices and established taxes (*mesada* and *media anata*) on their being filled. As the representative of the church, it collected tithes, an additional payment associated with the Crusades (*Limosna de la Santa Bula de Cruzada*), income from vacant ecclesiastical positions, and *mesada* and *media anata* for filled ecclesiastical positions. It collected Indian tribute and taxes on the importation of certain alcoholic beverages (*almojarifazgo*) and on commercial income (*alcabala*), which was commonly farmed out to collectors. Important for lawyers, it sold sealed paper on which most legal transactions and court filings needed to be written. It sold titles, requested "free gifts," and took forfeitures in various criminal actions. In 1799, it created the Consolidation Treasury (Caja de Consolidación), which in 1804 dissolved church lands held for pious activities and gave the church what it considered an appropriate return. The viceroy's treasury council (Junta Suprema de la Real Hacienda), which reported to the Board of Trade and the Council of the Indies, supervised all these revenues.[146] Each important city had royal taxation officials (*tesorero, contador, factor,* and *veedor*). The three tax courts (*tribunales de cuentas*) of México, Lima, and Bogotá decided questions of assessment of taxes and of the application of tax laws. Another such tribunal in Buenos Aires joined these in the late eighteenth century.[147] Havana and Caracas also had special *contadores*.[148] In the colonial period, many offices were sold, and some, such as the scribal offices associated with *cabildos* and *audiencias* (*escribanos, relatores*), might be sold at public auction to the highest bidder.[149]

Toward the end of the colonial period, various reforms were imposed to centralize power under Philip V and Charles III, both of whom looked to French models to achieve this goal. Secretaries (Secretarías de Despacho Universal) took over the functions of the Council of the Indies, and in 1770 the intendancy system was used to create another layer of regional royal power. For example, the Ordinance of 1783 gave the powers of taxation, justice, police, and war to the intendant for Río de la Plata. In 1788, similar intendants were empowered for Lima and New Spain.[150] From the early 1780s, each new political subdivision at the intendant level had a university-trained legal officer (*teniente letrado*) who ran the tribunals in each jurisdiction and served as an *asesor* to the intendant.[151]

The courts of the Spanish colonies had a complex hierarchy, jurisdictional boundaries, and internal structures. Various competing jurisdictions, along with the lessened, yet present, forces of the special *fueros,* exerted their influence. Despite their heavily weighted presence in the colonial economic centers, the penetration of legal institutions into the less populated rural areas was shallow. Nonetheless, the crown managed to maintain significant control from afar, and the courts of the region functioned to serve the interests of wealth and trade in the colonial centers for more than three hundred years.

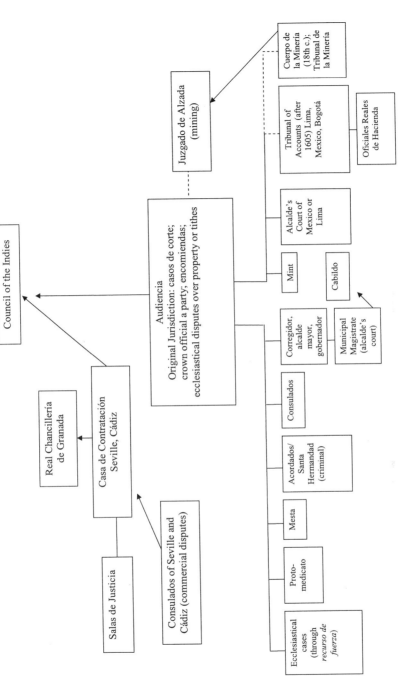

Colonial court structure: A simplified chart of jurisdictional relationships.
Bello Lozano (1983), 283, 337–348; Haring (1975), 98, 99, 121, 131, 157, 299, 300, 302; Howe (1968), 64, 65; Soberanes Fernández (1998), 53.

The chart contains the following boxes:

- Council of the Indies
- Real Chancillería de Granada
- Casa de Contratación Seville, Cádiz
- Salas de Justicia
- Consulados of Seville and Cádiz (commercial disputes)
- Audiencia — Original Jurisdiction: casos de corte; crown official a party; encomiendas; ecclesiastical disputes over property or tithes
- Juzgado de Alzada (mining)
- Cuerpo de la Minería (18th c.); Tribunal de la Minería
- Tribunal of Accounts (after 1605) Lima, México, Bogotá
- Oficiales Reales de Hacienda
- Alcalde's Court of México or Lima
- Mint
- Cabildo
- Corregidor, alcalde mayor, gobernador
- Municipal Magistrate (alcalde's court)
- Consulados
- Acordados/ Santa Hermandad (criminal)
- Mesta
- Proto-medicato
- Ecclesiastical cases (through *recurso de fuerza*)

Legal Education and Lawyers

Legal Education

LATIN American universities were modeled on European universities, and especially the University of Salamanca.[1] Having their own governing bodies and courts, universities had a significant amount of autonomy in colonial society.[2] They also fit into the broader matrix of social institutions found in the cities supporting them. Universities had ties to the local religious hierarchy and were usually led by a secular authority, a *rector,* and an ecclesiastical authority, a *maestrescuela.*[3] These interests did not always govern universities in harmony. For example, in the early years of the University of Mexico, the royal authorities of the viceroy and the *oidores* of his *audiencia* clashed violently with the archbishop and canons of the ecclesiastical *cabildo* over the control of the institution.[4]

Universities, faculties of law, and less formal centers of study played an important part in the perpetuation of the ruling elite of the colonies. For example, depending on the time and place in the colonies, entrance to studies required passing through a small trial-like examination, the *procesillo,* in which applicants established their racial purity (*limpieza de sangre*), religious conformity, and suitable familial and economic backgrounds.[5] Students and those with university degrees were distinguished in society by a dress code demonstrating their elevated status.[6] Studies not only served to validate the desired individual attributes of the degree candidate, but their completion, especially in law, benefited the entire family as it sought to exercise and increase its power and status through membership in the elite professions and alliances with other important families.[7]

Law students in a fully functioning colonial university, such as the University of Mexico, began with a preparatory classical education in the Faculty of Arts, followed by studies in one of the specialized faculties of theology, canon law, law, or medicine to obtain one of three degrees: *bachiller, licenciado,* or *doctor.* Examination methods varied from place to place and time to time, but some general characteristics may be observed. Candidates solicited the degree from the university by asserting that they had studied the requisite duration, held doctrinally conforming religious beliefs, and were racially pure. Examinations were conducted orally with debate on particular themes chosen either by the candidate or by a member of the faculty; for example, three doctors examined the candidate for *bachiller* for one hour, and the *maestrescuela* publicly questioned a candidate for *doctor* on his written thesis. The approval of the overseeing faculty officials was required, followed by oaths of loyalty to the crown and of religious conformity by the candidate. Celebratory public ceremonies increased with the level of the degree conferred.[8] A ceremonial satirical humiliation, the *vejamen,* in which a person chosen by the *maestrescuela* would remind, often gently, but occasionally harshly, the candidate of his faults and not to take himself too seriously, accompanied the granting of a doctorate from the University of Mexico.[9] Other universities had similar ritual jibes; the *vejamen* on awarding a doctorate at the University of Caracas could be a written rhyming verse.[10] In other universities, such as San Felipe in Chile, the doctorate was often awarded as a ceremonial addition to the *licenciado.*[11]

With relatively stringent social and economic entrance requirements and with significant study required for completion, typical Latin American law faculties in the colonial period only graduated ten or fewer students each year.[12] Advanced degrees were even rarer.

Until the eighteenth century, the formal structure of legal education during the colonial period was uniform and based on Salamanca. The European *ius commune* of Roman and canon law was taught by chaired professors (*catedráticos*) who read selected texts from the basic works of the *corpus iuris canonici* and the *corpus iuris civilis,* most importantly the *Decretals* and *Institutes,* usually covering the texts in a number of years.[13] These texts would be accompanied by related selections from their most common glosses, such as Accursius or Bartholomeus Brixiensis, which were used to explain the meaning of the primary texts.[14] Once available in the seventeenth century, Vinnius's commentaries on the *Institutes* were a popular text for providing explanation.[15] Professors were expected to divide their time between reading and explaining the text selected for presentation. Students were expected to memorize important sections of the texts. In daily lectures, professors read and commented on primary texts; students copied the texts and took notes. In less frequent conferences or disputations, students defended conclusions of law before the faculty and other students.[16]

Teaching positions in law were generally designated by university statute and were described in terms of the general text to be taught. In the University of Mexico, the faculty of canon law included: *Cátedra de Prima de Cánones* (the *Decretals of Gregory IX*); *Cátedra de Decreto* (Gratian); *Cátedra de Sexto* (the *Sexto*); and the *Cátedra de Clementinas* (the *Clementines*).[17] Its law faculty had chairs of law (the *Digest* and its *Inforciado*), and chairs for teaching the *Institutes* and the Codex.[18] The number of professors to cover this material could be expanded or contracted depending on personnel and resources. For example, in 1578, the statutes for San Marcos de Lima state that the law faculty included, "Prima de Leyes, Prima de Cánones, Instituta, Víspera de Cánones y Decreto."[19] Lectures were sometimes scheduled so that students might attend both the Roman law and canon law lectures during the same year.[20] Professors were appointed, at first by the viceroy and *oidores* of the *audiencia,* and later by the university's governing council.[21] It appears they were underpaid for their work, and this led to some professors delegating other people to read in their place.[22]

In the eighteenth century, and following peninsular requirements imposed in 1741, this classical curriculum was modified to include provisions on royal law, which were to be included in the presentation of Roman law, and the Spanish *Nueva Recopilación de Castilla* became one of the basic texts.[23] Despite this modification, the classical curriculum with its emphasis on the traditional *ius commune* sources was the standard fare in most colonial universities throughout the period. Numerous studies of libraries of law faculties and *audiencias* throughout colonial Latin America attest to the predominance of *ius commune* sources and particularly those associated with the *mos italicus,* or Bartolist, tradition of interpretation.[24]

Most main centers of commerce and government had some form of university legal education available, and by the end of the colonial period, a number of colonial universities had established faculties of legal instruction, including the Universities of Guadalajara (Mexico), San Marcos (Lima), San Francisco Javier (Chuquisaca), Caracas, Santo Tomás (Chile), San Felipe (Chile), and San Carlos (Guatemala).[25] In the Río de la Plata region, legal education began in 1681 with the University of Charcas. Having offered canon law since 1622, the University of Córdoba added Roman law based on the study of Vinnius's commentaries on the *Institutes* in 1791, and two years later added a chair of royal law. The University of Alto Perú offered courses in canon, Roman, and royal law.[26] Also somewhat later on the scene, colonial Bogotá provided a home to two law faculties. Students at the Rosario were examined and granted law degrees by the Universidad Tomística (Dominican), and those at San Bartolomé by the Universidad Javeriana (Jesuit). Little legal instruction was available at these universities before 1700.[27] Studying for university law exams outside of the universities was possible. Where the universities served only to confer degrees, such external study was necessary. There were several colleges and seminaries in New Spain that offered legal education in preparation for university exams, and this pattern existed elsewhere, particularly in larger cities.[28]

In the late colonial period, legal education followed an established pattern and was subject to various decrees to ensure its duration and content. For example, in New Granada in 1770, it was decreed by the *audiencia* that the postuniversity apprenticeship period (*pasantía*) would be increased from two to three years before full admission to practice and that the degrees of *licenciado* or *doctor* could only be awarded to those who had already completed the five-year *bachiller*.[29] Also in New Granada, a royal *cédula* of 1771 required five years of study to earn the *bachiller* and increased the apprenticeship period to four years.[30] To obtain the title of *bachiller,* students studied Roman civil law as it related to royal civil law (Vinnius and Juan Sala were the main texts), natural and national law, canon law, the *Siete Partidas* and the *Leyes de Toro*. These materials were taught through lecture, conferences, and acts.[31] In 1795, a required course in royal law (*derecho real*) was added.[32] Again in New Granada, in 1778 a Junta de Estudios was assembled to regulate legal education, and it required two years of canon law, two years of Roman and Spanish law, and a fifth year of "public law" which included natural and international law.[33]

Despite the addition of royal law to the curriculum, there was concern that university training created overly theoretical lawyers. To ensure a practical grounding, a four- or five-year period of practice was required before a graduate could present himself for membership in the bar (*abogacía*). Such practical grounding was not necessary for all graduates who studied law. Many chose careers that, while related to law, such as positions in the colonial bureaucracy, did not require the daily practice of law. For example, in late colonial New Granada, only about one-third of the law graduates went on to practice as lawyers, and a significant number of law graduates were also clergy who served as parish priests.[34]

Another way to foster practical knowledge was through practical academies, which aimed to train lawyers in the daily workings of the court and the royal law sources used there. In 1779 in Chile the Real Academia Carolina de Leyes y Práctica Forense was established to provide instruction in the most important sources of royal law, including the *Siete Partidas* and the *Nueva Recopilación de Castilla*. Teaching at the Carolina was in Spanish rather than the usual language of university instruction, Latin.[35] Works dealing with forensic practice, such as the widely used *Curia Philipica* of Juan de Hevia Bolaños (c. 1570–1623), also found a place in instruction at the Carolina.[36] Before 1800, similar academies were also established in Charcas and Mexico.[37]

Although of minor significance, some types of ancillary legal education were established through the lawyers' guilds, or *colegios*. For example, the Colegio de Abogados de Caracas attempted a form of continuing legal education for its members through an academy called the Academia de Derecho Público y Español, which presented lectures and writing competitions. The institution existed only from 1790 to 1797, due partly to its inability to locate suitable facilities and suspicion from the university that jealously guarded its monopoly on legal education. Attempts to revive the academy in the form of a school of court practice (*escuela de práctica forense*) in 1804 were unfulfilled.[38]

Lawyers

More is known about Castilian *abogados* in this period than their New World counterparts. *Abogados* were necessary to maintain the social and commercial activities of peninsular society and, as a class of individuals, were subject to both praise and criticism throughout the period. Criticism tended to focus on practitioners amassing wealth at their clients' expense by filing repetitious or verbose court papers. From at least the thirteenth to the nineteenth century, women were not permitted to serve as *abogados;* other laws prohibited Jews, Moors, excommunicates, heretics, criminals, and anyone with ancestors from these classifications from the profession.[39] Despite the concern for *limpieza de sangre* in the legal profession, several known *confesos* or *conversos* (converts) were able to practice as lawyers in Castile, and in the case of *licenciado* Pedro López de Alcocer, contributor to the *Nueva Recopilación,* to excel in the profession.[40] Clerics were prohibited from accepting clients, with a few limited exceptions such as representing the church or the poor. Judges were also prohibited from practice.[41] Such requirements were set by royal legislation.

After university training, a required period of practical training, and possible training in one of the academies, students were considered ready to request permission to practice before the courts. The exam was presented before the viceroy, judges, and other officials of the *audiencia,* as the controlling court of appeal. A successful candidate gave an oath and paid a fee before obtaining the title of *abogado.*[42] The oath required the candidate to practice faithfully, and the name of the *abogado* was inscribed in the records of the court. From Castilian judicial records, it appears that many of the requirements were taken lightly. An *abogado* of one of the royal *audiencias* was usually admitted to practice before other *audiencias* with little difficulty.[43]

Occupational choices for *abogados* were varied. Many chose to enter service in the colonial bureaucracy.[44] Others represented clients on a case-by-case basis, but some served institutional clients, such as monasteries or wealthy families, on salary. They might be assigned to indigent clients by the court. Guilds, like the Congregation of Lawyers of Madrid founded in 1595, assumed the representation of the poor as part of their religious and charitable activities. Nonetheless, *abogados* were expected to screen cases to make sure there was a valid claim.[45]

Abogados were entitled to compensation. Legislation generally permitted fees, *honorarios*, up to 5 percent of the value of the case. Early legislation setting maximum currency amounts fell out of use most likely due to inflation, but it is unknown to what extent even the percentage cap was followed in practice. The crown compensated *abogados* when they represented the poor. Compensation based on a part of the item or sum in controversy, or based on the contingency of winning the case, was prohibited, and fees were to be discussed with the client at the beginning of the case. *Abogados* on salary could not charge their clients more than the agreed salary. If a client refused to pay, the *abogado* could bring suit for the fees owed.[46] As part of representing clients, *abogados* owed them loyalty and secrecy; the *Siete Partidas* provided the death penalty for the most egregious breaches, but the usual penalty was a fine. Switching sides in litigation for better pay was a temptation some *abogados* fell to, but not without penalties on discovery.[47]

The Castilian *abogado* of the period held a high social status, particularly as assessed in the writings of lawyers. Special privileges for *abogados* included exemption from certain taxes, from imprisonment for debts, from torture, from their books being used to satisfy debts, and immunity while in court. In the eighteenth century, lawyers' guilds continued to press for the higher social status though stricter and stricter requirements of membership.[48] Throughout the colonial period, *abogados* wore distinctive dress in courts and ceremonies to mark their elevated status.[49]

From the earliest Spanish contact with America, *abogados* were needed to help with the legal affairs of the explorers. In 1499, for example, Columbus requested that an *abogado* be sent from Castile.[50] Such university-trained lawyers were not a favored group of individuals in the new territories, and in fact, from 1509 royal orders instructed the Board of Trade to prohibit *abogados* from traveling to the Indies without special license.[51] Evidently concerns about the litigiousness of Castilians and vexatious nature of lawsuits on the peninsula, prompted the crown to ban the travel of lawyers to Peru in 1529.[52] Cortés was among the first to request their exclusion from the newly conquered lands. The lawyers lucky enough to make it to the Indies were subject to substantial controls as later set out in book 2, title 24, of the *Recopilación* of 1680.[53] *Abogados* were subject to the *audiencia* for discipline, which might amount to a fine or suspension for improper behavior.[54]

Dislike or distrust of lawyers was a popular theme. In the sixteenth century, their practice was restricted or excluded in the colonial centers of Cuba and Mexico.[55] Even into the seventeenth century, they could be excluded from communities because they were seen as undesirable. Even though there may have been a paucity of lawyers in colonial Latin America, it is not clear that lawyers were always welcome in the community. For example, in 1613, the Buenos Aires *cabildo* refused to grant permission to enter the city to three university-trained lawyers because according to a *regidor,* echoing popular opinion, lawyers merely brought "suits, tricks, deceits, and other dissension."[56]

Distribution of *abogados* in the colonies was, as would be expected, uneven. Dependent on fees to survive, most practitioners stayed close to the centers of government and commerce.[57] *Abogados* tended to come from the same centers in which they were educated and practiced.[58] Some areas, such as the distant province of Texas, apparently never saw the presence of a practicing *abogado.* Even a scribe, also dependent on fees, was a rare occupant of such areas. Others, such as New Orleans under Spanish rule, had less than a handful of lawyers and scribes. Such scarcity away from the centers can be easily contrasted with the contemporary presence of more than one hundred *abogados* in Mexico City.[59] At the end of the colonial period in 1805, Caracas had a few more than fifty *abogados* practicing in the city, with another twenty-five or so practicing in other municipalities of Venezuela.[60] Even in remote areas, legal advice might be obtained from a scribe, a self-styled *procurador,* or an ecclesiastic.[61] On the average, at the beginning of the nineteenth century, there were usually between four and fourteen lawyers per 100,000 inhabitants in Latin America, depending on the particular geographic region.[62]

Toward the end of the colonial period, lawyers' guilds similar to those in Spanish cities, arose in larger colonial centers. The Ilustre y Real Colegio de Abogados of Mexico was founded in 1760 and served to ensure the social and racial character of those permitted to practice within the jurisdictional limits of the *audiencia.* Its members were generally Creoles rather than peninsular Spaniards, sons of professional families rather than the most elite families of the city, and educated at the University of Mexico rather than other centers of legal education.[63] Similar *colegios* were formed elsewhere in the Spanish colonies, modeled on the *colegio* of Madrid. In 1788, the Colegio de Abogados de Caracas was founded under the sponsorship of the *audiencia* to help control admission to practice before the *audiencia* and to further the racial and religious purity of the bar. The *colegios* also sought to benefit their members through providing religious and charitable services, through funerals and masses for dead members, and through legal services for the poor and Indians.[64] Determining who had the right to argue before the *audiencia,* they could monitor and admonish their members for inappropriate conduct. As an example of the *colegios'* enforcing colonial racial norms, one may note the case of Dr. Gil, who in 1792 was suspended from practice for four months by the *colegio* of Caracas for his dancing publicly with *mulatos* at a wedding.[65] In

1811, the Spanish Cortes acted to lessen the restrictions *colegios* could use to exclude qualified candidates from practice.[66]

Abogados benefited from the colonial regime and participated in the functioning of the colonial state. Not only in Mexico but throughout the Spanish colonies, lawyers were elite members of society, but usually not of the aristocratic layer.[67] The title of *abogado* imported a high level of social honor and prestige.[68] Thus lawyers were an easy target, and it is not surprising that the late colonial period witnessed numerous complaints about too many lawyers in society. One recent study in part attributes these complaints to a lack of legal work for the overall population of lawyers.[69] Concerns about the abundance of lawyers might also have been in some part a "politically motivated royal myth" created to counter the progressive activities of the profession.[70]

Procuradores

The position of *procurador* formed a separate class of legal practitioner in Castile. While the *abogado* was the expert in the legal sources and rules, the *procurador* handled procedural matters before the court—when and how to present the documents associated with litigation. From the beginning of the sixteenth century, Castilian *procuradores* were placed under the authority of the *abogados*. The line between procedural and substantive law was not always clear, and the permitted activities of *procuradores* remained unsettled. Nonetheless, the legal arguments set forth in the litigation documents were clearly the realm of the *abogado*.[71] Like his Castilian counterpart, below the *abogado* in professional status, the colonial *procurador* received less formal education. *Procuradores* assembled litigation documents often under an *abogado*'s supervision and handled various procedural aspects of litigation.[72] Distinctions could be made between types of *procuradores;* those *de hecho* served as agents for one client, those *de número* were approved by the *audiencia* and could even conduct a small amount of litigation before the courts. In some areas, *solicitadores,* below *procuradores,* assisted practitioners with investigation and obtaining business; they were largely self-trained.[73]

Scribes

The vast majority of legal work of the propertied classes was nonadversarial or administrative in nature. The frequency with which individuals made use of public scribes (*escribanos públicos de número*) reflected the legalism of the population and the bureaucratic structure of the colonial. Working from their own offices and compensated through a fee system for the work done, these scribes produced the daily documents of economic and social life in the colonies, including testaments, marriage contracts, transfers of property, letters of dowry, letter of payment obligations (essential in societies short of money), powers of appointment, manumissions, *censos* (perpetual monetary charges out of a principal sum often out of land, similar to a ground rent), and sales and mortgages of property. Public scribes have left behind a nearly endless amount of material. These vastly understudied historical sources, generally called notarial archives, report, in one way or another, on all levels of society; their detail and broad scope of daily dealings provide a rich source for social and economic historians. For example, one student of these records has noted the unexpected presence of wealthy women conducting property transactions and commerce in sixteenth-century Mexico.[74]

Judges

The *oidores* of the *audiencias* were university-trained lawyers and held a high position in colonial society. Perhaps because of the political activities of the *audiencias* and of the growing interest in the history of the legal profession, more and more recent scholarship has shed light on their activities and personnel.[75] The judicial path in Castile was marked by slow progress toward higher and higher positions over proven service, loyalty, and dedication.[76] In the colonies, judges were at first usually Spanish, but over time Creoles made inroads into this high judicial stratum.[77] Members of an *audiencia* were required to maintain social and economic distance from the territory in which they served; they were not to hold property in it, attend social functions, or receive favors.[78] They were not to marry local women.[79] Colonial judges were not to have their own houses, they were not to enter contracts or commerce, nor receive loans or gifts of money, called *dádivas,* or food.[80] Such social and economic isolation served the twin goals of impartiality and clear allegiance to the crown when enforcing royal interests locally. Although impartiality was seen as a requisite quality for these positions, recent scholarship has demonstrated that personal interest might be a factor in their decisions.[81] It is also clear that some judges and other restricted officials, however, sidestepped or ignored these requirements and conducted personal business and influence peddling that led to minor fortunes and landed estates, even in the regions where they served.[82] Some judges bought their positions and the crown's position on sale of judicial office followed its fiscal needs; during times of war or cash shortages, *audiencia* positions were sold.[83] When such positions were sold, dispensations from the rigors of the legal restrictions on economic and social activity might also be purchased.[84] Not all colonial judges peddled influence; some conducted their judicial duties with care, and it appears there was wide variation in the personalities and dedication of *oidores,* even from the earliest colonial times.[85]

The Council of Indies, which recommended candidates to the crown, selected judges and other high *audiencia* officials. Successful appointees had significant university training in law, had almost always served in lesser governmental positions, and had skillfully exercised the requisite patronage connections.[86] They were usually peninsular Spaniards, but some Creoles attained these positions.[87] Few were able to obtain appointments to peninsular councils, such as the Council of the Indies, from colonial posts. Exceptional cases, such as Juan de Solórzano's appointment to the Council of Indies from the *audiencia* of Lima, were possible.[88] Somewhat more typical of the early colonial period was the career of Alonso de Zorita who began as a law student at Salamanca, obtained several colonial positions including those of *oidor* in the *audiencias* of Española and then Mexico, and returned to Spain after this successful royal service to seek enough funds from the crown to live in Granada without running into debt.[89] Later in the colonial period, many *oidores* were the products of colonial education and experience, although crown policy vacillated on and reflected central authoritarian concerns on the question of whether it was better to have American- or Spanish-born judges.[90] As the crown reasserted control on colonial institutions in the second half of the eighteenth century, Spanish-born judges again were favored over American-born judges.[91] Local judges (*alcaldes ordinarios*) were not university-trained lawyers, but were required, in theory, to be literate and citizens of the city in which they served.[92] University-trained lawyers, where available, might serve as *asesores* in difficult cases.[93]

Juan de Solórzano Pereira.

Sources

ALTHOUGH scholars may disagree about the application of terms such as *public law* and *private law* to the Spanish colonial legal world, the distinction is useful in setting out the most important legal sources of the period. This chapter discusses public law sources first, particularly as they relate to perhaps the most important colonial legal source, the *Recopilación* of 1680. The chapter then addresses private law, especially the important *Siete Partidas,* and commentary sources. Last, the way sources were used in legal disputes in the colonial period is described.

The Spanish colonial law, or *derecho indiano,* was constructed out of the *cédulas,* provisions, instructions, letters, ordinances, decrees, and the like issued by or in the name of the crown. The different names attached to these different types of royal orders have more to do with a difference in the destination of the order rather than a difference in the issuing body.[1] *Cédulas* were the most common way for the crown to make laws for the colonies; provisions and *pragmáticas* were more formal and might be used for special situations such as where the crown wanted to assert its power directly or grant a favor by naming someone to a royal position. *Cartas* were letters answering questions by the crown's subjects and officials. *Ordenanzas* were groups of laws regulating entire institutions. Instructions provided minutely detailed rules for officials. Bourbon colonial rulers added decrees (*decretos*), orders (*órdenes*), and regulations (*reglamentos*), which were usually directed to colonial officials.[2] The history of colonial legal sources focuses on attempts, some successful and many others unsuccessful, to pull these various royal orders together into useful compilations for the courts and practitioners. These compilations were sometimes the result of official requests for such work, and at other times, they were undertaken through individual initiative.

Until 1614, Castilian law, as the laws of the colonial power, automatically governed and applied to the Indies. Thereafter, Castilian legislation did not automatically apply, but had to state specifically its applicability to the Indies.[3] Castilian law of the period was not a monolithic entity ready to be easily applied in the colonies. It suffered from a multiplicity of sources, *fueros*, special jurisdictions, special privileges, and its own shifting legislation. Indeed peninsular *fueros* could be so powerful that residents in the colonies might assert they could only be tried in the courts validly having the jurisdiction of the *fuero*, in other words, a particular court located in Spain.[4]

Laws aimed at the colonies reveal the crown's close supervision of its economic interests. Trade, royal governing institutions, and taxation were minutely addressed in legislation. Margadant has stated that the Spanish crown provided legislation that was a "distrusting law plagued with bureaucratic procedures," that led to "casuistic" forms of argument, so that colonial "practice and formal law were frequently divorced from each other."[5] Even if the letter of the law was not followed in practice, the texts themselves were considered important. By selective application of their provisions, the laws allowed local authorities to maintain power and demonstrate flexibility; by selective enforcement of their provisions, the laws allowed central authority to gain the same benefits.[6] Thus, the availability and knowledge of these texts were essential parts of colonial rule.

Numerous attempts were made to compile and organize the various royal materials related to regulating and governing the Spanish colonies. Ots Capdequí conveniently divides these attempted compilations into two groups, territorial and continental. The first territorial collections are from New Spain (Mexico). Following the wishes of a 1556 royal *cédula*, Maldonado, the *fiscal* of the *audiencia* of New Spain, prepared a collection called *Repertorio de las cédulas, provisiones y ordenanzas reales*. A few years later, another *fiscal* in Mexico, Vasco de Puga published a work later known as the *Cedulario de Puga* (1563).[7] This work chronologically republished laws affecting Mexico from 1525 to 1562.[8] Another Mexican collection, although with broader application to the Indies generally, was Alonso de Zorita's *Compilación para las Indias en general* (1574). Before preparing the draft, which has only recently been discovered, Zorita worked for twenty years in the *audiencias* of Santo Domingo, Guatemala, and Mexico.[9] Zorita's work was never published and never became a separate authority.[10] Peru, like its northern counterpart, also sought compilations of laws affecting the government of its region, and Viceroy Francisco de Toledo was asked to compile the legal provisions governing his territory, but it appears he did not accomplish the task.[11]

Peninsular institutions governing the colonies had better collections of legal sources, and the continental compilations applicable to the Indies were more numerous and successful. The first important project was by Juan de Ovando, a member of the Council of the Indies, jurist, and politician in the court of Philip II. Ovando attempted a compilation that went far beyond the mere collection of governing materials presented chronologically. Instead, he sought a topical division into seven books as follows: spiritual government, temporal government, justice, Spaniards, Indians, revenue, and navigation and trade.[12] Ovando not only sought to compile laws and reorganize them into a more useful structure but also suggested reforms such as placing experienced *oidores* on the council and other administrative reforms not directly touching private law.[13] Like so many of the attempts in the colonies, Ovando's work was neither readily nor entirely enacted by the crown. Except for the title concerning the Council of the Indies in book 2, which was enacted in 1571, Ovando's work did not govern as authority.[14]

Numerous similar projects followed, some more ambitious or successful than others. Four volumes of legal materials known as the *Ordenanzas de Encinas* were published by Diego de Encinas, an official of the Council of the Indies, in 1596.[15] Diego de Zorrilla, also an official of the council, continued this work, but little is known of how far it advanced. It appears that the only copy was forwarded to the drafters of the successful *Recopilación* of 1680.[16]

Following the structure of earlier Castilian works and abandoning a chronological presentation, Rodrigo de Aguiar y Acuña published his *Summario* in 1628. In this work, he attempted to publish only provisions that were in force, but the summary was never completed, and he died in 1629.[17] Antonio de León Pinelo who had been collaborating with Aguiar continued the work.[18] From about twenty thousand royal *cédulas* and orders, Pinelo produced a work of ten thousand laws.[19] The compilations discussed here were the most important, but there were numerous others.[20]

The public law of the Indies was successfully compiled in 1680 as the *Recopilación de Leyes de las Indias* (R.I. or L.I.), and should not be confused with other works with similar names. The *Nueva Recopilacíon* (1567) and the *Novísima Recopilación* (1805) are both Castilian sources of predominantly private law.[21] Providing the rules for government structures and institutions, this work was consulted and cited frequently, and it has been the subject of numerous studies.[22] In enacting the *Recopilación* of 1680, Charles II ordered that earlier, contradictory laws no longer held authority.[23]

Based on the works of Aguiar, León Pinelo, and perhaps Solórzano Pereira, the *Recopilación* was the most important source for public law until independence and was reissued numerous times during the period.[24] Its sources are laws emanating from the Spanish crown and peninsular royal bodies, but not from the colonial *audiencias,* viceroys, *consulados,* or *cabildos.*[25] The first edition was published in 1681 with reissues in 1756, 1774, and 1791. Updated versions were published in 1841 and 1864.[26] It is divided into nine books and 218 titles. At the beginning of each law, the text indicates its provenance, although the references are sometimes inaccurate. Despite being an attempt to set out the laws in force, the text is sometimes self-contradictory.[27] Topics covered by the *Recopilación* are as follows:

Book 1 the church, clergy, and ecclesiastical finances.

Book 2 the Council of the Indies, *audiencias*, the Juzgado de Bienes de Difuntos, and their personnel.

Book 3 the viceroy and military matters.

Book 4 discovery of new areas, establishing towns, coinage, and manual factories (*obrajes*).

Book 5 *governaciones, alcaldes mayores, corregidores*, special jurisdictions, and procedures.

Book 6 reductions of Indians, Indian tribute, *repartimientos, encomiendas*, Indian labor.

Book 7 moral and criminal offenses.

Book 8 finances.

Book 9 the Board of Trade, commerce between the colonies and Spain, and immigration to the colonies.[28]

Thus the *Recopilación* of 1680 covered a wide range of public law. Nonetheless, for the purposes of colonial private law, the work is also important. For example, there is much to be found on property law, commerce, family relationships, and the status of Indians.[29] Commentaries on the *Recopilación* were available and Cuervo, Palacios, Ayala, and Zurita wrote popular legal works based on it.[30]

The new Bourbon Spanish monarchy proposed many constitutional and legal reforms, and the colonial laws did not escape these changes. In 1719, Juan del Corral Calvo de la Torre, an *oidor* in the *audiencia* of Chile began to reform the *Recopilación* of 1680. A *fiscal* of the same *audiencia*, Tomás de Azúa, continued the task after Corral's death, and after Azúa's death, the viceroy appointed José Perfecto de Salas to finish the work. These attempts apparently produced no results.[31] In 1776, Charles III decreed that additions would no longer be permitted to the *Recopilación* of 1680 and that a new code of the laws of the Indies would be prepared, upon which no glosses or commentaries would be permitted. Under Manuel José Ayala, who had begun work on such a new compilation, a drafting committee including Miguel José Serrador and Juan Crisóstomo Ansotegui, high Spanish officials in organizations then governing the Indies, undertook the new compilation.[32] Ayala was born in Panama in 1726 and worked for its *audiencia* and then went to study law in Spain where he became an official and archivist to the Council of the Indies.[33] His *Cedulario índico* served as a basis for the committee's work. Book 1 was presented for publication to Charles IV, who decreed a law in 1792 approving the law of the new code. The work of the commission ended in 1799 with further laws enacted, and Ferdinand VII appointed a commission to reform colonial laws in 1817, but by then independence was well under way.[34]

The authors of these compilations were the elite of the colonial-peninsular legal system. Their professional lives demonstrate that on the highest levels of legal society there was a fluidity between colony and mother country. For example, Zorilla began in Spain, taking a bachelor's degree in law from Salamanca and his licentiate from Sigüenza, before working in Quito for many years.[35] Antonio de León Pinelo began in the colonies where he had served as an *audiencia* lawyer, a *corregidor* of the mining powerhouse Potosí, a representative of the city of Buenos Aires, and later in Spain, as a member of the Council of the Indies. Some might begin in Spain, make their professional mark in the Indies, and return to Spain as highly valued officials. Such was the case of Juan de Solórzano Pereira. He was born in Madrid in 1575 and studied and taught at Salamanca in both canon and civil law. In 1609 he was appointed an *oidor* of the *audiencia* of Lima and taught law at the university in Lima. He returned to Spain and became a member of the Council of the Indies from which he retired in 1654.[36]

Compilers were usually experienced judges and knew that such works needed to aid the profession in finding the applicable legal rule to a dispute. With this difficulty in view, the *Recopilación* of 1680 set out the rules by which private law rules were to be determined by the courts and practitioners. Law 2, title 1, book 2, refers the lawyer to the *Leyes de Toro* (1505), which, in turn, refers the lawyer to the *Ordenamiento de Alcalá* (1348). The *ordenamiento* provides a hierarchy of authority of itself followed by the local *fueros* and the *Fuero Real,* followed by the *Siete Partidas.* This was also the order provided by law in Castile under the *Nueva Recopilación de Castilla* (1567) and the *Novísima Recopilación* (1805).[37] Of these sources, the *Siete Partidas* was the most important for colonial private law.

In civil litigation, the thirteenth-century collection of laws known as the *Siete Partidas* (1265) was a usual source for private law in colonial litigation.[38] The Argentine legal historian Ricardo Levene writes: "The application of the laws of the *Partidas* was constant in the Indies. The judges of the Río de la Plata invoke them in almost all cases, as a legal and doctrinal source at the same time."[39] The contents of the *Partidas* are as follows:

Partida 1   The Catholic faith, the church and the *patronato.*
Partida 2   Kings, knights, war, and studies.
Partida 3   Justice, procedures, property.
Partida 4   Personal status, marriage, family law.
Partida 5   Commercial law, sales, leases.

Partida 6   Succession and testaments.
Partida 7   Criminal law.[40]

Written during the reign of Alfonso X, the Wise, the *Partidas* were most likely
the product of Master Jacobo, Fernando Martínez de Zamora, and Master
Roldán.[41] Ots Capdequí states that the most important sources of the *Partidas*
are the *corpus juris civilis*, the glossators, the Decretals of Gregory IX, and
the decretalists. Feudal law expressed in the *libri feudorum*, commercial law as
found in the *Roles de Olerón*, and the works of one of the compilers, Master
Jacobo, served as additional sources.[42] As mentioned earlier, the glosses on
the *Partidas* by Gregorio López were frequently used, although others, such
as Alonso Díaz de Montalvo, also commented on the work.[43] The rules of the
Partidas also found their way into the *Recopilación de Castilla* (1567), and because Castilian private law was colonial private law this *recopilación* was also
a valuable source in colonial practice.

Scholarly or doctrinal writings were an important supplemental source to
the texts of the laws. Frequently used peninsular sources such Juan Sala's *Ilustración de derecho real de España* (1803) and José María Álvarez's *Instituciones
de derecho real de Castilla y de Indias* (1818) were of great use to colonial lawyers,
and both works appeared in colonial editions.[44] Juan de Solórzano Pereira's
Política indiana (1647) is perhaps the best-known secondary work on colonial
institutions. It was first published in Latin (*De indiarum iure et gobernatione*),
but quickly thereafter translated into Spanish.[45] The work addresses the status
of Indians, encomiendas, the royal patronage, secular government, and royal
finances.[46] Solórzano has already been mentioned as a possible contributor to
the *Recopilación* of 1680 and was a student, and later professor, at Salamanca,
an *oidor* in the *audiencia* of Lima, a *fiscal* of both the treasury council and the
Council of the Indies, and at the end of his political and legal career, a member of the council.[47] Antonio de León Pinelo, whose compilation work also
led to the *Recopilación* of 1680, published an important treatise in 1630, *Tratado de confirmaciones reales, encomiendas, oficios y casos en que se requieren para
las Indias*. The work covers numerous topics of both public and private law
including *encomiendas, repartimientos*, pensions, and land grants. Pinelo was
first a student, then later a professor at Lima, was an *abogado* of its *audiencia*, a
corregidor of Oruro, and an *asesor* of the *corregidor* of the wealthy silver-mining
city, Potosí.[48]

Similar to the other works mentioned, Juan de Matienzo's *Government of
Peru* (*Gobierno del Perú*) addressed the structure of judicial institutions, *encomiendas*, mining, and landholding. Matienzo was a sixteenth-century jurist
who served as *oidor* of the *audiencia* of Charcas and collaborated with Viceroy
Francisco de Toledo.[49]

Although the *Siete Partidas* provided a basic framework of civil procedure, based on Roman law, for judicial proceedings, this body of rules was
supplemented by further peninsular legislation, including the *Leyes de Estilo*
from the fourteenth century and the late-fifteenth-century *Leyes hechas . . .
por la brevedad y orden de pleitos.*[50] *Audiencia* procedure was set out in Juan
de Hevia Bolaños's *Curia Philipica,* a standard work for colonial lawyers on
general aspects of litigation and appeal.[51]

In the eighteenth century, Manuel José Ayala produced several ancillary
works to his compilation efforts. His *Diccionario de gobierno y legislación de
Indias* presented colonial legislation alphabetically according to topic.[52] In
1804 he asked for permission to publish his *Origen e historia ilustrada de las
leyes de Indias.*[53]

In addition to commentary works on government institutions and private
law, two Spanish sixteenth-century treatises on commercial law were popular
sources in the period in the colonies: Fray Thomás de Mercado's *Summa de
tratos y contratos* (Sevilla, 1587) and Bartolomé de Albornoz's *El Arte de los contratos* (Valencia, 1573). Already mentioned, the treatise by Juan de Hevia Bolaños was a standard work for commercial law into the independence period
and was available in several subsequent editions.[54] The work covers all common aspects of land and sea trade, including markets, partnerships, trademarks, sales, usury, accounts, contracts, debts, shipping, customs, and the
like.[55] Commercial tribunals (*consulados*) both on the peninsular and in Latin
America used their own sets of rules. Particularly important for our consideration are the Ordinances of Bilbao confirmed first in 1560, replaced later by
the new Ordinances of Bilbao of 1737. These were adopted for use in the *consulado* of Cartagena and were highly influential texts in the colonial *consulados.*[56]
Similarly, in ecclesiastical tribunals, canon law was applied to disputes.[57]

The extent to which custom was a source of law has recently become a debated aspect of colonial Spanish legal history. In comparison to laws and commentary, custom and case law (jurisprudence) were relatively unimportant
sources.[58] Custom, however, might be a useful source in a few specific areas
such as trade and mining.[59] Some scholars have also seen custom as highly
influential in the ways royal Spanish law was implemented through relatively
autonomous and flexible colonial institutions to fit local circumstances.[60] Custom also continued to be a significant source for private law in the sphere of
Indian property and communities.[61] For example, during the early colonial
period, in disputes between Indian litigants, royal courts attempted to apply
rules formed from native tradition, and during the sixteenth century, Indian
litigants might strategically choose between Spanish royal law and indigenous
custom as applicable authority.[62]

By far the most common and influential source for private law in the colonial period was the *Siete Partidas*. Although royal legislation placed the *Siete Partidas* somewhat far down the list of authorities to be consulted, all the sources above it on the list usually contained no direct applicable provision concerning the areas of private law that found their way into the courts. Furthermore, in colonial America the *Siete Partidas* did not have to compete with the sets of jealously guarded regional rights and private rules of law found in the peninsular *fueros*.[63]

In the legal centers of the royal *audiencias*, lawyers and judges used a wide range of written sources beyond the *Siete Partidas* to advance or justify their positions. A study of civil actions before the *audiencia* of Santa Fe of Nueva Granada in the eighteenth century reveals the wide range of legal sources used by a mature colonial tribunal. The court uses various primary legislative sources including, among others, the *Siete Partidas*, the *Leyes de Toro*, *Municipales*, royal *cédulas*, the *Recopilación de las Indias*, the *Recopilación de Castilla*, and the *Fuero Real*.[64] It also makes use of commentary sources from Spanish, colonial, and the *ius commune* traditions, including Bobadilla's *Política*, the glosses of Antonio Gómez on the *Leyes de Toro*, Acevedo, Antonio de Ayala, Juan Gutiérrez on the *Nueva Recopilación*, Hermosilla, Matienzo, Inbáñez de Faria, Covarrubias, Salgado, Villadiego, Molina, Avendaño, Gregorio López's glosses on the *Siete Partidas*, the glosses of Febrero, Juan Andrés, Domingo Soto, Menochio, Baldus, Bartolus, Carleval's *Tratado de Juicios*, Antonio Canario, Serafino, Cartario, Parladorio, Cardenal de Tusco's *Diccionario*, and Montesquieu.[65] Likewise, in a usury case from the 1790s, one *procurador* displayed his knowledge of the topic by running through the various positions taken by Gaius, Paul, Scevola, Papinian, Doroteo, Tribonian, Azon, and Accursius.[66]

The variety and nature of sources used indicate that central tribunals undertook their task well within the tradition of the European *ius commune*, which was imported through legislative and educational channels to the courts of the New World, to the point of using late *mos italicus* sources until the end of the colonial period.[67] Collections of books indicating lawyers' familiarity with sources of the *ius commune* are found throughout the Spanish colonies, even in somewhat more remote areas.[68] This practice of citing numerous authorities in complex, important cases in central tribunals was not uncommon and continued despite a law from 1499 limiting lawyers' citations to only Juan Andrés, Baldus, Bartolus, and Panormitanus.[69] Nonetheless, the determination of the extent to which the *ius commune* infiltrated judicial decisions is greatly hindered by a prohibition of judges stating their reasoning for any particular decision. "It should be noted that we can never be sure of the exact judicial reasoning in the verdict, because the Castilian and, by extension, colonial legal systems forbade magistrates from issuing a written explanation (*sentencia fundada*) of their decision."[70]

In clear contrast to the sophistication of central practice, local officials with judicial power in peripheral areas settled legal disputes by applying what rules they could muster through summary procedures. They relied on what Cutter has described as the "inherent flexibility" of Spanish colonial law, especially as the *derecho vulgar* was applied in these areas.[71] Nonetheless, even in the remote areas studied by Cutter, there is evidence that parties cited the *doctores* in their arguments and that "some frontier magistrates did, indeed, consider *doctrina* in their judgments."[72] It also appears that even the most remote jurisdictions had a basic library of texts, which would have included the *Recopilación de Indias,* the *Nueva Recopilación de Castilla,* and the *Novísima Recopilación.*[73] The extent to which the *Novísima Recopilación* (1805) was authority in the colonies is debated, but there is evidence that its provisions were used in late colonial and early republic tribunals.[74]

In summary, there were a number of primary and commentary sources available to legal practitioners and judges in colonial Latin America, and in the legal centers, these individuals followed the continental *ius commune* tradition they had acquired in their university studies. By far, the most common source for private law rules in litigation was the *Siete Partidas,* but recourse was had to numerous other works of varying importance. In legal proceedings in peripheral areas, the use of sources and the complexity of legal argument diminished significantly.

Personal Status

COLONIAL Latin America was a socially stratified society. Social distinctions were made on the bases of race, sex, age, family lineage, religion, marital status, place of birth, occupation, wealth, and personal attributes.[1] The law reflected and reinforced many of these distinctions. There were consequently a multiplicity of juridical categories for individuals and entities subject to the law. Castilian, and consequently colonial, law recognized different levels of individuals based on birth. Other individuals claimed different or special treatment due to their being subject to a particular *fuero*, such as the ecclesiastical *fuero*.[2] Latin America also presented a host of new categories and distinctions that were expressed in legal rules. The legal significance of some peninsular distinctions was increased as certain groups were either favored or excluded from travel to the colonies. From the moment of European contact, at least two systems of social and legal distinctions were forced to interact, but the subjugated indigenous populations continued their own legal and social traditions of grouping individuals. Some of these indigenous distinctions were, in turn, adopted or indirectly used by the Spanish ruling population.

The *Siete Partidas* speaks of the free, servants, slaves, and the freed. Free people were either nobles or plebeians. Nobles enjoyed a socially, economically, and legally privileged status. They were exempt from certain taxes, were not subject to forfeiture or torture as punishment for certain crimes, and when guilty, received lighter prison terms. Plebeians received none of these special benefits. An important aspect of legal identity for a free man was whether he was considered a citizen (*vecino*) of the city in which he resided. In the colonies, at first this term only meant those who held an *encomienda* of Indians; by 1554, a royal *cédula* extended the term to mean one who owned a house and household in a city. As a result, from the beginning of the colonial period, property ownership carried political consequences. The status of *vecino* might be available to legitimate, mixed-race children, *mestizos* and *mulatos,* but according to contemporary sources most were born illegitimate.[3] Servants and slaves, of course, were subject to various social and legal detriments. Agricultural wage workers, *gañanes,* could rapidly fall into debt under a system completely stacked against them and become debt-peons who were effectively bound to the *hacienda.*[4] Their plight was arguably better than slaves. Because of its important place in the social, legal, and economic world of colonial Latin America, slavery is addressed in a separate chapter.

One way peninsular legal distinctions were applied to colonial activities was through restrictions on travel or on immigration. The crown tightly controlled legal travel and immigration to the colonies through the Board of Trade.[5] At first, only Castilians, and then later Spanish peninsulars were permitted the journey. Exceptions were made for artisans, and naturalization though marriage was also possible.[6] Only Castilians were permitted to trade in the Indies, to obtain *encomiendas,* and to fill prebends and ecclesiastical benefices. At first, these prohibitions extended even to people from other regions of Spain such as Aragon and Navarra, but the restrictions based on region diminished over time. In the 1550s, priests from Navarra were permitted to take benefices in the Indies. By the time of the *Recopilación* of 1680, Spaniards generally were permitted to travel to the Indies. Some restrictions continued to apply and the following groups were not permitted passage to the Indies: those from Moorish or Jewish family lines, those reconciled with or punished by the Inquisition, black "*Ladinos,*" Gypsies, married slaves who did not travel with their wife and children, unmarried women without license, and married people not accompanied by their spouses.[7] Application for a license of passage to the Indies had to be made in person to the Board of Trade and involved setting out the minutia of eligibility for passage.[8] By the eighteenth century, restrictions on foreigners traveling to the Spanish colonies were relaxed in practice, although they remained in the applicable royal legislation.[9]

Once present in the colonies, those born in Spain had a clear societal advantage, and almost all of the top government positions were reserved for those born on the peninsula. Children of Spanish-born parents in the colonies took on a separate, slightly lower, status in colonial society, *criollo* or Creole. Under the law, Creoles did not have any different status from the peninsulars, but they frequently had difficulty breaking into the highest levels of government or church service.[10]

Perhaps the most important social distinctions in the colonies were based on race. From the moment Spanish men encountered Indian women, racially mixed offspring were inevitable, and the general term *mestizo* was applied to these individuals. The possibilities of racial, and resultant legal, complexity were not limited to interaction between those of predominately Spanish descent and those of indigenous descent; millions of Africans imported as slaves to the colonies contributed to the myriad of possibilities and possible distinctions. Just as race, and racial categorization, had enormous social and economic consequences in the colonies, the law too reflected such distinctions. The law regulated slaves, slavery, and the slave trade. The public law of the Indies created separate governmental institutions for Indians, including rules establishing settlements and towns, their internal structure, the function of those Creole or Spanish individuals permitted to be in such settlements, and their relationship to the overall bureaucratic hierarchy of colonial rule.

Colonial private law addressed questions of property ownership by Indians, inheritance rights, and the extent to which indigenous rules of law would be permitted to apply to these populations. These examples demonstrate that racial distinctions were often at the core of both public and private law in the Latin American colonies. In many instances, racial distinctions provided the organizational category around which certain areas of the law were created and maintained. Racial categorization and the ruling elite's fear of miscegenation were also strongly present in other areas of the law, such as marriage. Because racial categories were essential for determining social and legal benefits, many have thought that colonial society and institutions made painstakingly strict determinations of racial lineage, categorizing individuals with a range of terms to indicate precise proportions of Spanish, Indian, or Africa blood he or she carried and translated these terms into a strictly enforced caste system. Nonetheless recent research challenges older perceptions of a strict caste system in the Spanish Indies.[11] Still, certain aspects of such a system are evident in the colonial laws related to marriage and family.

The *Siete Partidas* stressed the nuclear family and incorporated the Roman law of *patria potestad,* the father's authority over the family.[12] Majority was twenty-five years of age and women were held under the authority of their fathers, nearest male relative, or husbands. As a general rule, the husband managed the wife's property. A dowry (*dote*) was paid on marriage and was managed by the husband for the benefit of the wife and her children.[13] Dowries usually consisted of personal property and cash; slaves and real property were less common components.[14] In addition to the dowry, marriage brought with it a different set of property relationships. The husband might also make a marriage gift of property to the wife, called an *arras*. The wife was also permitted paraphernalia (*bienes parafernales*), consisting of her personal property and property individually acquired by her through inheritance or gift during the marriage. The property falling into these categories was immune from the financial misfortunes of the husband.[15]

New social factors present in Latin America forced royal legislation to adapt to these conditions. On one hand, greater flexibility was offered to permit valid marriage: impediments were reduced, parental permissions for blacks and *mulatos* were waived, and methods for transforming indigenous marriages to Christian marriages were provided. On the other hand, Spaniards imposed antimiscegenation laws, stipulated penalties for Spaniards who abandoned their wives in Spain, and the Council of the Indies was given some control over legitimization.[16] Laws applicable to the Indies demonstrated a clear policy of keeping married couples together in face of the new distances and mobility that were provided by and within the colonies.[17] An entire title (book 7, title 3) of the *Recopilación* of 1680 addresses married Spaniards in the colonies without their spouses.[18] Historians have recently documented a sixteenth-century prosecution for transatlantic bigamy.[19] Sixteenth-century laws also demonstrate the colonial coercive policy of encouraging marriage to the point of forcing single *encomienda* holders to lose their interests if they did not marry (1551) and of expelling singles from Spanish towns (1595).

During the early colonial period, cohabitation with indigenous women appears to have been a common, yet unapproved, practice and led to government sanctions, such as loss of inheritance, to discourage it.[20] This policy was justified with the dual crown goal of populating the colonies and setting Christian example for the Indians. It also probably served another important goal of limiting inheritance of *encomiendas*. Christian marriages between Spanish men and Indian women were officially permitted by royal *cédula* in 1514 and this was incorporated into book 6, title I, law 2, of the *Recopilación* of 1680. Thus a substantial legitimate *mestizo* population was possible.[21]

Ecclesiastical law was an important source of the family and marriage provisions of the *Siete Partidas* and played a significant role in later developments as well, especially as Spain closed ranks against the Reformation. Thus the Council of Trent was incorporated into Spanish law by royal *cédula* in 1564.[22] Legal aspects of Christian marriage were carried along with the church's conversion activities, and the public marriage of Indian elites was seen as an effective method to spread doctrine. Monogamous marriage clashed harshly with some Indian practices; in some areas nobles might have as many as two hundred wives.[23] Addressing polygamous families, the church wished to consider the wife with first sexual relations with the husband as the legitimate wife.[24] The problem for the church and Spanish authorities was short-lived; by the end of the sixteenth century, such communities had adopted Spanish ways.[25]

Trying to limit marriages between "unequals," a royal *pragmática* of March 23, 1776, required that adults under twenty-five years of age receive permission from their parents before marriage. The law severely punished those who married without permission, requiring the loss of dowry, inheritance, and rights in entailed estates.[26] Marriages between Spaniards and black or *mulato* women were particularly discouraged. The governing concern here was not miscegenation generally, because permission was not required for marriages between blacks or *mulatos*.[27] A decree of July 17, 1803, changed the ages to twenty-five for males and twenty-three for females. The need for parental permission to marry was cast in racial terms in 1803 when the viceroy expressed his concern to the king that nobles and those of pure Spanish blood (*limpieza de sangre*) were attempting to marry blacks, *mulatos*, and other castes. The king replied that even when one or both parties were above the age limit, royal assent through viceroy, president, or *audiencia* was required for such a union.[28] By 1805 all interracial marriages had to be approved by governmental authorities.[29] Laws aside, it appears that men of Spanish descent frequently had offspring, legitimate or otherwise, with Indian and black women in the sixteenth century, with *mestizo* women of mixed races in the seventeenth century, and with lighter-skinned *mestizo* women in the eighteenth century.[30]

Although royal laws and policy indicated that Indians were not suitable matches for Spaniards and Creoles, Indians were also seen as a group requiring special protection under legislation. Many of these efforts were in response to the well-documented contemporary abuses of native populations. For example, during the second half of the sixteenth century, the crown sought various methods to provide legal representation for Indians. This sometimes meant just adding the duties of serving as a legal representative for Indian parties to an already overtaxed official. The crown also accommodated the costs of prosecuting or defending Indians. For example, at first, Indian litigants were assessed court fee at a rate of about one-sixth the amount charged non-Indian litigants, but this order was suspended in the mid sixteenth century. Colonial institutions were also created solely for litigation concerning Indians, such as the General Indian Court of New Spain, which, despite a royal order prohibiting its hearing cases between Indians and Spaniards, decided such cases.[31] One historian of this tribunal concluded that the court served to relieve a certain amount of hostility of the Indians in the region and, thus "Indian riots and rebellions in Mexico were relatively infrequent in the colonial period."[32] The ways that Indian status was combined with landholding and exploitative labor practices are addressed in a separate chapter.

Race was not the only factor leading to disparate treatment under the colonial legal system. Some members of society were also subjects of particular legislation because they were seen as requiring special protection. As in Castile, the crown sought to provide legal representation for the poor, and during the second half of the sixteenth century, *audiencias* appointed legal officials, called *procuradores de pobres* or *abogados de pobres*, to serve the poor.[33] Children too were protected in the legislation for the Indies, and the colonial state recognized its obligation to find homes for abandoned and disabled children. Sale of daughters into marriage was prohibited by colonial legislation.[34] Illegitimacy was a significant social and legal disability in colonial society as well.[35] There were, however, means by which some illegitimate children could be legitimized through subsequent marriage, ecclesiastical petition, royal decree, declaration in a testament, or by a signed public instrument with three witnesses.[36]

Legislatively imposed restrictions on women were also justified under the guise of protecting them from the undue influence of the unscrupulous.[37] Generally, the status of Spanish and Creole women is not addressed in colonial legislation, and they shared similar status and disabilities as women on the peninsula.[38] Under Spanish law, women were excluded from political and religious power, and their economic activities were limited when compared to those of men. Nonetheless, in practice, women still might buy, sell, rent, and inherit property. As one scholar of Mexican women in the late colonial and early republic period writes: "They could lend and borrow money, act as administrators of estates, and form business partnerships. They could initiate litigation, be their own advocates in court, and appear as witnesses (except in wills)."[39] Nonetheless, as a general principle, married women required permission from their husbands to enter contracts or undertake legal obligations.[40] Furthermore, Kellogg's research indicates that some of the incapacities imposed by Spanish law simply were not followed in practice; for example, women litigated in their own name and served as witnesses in testaments.[41] Similarly, Lavrin and Couturier's work indicates women circumvented restrictions to engage in small-scale commerce.[42]

The status of Indian women was dramatically changed by the introduction of Spanish law in Latin America. Spanish conceptions of dowry and inheritance rights, associated with Spanish women, from the *Siete Partidas* and the *Leyes de Toro* were superimposed onto Indian women in colonial society. These codes favored the claims of the spouse and children above those of parents and siblings.[43]

By the late eighteenth century, the relationship between marriage restrictions and racial policy became increasingly complex. For example, in a case from 1790 brought in Santa Fe de Bogotá, María de la Mercedes Ferreiro brought an action against Pablo Serna for not fulfilling his promise to marry her. Pablo claimed that as a white he was prohibited by the *Real Pragmática* on marriage of 1776 from marrying María, a *mulata*. The *asesor* determined that Pablo was not white, but a *mestizo,* and the issue became whether the *Pragmática* extended to *mestizos.* The Fiscal of Santa Fe argued that it did not apply to marriages celebrated between *mulatos* or blacks, but did apply to *mestizos* because they were to enjoy the same rights as Spaniards as stated in Solórzano's *Política indiana.* María countered that the *Pragmática* was aimed only at Europeans and that Pablo was estopped from asserting the rule because others in his family were married to *mulatos*. A private reconciliation between María and Pablo produced a daughter, and Pablo offered financial support, but he still wanted the rule applied so that he would be free to marry another woman. The *audiencia* granted him the right.[44] This case indicates the complex social and legal consequences of personal status in the colonial period. Racial characterization mattered not only on a social and economic level, but on a legal level as well. In order to apply rules of law in which racial determinations were legally operative, the court had to assign race to parties. The case also indicates the manner in which marriage decisions and possibilities could be controlled by the legal status of the individuals involved.

In this way, personal status in colonial Latin America was dependent on a number of factors. Legislation seeking to protect often disabled those it sought to protect, as in the case of women and Indians. The importance of race in colonial public and private law is evident, so much so that its influence can be seen in the creation of certain public institutions as well as in essential aspects of private family relationships.

Land and Inheritance

"LAND tenure, with all its implications for social organization, the distribution of wealth, and the use of natural resources, is one of the least understood topics in colonial Latin American history," wrote one historian of landholding in colonial Mexico in the 1970s.[1] Although some advances have been made in the subject since then, the assessment is still accurate. With the exception of precious metal, land was the main form of wealth and the bedrock on which Latin American colonial society was constructed.[2] Land not only provided a stream of wealth to be used by the owner but also was frequently mortgaged in colonial times to provide security for loans.[3]

Original Spanish claims to land and the later asserted right to distribute it were based on the papal donations. Distributions were not to affect Indian rights, but this requirement was honored more in the breach.[4] Reflecting Spanish colonial legalism and its reliance on writings, distribution of land was accomplished through a series of documents. For example, the act of distribution (*repartimiento*) was accompanied by a royal *cédula* granting title.[5] One's claim to land often only matured on completing enumerated activities for a period of time on the property. From the 1530s, the viceroy or *audiencia* required that to establish complete ownership of land, a Spaniard had to reside on it for a period of four to eight years, work it, build a house, and promise not to transfer it to the church.[6] Grants of royal land could be used to raise revenue for the crown. By 1591, the crown moved to selling lands and offering them through contracts (*composiciones*).[7] These sales continued to require possession, cultivation, and residence of at least ten years for full ownership to be acquired.[8] During the reign of Philip II, Spain auctioned much *realengo* land, such as woodlands and areas set aside for hunting, to raise funds.[9] Grants might also create financial obligations to the crown, which could be collected as needed.[10] Colonial land titles were subject to periodic royal examination to confirm their validity, and such a *composición de tierras* was conducted in 1640.[11] In 1754, the crown inspected all titles from before 1700 and recognized prescriptive rights for lands cultivated since that date.[12] By the late eighteenth century, individuals who sought ownership of uncultivated lands were provided with methods to claim them.[13] In any event, royal confirmation was normally required for a valid grant of land. At first, the Council of the Indies confirmed grants; later, because this became administratively difficult in the eighteenth century, land judges (*jueces privativos de tierras*) confirmed the transaction without peninsular Spanish action.[14]

The aim behind attaching conditions that the land be worked and actively exploited was to encourage settlement rather than speculation, and in this way colonial laws supported the policy of populating America with Spaniards. Charles V established ordinances about this process in 1523, and Philip II promulgated another more important set of ordinances for population and discovery of new lands in 1573. This second collection of law, containing 149 articles, has been described as "a true code of colonization."[15]

Despite the legislative encouragement to work and to settle lands, the disposition and distribution of vacant royal lands continued to be a concern of the government. In 1735, a royal decree forbade the viceroy and *audiencia* from making grants of vacant land, but by 1754, the crown had reversed its position.[16] In the late colonial period, intendants could sell and distribute royal lands and, with compensation, even privately owned property that was not being cultivated.[17]

On the local level, *cabildos* assumed the power to distribute town lots to members of the community.[18] While the exact amount of land distributed varied, allocations usually made to a head of household included a town lot for a house (*solar de casa*), a garden (*suerte*), and somewhere between one hundred and two hundred acres for crops. Each family also shared rights to use the communally held town property. On the local level, occupation and use of the property for a number of years was also required to perfect a settler's claim, after which time the land was alienable.[19] The few studies addressing the social background of landholders during the colonial period indicate that they were mostly Creoles, with a substantial minority of *mestizo* holders.[20] Larger private grants, ranging in the thousands of acres, were also made to some town members for grazing livestock.

Where possible, a ceremony to transfer land was conducted by the *alcalde*, the grantee, and the neighboring landholders. They walked the borders of the property, placed monuments at crucial intersections where natural landmarks would not serve, and the grantee "plucked up grass, threw stones to signify their dominion over the land, and shouted 'Long live the King!'"[21]

The grantee received a *testimonio,* which was a copy of the documentation related to the transfer; the *expediente,* which included the petition for the grant; a report by the *alcalde;* the grant; and a recitation of the ceremony of possession.[22]

Settlers had rights to use various types of public lands, which were either held by the crown (*tierras realengas, tierras baldías*) or by the municipality (*tierras concegiles*). Grants by the crown were made from the *tierras baldías,* which were available for limited, shared agricultural and livestock uses. Much land held by the municipality was also used communally and was labeled according to the particular permitted uses (*exidos,* used for threshing, dump, stray animals; *montes,* used for wood and pasture; *dehesas,* fenced pasture; and *prados,* high-quality pasture). Other municipally held lands were reserved for municipal finances (*propios*).[23]

The cores of large estates often had their beginning in a royal grant (*merced*) for services to the crown.[24] Despite royal prohibitions on amassing too much land, powerful individuals built large estates through the seizure of unused, unclaimed, or Indian land. Provisions in the royal grants prohibiting alienation for a number of years after the grant were ineffective, and the use of undisclosed agents to request land for large estates was another method of sidestepping restrictions.[25] Land was purchased from Indians, and bolder estate holders simply exerted their force and encroached on the communal lands of neighboring towns.[26] The foreclosure on loans and mortgages of Indian lands provided an additional source for amassing estates.[27] In this way, the rules limiting the amount of land held by any individual and requiring royal confirmation of all grants were often breached in practice. Private landholding frequently exceeded the limits imposed. Land could even be acquired from those with contested rights to distribute it. For example, within colonial Mexico, the fourth marqués del Valle, an heir of Cortés's, sold numerous large grants at public auction based on his unusual seigniorial status.[28] Litigation and settlement with other landholders were additional ways of attaining lands to add to large estates.[29] In addition to rights in land, rights to water for irrigation were equally important in some areas, and similar methods were used to obtain these essential property interests.[30]

These larger estates were in some regions called *haciendas,* and the truly massive estates of several *haciendas* were referred to as *latifundios.*[31] Some of the largest estates achieved near self-sufficiency and asserted their own informal jurisdiction over their residents.[32] As legal entities, large farms (*haciendas* or *estancias*) included not only land and buildings, but also the slaves, animals, crops, machinery, and tools associated with them.[33] In turn, all of these aspects of the estate could be entailed using the *mayorazgo.*[34]

Entails or *Mayorazgos*

Lands were often held in a *mayorazgo* (or *vinculación*), a system of entailing that enabled lands to be passed on to selected individuals within a family, usually the first-born son in a primogeniture inheritance scheme. One writer on the *mayorazgo* defines it this way: "The right to inherit the left property, with the obligation that it is to stay whole in the family perpetually, and to belong to the next first born son in successive order."[35] The *Ordenanzas de Nuevos Descubrimientos, Nuevas Poblaciones y Pacificación de los Indios,* the ordinances for discovery and population of Philip II in 1573, granted to leading settlers (*poblador principal*) the privilege of establishing a *mayorazgo* over all one's property.[36] The institution became popular and was used by wealthy landholders with dynastic intentions and aristocratic aspirations throughout the Latin American colonies.[37]

When following primogeniture, *mayorazgos* were said to be "regular" according to *Partida* 2, title 15, law 2 of the *Siete Partidas;* "irregular" *mayorazgos* followed other patterns of succession according to the will of their founders.[38] Ots Capdequí lists twelve characteristics of the *mayorazgo* estate, which is addressed at length in the *Leyes de Toro:*

1. primogeniture passage (to pass as the succession of the crown of Spain);
2. indivisible nature of the estate;
3. the property is inalienable by the descendants of the founder in perpetuity;
4. the next taker is determined from the current holder by passing the estate to the nearest grade, males exclude females, the older excludes the younger of the same grade, with right of representation;
5. only legitimate descendants take;
6. only legitimate children of valid marriages or subsequent marriage take; legitimate children by royal grant or adoptive or assumed (*arrogado*) children are excluded;
7. descent and grade are determined from the holder not the founder;
8. succession is not by right of inheritance, but by right of blood;
9. ownership of property passes even if it is possessed by others;
10. all improvements pass to the next taker without having to pay the relatives of the deceased holder;
11. *mayorazgos* can be proved by writing, testimony, or immemorial custom;
12. the will of the founder governs the *mayorazgo*.[39]

The property in the *mayorazgo* usually passed on the death of the holder, but it might also pass to the next taker in the event of the holder committing lese majesty, sodomy, or heresy. The general isolation of the property from forfeiture for crimes of the possessor was an additional benefit. Only the founder could revoke or change the terms of the *mayorazgo*. The *mayorazgo* usually resulted in lands being held in a type of trust with a life estate to be given to the eldest son, and *mayorazgos* were most commonly used to establish primogeniture inheritance.[40] This inheritance pattern hindered a fluid market in land and concentrated power in wealthy families. It also might have reduced revenues from sealed paper used to transfer land regularly. As a result, the crown sought to limit *mayorazgos*. For example, in 1585, *audiencia* approval was required to establish a *mayorazgo*.[41] Royal license was required if the founder wished to place all his property into a *mayorazgo*, but if the forced heirs of the *legítima* were not injured, license was not required. Thus, in practice, there were two general types of *mayorazgos*, depending on whether all the settlor's property was put into it or only the portion after the heirs took their established shares under the usual inheritance pattern. The first type required royal license, the second was permitted under law 27 of the Laws of Toro. In 1789, the creation of new *mayorazgos* of the second type was prohibited and royal permission was again required to establish a *mayorazgo*. The crown used this procedure to gather information concerning the nature of the property and the founder's family.[42]

In theory, *mayorazgo* lands could not be mortgaged or sold, but royal licenses were purchased permitting the sale of such lands, and holders of *mayorazgos* also frequently managed to mortgage them to produce income from their life interests.[43] Significant debt seems to be a constant companion to entailed lands, and personal misfortunes and changing agricultural markets could lead holders of *mayorazgos* into substantial debt, forcing the sale of estates and greater mobility in ownership.[44] Nonetheless, as would be expected, lands held in a *mayorazgo* were generally more likely to be kept within a particular family.[45]

In the late colonial period, and in keeping with general European trends in the late eighteenth and early nineteenth centuries, Spain began to disfavor these institutions. In 1796, it imposed a 15 percent tax on *mayorazgos*.[46] During the independence and early republic period, most countries abolished *mayorazgos* through constitutional or statutory action.

The Church and Land

The status of the church as landowner reflected the gap between written law and practiced law in the colonies. Despite colonial laws prohibiting the church from holding lands, it became a large landowner in its own right and an important source of mortgages for landholders.[47] The exact extent of ecclesiastical ownership, outright or beneficial, of land is disputed, but contemporary accounts for Mexico range from 20 to 90 percent of all land.[48] In Oaxaca, the colonial church controlled about 25 percent of useful rural property.[49] Even if the smallest estimates are accepted, the amount is impressive. Not only could the church acquire land, contrary to expectations, it was also able to dispose of some of its lands by sale.[50]

Various legal devices were used to circumvent the prohibition of the church holding land. Through a chaplaincy, *capellanía*, land might be charged with a perpetual sum for the provision of pious works, usually to support a priest to say memorial masses for the soul of the deceased donor.[51] Thus many lands became encumbered with these obligations to the church. Where the administrators named in the founding documents could no longer act or payments were not met, the church often stepped in to administer the estate as its owner or sell the property.[52]

Furthermore, lay religious organizations, *cofradías*, might hold Indian or other land for the church. Just as a lay estate holder might amass lands through foreclosure on mortgages, so too the church, a major source of money lent, moved to repossess lands securing unpaid debts.[53] Church officials, as individuals, might also possess lands. "Individual clerics, vicars, and high church officials frequently possessed, in their own names, estates or mines in their parishes. Neither the original royal prohibitions nor the limitations imposed by the Council of Trent seem ever to have been enforced, even partially."[54] Thus, the church and religious were major figures in holding land and financing land transactions.

In the late colonial period, the crown, attempting to limit church power and increase revenues, began to attack church ownership of lands. In 1798, church lands became subject to a royal *cédula* requiring that they be transferred to the Real Caja de Amortización in return for a fixed 3 percent return.[55] This appropriation of church lands undermined carefully negotiated financial arrangements and forced many large estates to be sold under the new pressure of collecting the loans for which the church held them as security.[56] A crisis in Mexican landholding ensued.[57]

For most of the colonial period, the church was an important actor in the holding, distributing, and financing of land. It used various methods to circumvent royal prohibitions on its ownership of land, and at times merely ignored these aspects of royal laws. It would seem that for most of the period, the crown, with its powerful rights of the *real patronato* over the church, tolerated these infractions or may have viewed its relationship as so close to the church that there was little conflict in permitting the church to own and use lands.

Inheritance

The colonial written testament was a Spanish introduction founded on Christian ideas of the proper way to prepare for death. The theology and ministry of the necessity of testaments was carried with priests, and early religious manuals contained sample testaments.[58] Testaments were so closely linked to a proper Christian death, that intestacy might impede Christian burial.[59] After invoking standard Catholic formulae, the testator was identified in the testament and asserted that there were no impediments to testamentary capacity. Pious bequests usually followed, and the testator then disposed of houses, lands, and personalty. Executors (*albaceas*) were appointed in the testament and the document was signed in the presence of witnesses.[60] Following similar requirements, codicils (*codicilios*) could be used to supplement or change certain aspects of a testament.[61]

The *Siete Partidas* contained a well-developed system of property succession, and testaments and these rules are found in the Castilian sources that applied equally to the colonies, the *Nueva Recopilación* and the *Novísima Recopilación*.[62] Generally following Roman law, testamentary freedom was limited through the *legítima* that required a certain portion of the estate to pass to specified family members.[63] Legitimate descendants were entitled to four-fifths of the testator's property; depending on the particular circumstances, legitimate ascendants might be entitled to a smaller fraction. Where legitimate children inherited this portion, they did so in equal shares from either parent and without regard to sex.[64] Adopted, assumed, natural, and spurious children did not receive a forced share, but could take the portion over which the testator was free to devise, and in the absence of legitimate children, might take a portion by intestacy. For example, according to the *Siete Partidas,* natural children might inherit two-elevenths of the estate, if the father left no legitimate ascendants or descendants. Furthermore, illegitimate children could take the entire estate by testament if the testator was free to devise all the property.[65] Certain classes of individuals, such as children of priests or nuns and clerics assisting the testator at death, were prohibited from inheriting property.[66]

Disinheriting remained a technical possibility, but involved rather grave justifications.[67] The *Siete Partidas* and the *Leyes de Toro* favored the spouse and children above parents and siblings.[68] Through a *mejora,* a limited specific devise to certain family members, testamentary freedom might be exercised over as much as one-fifth to one-third of the estate, but the inheritance provisions were generally protective of the spouse and children as primary beneficiaries.[69] Therefore, even though the *mejora* gave some latitude for the testator to direct the disposition of his property, this portion too was required to be devised to members of the testator's family.

The portion not allocated through this forced heirship scheme was available for the testator to dispose of freely; in fact, however, this portion was usually given to the church for the good of the testator's soul and the forced heirship provisions appear to have developed to provide better for the family in light of a testator's desire to make even larger gifts to the church.[70] Decedents also sought ways to further the familial line in the first-born son despite the rules of inheritance benefiting children more generally. The *mayorazgo* is the best example of these practices, but others, including pious gifts that benefited a particular son and inter vivos gifts, were available under Castilian law.[71] Other provisions governed the partition of inherited property between beneficiaries and the ability to exclude some property for the benefit of the children of a testator's first marriage when he entered into a second marriage.[72]

Testaments were required to follow various formalities that helped to ensure the careful consideration of the testator and the genuineness of the document.[73] Nonetheless, upholding the intent of the testator was often paramount, even to the technical formal requirements of the testament. In a Maracaibo case decided in Santa Fe de Bogotá in 1756, the testatrix died while writing a clause manumitting a slave and her son. Despite the defects in the execution of the testament, the court manumitted the two people.[74]

A special, less formal testamentary regime was established for Indians, and safeguards were imposed to ensure they would not be overly influenced by clerics in the disposition of their property.[75] Examples of such rules are found in laws from 1580 and from 1609.[76] In a survey of Mexican Indian wills during the colonial period, Kellogg has noted the cultural shifts recorded in these documents as Indian ideas of inheritance, land, and family were gradually merged with their Spanish counterparts.[77]

Certain new institutions were required to carry out the distribution of property in the colonies, as well as its safe delivery to beneficiaries on the peninsula. Book 2, title 32, of the *Recopilación* of 1680 addresses colonial probate, and eventually every important city had probate judges (*juzgados especiales de bienes de difuntos*). A special chest with three keys (one each for the *juez,* the *fiscal,* and the *escribano*) held decedents' property that was sent to the Board of Trade for eventual distribution.[78]

Concluding Comments

Thus land was obtained, amassed, financed, and distributed in various ways in colonial Latin America. Recent studies have indicated that the market in land was more active than one might expect. Land was not merely obtained and then entailed or devised. Despite the concerns of the upper classes for entailing lands, and the interest of the middling classes in testaments, in some areas it appears that sale was a much more common method of transferring land than inheritance.[79] Diverse groups had different ideas about land holding. In contrast to Mexican Indians, for example, Spaniards seemed to have been more concerned with keeping family lands together.[80]

By the late eighteenth century, colonial land law had grown to include numerous facets responding to the needs of those exploiting property. To the institutions of mortgages, *mayorazgos,* testaments, and sale, complex duties, rights, and obligations became recognized in the land law, which by this period addressed such topics as drainage; sewers; aqueducts; servitudes for light and view; regulation of sounds, smoke, and odors; party walls; and even esthetic considerations. Where land was tied to economic activity such as loans, mining, and agriculture, extensive laws were enacted to govern these areas.[81]

Commercial Law

T HE extraction of wealth and the concomitant exploitation of native and imported labor were the overall aims of colonial commerce.[1] Geographical distances from Spain, the enormous size of the new colonies, and the lack of an established colonial infrastructure and available commercial tools hindered such activities. Spain responded to these aims by creating a new commercial framework. The crown established new colonial institutions and legal machinery, and adapted and expanded existing governmental structures and legal rules to the new commercial environment. The crown created new institutions, such as the Board of Trade and the colonial *consulados,* that grew on both sides of the Atlantic to further these aims. It enacted new provisions concerning trade, mining, and agriculture, and it put into service older forms of private law for a more complex commercial world.

Maritime Trade

Perhaps the most important aspect of trade for Spain was the control of maritime trade and shipping. Excluding substantial contraband traffic, all trade with the Latin American colonies ran through Spain so that the Spanish crown and merchants profited at several steps of any particular transaction. Only a few select ports in the colonies were officially open for trade, Veracruz in New Spain, Cartagena in New Granada, and Nombre de Dios (Portobello) on the Isthmus of Panama.[2] In the rare moments when the system operated smoothly, large flotillas of merchant ships crossed the ocean twice a year, to deliver and pick up goods.[3]

The main institution for keeping track of this commerce and settling related disputes was the Board of Trade. Established in 1503, it served as civil and criminal court, administrative agency, tax collector, and oceanic and navigational research institute. There was also a *consulado* for colonial trade, the Universidad de Cargadores de las Indias.[4] The crown established this *consu-*

lado, which was modeled on the *consulados* of other Spanish trading cities, in 1543. A prior and two consuls who served as judges constituted its staff. Having a broad jurisdiction based on trade and commerce, the *consulado* removed some of the legal burden from the Board of Trade, whose members retained an appellate jurisdiction. Arguments were to be presented without the use of writings prepared by lawyers, but ordinances of the board in the 1550s and 1580s permitted university-trained lawyers to advance arguments.[5] Both the board and *consulado* were located in Seville, until 1717 when the Board of Trade relocated to Cádiz, which provided a larger port.[6] The important place these matters had in the colonial system is indicated by their extensive treatment in the *Recopilación* of 1680; provisions regarding these institutions, their personnel, procedures, and contracts associated with sea trade fill hundreds of pages in book 9 of the work.[7]

Shipping was subject to various systems of taxation. The complex system of *almojarifazgo* of import and export duties based on valuation, was replaced with a streamlined system in 1720 based on the size, weight, and number of articles shipped.[8] Religious houses often took advantage of their tax exemption to serve as "depositories and distributing centers for contraband goods."[9] Spanish control of shipping was substantially eroded in 1713 when the Treaty of Utrecht gave England an exclusive right to import slaves into Spanish possessions and to send yearly a ship with five hundred tons of European merchandise.[10] In the 1760s, Caribbean ports were permitted to trade directly with peninsular Spain, and customs duties were further simplified to a set percentage of value of the goods shipped.[11] Throughout the eighteenth century, there was substantial debate concerning the best way to restore, maintain, and improve Spain's place in transatlantic commerce. Ideas of continuing and revitalizing a tightly controlled Spanish flotilla system competed with newer ideas of open commerce with many fewer restrictions on trade in and with the colonies.[12] By 1778, the crown released the Spanish colonies from the flotilla system.[13] Trade greatly expanded under these new conditions; older commercial centers came back to life, and newer centers were born.[14]

Mining and Agriculture

One of the greatest sources of wealth in colonial Latin America was precious metals. Spanish explorers quickly found the silver and gold they had sought in Latin America. Mineral rights belonged to the crown and could be privately exploited only with permission.[15] As one of the main goals of exploration and one that panned out relatively early in the colonial period, mining was subject to significant legislation from Spain. In 1589, colonial administrators adopted the *Ordenanzas de Toledo* (after Viceroy Francisco de Toledo of Peru), which went into effect throughout the colonies; in 1683 Spanish authorities expanded these ordinances under the name *Ordenanzas del Perú.*[16] Methods of discovering, claiming, owning, and operating mines were minutely detailed in these ordinances.[17] Mining was treated extensively in the Castilian *Nueva Recopilación,* which incorporated two earlier sets of ordinances on mining (*Ordenanzas del Antiguo Cuaderno* of 1563 and law 9 of the *Ordenanzas XX del Nuevo Cuaderno* of 1584) upon which in 1761 Francisco Javier Gamboa wrote a compilation and commentaries.[18] These commentaries were in turn a major source for the next set of mining ordinances, the *Ordenanzas de Aranjuez* of 1783 (*Ordenanzas de Minería de Nueva España*).[19] These ordinances were applied to Peru in 1785, and then extended to Venezuela, Guatemala, New Granada, and Chile.[20] The mining Ordinances of Aranjuez of 1783 took a broad view of the topics to be covered and addressed the operation of mines, the resolution of mining disputes, the structure and function of the mining guild, the regulation of labor, the financing of the trade, the required technical training for miners, and the privileges of guild membership.[21] Precise rules, based on measured distances, allocated the portions of a mine to be given to the discoverer, the owner of the land, and the king.[22] Generally, active and uninterrupted work on the mine was required to maintain one's claim; a period of idleness as short as twenty days might compromise a mine owner's title.[23] It is no wonder that Indians and slaves were pressed into continuous labor not only to remove as much metal as quickly as possible but also to assert effectively one's claim to the property. Indeed, one of the requirements for keeping a mine active was to have either eight Indians or four slaves working it.[24]

Colonial mining law's degree of complexity can be gathered from one legal historian's attempt to summarize the development of this area of law. After characterizing it as "variable" and "contradictory," Ots Capdequí notes that at first, all mines were royal property, but could be privately exploited with a payment to the crown of 20 percent (*quinta*) or sometimes less. By the time of the *Ordenanzas de Toledo* (1589) the regime changed so that those staking a claim had to reserve the richest vein for the crown called the *mina de su majestad.* The *Recopilación* of 1680 appears to have abandoned this requirement, instead letting everyone exploit mines on payment of the *quinta.* The mining ordinances of 1783 provided even more specialized legislation.[25] With many laws on the topic, great wealth at stake, and numerous potential competing claims for precious metals, ready means of settling mining disputes were essential for maintaining peace and for the efficient extraction of Spain's lifeblood. The mining guild established courts of both original and appellate jurisdiction to hear cases arising in this industry. Mining districts had a provincial court of delegation (*diputación territorial*) whose appeals (after 1793) in New Spain ran to the central mining tribunal in Mexico City.[26]

An *alcalde de minas* served both administrative and judicial aspects of mining using summary procedures. His decisions could be appealed to the *audiencia*.[27] By 1780, the General Tribunal of Mining (Tribunal General de Minería) regulated the industry in New Spain.[28] Although the ordinances required that proceeding be oral and without the involvement of lawyers, the judges, who were miners, relied on legally trained *asesores,* and the parties too soon made use of lawyers in their arguments to the court.[29] Appeals were made to a court known as the Juzgados de Alzadas, composed of two mining representatives and a judge of the *audiencia*.[30]

Another associated method of extracting wealth through land was animal farming. Like the institutions and rules that grew up around the special jurisdiction of mining, a separate body of law and institutions were applied to grange animals. Because of its important place in the peninsular and colonial economy, animal farming was subject to the special jurisdiction of the *Mesta,* which battled cattle rustling and furthered the interests of the large farms. The members (*hermanos*) of the *Mesta* and it officials (*alcaldes*) met regularly to promote their interests, often acting to exclude Indians from these activities.[31]

Contracts and Obligations

Writing in 1952, Ots Capdequí reported that the history of the law of obligations in the Indies had not yet been written.[32] More recent works indicate that little is still known about the law of obligations or contracts in colonial Latin America.[33] Focusing his inquiry on the *Recopilación* of 1680, Ots Capdequí noted that the work does not treat obligations and contracts systematically, nor does it present general theories or principles concerning them.[34] Because of its general emphasis on public law, institutions, and particular areas of commerce, such as maritime trade, the *Recopilación* may not have been the best place to seek a general statement of contract law. The provisions of the *Siete Partidas* concerning promises and obligations address such aspects of reciprocal promises, contractual capacity, representation of parties, the types of promises, performance, interpretation, damages, and defenses such as coercion.[35] Separate sections of the *Siete Partidas* address sales, purchases, and exchanges.[36] To what extent these rules were able to give rise to a general law of contracts in Latin American colonial practice is unknown. Colonial contract law was not a unified body of principles extended to all subject matters. Instead, each area of law had its own individual rules for contractual transactions. Perhaps no general theory of contract under colonial law was necessary; there were individual enforceable agreements that fell within the certain ambits of real property, mining, maritime trade, or commerce, and these areas were sufficiently well developed to meet the needs of those people transacting in such areas.[37]

Colonial law limited contracts based on capacity to contract or subject matter. Beyond the expected incapacities related to sex and age noted in the discussion of personal status, certain individuals such as royal officials and their family members lacked capacity as a means of limiting potential abuses and of economically isolating them from the population. Other classes of individuals also lacked capacity; for similar reasons, clerics and foreigners were not permitted to form commercial contracts. Other restrictions were placed on certain kinds of goods, such as specific spices, dyes, precious metals (including mercury needed for silver extraction), fruits, and beverages.[38]

One very important aspect of the law dealing with contracts and obligations was the creation and enforcement of debt. Trade, mining, social position, and personal comfort often ran on an engine of debt, and the law developed numerous methods to supply and secure this essential part of colonial life and economy. Imprisonment for debt was a possibility, although various classes of individuals were exempt.[39] Security for loans could be created in land, or money payments could be extracted from giving up rights in land without relinquishing ownership. Even under the *Partidas*, various contractual relationships could be established to provide either lump-sum payments or annual pensions out of land. Thus, one important aspect of contract was the *censo*, set out in the *Partidas* and containing elements of a lease and a sale and purchase.

Three common types of the *censo* were the *enfitéutico*, the *reservativo*, and the *consignativo*. The *enfitéutico* was when someone transferred, in perpetuity, for lives, or a term of years, real property or the use of real property to another in exchange for a series of payments or an annual pension. The grantor had a right of entry if the payment was not made (*comiso*), or if the holder wanted to sell his use (*tanteo*). The grantor also had a right to a percentage if the holder sought to alienate the use.[40] Nonetheless, the use could be alienated within limits, excluding, however, transfers to ecclesiastical corporations, *mayorazgos*, clerics, women, or very rich or very poor persons.[41] With the *reservativo*, an annual pension in fruits or money was reserved, but it did not have the security of the rights to reenter or a percentage on alienation. Still, it could be canceled (*redención*) by delivering money within the legal interest limits, to produce income equal to that of the *censo*.[42] With the *consignativo*, someone purchased from the owner of land an annual pension for a payment in cash; here the ownership and use of the land stayed with the owner.[43] *Censos* were commonly employed in the colonial period for real property financing and transactions, and the church was skilled at using them to lend on and transfer real property.[44]

Commercial law was not found in the colonial and Castilian law of general application; there was, of course, a very important body of commercial law applied exclusively to commerce in commercial tribunals. There were numerous sources of commercial law. For example, book 9 of the *Recopilación* of 1680 discusses commerce and commercial tribunals such as the Consulado de México, which was to be modeled on similar tribunals in Seville and Burgos and to use the ordinances to those tribunals.[45] In the late colonial period, one important, unifying source for commercial rules was the *Ordenanzas del Consulado de Bilbao* (1737), based on French ordinances and the works of Colbert.[46] This work, often referred to as the *Ordenanzas de Bilbao,* addressed many aspects of commercial and maritime law, including how to organize commercial enterprises, contractual obligations, and commercial paper. The provisions of the *Ordenanzas* date from as early as 1429. Philip II applied them throughout the Spanish empire in 1560, and in 1737 Philip V reaffirmed that they controlled commercial matters.[47] They were accepted as useful rules in Latin American colonial dealings and often governed legal aspects of commercial affairs until replaced by national commercial codes in the mid nineteenth century.[48] Commercial laws might be summarized or described in other works, for example, the often-used *Curia Philipica* by Hevia Bolaños. By the late eighteenth century, commercial sales contracts were common, and the courts applied doctrines of fraud, deceit, and good faith to void sales and rental contracts.[49] Courts also recognized that agriculture and commerce must both be accommodated under a contractual regime to benefit the colonial state.[50]

Business Associations

Just as the regime of contract law was divided amongst the various important sources of civil, commercial, and public law, so too was the organization and operation of the various forms of business associations. The *Siete Partidas* generally followed the *corpus iuris civilis* and its commentators concerning civil and mercantile partnerships.[51] Thus the *Siete Partidas* provided general rules concerning the formation, nature, allocation of profits and losses, debts, and dissolution of business partnerships.[52] The *Siete Partidas* shared their authority in guiding companies with the *Ordenanzas de Bilbao,* which often provided somewhat different rules. For example, the two bodies of law differed on the liability for debts incurred by the partnership.[53] These sets of laws had various limitations for creating larger business enterprises. For example, share companies were not addressed by either set of laws, but could be created by building on the principles set forth for partnerships. Similarly, some sets of specialized laws, such as mining ordinances, contemplated business forms similar to the share company.[54]

Laws and practices providing for business partnerships (*sociedades mercantiles*) continued throughout the colonial period. The members needed to sign an agreement (*estatutos*) before two witnesses and a scribe. An accounting would be held every year and profits or losses distributed to the members who were under an obligation to conduct themselves in a trustworthy and faithful manner toward the other members. Disputes were under the jurisdiction of commercial tribunals.[55] Some share companies, lacking corporate status, were used during the colonial period, particularly to finance and to enjoy the profits of individual expeditions.[56] Ongoing trading companies formed as joint-stock companies were a later colonial development because business ventures and partnerships were usually formed on an investment-by-investment basis.[57]

In general, the colonial market was highly regulated by both royal law and commercial practices. On the consumer side of transactions in the colonies, goods were legally bought and sold in markets, fairs, and shops. Provisions were made to ensure standard weights and measures, and markets for necessary goods were subject to price controls by *alcaldes ordinarios* who had the power to set just prices for goods.[58] Prices were also set for foodstuffs and drink to provide a modest profit for the seller.[59]

Trade generally required minimum functioning systems of insurance, bills of exchange, and bankruptcy.[60] Colonial law also provided for the extension of some protection to trade and makers marks. Generally, outside the area of royal monopolies and licenses, there was little legal protection of what one today considers intellectual property. Nonetheless, nascent provisions designed to protect intellectual and industrial property rights became more common in the late colonial period. By the early nineteenth century, Spain was following the lead of France in this area of the law.[61]

Slavery

AT the time of Spanish conquest, the institution of slavery was already well known to both Spaniards and Indians. Indeed, slavery was deeply ingrained in the Spanish mentality and was "taken completely for granted as an ancient tradition."[1] Nonetheless, slavery on the Iberian Peninsula was very limited when compared to the colonial expansion of the institution.[2] Slaves were used to provide all sorts of labor, and in the colonial period few questioned either the morality or legality of the practice. Two general types of slavery, African and Indian, existed in the colonies. Early royal legislation prohibited Indian slavery, except in certain circumstances, but African slavery was used throughout the period.

African Slavery

African slavery existed in the region throughout the colonial period, and slaves were brought to Latin America from the beginning of European contact.[3] The conquistadors brought personal slaves with them, and slaves served aboard Spanish ships. Although as early as 1501, African slaves were among those classes of people prohibited from traveling to the Spanish colonies, leading Spaniards obtained royal licenses to bring African slaves with them, first to the Antilles, and shortly thereafter throughout the Spanish colonies. It appears that the earliest African slaves in the Spanish colonies had a higher place in society than conquered Indians. They might purchase their freedom and might even become assimilated into the Spanish levels of society, all due to their association with the conquering Spaniards. Nonetheless, by 1570 such possibilities of gaining liberty and joining the ruling segments of society were no longer available in the more settled areas such as Mexico, Peru, and Chile. Throughout the period, not all blacks in the colonies were slaves, and some free blacks were entitled to the rights of a Spanish subject.[4]

Spaniards and Creoles viewed African slaves as a good source of labor, especially after the Laws of Burgos of 1512 limited their hopes of fully exploiting Indians. The sources of Indian labor were not only limited by legislation, but also by a dramatically declining population. In areas such as Central America, the coastal areas of Venezuela and Colombia, and southern Mexico where the labor market was hit the hardest by rapidly diminishing Indian populations, African slavery moved in to fill the gap, especially for agricultural production. Where a large supply of indigenous workers could be exploited, such as in the mines of Peru and Colombia, African slavery never displaced the labor of Indians.[5]

The main justifications offered for enslaving Africans were that they were criminals condemned to death commuted to slavery, or people already having slave status in Africa, usually through capture in war, or people taken as slaves through license from African sovereigns.[6] Shortly after the slave trade to Spanish colonies was running, however, it appears that very few of the estimated 1.5 to 3 million people violently wrenched from their homes and sold though a massive and highly profitable machinery had been actually taken into slavery though capture in "just war," as their documentation usually recited.[7]

Profit from slavery was possible on both an individual and commercial level. Officials appointed by the Council of Indies were permitted to import African slaves, on the theory that they were prohibited from using the personal services of Indians. The officials were also exempt from taxes and duties on the importation of slaves, and thus used this as a means of importing and then, even though not officially permitted, selling them for a quick profit.[8] With great sums to be made in the slave trade, the crown moved quickly to regulate the commercial aspects and to adapt institutions to this commerce over the centuries of colonial slavery.

On a commercial level, at first, the legal instruments (*asientos*) authorizing the importation of slaves to America created a monopoly for the holder for a certain number of years for a certain number of slaves.[9] For example, quite small in quantity, "the first license was for 4,000 African slaves in five years" granted in 1518 by Charles V to one of his favorites.[10] The Portuguese controlled the African ports where slaves were obtained, and slaving was necessarily a complex international maritime activity.[11] With this in mind, the Board of Trade and the *consulado* of Seville took over the issuing of exclusive licenses from 1532 to 1589. These licenses were granted to royal officials and clergy, those who had helped in the conquest, local powerful *cabildo* members, individuals favored by the crown for their service, and private merchants and businessmen.[12] "It was only rarely and under specifically controlled conditions that those involved in shipping the slaves were also allowed to market them at their eventual points of destination."[13] Thus smaller slave traders handled distribution in the colonies after the slaves had arrived in the legal ports of entry. Even though the crown required almost all commerce to adhere to the set schedule of travel with the fleet between the peninsula and the colonies, slave ships, because of their unexpected arrival from Africa and the fragile nature of their "cargo," were permitted to travel outside the regular pattern of the fleet.[14]

From 1595 to 1640, licenses were granted directly to the Portuguese, reflecting the union of the Spanish and Portuguese crowns under Philip II during that period. Although the Portuguese successfully saturated the permitted market, there were still many areas seeking slaves but prohibited by the licenses. A booming slave smuggling industry, centered in the Río de la Plata, provided slaves for Chile, Ecuador, Peru, the River Plate region, Tucumán, and Upper Peru (present-day Bolivia).[15]

The slave trade in the second half of the seventeenth century was marked by an active Brazilian smuggling business, while the Board of Trade and the *consulado* of Seville granted legal Spanish monopolies from 1651 to 1676. Genoese and Dutch slaving companies reached significant agreements with the crown in this period. New methods of measuring the number of slaves shipped, moving from measurement based on *piezas* to tonnage, increased the possibilities for exceeding the limits imposed by licenses as well as for inhumane conditions in transport. The *pieza* system involved measuring the height of the slaves: a full *pieza* was a male slave 5 feet, 7 inches tall; fractions of a *pieza* were assigned to slaves under that height. Under the tonnage system, at first one ton was one slave, the crown then accepted three slaves to a ton, but the practice was to include up to seven slaves to a ton. Earlier slaving ships had a capacity of about 100 tons, later the average was around 220 tons, with 500 tons being the largest slavers used during the period.[16]

Portuguese and Spanish activity was replaced during the first half of the eighteenth century by French and English slaving enterprises that became the major supplier to the Spanish colonies. Freer trade in slaves began in the second half of the eighteenth century. The erosion of Spanish monopolistic trade policies, a booming smuggling trade, and the English control of Havana for part of the period all led to a slow broadening of permissible slave trade with Spanish colonies. During this period, new ports were opened to direct importation of slaves and various restrictive duties were dropped in 1765. Free trade of African slaves was permitted for a number of important colonial provinces such as Caracas and Cuba in 1789; two years later the viceroyalties of Buenos Aires and Santa Fe de Bogotá obtained the same status. By 1793, colonials were permitted to launch their own slaving ventures to Africa.[17] "By 1804 all the major ports of Spanish America had rights of complete freedom of trade in African slaves."[18]

Slaves were used to produce agricultural goods for local consumption and export, especially on large tropical plantations. Other tasks slaves were forced to undertake included construction projects, serving municipal or religious institutions, transporting materials and goods by water or overland, and constructing and maintaining public works. Some slave owners hired out slaves for short periods.[19]

Along with the social institution of slavery, there was a well-developed body of law. Roman law, the root of Castilian law, not only recognized slavery but addressed it at length. Many of the Spanish *fueros* provided for slavery, and in turn, the cornerstone of Castilian and colonial Latin American private law, the *Siete Partidas* also provided legal rules governing slavery.[20] Several chapters of book 8 of the *Recopilación* of 1680 address slavery. For example, title 18 provides regulations for the disembarkation of slaves without royal license, prohibits transportation of slaves already in the colonies to Peru, levies a port tax on slaves arriving in Cartagena to fund the capture of escaped slaves, prohibits *audiencias* from freeing slaves, and provides methods of accounting for live and dead slaves at various points in the slaving passage.[21]

Other regulations, such as the Black Codes, *Códigos de Negros*, from the late eighteenth century, provided minute rules concerning the treatment and obligations of slaves and were the products of colonial drafting. These provisions were not universally applied throughout colonial Latin America but were limited to smaller geographic areas, such as the Caribbean island of Santo Domingo, where the *Código Negro Carolino* attempted to borrow the perceived economically and socially successful aspects of French slave law of the *Code Noir* and apply them to newly imported slave labor for Spanish agricultural expansion on the island.[22] Further regulations "prohibited slaves from carrying arms, wandering at night without permission of their owners, going into the Indian markets, entering private property, cutting down trees, and engaging in commerce."[23] Some regulations concerning the treatment of slaves are in retrospect particularly ironic. For example, one provision requires slaveholders to send slaves to churches or monasteries to be instructed in Catholicism.[24] Furthermore, laws concerning slaves attempted to maintain certain societal barriers between races in the new social environment of the colonies. Blacks, slave or free, were prohibited from living with Indians and Europeans.[25]

Other rules, usually directly adopted from Castilian sources such as the *Siete Partidas,* addressed the private law aspects of property ownership in slaves, including methods of transfer, inheritance, and manumission.[26] The rules for manumission were intricate and depended on the duties the slave performed, the personal relationship of the owner to the slave, and the age of the owner among other factors. Other activities led a slave to freedom under Castilian law, such as marrying a free person with the owner's knowledge or being appointed the owner's heir.[27] Testamentary manumission was not uncommon as an act of Christian charity.[28] Rules also governed the punishment for slaves who had escaped and the division of expenses for their recapture.[29] The jurisdiction of the Santa Hermandad was expanded to the capture and return of slaves who had escaped.[30]

Some legal developments surrounding slavery appear to have arisen from customary practices or substantial extensions of the legal texts. The ability of a slave to purchase his or her freedom by himself, herself, or through another, *coartación,* was an important aspect of the law of slavery. Once a down payment was made, the slave acquired the new legal status of a *coartado.*[31] *Coartación* has not been studied enough to ascertain its prevalence throughout colonial Latin America. It appears to have been an established but seldom-used practice by the mid eighteenth century.[32] Some areas, however, such as nineteenth-century Cuba, had a significant population of *coartados.* Indeed, Cuban slaves had a right to initiate self-purchase.[33]

In other ways, possibilities for freedom were more limited in the colonies. The special circumstances of the colonies, including racial population distributions and the fear of slave revolt, required that some established Castilian rules, such as that granting free status to the offspring of a slave, be specifically modified by royal act. In this case, offspring of slaves were slaves. Thus the child of a woman, who was a slave, was a slave. The child of a man, who was a slave, and a free Indian wife was also a slave on the theory that the mother was to be considered a slave. Owners of slaves who fathered children with them often freed their children.[34] Another adaptation of the Castilian laws concerning slavery was the status of a slave who married a free person. Under the *Siete Partidas,* a slave who, with the owner's consent, married a free person became a free person. Recognizing that because Indians were free persons under Castilian law and because a slave who married an Indian would as a result become free, the crown saw the potential dilution in slave population and provided a law that maintained the slave status of slaves who married free persons. Thus, the policies of encouraging Christian marriage and securing property rights in slaves were harmonized.[35]

In 1789 there was an attempt to restate the laws governing slavery in the colonies by royal decree, the *Real Cédula de su Magestad Sobre la Educacíon, Trato y Ocupaciones de los Esclavos, en Todos sus Dominios de Indias e Islas Filipinas,* which included limits on the corporal punishment of slaves by their owners. The decree was suspended from local application to colonial slaveholding areas because of its potential to stir excitement and insurrection. The local slaveholders believed their treatment of slaves was appropriate, perhaps even more charitable than in other contemporary slave societies, without additional guidance from the crown.[36]

Despite suffering substantial legal disabilities, slaves, under certain circumstances, might testify in colonial Latin American courts. It appears that their testimony would only be admitted where other, more respected testimony was unavailable. For example, in an eighteenth-century case concerning adultery, the Santa Fe de Bogotá *audiencia* stated that "in domestic affairs and in hidden crimes, the law permits the slave to testify; because in these cases the truth is revealed by the only method through which it can be communicated."[37]

The independence period affected the slave trade on both a practical and theoretical level. With the outbreak of war, the slave trade could no longer be conducted because of the dangers of marine travel. Furthermore, in some areas, production by slaves became uneconomical and reliance was placed on paid workers or semislave debt peons, often the children of slaves.[38] In the independence period, movement from one group to another in society became somewhat easier, but the period was also marked by a reinvigoration of harsh colonial provisions that had fallen into disuse; one author cites the Puerto Rican *Reglamento de Esclavos* (1826) as an example, and Havana enacted regulations as late as 1842.[39]

Indian Slavery

At the beginning of exploration and colonization, some Indians were enslaved. Slavery existed in preconquest societies, and Columbus in 1495 and Isabel in 1496 made references to Indian slaves. Slaves from before the conquest remained slaves, and slaves could be made from those taken as prisoners in a "just war." In the 1520s, for example, "the Spanish branded and sold as slaves thousands of captured Quiches and Cakchiquels. The king's treasury received the yield from one-fifth of all slaves sold."[40]

Legislation affecting slavery was common. Branding slaves was abolished in 1532. Their being sent to Spain was prohibited by the crown in 1536. When slavery resulting from "just war" conquest was abolished in 1530, it appears Spaniards found it easier to kill those who lost on the battlefield. The practice of taking slaves however continued until the New Laws of 1542, which confirmed the 1530 prohibition. The New Laws were the result of the Dominican Bartolomé de las Casas's advocacy on behalf of the Indians, and he continued his work with the publication of *The Indians Who Have Been Made Slaves* (1552), which received substantial criticism in the colonies. The New Laws resulted in a civil war in Peru, but other areas chose to ignore the legislation and make slow progress toward the abolition of "just war" Indian slavery. Indians who proved their unjust enslavement received exemption from tribute payments for three years and lifetime exemption from forced work.[41] Enforcement of protective laws proved to be politically and practically difficult.[42]

Indian labor through *encomiendas* and other unquestioned colonial institutions discussed in the next chapter provided a ready replacement to Indian chattel slavery. Thus Indian slavery was abolished early on, although Indians continued to be subject to deplorable conditions and treatment and were readily exploited for their labor.[43]

Indian Status and Indian Land

THE native populations of the Spanish colonies were new to Spanish experience, thought, and in turn, law. From the colonizer's point of view, the nature of proper relations with these people remained a persistent question. How were they to be incorporated into Castilian social and legal structure? One overriding consideration was the duty of the Spanish to evangelize amongst the Indians. This was a crown obligation on which the very claim to America rested.[1] Numerous concerns and different interpretations arose concerning Indian status, labor, protection, and land. A significant amount of legislation in the colonial period addressed these concerns, yet in perhaps no other area of Spanish colonial private law was the gap between law as written and law as practiced so apparent as with the legal regime addressing Indian status and Indian land ownership. Practice throughout the period flew in the face of repeated institutional and legislative attempts to lessen the oppression of occupier on inhabitant. From the sheer volume of legislation, it appears that the crown did not give up easily; book 6 the *Recopilación* of 1680 is dedicated exclusively to these questions and contains more than 170 pages of laws.

As the institutions and laws related to Indians are discussed in this chapter, it is well worth remembering that Spanish legal and social planning for Indians was applied to a rapidly shrinking population during most of the colonial period. It is estimated that Indian population in this area of America at initial Spanish contact was about 35 million and this had withered to about 750,000 by 1650. From this date, the population began to increase again. Causes for the rapid decrease in population included disease, war, changes in diet, flight, and oppression. During the same period, about 500,000 Spaniards had moved to America.[2]

Indian Status

In theory, Indians were considered free vassals of the crown, and chiefs (*caciques*) were the equivalent of nobility.[3] Furthermore, certain native nations that aided the Spaniards enjoyed royal privileges that were eroded over the colonial period.[4] In some areas, Indians were politically organized on the local level into towns that followed Spanish models of government.[5] Shortly after conquest, abuses of the Indian population, especially abuses related to the unauthorized or overzealous exploitation of Indian labor, led to various institutional and legislative attempts to protect Indians. Ricardo Levene places laws concerning the protection of Indians and their legal status into four periods centered around the following enactments: the Laws of Burgos (1513); the New Laws (1542); the law of 1601 concerning forced work; and the abolishing of the *encomienda* (1721).[6]

As early as 1501 the Spanish crown sent officials to maintain the freedom of Indians. Nonetheless, Spanish policy was that Indians could be required to work in the mines as paid workers, not slaves. Not unexpectedly, in just two years, additional laws were enacted to prohibit Indians from moving away from Spanish mining centers.[7] The same year, 1503, also witnessed the legalization of forced labor by free Indians as well as attempts to protect them, such as the requirement that each Indian was to have a house and land that could not be transferred.[8]

The Laws of Burgos were begun in 1512 and completed in 1513 in Valladolid. The product of heated theological debate, these laws established that Indians were free beings, that they ought to be instructed in the faith, and that they might be compelled to work within limits for compensation.[9] In 1537 Pope Paul III drew similar conclusions and in the bull *Sublimis Deus* determined for Christianity that Indians were capable of conversion, capable of owning property, and not subject to enslavement.[10] The Laws of Burgos, by singling out the indigenous population as legal subject, began a long line of colonial legislation in which Indian status became a juridically distinct category, apart from those juridical categories already present in Castilian law.[11] The Laws of Burgos set out minimum requirements for food, clothing, rest, a maximum work year of nine months, and prohibitions against forcing children under fourteen and pregnant women to work. It also provided that Indians could not be used as beasts of burden.[12] An additional important exemption for Indians was that they were not subject to the jurisdiction of the Inquisition.[13]

The principles of Burgos were not put into effect, and the Spanish treatment of the Indians continued to be criticized. One *encomendero*, Bartolomé de las Casas, converted from these exploitative practices, became a Dominican and wrote an influential polemical work against the Spaniard's treatment of the Indians, his *Historia de las Indias*. He also played an important role in the drafting of more protective legislation, the New Laws of 1542, which, in part, abolished personal services as part of the *encomienda* but provided the owner the right to collect Indian tribute.[14] The laws led to various officials being sent out to enforce their protective provisions of the Indians and in the words of Ricardo Levene "converted a nation of slaves to freedom with the stoke of a pen."[15] This it did, at least on paper. The New Laws sought not only the protection of Indians, but also the social control of the *encomenderos*, those legally exploiting Indian labor, so that they might not approach the power of the peninsular nobility.[16] The New Laws prohibited new *encomiendas*, new enslavement of Indians, and required the release of slaves where title could not be demonstrated.[17] The laws of 1601 did not try to make such great advances and were more cautious.[18]

The Ordinances of Alfaro (1612) were first applied in the region of Paraguay and addressed questions of the government of the reductions, and the social, legal, and economic relationship of the Indians to Spaniards. Francisco de Alfaro, a university-trained lawyer (*licenciado*) who served as *fiscal* and *oidor* of the *audiencia* of Charcas, drafted these ordinances in the 1590s and 1600s as a way to better enforce the protective laws.[19] Alfaro's work was incorporated into laws decreed by Philip III in 1618, which were subsequently incorporated into the *Recopilación* of 1680.[20] These laws prohibited *encomiendas* of personal services in Tucumán, Río de la Plata, and Paraguay; granted Indians freedom of contract for their services; required compensation to *mita* Indians; prohibited their removal from reductions; regulated tribute; mandated support for them by the *encomienda;* and prohibited Indian women from leaving an Indian town to have a Spanish child when she had Indian children living in the town.[21] Some preliminary research indicates that where the Indian populations were small, the legislation protecting their interests was better enforced.[22]

Although common in many preconquest societies, the payment of tribute was an additional burden enforced against Indians. As a general rule, Indians between eighteen and fifty years old were required to pay tribute in money or kind to either their *encomenderos* or to the crown. *Caciques,* their oldest sons, Indian *alcaldes,* and women were generally exempt from tribute. Groups of Indians tied to the land for services (the *yanaconas* of Peru) and certain Indians who helped during the conquest (the Indians of Tlaxcala, Mexico, for example) were also exempt. Indians who submitted to Spanish authority peacefully were given a ten-year exemption. Visitors (*visitadores*) determined the appropriate rate of tribute (*tasación*), which could not exceed the preconquest rate.[23]

Advancement for Indians in colonial society was blocked by both official and unofficial means. Early Franciscan attempts to train Indians for the priesthood were crushed by other clergy, and Indians were barred from ordination from 1555 to 1591.[24] Also in the sixteenth century, Indians were prohibited from owning horses without a license.[25] Perhaps the most common view of Indians in the colonies was that they provided a significant, and at first seemingly endless, supply of cheap labor for mining and agricultural exploitation. Various complex institutions grew up in colonial legislation that facilitated the exploitation of Indian labor, in many instances shifting the rights granted to use Indian labor into something akin to property. The most important of these institutions were the *encomienda, repartimiento, mita,* and *reducción.*[26]

Encomiendas

Spaniards saw Indians as a free source of labor. This was not necessarily new, and many Indians had been subject to forced labor before conquest and colonization. Under the legal structure of the *encomienda,* Spaniards were entitled to receive the work of groups of Indians in exchange for Christianizing them. Through this institution, groups of Indians were assigned to provide labor and tribute to the holder of the *encomienda.*[27] The crown probably saw the institution as a revenue neutral way to compensate conquistadors, to incorporate Indians into the colonial economy, and impose military duties on the leaders of the *encomiendas,* the *encomenderos.*[28] Early on, this institution was seen as temporary, lasting up to three years, and each Spaniard could have an *encomienda* of between thirty and eighty Indians.[29] Indians were assigned to a particular Spaniard by written deed or patent.[30] Widespread distribution of *encomiendas* never became the rule and they were reserved for the aristocracy. Many *encomiendas* exceeded the legal limit on the number of individuals and contained thousands of Indians. In the first half of the sixteenth century, there were about five hundred *encomiendas* in New Spain, and Peru had about an equal number during its colonial period.[31]

Despite numerous legislative efforts to control *encomiendas* during the first two hundred years of colonization, the institution flourished in many different forms and investigation of the *encomienda* has revealed wide gaps in legislative requirements and practical institutions.[32] Laws set requirements for the capacity to be an *encomendero;* the inability to alienate, divide, or mortgage *encomiendas;* the requirement that the *encomendero* be resident on the property; the confiscation of tribute collected by the owner; and the methods of setting and nature of tribute.[33] Most royal and ecclesiastical officials were prohibited from possessing *encomiendas.*[34]

Despite the initial view that *encomiendas* were temporary institutions, the provision of the New Laws of 1542 that they should revert to the crown after the death of the first holder led to violence in Peru, and the crown did not enforce the provision. The inheritability of *encomiendas* was a focal point of the struggle for economic and resulting political power between colonial aristocracy and the peninsular crown. *Encomiendas* were extended from two lifetimes (1536) to an additional lifetime with a payment to the crown (1629), and again with a payment to the crown to four lifetimes (1704).[35] These attempts to perpetuate the *encomienda* in the private hands of the aristocracy were, for the most part, unsuccessful due to a failure of lineage.[36] "Before 1570 about three-quarters of the *encomienda* income in the Valley of Mexico had reverted to the Crown, and so extensions of *encomiendas* for third and fourth lives had little significance."[37]

There were many similarities between *mayorazgos* and *encomiendas*. *Encomiedas* were passed by primogeniture, and as early as a royal provision of 1536 extending them to two lifetimes, it was recognized that they would pass first to the oldest son, then to the daughter, and afterward to the wife.[38] They were also indivisible and inalienable.[39] Natural children, religious, clerics, and those who already had an *encomienda* were excluded as takers.[40] These rules related to the succession of *encomiendas* are set out in title 11 of book 6 of the *Recopilación* of 1680. The primogeniture inheritance scheme established in 1536 was tied to the provision of a knight to fight for the crown.[41] Passage of the *encomienda* was by operation of law, and various usual rules did not apply. For example, the right of representation did not apply, nor did it matter if the last possessor had not appointed an heir or had attempted to disinherit him. The possessor could do nothing to prejudice the successor and if a successor was also the universal heir, he could elect to take the *encomienda* and waive his right to the inheritance. Generally, *encomiendas* were not charged with the decedents' debts or as assets for calculating the *legítima*.[42]

The Ordinances of Alfaro of 1612 directly affected *encomiendas* by seeking to end forced personal services by Indians and to replace these services with compensated work. At first accepted on the regional level, the Council of the Indies did not approve them all, but in 1618, Philip III ended *encomiendas* for personal services in Río de la Plata, Paraguay, and Tucumán, a provision later incorporated in the *Recopilación* of 1680.[43] During the mid seventeenth century, the crown placed exactions on *encomiendas* to better its fiscal situation. Over the following decades, the financial benefits of holding *encomiendas* were reduced by these demands.[44]

The harshness of the *encomienda* system on Indian life was reflected in its being a major cause of the Pueblo Revolt in Mexico in 1680.[45] In 1701 all *encomiendas* held by nonresidents were transferred to the crown and the institution was abolished by royal decree in 1718.[46] Further laws of the 1720s repeated the abolition and provided for some discretional compensation to *encomenderos* and even substantial exemptions. The Yucatán, Chile, and Paraguay received favorable treatment under this legislation. *Encomiendas* continued under this uncertain condition during most of the eighteenth century.[47] In some areas of colonial Latin America, such as Quito, the *encomienda* was transformed into a less burdensome head tax.[48]

Repartimientos and Mitas

Periodic Indian services were exacted by the Spanish under the names of *repartimiento,* in Mexico, and *mita,* in other regions.[49] Early in the colonial period, assigning the labor of a chief and his people to a Spaniard's *encomienda* was called a *repartimiento,* but as seen above, the *encomienda* was soon equated with a property right.[50] The exclusion of Indian personal service from *encomiendas* did not mean that Indians were completely free from such exactions. The *repartimiento* required that Indians provide personal services to Spaniards on a rotation system, often one week out of four, and, like the *encomienda,* was supposed to be a temporary institution. In return for the services, the Spaniard had to pay a fee to the crown and also pay the workers. Judges of the *repartimiento* determined the appropriateness of work for Indians. *Repartimientos* were abolished in the Guadalajara *audiencia* of colonial Mexico in 1671.[51] Even in areas where *repartimientos* were prohibited for particular purposes, such as agricultural work, after 1609, they continued to be abused and permitted for limited needed types of production. Furthermore, the number of Indians forced to serve was supposed to be adjusted according to the overall population of Indians available. These calculations, almost always resulting in a decline in the number of Indians forced to labor, were often delayed for years.[52]

The Spanish Cortes abolished *repartimientos* in 1812.[53] Aspects of the *repartimiento* nevertheless lasted until the independence period, above all in mining enterprises. Laws further regulated them to avoid workers being bound to Spaniards through debt peonage.[54] Debt peonage bound Indians to provide labor for money advanced to them. Although limits were placed on the total amount advanced to one Indian, usually about three months' wages, the system was abused until the early nineteenth century. Originally permitted to move from an estate, debt peons were later subject to restrictions of movement in the eighteenth century.[55] Some estate owners refused to let debts be repaid and, contrary to established civil law, attempted to make the debts inheritable so that future generations too would be bound to serve as debt peons.[56]

Playing off preconquest requirements for personal services discussed earlier, the *mita* can be seen as a type of *repartimiento* in which the Indian leader chooses the workers who will serve for compensation, for example, up to 4 percent of the Indian population in Mexico at a given time.[57] Mining, agriculture, farming, and domestic work could all be done through a *mita* on a rotation basis, which varied between ten days per year for mining to three or four months a year for pasturing animals. In Peru, the maximum Indian population serving in a *mita* was capped at 7 percent. *Encomienda* Indians could also be subject to *mita* service.[58] Where Indians cultivated land for Spaniards, their tribute payments might be reduced for the work, and they might receive land to work for their own benefit as well as the Indian community's benefit. Mining *mitas* were legally abolished as early as 1549 for New Spain and slightly later for Peru and New Galicia, but they continued in practice and were even subject to later legislation under the *Ordenanzas* of Toledo, which were later incorporated into the *Recopilación* of 1680.[59]

Indian labor, along with slaves and convicts, might also be used for manufacturing purposes in sweatshop-style factories, *obrajes*, often dedicated to textile production.[60] It is estimated that at given moments in the colonies more than twenty-eight thousand Indian workers were laboring in Quito, with thousands also forced to work in smaller centers such as Mexico.[61] As manufacturing increased during the late colonial period, these small factories became lucrative, but were highly dependent on ample labor supplies. By the 1750s the Protector of the Indians might bring legal action to ensure that Indians were not forced to stay in the area of work and that they were compensated for their work.[62]

Reductions

Indians not subject to an *encomienda* might be gathered together in groups called *reducciones* or *congregaciones* with some administrative independence under their own *alcaldes* and *alguaciles*.[63] This legal device for obtaining Indian labor in exchange for religious conversion was often used by regular cleric, then secular, then lay *encomenderos*.[64] In typical form, a few hundred households were grouped under their leader (*cacique*) who would then monitor the provision of a rotation of one-third of the labor force to work in mines, or otherwise. In theory, the earnings of the mine would be divided between the king, the *cacique*, and the workers.[65] Even though laws regulated this institution, leaders of the reduction could easily appropriate the share destined for the communal treasury (*caja de comunidad*).[66] Nonetheless, the communal treasury was earmarked for hospitals, widows, orphans, the sick, the payment of tribute assessments, the costs of missions, and education, some of which must have been achieved.[67]

Government officials were appointed to the reductions according to population, and because Spaniards were not permitted to reside on reductions, they could only use them as stopping points during journey.[68] In peripheral areas, missions run by regular clerics also redefined Indian landholding and the provision of services.[69] Reductions later bore the name *corregimientos* when their operation had been transferred to a royal official, the *corregidor de pueblos de indios*.[70]

Reductions carried with them a parcel of land, called the *resguardo,* extending one league from the center of the population. The *resguardo* was divided into three parts: one distributed among the families for their own cultivation, one for communal pasture, and one worked for the community on a rotation basis by the Indians for their communal treasury. These activities could be turned into money payments by using the land as the basis of a *censo*.[71] These and other aspects of reductions are addressed in the *Recopilación* of 1680.[72]

Although Spanish practices generally attempted to construct Spanish society in the colonial areas, some saw the new land and population as an opportunity to build new Utopian societies. Trained as a lawyer, Vasco de Quiroga served as bishop of Michoacán in the 1530s. Inspired by More's *Utopia,* Quiroga attempted to set up Indian villages where property was held in common with houses and gardens assigned to the inhabitants. The success of these early projects led to the mission (*misión*) system imposed by later orders.[73] Missions were effective means of establishing legal claim to territory and flourished in the early sixteenth century. Missions were similar in structure to the reductions and other municipalities, but were usually established in uncolonized or frontier areas and were often headed by a Jesuit priest until the society's expulsion from Spanish Latin America in 1767. The Paraguay missions were the most famous.[74] Although the general rule for missions was that property such as lands, cattle, and crops were held in common, by the eighteenth century, mission Indians were sometimes individually given a cottage and garden that could be passed by will.[75] Missions were abolished by royal decree in 1803.[76]

These various institutions, under various names, were used to extract labor and tribute from Indians. Legislation prohibited the use of Indians for personal service, but these laws were ignored.[77] Some institutions, like the *repartimiento* and *mita,* were considered by colonial powers to be temporary, until they could be replaced with systems of paid labor or African slaves. When such institutions were abolished in name, they continued in fact, with debt-induced peonage creating additional holds on the workers.[78] Thus, in the exaction of services from Indians, some historians have observed a general progression of legal institutions for the exploitation of labor from *encomienda* to *mita* to debt peonage during the colonial period.[79]

Indian Land Ownership and Assertion of Property Rights

Indians were not merely suppliers of labor in colonial society, they also made up important segments of society that served to challenge, use, and appropriate colonial institutions and laws. As mentioned in Chapter 6, in theory lands were not to be acquired by Spaniards when this disrupted Indian rights. Furthermore, Indian lands were not subject to forfeiture for crimes, nor could they be forcefully liquidated to satisfy debts.[80]

In the early colonial period, the crown respected Indian land rights. At first Spaniards appeared to have little interest in agricultural pursuits, and as long as Indians were supplying needed food, there was no need to deprive them of their land.[81] Spaniards needed and sought to control labor, not land. Although some generalizations may be made about Indian landholding, it appears there was little uniformity throughout the region, or indeed, within regions.[82] Indian landholding could be based on ownership at the time of conquest, royal or viceroyal *merced* (grant), recognized claim through a title inspection (*composición de tierras*), purchase, or inheritance.[83]

Two general types of Indian landholding can be noted during the colonial period. First, was the *cacicazgo,* estates held by native chieftains that had legal properties very similar to *mayorazgos.* These were usually granted to chieftains who had aided in the colonization and Christianization efforts of the Spaniards.[84] To claim these rights, *caciques* usually converted to Christianity and adopted Spanish aristocratic lifestyles. The lands were worked by *terrasguerros* who lived on the *cacicazgo. Cacicazgos* usually followed a primogeniture inheritance pattern, but the rule was not without exception for local practices, and female descendants sometimes took the property even when there was a surviving male heir.[85] *Caciques* used various methods to expand their holdings, including litigation, frequently against other Indian landholders. Just as with *mayorazgos, cacicazgos* presented difficulties for their holders who often had to encumber and lease their holdings to obtain income streams that would permit them to carry on in aristocratic comfort.[86] Most *cacicazgos* were diluted over time, giving way to expanding landed estates held by Spaniards, and the social status of the hereditary nobility of the *caciques* rapidly diminished. Nonetheless, in some regions, such as Oaxaca, *cacicazgos* survived into the late colonial period.[87] Legislation was enacted to ensure that *cacicazgos* passed according to the wishes of the Indian holder.[88] Lands of lesser nobles were not held in *cacicazgos* and were not subject to the restrictions on alienation or the primogeniture inheritance pattern. These two noble landholding classes often provided the members of the Indian *cabildo* where such political subdivisions existed.[89]

The second type of Indian landholding was on the peasant level. Despite numerous forms of communal holding and the possibility of private holding, it appears that the crown only recognized and enforced the communal holding of Indian villages or towns. It would uphold these communal rights against private parties seeking to control such lands. Small individual family holdings were recognized, and Indians in New Spain almost always made testaments devising these holdings.[90] Individual holdings were also a part of the *encomienda* system; plots of agricultural land were carved out for Indians as their own property.[91] Land of intestate Indians who died without an heir did not completely escheat to the crown, but a portion was returned to the community to help with tribute payments.[92]

In the last days of the colonial period under the Spanish Constitution of 1812, *mitas* and personal services were prohibited, and importantly, legislation attempted to place the lands that were earlier held in common into Indian hands. At the same time, other legislation paradoxically affirmed certain communal rights in land. Thus, changes in Indian landholding to increase private ownership and commerce were seen as necessary, but how to effect these changes remained uncertain. These attempts were not put immediately into place because in 1814 the laws adopted by the Spanish Cortes were abrogated. In 1821, for example, under Iturbide, the legislation sprang to life again and lands were reapportioned into private hands.[93] As Andrés Lira wrote, "The destruction of indigenous life was the only way to integrate Indians into the constitutional regime of the new nation."[94]

In some regions, Indians were at first quite successful in pressing claims to land based on pre-Hispanic ownership, although the usefulness of such claims declined in the mid seventeenth century.[95] In summarizing his work on the General Indian Court, Woodrow Borah states:

Land and property rights constituted the largest category of disputes. As one acerbic writer of the later eighteenth century commented, "On all the face of the globe there is no place with more suits over lands despite the fact that this new world has immense untilled and unsettled regions." Indian towns and villages would fight each other or hacendados for decades and even centuries over boundaries, frequently spending on the suits far more than the value of the land in dispute. Contrary to a widely held current opinion, Indian towns and villages fought more with each other in these suits than with Spaniards.[96]

Reports on the litigiousness of Indians vary. The Indians of central Mexico were viewed as being very active in court.[97] The Indians of Oaxaca also actively protected their interests in lands, not only against Spaniards, but often against other Indians in the courts.[98] Similar findings have been found for Indians in Peru during the period.[99] Such suits would commonly begin with a plaintiff's compliant followed by supporting documentation and interrogatories. The defendant would respond with similar proof and the *procuradores* then would summarize the positions of their clients. These materials would be capped off with the judge's decision.[100] In colonial litigation in Mexico, although Indians served as witnesses in disputes involving other Indians and those involving Spanish litigants, Spanish witnesses did not serve in disputes between Indians.[101] Interestingly, before 1650, in litigation involving Indians before the Mexican *audiencia*, women litigants, either as plaintiff or defendant, were more common than men. After 1650, the presence of Indian women as litigants decreased and husbands often represented their wives, perhaps reflecting a decline in women's legal status.[102]

Family relationships were often expressed and even defined in property disputes. This was particularly true as Indians might characterize or label polygynous family structures to fit Spanish, Catholic notions. In fact, multiple spouses might be presented to the courts under the socially acceptable guise of "slave woman."[103] Indeed, "Indians were able to possess slaves and did so, though the total number was comparatively small."[104]

Kellogg has also noted a shift in the way property was perceived among colonial Mexican Indians. She notes the shift from communal to individual rights over property and, in the late sixteenth century, the shift from the key concept of the rights within the household complex to the land itself as the object of litigation.[105] Furthermore, this period marked the adoption of various Spanish legal concepts by Indian litigants, including the *quinto*, the *heredero*, dowry, and the importance of documentary evidence.[106] Litigation under Spanish law could be an effective strategy of Indian resistance. Issues of land, tribute, and labor could be resolved in court to the benefit of native plaintiffs, and even litigation itself could hinder those seeking to enforce labor and tribute obligations. Judicial inspections could also be brought about through Indian complaint. The success of these tactics in substantially reducing labor and tribute in at least one area of Peru has been well documented.[107] Despite a few victories in the courtroom, Indians were, of course, dispossessed of their lands over the long term.[108]

Part II

Independence and the Nineteenth Century

Constitutions, Codes, *Caudillos,* and Commerce

PRIVATE LAW AND NATION BUILDING

W ITH unwitting irony the countries that struggled so hard to shed the Spanish yoke turned mostly to borrowed European sources in constructing their new national legal systems. France, and to a lesser extent the United States, provided the political philosophy and other legal models that could be easily co-opted. From the beginning, revolutionary leaders sought to establish new rules of private law. Indeed, in 1822, both O'Higgins in Chile and Santander in Gran Colombia proposed the French codes as new legislation.[1] Thus, there was something that intimately tied a new country to new law; national law was an expression and exertion of national identity. Bolívar sought new laws as early as 1819 when he rejected colonial Spanish law this way:

In asking the stability of judges, the creation of juries and a new code, I ask the Congress for the guaranty of civil liberty, the most precious, the most just, the most necessary thing, the only liberty, for without it the rest are nothing. I ask for the correction of the saddest abuses of that excess of Spanish legislation that like time collects from all ages and from all men, from the works of dementia as well as those of talent, from sensible products as well as extravagant ones, from the monuments of genius as well as those of whim — this judicial encyclopedia, a monster with ten thousand heads, which until now has been the whip of the Spanish peoples, it is the most refined torture that the wrath of heaven has permitted to let loose on this unhappy empire.[2]

Bolívar sought not only to replace Spanish law but to suit the new laws to the new country. This meant rejecting certain foreign models as well. In the same speech he declared:

Does not the Spirit of the Law say that it should be characteristic of the people who make it? that it is a great coincidence that the laws of one nation are able to suit another? that the laws ought to be relative to the physical characteristics of the country, to the climate, to the nature of the terrain, to its location, its extension, to the type of life of its peoples? that it ought to refer to the level of liberty the constitution may permit, to the religion of its inhabitants, to their inclination, to their commerce, to their customs, to their manners? Here is the code we ought to consult, not that of Washington![3]

Generals and legislators knew that the control of private law was the control of the nation. It was a lesson they had learned from the colonial Spanish law in Latin America. Thus, they saw an intimate connection between nation building and law reform. New private law rules, and especially rules related to property and inheritance, controlled the structure of society and, in turn, channeled significant political power to the authority creating those rules. It is not by accident that several early attempts at codification began not with the provisions dealing with the legal status of persons, as the French Civil Code of 1804 would indicate as the logical starting place, but with the provisions dealing with the inheritance and succession of property.[4]

The general method was to enact a new constitution granting legislative authority to a congress that would then enact a series of codes. The nature and content of these codes will be discussed later. Here, the way these codes generally relate to nation building and the centralization of power is examined. Latin American codes have often been seen exclusively as important steps along the way to the creation of a liberal state. A code "is characterized by the claim to construct a 'new,' 'complete,' and 'definitive' legal order," according to Manlio Bellomo.[5] Codes could rewrite the structure of society and strip away feudal privileges imbedded in social rank and nobility. Codes offered the possibility of etching enlightenment values of life, liberty, and property into new law. Thus, Bellomo sees codes after the French Revolution as distinct from earlier codes:

After the [French] Revolution, codes produced a unity of the legal subject that replaced the plurality of legal subjects of the eighteenth-century law codes. Henceforth it was not only possible, but mandatory to legislate solely and in unified fashion for the "citizen" rather than for the "noble," the "bourgeois," and the "peasant."[6]

It was this promise of a new society that made codification an essential block in building new nations.

There was, and is, however, another less recognized side to codification, especially in its relationship to Latin American codification.[7] Once the war had been won, generals sought control through law codes. This was a lesson taught to nineteenth-century Latin America by Napoleon. Codes supplied the optimal method of legal control for the consolidation of political power. As one noted historian of codification writes:

If we now look at codification not simply as a technical instrument in the formal organization of law, but as a means of *the political power of the state to assert a central will uniformly in the whole community,* then we can explore yet another feature generally characteristic of codification. In respect of its ultimate effect, codification is nothing but a means for the state to assert its domination by shaping and controlling law.

As a matter of fact, codification is the means, and also the product, of the transformation of law from its role being an agent of preserving the traditional framework of everyday life to being an agent to formulate and also to assert the arbitrary will of the ruler, effective by its formal enactment and open to further development in any direction through formally controlled processes.[8]

Other scholars of codification have noted this relationship as well.[9] Generals, autocratic regimes, such as Chile during the Portales era, and more recent victors through coups d'état have quickly grasped this concept. If one monopolizes the sources of law and controls the people's property and familial relationships, one controls the country.

The process from colony to independence to fully functioning state was often not direct and immediate. Jeremy Adelman's recent study on the development of private law in Argentina provides wonderful insight into legal change in the intervening periods, which were often characterized by the ruling institution of the *caudillo.*[10] On gaining independence, Argentina entered into a period of rule by such *caudillos,* notably Rosas. Argentina under *caudillo* rule was not characterized, as many have assumed, as a system with no law, but rather as operating under a system of "quasi-law."[11] "Rosas and his filial type ruled though an incomplete (not absent) legal order," writes Adelman.[12] Wealthy from trade in the 1840s, merchants supported Rosas, as did the holders of large rural estates who were able to amass large holdings despite partible inheritance laws and the uncertainty of the law related to property holding generally.[13] The uncertainty and incompleteness of the legal order were the seeds of overturning Rosas's rule. Adelman writes:

Merchants and their landed cousins thrived off Rosas's preservation of Buenos Aires' grip on Atlantic trade; private capital needed to preserve political power of the regional capital. On the other hand, by ruling through quasi-law, he did not create *public* institutions of governance to allow property owners to contract under stable and credible conditions. This was a transition, but under Rosas, one that would remain by definition. In the end, it was the internal contradictions of his quasi-legal regime that prevented the new capitalists of Buenos Aires from fully identifying with his brand of rulership.[14]

At the same time that wealthy classes sought sound public institutions to support their contractual relationships, lawyers increasingly ran the traditional commercial forums (*consulados*), which became more formal and impersonal. This provided further impetus for merchants and landholders to seek new forums and to embed a stable private property regime into public law and institutions.[15] These pressures led lawmakers to establish provisions in the Argentine Constitution of 1853 for the mandatory drafting of civil, commercial, mining, and penal codes.[16] As a result, Vélez Sársfield and Acevedo drafted the commercial code for Buenos Aires, which was enacted in 1859, even before the civil code was enacted. The commercial code gained national application in 1862 when tension between Buenos Aires and the Confederation subsided. Seven years later, the civil code was enacted and the two codes were harmonized in 1889.[17] Adelman sees the commercial code in this light as succeeding "to inscribe rights into a formal code that would doctrinally exhaust—and therefore make unassailable—contract and property law."[18] Thus the inability of the *caudillo* to recognize the essential relationship of property to code to nation led to his political substitution by the interests of capital in Argentina.

Another example may be drawn from Iván Jaksić's recent work on Andrés Bello. Bello's difficult trajectory toward being Chile's most respected codifier has been sketched out in the chapter addressing codification. The discussion of Bello here seeks to place the project of the civil code into the context of the construction of nations in Latin America. Much of Bello's thought may be viewed as essentially conservative because of his desire to adapt the old to the new, to pull out the best of Roman and Spanish colonial law and adapt it to newly independent countries. In many ways, most of Bello's work, legal and nonlegal, centered on the idea of the construction of new nations in Latin America. Even on the legal side of this prodigiously productive intellect, the civil code was not the only work leading to this goal. As Jaksić has demonstrated, Bello's works on international law were aimed at the recognition of newly independent Latin American countries in the international community.[19] His work in Roman law was to introduce students to the elements necessary to understand the laws of the new country.[20] His nonlegal works, such as his famous work on Spanish grammar, also addressed the new countries of Latin America. "Indeed, the purpose of the *Gramática* was to provide such an instrument of unity, and it was specifically to a continental audience: 'I do not claim to write for Spaniards. My lessons are aimed at my brothers, the inhabitants of Spanish America.'"[21] Concerning the creation of new nations for Bello, the rule of law was essential.[22] Republics for Bello were political entities based on the rule of law.[23] Indeed, for Bello, who was born a Spanish colonial, witnessed the independence from Spain in Caracas, served Gran Colombia, lived many years in England, and whose greatest political achievements were in Chile, the idea of homeland was problematic. Relying on a linguistic turn far ahead of its time, Bello replaces traditional notions of geography with the security provided by stable law-governed societies this way:

Certainly the soil on which we were born is not necessarily our homeland, nor is the land where we have chosen to spend our lives. Nor are we ourselves that homeland, for we are not sufficient for all our needs, nor can we think of the people who live with us as lawless, for in that case they would be our greatest enemies. Therefore, our true homeland is that rule of conduct indicated by the rights, obligations, and functions that we have and that we owe each other; it is that rule which establishes public and private order, which strengthens, secures, and imparts all their vigor to the relationships that unite us, and forms that body of associations of rational beings in which we find the only good, the only desirable thing in our country. Therefore that rule is our true homeland, and that rule is the law, without which everything disappears.[24]

Perhaps no locus served a better place to set out rights, obligations, and functions for Bello than his civil code. With each phrase and each article of the code, Bello was drafting in his mind a yet constructed homeland not only for himself but also for the entire Chilean nation. This alone must have provided him with the fortitude to continue with the arduous project of several decades.

Nonetheless, the appropriate conditions were needed to have a draft code come to fruition. Bello's project would probably have come to naught were it not for the atypical, sound economic condition of Chile during Bello's work, and the autocratic stability of Chile provided by Diego Portales and his political progeny that continued from 1830 until at least 1861 or 1891, depending on the historian of Chile questioned.[25] President Montt, elected in 1851, wholeheartedly supported the project and Montt beforehand was a member of the drafting committee appointed in 1840.[26] Along with Bello and Ocampo, Montt was actively involved in the revision of the code and delivered the Bello-authored message to Congress in 1855, which led to the successful enactment of the code.[27] Bello's own persistence was, of course, an essential element in the success of the project.

In this way, private law shaped and built the new nations of Latin America. It enabled countries to shed colonial private law rules related to land and inheritance, and it permitted certain movement toward more socially progressive positions regarding slavery, the status of women, and illegitimate children. Private law enabled the freer movement of property in the market and could provide a necessary state-enforced property regime that favored commerce and economic growth. Indeed, private law was an essential building block in the construction of the Latin American homeland.

Private Law and Independence

THE newly independent republics of Latin America faced a number of similar difficulties. Despite their recent independence from Spain and their political independence from each other, they shared some common experiences, heritage, and challenges. Nonetheless, many of the newly independent countries fought internal struggles concerning the political directions they would take. Internal divisions were often between liberals and conservatives, and these ideologies were foundational aspects of political and legal developments in the region. Very generally, liberals embraced the equality of persons and tended to be associated with anticlericalism and republican values in the Enlightenment tradition. Liberals often favored local or provincial autonomy and an economy free from state influences. Liberal ideas were certainly important in the independence period, but they were to become profoundly influential in political and legal developments in the mid nineteenth century. Conservatives usually endorsed a continuity with Spanish models; the favored status of the church; and a strong, central government. An overarching political phenomenon was *caudillismo*, authoritarian local control by an individual who held informal or formal military and political power, usually over a mostly rural population. Thus, in many areas, while liberals and conservatives debated, drafted constitutions, or waged civil war, the *caudillos* governed in rough fashion.[1] The conflicts between federalists and centralists and between liberals and conservatives were found throughout the region and significantly impacted legal and political development in many countries, including Argentina, Mexico, and Venezuela.[2]

Just as legal institutions and law were central to maintaining the colonial state for Spain, so too they formed the core around which new nations were assembled.[3] Both constitutional law and private law were seen as needing substantial changes to bring about the success of new countries.

Constitutional change came immediately. In early constitutions perhaps the greatest influence on general political viewpoint and structure were the French writers: "The works of the eighteenth century French philosophes, particularly Rousseau, Voltaire, and Montesquieu, were highly influential with the creole elite, and were reflected in the strong emphasis placed upon human liberty, republicanism and equality in the basic documents."[4] Independence brought about immediate change in the public institutions creating and administering law. New legislative bodies were constituted, and new courts and court systems were established under new constitutional provisions. The immediate challenges of staffing and financing these institutions in the new countries were often insurmountable for new governments. Areas that in colonial times complained bitterly over the surplus of lawyers, now had difficulty finding qualified people to sit as judges; outlying regions continued to be underserved. For courts that were adequately or even marginally staffed, it was not clear that the new treasuries would be able to provide the needed compensation to keep them running. Wartime interruption of trade led to economic depression. National debts from war and the related decline in national profits from mining, agriculture, and trade often meant that the constitutionally contemplated structures of national court systems had to be drastically reworked to meet the financial realities of the nation. Countries that settled on constitutions providing for federal systems shifted the problems of public and private law reform to the constituent states, which were usually in no better organizational or financial condition to undertake the tasks.

Changes in private law were much slower, and substantial changes did not come about until the mid nineteenth century when, after a host of political issues worked their way through the societies of these countries, legislatures could turn toward revising their disorganized colonial legal legacies. Consistent with the republican and liberal values imported with independence, there was a general desire to do away with royalty, monarchy, status, and privilege. Thus one political aspect of the revolution had a direct and immediate influence on private law; independence thinkers sought to replace the multiplicity of juridical objects on which the law operated—royalty, cleric, merchant, gentry, Indian, slave—with one juridical object, the citizen. This was expressed both on the public law level, constitutionally, and on the private law level, legislatively. The abolition of slavery after independence transformed Latin American society and private law. Other examples include the abolition or substantial limitation of *fueros* and the abolition of *mayorazgos*. Countries debated the place of the church, the army, and the large landholders.[5] In the first half-century of independence, some countries, like Mexico, sought to reposition the place of the church where new laws reflected social reforms, such as laws establishing civil marriage and bettering the plight of illegitimate children. Such reforms moved in or out according to the political tide.[6]

Although numerous attempts were made at legislating radical social changes on the levels of constitutional law and private law, there were no radical legal changes in private law. First, constitutional and legislative changes did not take immediate social effect. Those of Spanish descent, clerics, men, and property owners were still socially privileged, and these modifications did little to change this. Indians, blacks, women (especially married women), and the poor continued to suffer from numerous private law incapacities. In many ways, the political and constitutional rhetoric was incapable of making immediate social change. Second, the main sources of private law remained the same, and so the private substantive law found in those sources remained the same. The colonial sources of private law lived well into the middle and, in many cases, the end of the nineteenth century. Dramatic change in private law was not a product of independence; it would come only during later and more politically stable periods.

If private law did not face immediate change after independence, it was not for a lack of direction or ideas. In fact, most constitutions of the new republics indicated the belief that legal reform was close at hand by asserting that the laws in force would remain in force until such time as new laws were enacted by the legislature. The French codes, above all, served as ready and attractive pieces of legislation to be suggested for adoption by new countries, and numerous influences prodded drafting committees and legislatures toward eventual codification. These included the successes and availability of European codes, their qualities as "talismans" as Jonathan Miller would put it, the circulation of Bentham's works on codification and his individual communications with Latin American leaders, the general cultural pressure of Europe and especially France on the newly independent countries, and the Roman law foundations of the European codes.[7] A few countries moved very quickly to enact European models. Other countries found that the process of thoughtfully revising European codes to fit the particular needs and circumstances of the country, as urged by Montesquieu's *Spirit of the Law*, was a difficult, time-consuming task, riddled with possible political objections and stalemates.

Reform in private law could not be delayed or neglected forever. The very notion of the term *independence* meant that the new nations would have to be free of colonial Spanish law, or at least appear to be free of it, and the process of establishing national law was certainly encouraged by desires to create a new nation with its own laws. Thus the very act of establishing new national law was an assertion and validation of national identity and power. Within a country, the control of private law, and particularly the control of new private law rules, was important for the assertion of internal political power. Even minor changes to the laws concerning property, inheritance, *fueros,* and legal status created clear winners and losers; governments were not immune from using private law reform to reward friends and punish enemies. Private law reform could also serve to cap off a successful centralization of power, and in the battle between federalists and centralists in several countries, once gaining victory, centralists moved to establish civil and commercial codes on a national level. By controlling the sources of law on a national level, central governments suppressed potential regional variation and asserted even greater say over the daily affairs of individuals by controlling the legislation that touched these aspects of life.

Similarly, in regions where complete and active state control and institutions were impossible, local rulers might also move to control these aspects of economic and daily life. The interests of *caudillos* and federalism could shape regional and provincial private law as well as the more evident public law.[8] Thus, independence unsurprisingly led to greater variation in both institutions and rules of private law when compared to the colonial period. With different nations, each building separate legal structures and rules to respond to the needs or demands of their populations, variation in these aspects became inevitable. New possibilities, however, were also present in this variation. As particular countries attempted institutional experimentation or drafted new codes, these aspects of independent legal development became available sources for other countries. Where one country had expended great effort in designing a new civil or commercial code, this code became a useful starting point for other countries that might have structures, populations, and economies that were closer to the Latin American donor than to European counterparts.

Independence also changed the legal profession and legal education. Many royal judges and *audiencia* officials, with royal favors having been granted them, chose to side with Spain during independence. Others, however, chose the side of independence, but the divided loyalties of the bench reduced the pool of valuable legal talent for newly independent countries. Lawyers too were divided. With wealth and privilege under the colonial system, lawyers were paradoxically instrumental in the independence process from Spain. They were involved with the political and juridical institutions that led to the break from Spain, somewhat less involved with military activities during the wars for independence, and then very active in the creation of new constitutional, political, and legal structures in the independent countries.[9] Nonetheless, shortages of qualified lawyers did much to hinder the successful creation and staffing of legal and political position.[10] Relatively traditional in outlook and method, the law faculties did not move rapidly to revise the curriculum for law students, and indeed, the law school curriculum during the decades following independence often reflected the political battles between conservative and liberal ideological forces.

Independence from Spain left many aspects of legal institutions and private laws unsettled. While public law institutions, such as the courts, needed to be provided immediately to fill the void left by the collapse of colonial institutions, private law rules continued mostly unchanged in spite of the sweeping political changes. Successful reform in either area was difficult. New institutions needed capable individuals and effective financing, both scarce commodities after violent battles that often left the republics still internally divided about the direction they should take. New private law was even slower in replacing colonial law. Because the rules reflected political choices, these choices had to be determined first. Unreflective adoption of European codes was not a solution, and the well-considered appropriation of these sources required the same scarce items that hindered the building of effective institutions, legal talent, and available funds, even if the underlying goals of a new private law system were within the reach of a country's grasp.

Structures and Courts

INDEPENDENCE led to new institutions created under the new constitutions of the separate republics.[1] Governments legitimized themselves
after independence by creating and staffing judicial institutions among other
means. Bolívar, for example, published more than thirty decrees related to
the courts and their judges between 1817 and 1830.[2] Despite the solidity constitutional language might imply, many of these institutions were in a fluid
and uncertain condition during the early decades of the nineteenth century.
Institutions depended on political stability, state financial resources, and the
quality of and number of personnel available to fill essential positions. It was
usually only after several decades of instability and experimentation in court
structure and jurisdiction that countries undertook substantial legislative reforms on these topics, producing, in the later half of the nineteenth century,
pyramidal systems based on geography and jurisdictional amount.[3]

In some areas, because independence crept in though juntas maintaining loyalty to the Spanish crown (Ferdinand VII), there was at first no great
revolutionary zeal to shake royal institutions. For example, in Río de la Plata,
which later became Argentina, during the May Revolution of 1810, the *cabildo* transferred jurisdiction in all causes not involving the government to the
royal *audiencia,* and the *cabildo* itself functioned under the rules for open *cabildos* set out in the *Recopilación* of 1680.[4] By June 1810, in the same region,
royal *oidores* were removed and replaced by new judges (*conjueces*) who were
to dress the same way as the *abogados.* These new judges were still to swear
allegiance to the king, Ferdinand VII.[5] The provisional government of Río de
la Plata repeated the structuring of new courts in its decree of 1812.[6] During
these uncertain, initial periods, colonials often desired to set the movement
toward independence into actions that could be legally justified.[7]

New court structures were part of new government structures, and no-
where was the change so immediately felt as in the judicial review of lower

court decisions. The solution in Río de la Plata, again as an example, was to enact a new system of appeals in June 1811. Where appellate procedures formerly brought cases before the king or Spanish bodies, these cases were now to be brought before the provisional junta.[8] An 1812 draft constitution for the United Provinces of Río de la Plata provided for a supreme court for the republic, superior courts for each province, and local judges.[9] This evidently followed the structure introduced earlier that year through a provisional decree, the *Reglamento de Institución y Administración de Justicia,* which established an appellate tribunal, the Cámara de Apelaciones.[10] Several notable Argentine judges staffed the first *cámara,* including Manuel Antonio de Castro, who would contribute much to separating the court's judicial functions from political considerations and would establish a sense of Argentine judicial independence.[11]

Generally speaking, the constitutions of the United States, France, and Spain strongly influenced the framers of the new Latin American constitutions.[12] The notion of separation of powers was foreign to colonial practice where multiple functions and duties might be placed in the same institution or person.[13] Such practices continued in the early republic period. The expressed constitutional desire for a separate judiciary competed with established experience and revenue difficulties; the doctrine of the separation of powers often yielded to these restraints. For example, in Charcas (Río de la Plata) in 1813, the governor also served as the president of the appellate court (*cámara de apelaciones*). *Alcaldes de cabildo* were the first instance judges in Buenos Aires until 1821 when university-trained judges replaced them.[14] In Chile, too, some positions of *alcaldes* continued with judicial functions for most of the nineteenth century.[15]

Existing colonial institutions could be expeditiously modified to meet pressing judicial needs of the new countries. For example, even before new constitutions were drafted, *audiencias* might be transformed into purely appellate tribunals.[16] These institutions were then further modified when a congress enacted a constitution, and early national constitutions usually created a single supreme court that took over the judicial functions of the colonial *audiencia.*[17] This court was often later divided into jurisdictional divisions (*salas*), such as civil, criminal, administrative, and labor. Lower appellate courts and courts of original jurisdictions were created along geographical lines.[18] As Linda Arnold has demonstrated for Mexico, such transitions might be fraught with difficulties related to personnel, jurisdiction, finances, and the new position of the tribunals within the political order.[19]

Independence brought experimentation in creating judicial structures, and most of the new republics entered a period of institutional instability, creation, and re-creation.[20] For example, in Río de la Plata, a local system of lawsuit clearinghouses (*tribunales de concordia*) was established using the *procurador síndico,* two *regidores* of the town council, and at times another judge as personnel. This was a system of free, forced arbitration, and in the event the parties did not agree to the panel's determination, the panel would decide if the matter could proceed to court or not. Permission by the panel to proceed to court was also based on jurisdictional limits: below five hundred pesos, the panel's determination was final; for higher amounts, the panel's decision of finality could be appealed to the governors. Initial complaints in the courts had to include the panel's determination.[21] Such panels also had jurisdiction over verbal injuries without damage to body or property, no doubt providing an important locus for airing personal conflicts and damages to reputation. Their procedure was oral, prohibiting writings, and quick. The experiment was over by 1815 when it was abolished by the Provisional Constitution of 1815 (*Estatuto Provisional*), but it left a legacy of providing an example for other institutions (the Juzgados de Concordia of 1835 in Córdoba, for example) and more importantly the idea that attempts at conciliation were necessary before initiating legal action.[22] Bolívar too in his draft constitution for Bolivia and decrees wanted to make conciliation a necessary step before trial.[23] Along with experimentation in structures, countries also debated and attempted various models of selecting judges. For example, in the 1820s and 1830s, Chile considered appointment by the president, election by the provincial assembly, and election by congress, before settling on presidential selection in its Constitution of 1833.[24] Similarly, the course of Mexico's judicial history reveals several different methods of selecting judges.

With new courts, appellate jurisdictions and structures were often tentative and varied greatly in the early independence period. For example, in operation as early as 1811, the Argentine Tribunal Extraordinario, as an appellate tribunal, was a changing yet permanent part of the judicial structure until its abolition in the mid nineteenth century.[25] Nonetheless, the 1853 Constitution created a similar institution.[26] Intermediate appellate tribunals were commonly in use. For example, from 1815 to 1829 a case might pass from a university-trained judge of first instance, to a judge of the Alzada de Provincia, to the Cámara de Apelaciones, and then finally to the Tribunal Extraordinario.[27]

The judicial system of Argentina was reformed in 1821 under Manuel Antonio de Castro and Bernardino Rivadavia, then minister of the government. With the dissolution of the *cabildos* of the province of Buenos Aires, a vacuum was created where original civil and criminal jurisdiction had once been in the *alcaldes* of the local government. Justices of the peace (*jueces de paz*) for each parish and five university-trained judges (*jueces de primera instancia*) were distributed regionally throughout the province (two in the capital, three in the country). These reforms sought the creation of a university-trained, decentralized, government-paid, stable, and tenured judiciary. Nonetheless, legally trained individuals willing to serve as lower judges were scarce during this period and expectations had to be lowered.[28] Authorities removed the requirement of university training for the country judges in 1825.[29]

As the case of Argentina under Rosas demonstrates, even under autocratic rule, there was wide variety and experimentation in establishing judicial institutions and appellate structures. Institutional rearrangement was even more likely after the removal of a leader like Rosas, especially where competing factions expressed varying views on constitutional and institutional issues.[30] The new Argentine Constitution of 1853 contemplated a supreme court (Corte Suprema de Justicia) and intermediate appellate tribunals along the United States model. Judges served during good conduct and received set compensation. The jurisdiction of the Supreme Court was very similar to that given to the U.S. Supreme Court, including cases under the constitution, confederation laws and treaties, conflicts between public powers within the same province, cases with ambassadors as parties, admiralty and maritime jurisdiction, challenges to ecclesiastical authority (*recursos de fuerza*), where the confederation is a party, cases between two provinces, the citizen of a province and another province, or citizens of different provinces.[31] After political and constitutional upheavals and a civil war in the early 1860s, judges for the Supreme Court were finally appointed in 1862.[32] In the same period, Argentina established a system based on geography of lower courts in city neighborhoods, districts, rural departments, and an appellate tribunal.[33]

Theoretical works or foreign models could also have significant impact on the structure of judicial institutions. An example is Bellemare's *Plan General de Organización Judicial* (1829), which provided for judicial police, judicial assistants to bring suits for creditors, justices of the peace, jurisdictionally segregated courts of first instance (civil, commercial/maritime, and criminal), and a high court of justice. Personnel under the *Plan* included high government legal officials, criminal juries, bar associations, and an association of scribes. The *Plan* called for the abolition of certain colonial offices or institutions such as *procuradores*, the *consulados*, and the *tribunal de alzada*. Importantly, the *Plan* also sought the establishing of birth, marriage, and death registries.[34] In Argentina, for example, during the government of General Balcarce, many of these ideas were repeated in proposed reforms but were not enacted because of political instability before Rosas assumed power in 1835.[35] Similarly in the later nineteenth century, Chile revealed a passing interest in common law models, including ideas of drawing the judiciary only from experienced lawyers, rather than using a system of independent career tracks.[36]

The early Mexican experience provides another example of these changes.

Even before Mexican independence in 1821, Mexican courts were undergoing substantial change as a result of peninsular and American influences. Mexico participated in the Spanish Cortes from which the constitution of 1812 and legislation concerning court structure were promulgated. Although this constitution was of limited application in Mexico, it was in place long enough for some judicial reforms to take root. Special jurisdictions were limited to the ecclesiastical and military sphere, reducing substantially the more than twenty areas of special jurisdiction listed for the period by Arnold.[37] The colonial *audiencia* was transformed into an appellate tribunal.[38]

It was not until after the first independence constitution, the Constitution of 1824, that the judiciary was completely restructured for the new state. This constitution addressed the judicial power of the state and provided for the election by state legislatures of the justices of the Supreme Court. The court, composed of eleven justices, was divided into three divisions. This constitutional provision also addressed the qualifications for judges, the jurisdiction of the courts, and the lower federal tribunals on the circuit and district level.[39] Eight circuit and twenty-eight district courts were established.[40] Under this federal constitution, state courts were also possible, and state constitutional provisions provided for state and local courts as well until the country took on a more centralized structure in 1835. As one might expect, throughout this period, finding qualified individuals for all these positions and finding sufficient sums to pay them were immense challenges for the fledgling government, and various modifications were made along the way, including the more or less ad hoc use of substitute judges by the early 1830s.[41]

A new constitution, effective 1837, did not mean that judicial institutions fell into a static structure. In fact, with political power moving toward centralization, in the mid-1830s, the Supreme Court gained greater control over the country's courts. At first, local and departmental courts were not abolished, but their staffing and procedures were left in the hands of the Supreme Court. Authorities harmonized the jurisdiction of the Supreme Court with the powerful jurisdictions of the military and ecclesiastical courts in this period as well. The text of the 1837 Constitution reflected these reforms, as well as the abolition of the departmental tribunals. Financial and personnel problems made the elegant structure of this constitution falter, and indeed reports concerning the administration of justice during the period indicated that many of the reforms had not taken place. In some areas there was just no one to fill the position and no money to pay the judge; in other peripheral areas, the central authority of the Supreme Court was unable to act meaningfully because lower courts did not supply the needed information. Nonetheless, the overall centralizing trend, the increase of power in the Supreme Court, and its willingness to act even through its constitutionally permitted power of initiating legislation, were evident.[42] Separate commercial tribunals moved in and out of favor during the period.[43]

Mexico continued to reform judicial institutions substantially during the Santa Anna period and its increasingly powerful executive branch. The continuation of the Supreme Court throughout the political turmoil of the period was a product of its political savvy and power, its willingness to continue to sit during uncertain times, and perhaps the need of the executive to rely on the stabilizing force of a continuous judiciary. In 1840, it established new procedures, and throughout the 1840s and 1850s new laws addressed court structure, jurisdiction, and finances.[44] The Constitution of 1843 (*Bases Orgánicas*) granted judicial power to a supreme court of eleven judges and the lower courts. The jurisdiction of the Supreme Court was also delineated with care in the document, and the existing tax, commercial, and mining tribunals were to continue with their limited jurisdictions.[45] Likewise, the ecclesiastical and military *fueros* continued to a significant extent.

In 1846, the federalist Constitution of 1824 was reestablished as the fundamental constitutional law of the country under the coup led by General Salas, and the Supreme Court again lent its hand to reestablish the departmental courts. The following year, however, the center of government and the Supreme Court moved to Querétaro; when the occupation of Mexico City by the United States ended, the court returned there in 1848.[46] By the early 1850s the Supreme Court was overtaxed with work, particularly because in addition to its national duties, it also served as an ordinary court of appeals for the Federal District under the 1824 Constitution still in effect.

In 1853 Santa Anna ruled Mexico again with broad-ranging executive powers, and a law to reform the judiciary placed the powers of judicial appointments in the executive, which replaced several justices of the Supreme Court. In 1855, the *Ley de Administración de Justicia y Orgánica de los Tribunales de la Federación,* often called the *Ley Juárez,* reformed the entire judicial system of Mexico.[47] This law, along with the *Ley de Desamparo* of the same year, dissolved the sitting Supreme Court and created another to replace it. Removing the court's ordinary jurisdiction in the Federal District, this law placed the judicial power under the supervision of the executive power by making all judicial appointments the prerogative of the executive and asserted that the state had the sovereign power to limit the military and ecclesiastical jurisdictions. This last assertion was met with extreme protest from the church and created a political shake-up in the government.[48] After the War of the Reform (1858–1861), the replaced justices signaled their acquiescence by accepting the reestablishment of the Supreme Court, and some even took positions on it. Thus, the executive domination of the judicial power in Mexico was complete and would continue well into future.[49] The ecclesiastical and military *fueros* as areas of broad power had been effectively abolished, and the Constitution of 1857 abolished the ecclesiastical courts.[50] Each important political turn encompassed some changes to the judiciary. For example, the jurisdiction of the Mexican federal courts was defined again in 1884.[51] Court structure, likewise, was further delineated in 1896.[52] Under a federal system, as in Mexico, state courts also needed to be structured and staffed, and states enacted their own laws for these tribunals.[53]

As seen in the example of Mexico, along with the streamlining of the regular courts, countries moved either to abolish or to consolidate jurisdictions based on the Spanish *fueros*, although many did not move as quickly, nor as drastically, as Mexico.[54] Furthermore, certain *fueros* like the ecclesiastical or military privileges were too powerful or ingrained into society to be summarily removed. The benefits of asserting such jurisdiction might have been illusory. Running counter to general expectations, recent research has indicated that the assertion of a *fuero* by a party might not have resulted in any better chances of winning one's case before the specialized tribunal.[55] The political forces reducing the number of specialized jurisdictions and *fueros* succeeded in abolishing courts dedicated to Indian parties, such as the Juzgado General de Indios, but the effect of such constitutional and philosophical shifts on Indian life remains to be studied.[56] Specialized courts for merchants were reviewed with a desire to treat all parties and disputes equally. In the 1820s and 1830s in Colombia, the *consulados* of Guayaquil and Cartagena shifted into and out of existence as various proposals for setting up regular tribunals were enacted and repealed.[57] Also in the 1820s, Mexico suppressed the specialized jurisdictions of its *consulados* and of its mining tribunal.[58]

Most newly independent states claimed that the patronage of the church was attached to sovereignty rather than to the crown. Thus, independence led to a renegotiating of the place of the church in society and as a legal institution. Remaining ecclesiastical jurisdiction was also called into question. The Inquisition was inconsistent with the Spanish Constitution of 1812, and the new republics also moved quickly to abolish its presence.[59] In the early 1810s, Río de la Plata abolished the Inquisition and transferred its jurisdiction to the ordinary ecclesiastical courts.[60] The ecclesiastical jurisdiction itself was limited during the same period by cutting off the church from any hierarchy outside the state and granting the bishops their "original faculties" during the temporary lack of communication with the Vatican.[61] Argentina, in 1813, declared its clergy free from ecclesiastical authorities outside its territory and this was continued until new agreements could be established with Rome.[62]

Another important procedural and administrative development in this period is associated with the removal of church control over various aspects of family law. With the church's jurisdiction being taken over by ordinary tribunals, civil registers encroached on the church's service as the official record keeper for births, marriages, and deaths as well as other public events. For example, with the secularization of marriage in 1859 and the general restriction on the power of the church during the period, Mexico instituted a system of civil registers in 1857 to keep information regarding births, deaths, adoptions, paternity acknowledgements, and other documents indicating family status, formerly held only by the parish records.[63] Expressing important shifts in political and social power, these changes in private law and institutions frequently created dilemmas for individuals wanting to comply with both secular powers and religious authority.[64]

New hierarchies of courts often accompanied new procedural law. The earliest civil procedure laws at first reflected the experimentation and uncertainty found in new court systems, and like the courts in which they were to function, were provisional and incomplete.[65] For example, although substantial reforms in its substantive law were decades away, Venezuela adopted a code of civil procedure in 1836 drafted by Francisco Aranda. The code modernized many aspects of procedure and increased the simplicity, clarity, and speed of proceedings.[66] This code, with additions adopting Italian and French innovations, was still the basis of Venezuelan civil procedure in the 1980s.[67] Foreign sources for procedural laws were influential in other countries as well. Using the Spanish *Ley de Enjuiciamiento Civil* of 1855, itself based on the third *Partida,* as a model, Mexico reformed its civil procedure before district and territorial courts in 1857.[68] Chile, however, did not break away from colonial procedures completely until the enactment of its Code of Civil Procedure in 1903.[69]

A Mexican law in 1841 that required all civil, ecclesiastical, and military courts to cite the law upon which their decisions or judgments were based represented an important procedural, and indeed substantive, provision of the period. Because this provision applied even to the most summary proceedings, it was soon corrected by decree to exclude cases of the first instance, but continued to be in effect for any higher decisions.[70]

Many innovations and clarifications were not immediately brought into play in the newly established courts but came instead with the introduction of successful and comprehensive codification somewhat later in the century. Other innovations, such as juries, were discussed, but never put into effect. For example, Río de la Plata proposed juries in the early 1810s and the 1853 Constitution incorporates their use, but they were not put into effect.[71] Likewise, the Colombian Constitution of 1821 states: "One of the first cares of Congress shall be to provide for jury trial in certain kinds of cases until the advantages of this institution become well known, at which time it shall be extended to all criminal and civil cases to which it is usually applied in other countries with all the forms adapted to this mode of procedure."[72] Attempts were also made to provide greater access to courts by reducing costs, and movements toward an inexpensive or free judiciary were part of the modernization of the courts.[73]

Of course, not all legal disputes had to end up in front of a court, and as mentioned earlier in this chapter, governments encouraged various forms of alternative dispute resolution even in the early decades of the new countries. Such alternative means of settling legal disputes made great sense where there was a scarcity of judges and institutions to handle cases. Formal judgments for conciliation became institutionalized in the beginning of this period, as did arbitration apart from the court system.[74] Conciliation (*conciliación*) could be particularly important in areas where legally trained individuals were absent. For example, legislation from Mexico in the mid-1830s indicates that parties to a dispute selected respected individuals (*hombres buenos, apoderados*) who would attempt to reach a settlement between the parties and propose it to the *alcalde*. On examination by the *alcalde*, an agreement by the representatives would bind the parties. If there were no agreement, the *alcalde* would summarily decide the matter. If the parties did not accept the decision, they could proceed with a more formal, written procedure.[75]

Legal Education and Lawyers

INDEPENDENCE brought new ideas about society, government, and law that were reflected in legal education and the profession. Ideas of human equality paradoxically meant that a broader range of students would be pulled into the elite world of legal studies and practice. Law provided social mobility. Legal education, as training for the governing classes, was subject to close governmental scrutiny and to contested rivalries of liberal and conservative views that could reach into minute curricular choices. In the mid nineteenth century, as codification became a reality, the mostly conservative traditional nature of legal education was challenged by new ideas of liberalism and legal science. Law curricula would eventually shift from the colonial substance and methods of the European *ius commune* to incorporate national law, and as needed by new countries, international law. Legal education during the century also would adapt to jurisprudential trends that moved from natural law to "science of law," or positivist traditions.[1] Legal education also addressed the perennial concern of how theoretical or practical instruction should be.

Legal Education

Independence brought significant changes in legal education, although not, at first, in the legal curriculum. Certain families and regions that did not have access to legal education were given the possibility of study though programs awarding children of fathers who died in fighting for independence the opportunity to study, and this meant that some children of moderate means were admitted. Colonial prohibitions dealing with race and illegitimacy were reduced, so that these impediments became occasionally surmountable by particularly worthy or lucky applicants. Revolutionary and constitutional ideas of equality filtered their way into academic admissions and government service. All of these changes led to legal studies as being a possible means of upward mobility, much more so than it had been in the colonial system.[2] Another way independence led to broader opportunities for legal study was an increase in the number of provincial *colegios* where students could study law in preparation for exams administered by the existing universities. In New Granada, this trend began in the mid-1820s and increased significantly in the 1830s and 1840s. Additional degree-granting universities were also established in smaller centers of the new republics, such those in Cauca, Popayán, and Cartagena, in Colombia, for example, which grew from local *colegios*. As the central and regional universities were given the power to issue their own degrees, the church's, and in the case of Colombia, the Dominicans', monopoly on education was broken.[3] Exercising their degree-granting power to the very end in 1826, the Dominicans "generously issu[ed]" law degrees contributing to the number of lawyers in the period.[4]

Similar patterns can be observed throughout the region. Shortly after gaining independence, Mexico in 1823 gave regional *colegios* authority both to hire law professors and to give law degrees, thus spreading the possibility of legal study into the less populated areas of the country. While political differences in Colombia affected the content of the curriculum, political disputes in Mexico went to the very core of whether there would be a central national university offering legal instruction; between independence and 1867 the University of Mexico was disbanded three times. The first time, in 1833, was to replace it with a new educational system based on wide-ranging reforms, but Santa Anna reestablished the university the following year. The second disbanding was equally as short lived during 1857, and the final disbanding occurred in 1865 under Maximilian. Nonetheless, legal instruction continued during these periods, even in Mexico City at the *colegios* of San Ildefonso, San Juan de Letrán, and San Gregorio. Backed by important educational reforms in 1867, government officials established the Escuela Nacional de Jurisprudencia in 1868 and placed it in the former building of San Ildefonso; the Escuela Nacional soon became the premier school for legal instruction in the capital. The following year it found a new home at the former convent of the Incarnation.[5]

Law faculties continued to teach the traditional courses established in the colonial period, with great emphasis on Roman and canon law, which remained the mainstay of legal training throughout the period.[6] For example, the curricular content of legal studies at San Ildefonso included natural, Roman, and Mexican law as well as the English language, which were taught in the first year. English was extended throughout the second year, and the second, third, and fourth years had the same topics — Roman, canon, and Mexican law. This led to the degree of *bachiller*. Three more years of forensic practice and procedure with touches of international, mercantile, and administrative law, topped off with political economy led to the *licenciado* degree. The degree of *doctor* was granted after an additional year of study dedicated to legal philosophy, comparative legislation, and the history of treaties.[7] A similar curricular emphasis was found in the legislation of 1867 for studies at the Escuela Nacional de Jurisprudencia, although this new institution offered the title of lawyer (*abogado*) or notary, rather than the colonial-styled degrees.[8] The course on comparative legislation predominantly addressed comparative constitutional law between the United States and Mexico, and indeed over the decades following the establishment of the school, school officials significantly expanded the curriculum. The adoption of codes of law for the federal district and territories led to their use and exposition in the classroom as basic teaching texts.[9] The method of instruction remained the same as in the colonial period: the professor read the text, explained its philosophical and historical background, and sought repetition from students indicating sufficient memorization.[10] The curriculum of the national school provided the model for the provincial schools, and the traditional content, methods of instruction, and the manner in which these were followed as models by others teaching law throughout the country are representative of what occurred in many countries of the region in the late nineteenth century.

This concentration on the classical curriculum led to concern about how to train contemporary, useful lawyers, especially when most countries recognized a need for trained legal minds not only in the judiciary but also in many other positions in political life and government service. The colonial concerns that university legal training did not provide a practical grounding were repeated. Addressing some of these concerns, several countries modified the institutions and systems of legal education. For example, Argentina established the Academia de Jurisprudencia in 1815, and Manuel Antonio de Castro served as its first director and Antonio Sáenz as its president.[11] Because university legal training was seen as not providing the necessary familiarity with present-day law, the academy was established to give future lawyers an additional two years of education in practical legal matters. In Levene's view, the instruction at the academy only highlighted the poor state of the substantive national law, and this, in turn, led to a push for new, codified laws.[12]

The University of Buenos Aires opened a faculty of jurisprudence in 1821. Sáenz was instrumental in this faculty as well and took a chair in natural law from which he taught what became fundamental principles of Argentine law. Pedro Somellera, who worked on commercial tribunals and procedure, held a chair in civil law. Influenced by Bentham, he brought similar enlightenment principles into the classroom.[13] A chair in legal history was added to the university through student pressure because they believed that legal history, incorporating constitutional history and codification, was a needed, practical discipline.[14] An additional course on political economy was taught from Mill's *Elements*.[15] The number of courses and length of years to complete legal study were increased from the 1820s to the 1870s. The emphasis of earlier years on practical education was shifted to the study of legal science and the newly enacted codes during the same period.[16] José Dámaso Xigena founded another academy in Córdoba in 1821.[17] The University of Córdoba also granted law degrees through its faculty of arts and by presidential decree in 1827; the bachelor's degree in law from Córdoba was made the equivalent of a doctorate from the University of Buenos Aires.[18]

Colombia changed the legal curriculum shortly after independence. Various political forces drove the content of the course of study in Colombia; Bentham's works in the classroom became a focal point for the debates, and both Bolívar and Santander decreed aspects of legal education in the area. Because the appropriateness of Bentham's work in the legal curriculum was often disputed, the use of Bentham in legal education was contentious throughout the region during the first half of the nineteenth century.[19] For example, Quiroga de la Rosa and others attacked Bentham's works in Argentina in 1829.[20]

Colombian legal education in 1826 provided for six years of study. The first three led to a bachelor's degree, and the last three to a doctorate required for practice. The first three years included courses on universal, civil, and penal legislation; constitutional law; administrative sciences; Roman law compared with national law; and ecclesiastical law. The last three years included more Roman law, canon law, church history, political economy, international law, and treaties.[21] Although this plan only lasted two years because it was seen as being too demanding and overly broad, it indicates the general subjects taught and the ideas behind legal education in Colombia during the period.[22] It also appears that the time required might be substantially shortened by taking several courses in one year (*cursos simultáneos*), a practice that was not prohibited until 1840.[23]

Means notes that the curriculum was to prepare students for political leadership, rather than exclusively legal practice.[24] Yet reforms in the curriculum in the 1830s and 1840s indicate that it remained highly focused on Roman civil law, national civil law, and canon law.[25] The 1842 plan of studies tried to make legal education more practical: courses included Roman law; national civil law; constitutional and administrative law; criminal law; international, commercial, and maritime law; political economy; and public and ecclesiastical law.[26] Rufino Cuervo introduced another short-lived plan of legal education in 1847. Under his plan a doctorate in law required six years rather than the earlier five, and commercial law was made a required course for both students pursuing a bachelor's degree or a doctorate. The main aspects of his plan were to centralize control and impose national curricular requirements.[27]

The politically liberal educational reforms of 1850 drastically transformed Colombian legal education. The decree provided for freedom of profession, which was interpreted to mean that a law degree was not a prerequisite to practicing law. Although a law degree was still most likely seen as a good thing for a lawyer to have, the decree eroded the position of legal education in the country. Under the decree, jurisprudence was to be taught at Popayán and Cartagena, but not in the public national *colegio* in Bogotá. The Rosario, which had offered legal instruction in the colonial period, would be reopened.[28] Until their expulsion in 1861, the Jesuits at San Bartolomé in Bogotá also taught a three-year law course that included offerings in civil and commercial litigation.[29] Only the doctorate, requiring the passage of eight subjects, was retained. The curriculum was limited and some courses, such as commercial law, were dropped.[30] In the late 1860s legal education in Colombia improved with the reopening of San Bartolomé, the course of legal study newly available at the Rosario, the Colegio of Boyacá increasing its law offerings, and the plans for a four-year law school attached to a new national university.[31] By decree in 1872, a three-year curriculum required Colombian law students to study constitutional law, civil and penal legislation, political economy, introduction to law, Roman law, national civil law, international law, judicial organizations and evidence, comparative legislation of the union, and comparative judicial organization of the union. Means notes that the content of Colombian when compared with contemporary U.S. legal education was focused more on public law and on legal and political theory than on private substantive and procedural law.[32]

Latin American legal education in the nineteenth century was linked to political power. It was not confined to education for lawyers and judges; legal education was the predominant preparation for a politically active life in government and a host of other influential slots in society. The structure of legal education was legislatively controlled in many countries, even to the point of prescribing or prohibiting individual texts for certain courses. By the early twentieth century, legal education had been laicized, earlier required courses in theology and particularly canon law having been removed to different faculties. Legal education also sought to provide a broader political education rather than a strictly professional, instrumental course of study. These changes reflected the watchful eye of the political powers and their concern that what went on in the law classroom could shape their countries' futures.[33]

It is very difficult to determine the quality of legal education provided in law faculties during the early and middle nineteenth century. Some evidence indicates that students might receive law degrees after cursory study under less than ideal conditions.[34] Nonetheless, judging from the successful legal reforms of many countries in the second half of the nineteenth century, some students must have benefited greatly from their studies, at least well enough to guide their countries' law and institutions into modern systems responding to the economic and, on occasion, social needs of the population.

Lawyers

The evidence concerning the distribution of lawyers in society during the independence and early republic period is not clear. Some sources indicate that there were too many lawyers, and yet there were not enough to meet the new countries' demands to staff their nascent judiciaries. For example, at independence in Río de la Plata, there was a general popular concern about an excessive number of lawyers.[35] General opinion during the early republic period was that there was a shortage of qualified lawyers. Factors resulting in the scarcity noted by Victor Uribe-Uran included the royal repression of lawyers, the flight of royalist lawyers during the independence period, and the disruption of legal education during war.[36] Just as the relative numbers of lawyers shrank, the newly created judicial institutions of the new republics were calling them to serve as judges, often far away from the comfort of the large cities that have always been homes to the successful practitioner.[37] Finding public funds to pay those who filled such judicial positions was an endemic problem.[38] The scarcity of qualified lawyers was, as it had been in colonial times, most evident in the peripheral areas. These outlying areas continued to have a paucity of legally trained individuals in both governmental and private roles. Peripheral areas served by lawyers were exceptional. It appears that there was during the independence period, as in the colonial period, an adequate supply of lawyers in the centers of power such as Bogotá.[39]

Lawyers in the early republic period continued to be members of the elite, ruling classes, and indeed every elite family would seek to have some legally trained members to complement those in the church, government, military, and income-producing activities. Recent study has demonstrated that legal training provided upward mobility in society as well, as families broadened their circles of influence.[40] The ways in which lawyers deterred or contributed to the independence movement in Latin America is only beginning to be understood. Some lawyers were instrumental in establishing the first independence *cabildos*. Sometimes, however, lawyers showed their royalist colors, for example, when twenty-one lawyers in the Buenos Aires *cabildo* of August 14, 1806, voted to grant the viceroy a pension.[41] Others, of course, after independence were to become actively involved in building the new court systems, drafting early constitutions, and reforming all aspects of substantive and procedural law.[42] At first, it is puzzling to see the elites, those favored under the monarchy, turn against their benefactors and support revolution.[43] It appears that one source of the drive for independence may have been the crown's unwillingness to negotiate and to bargain with elite sectors of society, including lawyers, and thus, they turned away from Spain because there was nothing to be gained in continuing the extant political relationship.[44] Recent scholarship has emphasized the role of lawyers in the independence movement as a result of their stepping in to initiate a "revolution from above" to address the collapse of Spanish rule during the French occupation. This analysis calls into question or at least supplements the traditional explanation of revolution stemming from disaffected Creoles who were excluded from local political power by peninsular favorites. Although American Creoles had greater access to such positions before the middle of the eighteenth century, from the 1750s, they were increasingly excluded, and this too must have bolstered revolutionary sentiment.[45] Regardless of the causes of revolution, lawyers were ready to assist in the independence movement and in the establishment of independent *juntas* exercising autochthonous power. Indeed, in some areas, lawyer involvement was a key factor in the creation of such institutions. Uribe-Uran has summarized lawyer participation this way, "Lawyers were the most conspicuous leaders of the movement for independence that started with the creation of *juntas supremas* in the major cities of the Viceroyalty of New Granada, including Bogotá itself on July 20, 1810. . . . Lawyers' apparent dominance in the several juntas that started the movement to unseat the colonial authorities was bound to affect the extent and nature of that movement."[46] It should be noted that at least in the case of independence in New Granada, lawyers' involvement in "the revolution was not motivated by the content of legal education" which, as noted above, stayed conservatively classical during the period.[47]

When the independence movement suffered defeat, for example in New Granada in 1816, Spanish forces executed lawyers who had participated in independence activities. In that year alone, more than twenty-five lawyers were executed for their revolutionary activities, and the Spanish commander was known to have been particularly harsh with lawyers as a group.[48]

Not all lawyers were killed as a result of revolutionary involvement, and of course, even during the independence decades, students continued to study law, although education was easily disrupted and at times halted because of war and political turmoil. In some ways these newly trained lawyers served to link two generations of the profession, those who were trained in a colonial system and had been through the independence period and those who only knew postindependence legal education, practice, and institutions. Uribe-Uran has labeled this a "transitional generation" of lawyers who served as "high-ranking lawyer-bureaucrats and congressmen."[49]

By the middle of the nineteenth century, government, usually first through the newly created supreme courts, and then later through the legislatures, began to regulate the legal profession, attempting to set forth minimum standards for practice, often in an attempt either to require more training for *procuradores* or to exclude them clearly from the more distinguished ranks of the *abogados*. The regional or national *colegios de abogados* joined in the self-selection and protection process, although in the earlier years of independence at least one such organization, the Colegio de Abogados of Caracas was prohibited from reestablishment because of its association with the nobility and over-exclusivity in the practice of law.[50] Some of the increased regulatory activity may have been in response to a rapidly increasing number of lawyers during the mid nineteenth century, which has been observed in some regions.[51]

Where or when *caudillos* or dictators ruled, lawyers were very often politically aligned with these interests. Indeed, some scholars have asserted that during this period under these conditions, lawyers functioned more as politicians and less as representatives of individual clients. Surely, lawyers served as an essential bridge into civil power for military power.[52] Nonetheless, it appears that in some countries their cooperation went only so far, for when the rule of law (particularly private law assuring property rights) became too personally tied of powerful leader, lawyers might lead the charge for new government.[53] In either case, lawyers in this period were an elite group often linked to political power and government service.[54]

Elite lawyers might have several phases of their careers, often alternating between judicial and legislative positions as well.[55] For example, between 1860 and 1910, the Argentine José Olegario Machado served as a legislative representative, a judge, law professor, and an author of important legal works, including the first major commentary on Vélez Sársfield's civil code of Argentina and a treatise on contracts.[56] Such diversity in professional activity was typical of lawyers at the top of the profession. Most were not able to break into this layer where the greatest mobility existed.

Scribes and notaries became increasingly important to the commercial expansion of the republics. While their presence was well established in the large colonial centers during the Spanish period, these officials found new demand in the smaller regional centers as their assistance with contracts, mortgages, and other commercial papers was needed. For example, the city of Rosario, Argentina, obtained its first notary in 1852. Shortly afterward, the city obtained its first commercial *consulado* and commercial tribunal. By 1856, two Spanish notaries had moved to the city to practice and were joined by another from Buenos Aires. By the end of the century, this regional center with a population of about 100,000 had fifty-five notaries.[57] The practice of these individuals during the nineteenth century continued much as it did in the colonial period, and colonial practices were not easy to shake. The Argentine law for notaries of 1867 stated: "Notaries shall continue to provide public documents in the form prescribed by law 13, title 23, book 4 of the *Recopilación Castellana*."[58]

During the early republic period, at first legal education and the social status of lawyers did not change. Law students and the legally trained served not only as lawyers and judges, but also as politicians and leaders of society. Indeed, lawyers had helped topple monarchical control and ushered in new governmental structures. Independence did not mean that political battles were at an end, in fact, in determining the future course of nations, new governments were cautious of innovation in legal education and wary to ensure that lawyers were subject to close governmental control. Lawyers continued to be members of elite families and contributed to their social power. Other legally trained officials, such as scribes and notaries, filled the increased demand for professionally prepared and recorded personal and commercial legal documents.

Sources

THE sources of private law did not change immediately on independence. With few exceptions, new countries continued to use the colonial materials for questions of property, testaments, family law, contracts, and commerce. The provisions of new constitutions sanctioned appeal to these sources and laws governing procedural aspects of newly established courts. By the mid nineteenth century, codification radically changed the structure and content of private law. This chapter addresses precodification sources, practioners' works, and treatises. It also notes some of the concerns raised as countries moved toward codes. The process and nature of codification are discussed in the next chapter.

While independence ushered in many new changes in constitutional law and government structures, the sources of private law after independence generally continued to be those used before independence. The continuity of private law was often incorporated directly into the constitutional provisions of the new country, which usually indicated that Spanish law would control until the contemplated new codes drafted for the country were enacted. The constitution of Colombia of 1811 stated:

Article 72. The laws which, for these and other cases, now operate in the tribunals of the Union are those which have hitherto governed us insofar as they are not contrary to the present pact, nor incompatible with the actual state of things, nor prejudicial to the political situation of the Kingdom or Provinces of New Granada.[1]

The new constitution of Colombia in 1821 stated:

Article 188. Laws hitherto existing are hereby declared to be in full force in all matters and cases not directly or indirectly repugnant to this Constitution or to the decrees and laws which Congress may enact.[2]

Similar savings clauses are found in other early constitutions throughout the region.[3]

Some modifications were immediately made to private law, particularly to neutralize societal privileges, such as changes to the law of slavery, entails, and the *fueros*. As governments enacted their own piecemeal legislation addressing particularly pressing areas of private law, these new laws governed and replaced the colonial law on the legislated topic. Faced with recent republican legislation piled on top of the colonial legislation, lawyers and judges had the difficult task of determining applicable rules of law. Throughout the nineteenth century and before the enactment of topical codes, lawyers sought guidance from treatises and legislation to determine the weight of various authorities. For example in Mexico, the widely used treatise by Febrero gave the following order of authorities in 1834:

1. Legislation of the Mexican congresses
2. Decrees of the Spanish legislature given before independence
3. The last royal *cédulas* and orders sent to America
4. Sets of royal orders on particular areas of law
5. *Recopilación de Indias*
6. *Recopilación de Castilla, Nueva y Novísima*
7. *Ordenamientos Real y de Alcalá*
8. *Fueros Real y Juzgo*
9. *Siete Partidas*[4]

Just as in colonial practice, the judge or practitioner would often read down the list to the *Siete Partidas* to find a law applicable to a particular dispute. Practice in many areas stayed the same for decades, usually until codification of the area of law. For example, surveying Mexican wills from 1789 to 1840, one scholar noted no substantial changes in their text.[5] Use of authorities in private disputes continued much the same as during the late colonial period, although the range of sources might be expanded to include newer European sources, such as the French civil code.[6] But continuity was the usual situation; in Mexico, a law of 1837 required the use of all legislation from before 1824 that was consistent with the norms of an independent state.[7] Likewise, colonial classics, such as Hevia Bolaños's *Curia Philipica*, might be reworked into national editions, such as Galván Rivera's *Curia Filípica Mexicana*.[8]

Rules stating the order of legal authorities were frequently incorporated into the legislation addressing the civil procedure of newly established courts. Following on the general constitutional provisions to continue colonial law in force except where it conflicted with new law, legislation often had to be more specific and the ranking of sources was complex. For example, the applicable Colombian provision found in the civil procedure law of May 1, 1825, read:

Article 1. The order in which the laws in all the tribunals and trials of the Republic, civil, ecclesiastical, and military, both civil and criminal, is the following: First, those decreed or to be decreed by the Legislative Power; Second, the *pragmáticas, cédulas,* and ordinances of the Spanish government in effect until March 18, 1808, which were in observance under the same Spanish government in the territory forming the Republic; Third, the laws of the *Recopilación de Indias;* Fourth, the laws of the *Nueva Recopilación de Castilla;* and Fifth, the laws of the *Siete Partidas.*

Article 2. In consequence, none of the laws, *pragmáticas, cédulas,* orders or decrees of the Spanish government after March 18, 1808, will have any effect or force in the Republic, nor those set out in the article above which directly or indirectly are contrary to the Constitution or to the laws and decrees which have been given or are to be given by the Legislative Power.

Article 180. Until a complete code of civil procedure is given by the Congress, the tribunals and judges of the Republic are to conduct civil causes according to the dispositions of this law. In cases not foreseen in this law, tribunals and judges shall use the laws in force according to the first chapter of this law.[9]

Most newly independent countries adopted similar rules, often in setting out the structure and workings of newly established systems of courts and their procedure.[10]

Presented with the labyrinth of colonial legal sources and the possibility of superseding national legislation, lawyers sought works summarizing or at least compiling these various materials. As a result, preindependence laws and newer legislative acts were rearranged for professional use, and these collections served a legal community that did not yet benefit from the organizational elegance of codification. An example compiling Spanish law is Juan de Sala's *Ilustraciones del derecho real de España*. It follows an institutional structure and gives references to the *Siete Partidas* and other texts. Very popular, it went through several printings in the first half of the nineteenth century. In the 1840s, several country-specific editions were published in Paris for Latin American use, including a *Sala Hispano-Mexicano*, a *Sala Hispano-Chileno*, and a *Sala Hispano-Venezolano*. Also popular in the same period was Joaquín de Escriche's *Diccionario razonado de la legislación civil, penal, comercial y forense*.[11] Another example of such compiling works is Lino de Pombo's *Recopilación de leyes de Nueva Granada formada i publicada en cumplimiento de la lei de 4 de mayo de 1843* (1845) that organizes legislation around seven topic areas.[12]

As would be expected, in peripheral areas of the republics, customary practices, rather than written legislation, were often the basis of deciding cases.[13] While recent legislation may have made important changes in some areas of the law, it is unlikely that these were either important in or effectively transmitted to outlying areas. Where changes may have been fundamentally important to some people, such as changes in the law of slavery, others interested in the perpetuation of the status quo were able to hinder and even to block such changes from being put into effect in the peripheral areas.

The most important change occurring to the available sources of law in Latin America from independence to the beginning of the twentieth century was the success of the codification movement. The nature of this movement, its methods, and results are discussed in the next chapter. From the standpoint of sources of law, codes and codification changed almost everything. Successful codification of an area of law changed the very nature of that area. How students studied that area of law, how lawyers and courts approached it, how they interpreted the rules provided by the code, and what secondary materials they used to understand it all changed.

Some attempts at codification were premature, and the mere, unthinking borrowing of European codes led in instances to confusion concerning governing provisions and desuetude resulting from a lack of institutions or personnel described in the codes. Some have seen the wholesale borrowing of codes as an indicium of legal underdevelopment. There was significant debate in Latin American countries about the quick adoption of continental sources as the most beneficial method of modernizing law, especially as countries were entering the era of codification. European sources could lead to a self-critique that encouraged the appropriate creation and adaptation of sources to the particular characteristics of the country, and some cautioned against the facile acceptance of continental sources. For example in Argentina, Juan B. Alberdi's *Fragmento preliminar al estudio del derecho* (1837) followed the thought of Savigny and Lerminier in stressing the importance of national characteristics and history in legal systems.[14] In 1838, Marcos Sastre's *Ojeada filosófica sobre el estado presente y la suerte futura de la Nación Argentina* complained of the error of imitating foreign institutions and structures instead of following national solutions extracted from the character of the country.[15] Nonetheless it appears that national political events did little to hinder the long-term influence of European sources. For example, lawyers and legislators in Mexico seemed to have forgotten the failures of Maximilian's empire, and the poor relations with France in the late 1820s, when Veracruz was bombed by a French flotilla in a strong-arm debt collection tactics, seemed even more remote.[16] With the general adoption of European-style codes, usually with European content, the nationalist protests concerning this issue greatly diminished.

When codification successfully took, it meant that the usefulness and availability of the legal rules increased dramatically. Laws addressing a single area could be published, bound, and circulated in small compact and relatively inexpensive volumes for use by legal practitioners and those in business affected by certain areas of law. Lawyers and judges could also take advantage of a growing body of works, such as the important annotated version of Colombia's civil code by Manuel J. Angarita, *Código civil nacional concordado y leyes adicionales concordadas y comentadas*, published in Bogotá in 1888, annotating and updating the codes.[17]

Successful codification also meant that the countries adopting these sources had, once again as they did during the *ius commune* period, much in common with each other and much in common with the advanced countries of Europe. Furthermore, the full panoply of European interpretive tools aimed at codes was applicable and readily appropriated by the Latin American countries, particularly where the tools were in comfortable languages for Spanish speakers. After codification, the most important development in Latin American private law during the nineteenth century was probably the influx of continental sources as interpretive tools to the codes. Roman law continued to be an important tool of interpretation, and the use of Roman law in this way may have developed in unique ways in Latin America.[18]

Although a tradition of treatises and commentaries was in existence in colonial times, it greatly increased in the nineteenth century. Where new national laws were based in part or in whole on foreign sources, these sources and their commentaries became valuable guides for the practitioner and judge. Annotated codes and commentaries incorporating references, abstracts, or quotes from European sources were, and to some extent continue to be, common.[19] The increase in such sources was dramatic in the second half of the nineteenth century as universities turned out more law graduates and countries moved toward greater economic strength and political stability. In many areas of civil law, French sources led the way.[20] For example, in 1875 José Machado published a commentary on the contract provisions of Vélez's Argentine civil code. In the course of his study, Machado drew analysis from and comparisons with more than fifteen French sources, including Pothier, Demolombe, Toullier, Marcadé, Mourlon, Aubry and Rau, Larombière, Duranton, Merlin, Dalloz, Taulier, Demante, and Acollas.[21]

Spanish sources too were, as would be expected, very influential even from the earlier part of the nineteenth century. A treatise sitting on the border of pre- and postcodification thought is Eugenio de Tapia's *Tratado de jurisprudencia mercantil* (1828), which, according to Means, reflects the state of Spanish commercial law before its codification but with the then twenty-year-old French commercial code as an organizational backdrop.[22] One important treatise on civil law was José María Alvarez's *Instituciones de derecho real de España*. A Guatemalan edition of the work was published in 1818–1820, and peninsular editions were also available. Working from the 1829 Madrid edition, the Argentine codifier Vélez Sársfield prepared his 1834 edition published in Buenos Aires.[23]

Latin American countries developed their own legal doctrine as well, and by the mid nineteenth century one enters a period in which a complete list or description of such treatises is not within the scope of this work, but a few examples are offered here. Mexico developed an important body of domestic writings on legislation from an early date; even in the midst of political turmoil, several works on civil legislation and legal commentary were available, including those of Basilio José Arrillaga, Juan R. Navarro, and Vicente García Torres. Later in the nineteenth century examples abound.[24] Under the rule of Porfirio Díaz (1876–1910), Mexican authors wrote numerous treatises on civil and commercial law, including Jacinto Pallares's *El derecho mercantil mexicano,* J. A. Mateos Alarcón's *Lecciones de derecho civil,* and A. Verdugo's *Principios de derecho civil mexicano.*[25] In Argentina, an influential procedural treatise was Miguel Esteves Sagui's *Tratado elemental de los procedimientos civilies en el foro de Buenos Aires* (1850).[26] Some countries took a bit longer to develop a significant indigenous treatise tradition. Treatises addressing private law in Colombia belong to the twentieth century. Only a few earlier works are noted in a useful bibliography of Colombian law: a program of study of the civil law from the Rosario from 1888, Justo Arosemena's "El Matrimonio ante la ley" in the *Revista Latino-Americana* (Paris, 1874), and Venancio Ortiz's *De la propriedad en la Nueva Granada* (Bogotá, 1852).[27] Fernando Vélez's influential *Estudio sobre el derecho civil colombiano* was published in 1898.[28] Although these works were written for Latin America, European works continued to be important sources on which they were based. These sources became available in Spanish through importation of translations published in Spain or translations published in the particular country.[29]

The use of European code provisions, European organizational structures for law, and European doctrine had a powerful impact on Latin American law and legal development. Law students and lawyers tended toward an international intellectual outlook that included training in European languages, French most of all, and readily made these foreign sources their own. Furthermore, since European law provided a great deal of intellectual framework and content of Latin American law, further adoption and appropriation of European models and indeed European improvements were relatively common.

Government officials and publishers developed improved methods for publishing, disseminating, and organizing national legislation in the later half of the nineteenth century, and even the regional centers of federal states making up countries like Colombia, Argentina, and Mexico at different periods published editions of their provincial legislation. More modern and comprehensive treatments of legislation in which even superseded laws might be published for study, did not fully develop until the twentieth century. An example of this is the forty-seven-volume work by Dublán and Lozano, *Legislación Mexicana,* which covered Mexican legislation from 1687 to 1909.[30]

Newspapers provided an essential link to legislative activity and legal developments in Latin American countries. Newspapers intended for general readership, although almost always with a clear political predisposition, were important forums for the discussion and debate of proposed legislation as well as the publication of new laws.[31] The nineteenth century also witnessed the growth of newspapers dedicated exclusively to legal affairs. For example, in the later nineteenth century, legal periodicals flourished in Mexico.[32]

Although it is a common refrain that civil law jurisdictions do not rely on case law for the creation of legal rules, this oversimplification has been appropriately questioned, even in the introductory literature.[33] As early as the mid nineteenth century in Mexico, for example, the Supreme Court was willing to assert that certain questions of state constitutional law had been decided previously and would not be reexamined based on the applicability of the prior decision.[34] Mexican judicial decisions would not be widely available until the twentieth century.

The beginning of official publications marked a final important aspect in the type and availability of sources of law during this period. For example, reports of Argentina's Supreme Court became available from the 1860s, and the official reporter of the Colombian Supreme Court, the *Gaceta Judicial,* began in the 1880s.[35] Official publications related to legislation and the activities of central governments were even more common by the late nineteenth century. Some attempts at official publications of laws and government notices dated from an even earlier period, such as the official bulletin (*Diario del Imperio*) established by Maximilian in Mexico in 1864.[36]

The sources of law slowly changed over the course of the first half of the nineteenth century. For private law, these sources continued to be very similar to the colonial sources. Rapid change occurred in countries once codification replaced the colonial system of legal rules. The newly effected constitutions and codes went hand in hand to guide both public and private law. The codes, and above all the civil code, formed the central documents for thinking about the law, and indeed they formed the basis of the entire structure of legal rules. The placement of laws in one code or another defined the areas of law. Works interpreting, annotating, and explaining the codes became the central sources of law for the lawyer. In the next chapter, I examine how the dramatic change in codification occurred.

Andrés Bello.

Codification

Codification in Constitutions

NATIONAL officials and legal specialists understood that civil law was integral to establishing new countries and their institutions.[1] Lawyers, professors, judges, and politicians criticized the confusing, labyrinthine nature of the postindependence civil law.[2] When replacing this system of law, Latin American countries turned to the legal systems of other countries, borrowing and transplanting these foreign laws. The very process of codification was consistent with liberalism and the shedding of the Spanish colonial past and its hierarchies. Notions of rational lawmaking and of law as a science informed the content and structure of codification. Codes not only established rules for the regulation of conduct and the resolution of disputes but also served as important methods of transmitting legal knowledge.[3] In this way, codes fit well into an agenda of rationally restructuring society in accordance with egalitarian, enlightenment values.[4]

New governments and their constitutions assumed that new laws would accompany the shift to an independent state, and constitutions frequently referred to codes when addressing the powers of legislative bodies. One of the enumerated powers of the Congress in the Colombian Constitution of 1830 is "to draw up national codes of all kinds and to enact laws and decrees necessary for the regulation of the different branches of the administration, and to interpret, amend, and annul existing legislation."[5] Provisions for codification are found as early as 1811 in the Constitution of Tunja (New Granada).[6] Likewise, the draft constitution of 1813 for Río de la Plata stated that civil and commercial codes were to be prepared for the country.[7] Thus the idea of codes and codification were sometimes explicitly stated in the constitutions of the new republics and sometimes only implicitly under the general legislative powers described. Codes, as such, were not mentioned in the early constitutions of Mexico.[8]

Even if not specifically mentioned in the constitution of a new republic, codifying civil and commercial law was frequently discussed in the 1820s and 1830s throughout the newly independent states of Latin America.[9] The excitement frequently ended with the appointing of a committee to draft codes, usually composed of overburdened members of the new governments who had little extra time to draft comprehensive legislation. Mexico experienced this in 1822.[10] Ecuador and Venezuela experienced the same thing in the late 1830s.[11] In at least one situation, codification took legislative precedence to drafting a constitution; but after debate, the Ecuadorian legislature decided it could not move forward with the civil code until it had first drafted and adopted a constitution.[12]

The general pattern was for the constitution to provide the delegated power to the national congress, which was then authorized to commission drafters who would revise a particular area of the law. This draft would then be enacted by the congress, and the earlier legislation governing the area would be simultaneously repealed. Legislation or decrees effecting this procedure might cite the appropriate constitutional provision as authority. Naming a commission to begin codification of Peruvian law in 1825, Bolívar decreed in Lima:

Considering:

1. That according to article 121 of the Constitution all the laws which are not in opposition to its principles or to the system of independence ought to govern while the civil and criminal codes are prepared;
2. That the rule of the Republic urgently demands this preparation in accordance with the fundamental law, and as the only way to avoid the doubts and contradictions that frequently are observed in the application of the law;
3. That this object cannot be achieved except through a plan of civil and criminal codes which are formed by a special commission which facilitates the work of the Congress, I have come to decree.

I decree:

1. A commission is named composed of the President of the Supreme Court of Justice, of Doctor Don Francisco Valdivieso, of Doctor Don José Cabero y Salazar, of the President of the Superior Court, of Doctors Don Miguel Tadeo Fernández de Córdoba, Don Ignacio Ortíz de Ceballos, Don José de Larrea y Loredo, Don Manuel Tellería, Don Ignacio Moreno, Don José Armas, Don Justo Figuerola y Don Agustín Quijano, formerly the Count of Torre Velarde.
2. The object of the commission is to make drafts of civil and criminal codes, and present them, as soon as possible, to the government, so that it may submit them to the Congress.

3. In necessary cases, the commission will speak to the ministers who, according to their departments, ought to have intervention in this work.
4. The Ministry of State in the Department of Government is charged with the execution of this decree.[13]

This decree, as many similar decrees in the early part of the nineteenth century, came to little. It appears that political instability, even anarchy, overworked and scarce legal talent, lack of additional pay for such work, difficulty in obtaining sources, and the personal attributes of commission members often led to the postponement of such codification proposals.[14] Most countries would have to wait for the later half of the nineteenth century to enact codes of law, most likely due to, as expressed by Means, the scarce resources for codification and a lack of ways to mobilize them.[15] At the beginning of the national period, codification efforts were often unsuccessful because of lack of funding and political instability.[16] Thus, for codification to be undertaken successfully, countries needed to fund sufficiently the efforts of drafters and to provide a politically stable enough environment for a consensus to be built concerning the more controversial provisions of the code. Available legal talent was also scarce.

Codification was often seen as a package of comprehensive and interlocking codes. It might follow the five areas of law in the Napoleonic codes: civil, commercial, criminal, civil procedure, and criminal procedure. Indeed, Haiti in 1825, and thus the Dominican Republic, which was under Haitian occupation at the time, adopted these codes. Bolivia's precocious adoption of the French civil code dates from 1830.[17] A similarly influential source, Bellemare's *Plan General de Organización Judicial* (1829), speaks of enacting six codes.[18] The center from which the other codes emanate was the civil code addressing private law between individuals. The typical structure of a civil code is set out in the French Civil Code of 1804, which has three divisions: persons, property, and the modes of acquiring property. Thus a sampling of legal areas covered by a civil code typically include marriage and divorce, children, adoption and guardianships, types of property, usufructs, servitudes, successions, inheritance, wills, contracts, obligations, certain types of partnerships, loans, and mortgages.[19]

Of course, the various Latin American countries and congressmen that used French structure and content modified them for their own civil codes. For example, the extent to which codification in Peru from 1847 to 1852 adopted or rejected French structure and substance has been a topic of recent exploration.[20] Different countries in Latin America borrowed and adapted language from other Latin American codes.[21] Other codes and sources were instrumental in Latin American codification, particularly the works of Jeremy

Bentham.[22] This chapter will focus on efforts to codify civil law and procedure; the codification of commercial law is discussed in Chapter 18.

Codification and Political Structure: Mexico

Codification could also be the playing field for competing interests and views of political power.[23] For example, federalists might wish to codify law on a state or department level rather than a national level, and the struggle of Mexican states and the Mexican federal government to enact a civil code during the second half of the nineteenth century illustrates this conflict. In Mexico, some commentators spoke out in 1824 in favor of a federal civil code, but when the Mexican Constitution of 1824 was not in force during the late 1820s and early 1830s, Oaxaca enacted a civil code, and Zacatecas, Jalisco, and Guanajuato all moved forward with plans and drafts.[24] Oaxaca was the first Mexican state to have such a code, in 1828.[25] The authority to adopt civil and commercial codes was then assumed by the federal government through the Constitution (*Bases Orgánicas*) of 1843.[26] In 1846, codification returned to the state level, and Oaxaca's civil code returned to life, only to be abolished by decree of Santa Anna in 1853.[27] Under Juárez and the Mexican Constitution of 1857, legislative authority was again placed in the states, and Justo Sierra was asked to prepare a draft of a civil code for Mexico, which was adopted for the Federal District and territories and which was put forth by the federal government as a model for states to adopt.[28] After being adopted by only Veracruz, Justo Sierra's code was sent to a commission for revision just as the imperial government of Maximilian came to power. The commission worked through the change in government, and the first two books were enacted under Maximilian in 1866.[29] Indeed, the content of the Sierra draft and the later draft under Maximilian did not change concerning such politically and socially sensitive matters such as the civil register and the definitions of marriage and divorce; despite Maximilian's conservative power base, the codes enacted under his rule continued Juárez's more liberal reforms.[30] Thus attempts to codify the civil law were successfully begun when Justo Sierra's draft code was posthumously published in 1861 and submitted to Maximilian's imperial commission in the mid-1860s. After Maximilian's ouster, a new commission (Yáñez, Lafragua, Montiel, Dondé, and Eguía Lis) modified the work with the draft Spanish Civil Code of 1852 and Andrés Bello's Chilean Civil Code of 1855 in mind.[31] At the same time, after the fall of the Mexican Second Empire in 1867, the country returned to a federalist structure during Juárez's third term and the 1857 Constitution. Several states moved forward with a civil code, and the state of Mexico enacted a civil code in 1870, again apparently based on Sierra's code.[32] The same year the republic moved to enact a civil code also based on Sierra's work, which after revision by a commission, became the

Mexican Civil Code of 1870, and this civil code for the Federal District and Baja California served as a model for state codes. Some states chose not to follow its provisions. For example, Veracruz apparently had a civil code from 1868 drafted by Fernando de Jesús Corona.[33] It was, however, this Mexican Civil Code of 1870 that became the basis for almost all of the individual state civil codes. It was enacted regionally, sometimes with minor modifications, over the following four years in sixteen of the states.[34] The 1870 code also served as the model for the Civil Code of 1884, whose only significant substantive changes reduced the fraction of the estate subject to forced distribution to heirs (*legítimas*) and altered divorce law.[35]

Chilean Civil Codification: Andrés Bello

Perhaps the most influential civil code in Latin America has been Andrés Bello's Chilean Civil Code of 1855.[36] After its preparation and adoption in Chile, this code served as a model and important source of civil law in the entire region. It was adopted in El Salvador, Ecuador, Venezuela, Nicaragua, Colombia and Honduras; it was a main source and influence on the civil codes of Uruguay, Mexico, Guatemala, Costa Rica, and Paraguay. The arrival of Bello's code even put an end to one country's own efforts at codification. In Ecuador, several codification commissions worked diligently throughout the early 1850s, only to set their work aside in 1855 to make minor revisions to Bello's code, which was quickly adopted.[37] Similarly, Julián Viso's draft civil code based on Bello's work was adopted by the Venezuelan legislature in 1862.[38]

Bello was born in Caracas in 1781 and got an early classical education there. By 1797, he served as a private tutor to Simón Bolívar, who was just two years younger than Bello. Bello later joined Alexander von Humboldt's expedition and then took several administrative and lower political appointments in the early 1800s. He was appointed an official to accompany Bolívar to England in 1810 and remained there until 1829. In England, Bello supported the Latin American independence movement, worked on the papers of Jeremy Bentham, and spent significant time in the British Library studying Roman and medieval Spanish law. With his pleas for a better position from Bolívar unanswered, Bello left for Chile in 1829. In Chile, he taught Roman law, consulted on various government legal projects such as the drafting of the Chilean Constitution of 1833, and entered into a long period as a senator after obtaining Chilean citizenship. It was in the Senate, and particularly as a drafter on various commissions and individually, that Bello wrote the work that would become the Chilean Civil Code of 1855. In the late 1850s, Bello removed himself from an active public life and turned his attention to writing literary works. He died in Santiago, Chile, in 1865, at age eighty-four.[39]

Bello's code successfully wove together modern European codes, particularly the French Civil Code of 1804 (the *Code Napoléon*), the medieval Spanish law of the *Siete Partidas,* and Roman law to create a code that was a great step forward for civil law in Chile and, in turn, that was easily adopted in countries with similar economic, social, and cultural conditions. Although substantially the product of Bello's own work, the code would not have come about were it not for the political stability of Chile's autocratic regimes during the Portales era nor the direct presidential support Bello received in his efforts. Numerous factors played into Bello's construction of the code, including the works of von Savigny, the French commentators on the civil law and the French civil code, the writings of Jeremy Bentham, and various European codes of civil law.[40] Bello's code had four sections: persons, property, inheritance, and contracts and obligations.[41]

Although the French Civil Code of 1804 was the Northern Star by which other Latin American civil codes oriented themselves, the Spanish civil code and other European codes also served as important models. Sierra's code for Mexico, for example, made substantial use of the draft Spanish Civil Code of 1852.[42] The Venezuelan Civil Code of 1862 was revoked the following year and, again under the guidance of Viso, was replaced by a code modeled on the Spanish Civil Code in 1867.[43] This code was replaced in 1873 by one modeled on the Italian code, itself grounded in the French Civil Code of 1804.[44] The mere existence of a new European code could even be the driving force for Latin American countries to reform their law to conform to the new code, such was the case of Mexico in 1884, which repealed the 1880 text of its code of civil procedure, based on the Spanish Code of 1855, to substitute a new text, based on the Spanish Code of 1881.[45]

Argentine Civil Codification: Dalmacio Vélez Sársfield

Perhaps the second-best-known civil code of Latin America is the Argentine civil code drafted by Dalmacio Vélez Sársfield.[46] Vélez, the central figure in Argentine codification, was born in Córdoba in 1800. He studied at a Franciscan convent and later the College of Monserrat. He received his bachelor's in civil and canon law in 1820 from the Faculty of Arts of the University of Córdoba.[47] It is likely that his studies there included the works of Vinnius (1558–1657), Heineccius (1661–1742), Cujas (1520–1590), the Napoleonic codes, and later Aubrey and Rau's *Cours de droit civil Français.*[48] His hopes of practicing in Buenos Aires were frustrated by political circumstances at the time, but he became a protégé of the legal officer and law professor José Dámaso Xigena whose Academy of Jurisprudence was opened in Córdoba in 1821 where Vélez served as secretary. He was admitted to the Buenos Aires bar in 1823.[49] In the mid-1820s, Vélez served as a deputy to the Constituent Congress of 1824 and was a professor of political economy at the University of Buenos Aires. Under the dictatorship of Rosas, Vélez left Buenos Aires and returned to Córdoba. During the 1830s, Vélez dedicated himself to legal studies and writing. With the help of another mentor, Manuel Antonio de Castro, Vélez's work flourished, and he contributed introductions and substantial editorial additions to two important legal texts in the period: the *Instituciones del derecho real de España* by José María Alvarez and the *Prontuario de práctica forense* by Castro. Alvarez's text would serve as a standard pedagogical work in civil law in Argentina from its publication in 1834 until the 1850s.[50] During the mid-1830s, Vélez worked on the legal status of the church and ecclesiastical law.[51] His property being subject to confiscation by a decree of the Rosas regime in late 1840, Vélez fled to Montevideo in 1842 and returned to Argentina in 1846, subsequently freeing his property.[52]

In the early 1850s with the fall of Rosas, Vélez became involved in national politics, the perfect platform for launching his desires for codification. In 1852 the president of the confederation created the commission mentioned above to prepare codes. Vélez and Carlos Tejedor prepared the 1854 Constitution of the State of Buenos Aires, and Argentine politicians selected Vélez and Eduardo Acevedo to draft a new commercial code, which was enacted in 1859.[53]

In 1863, President Mitre charged Vélez with preparing a civil code. His life's work could be poured into the project.[54] In less than a year, Vélez had prepared the first part of the code on persons, with cross-references to European and American codes. The final part was published in 1869 and the entire code was enacted into law effective January 1, 1871.[55]

Vélez consulted numerous Latin American and European models, including Bello's code, Freitas's Brazilian code, and the French Code of 1804. French commentaries were also an important source for Vélez, and he pulled provisions and thoughts from an incredible array of sources and applied a "scientific" method to drafting the work.[56] Citing the work of Borchard and Eder, Karst and Rosenn are paraphrased to provide quick summary of Vélez's sources this way:

NUMBER OF ARTICLES	SOURCE
1200	Teixeira de Freitas's draft code for Brazil (1856–1865), an exhaustive, detailed work containing 4,908 articles
700	Aubry and Rau, two Strasbourg law professors who published a five-volume treatise on civil law between 1838 and 1847

300	García Goyena, author of a four-volume draft and commentary of a civil code for Spain published in 1852
170	Bello's Chilean civil code
145	French civil code
78	Zachariae, an 1808 German commentary on French civil law
52	Louisiana civil code
52	Demolombe, French commentator
50	Troplong, French commentator
27	Acevedo's draft civil code for Uruguay
18	Chabot, French commentator
15	Maynz, Belgian commentator
12	Molitor, Belgian commentator[57]

Karst and Rosenn conclude that "the remaining articles were taken from miscellaneous codes and commentators. Almost none of the Argentine Code's 4,051 articles are original."[58] Vélez too explicitly stated the sources for his work: the *Partidas;* the *Fuero Real;* the *Recopilaciones;* European and American codes; the French civil code; Aubry and Rau; Pothier, Troplong, Duranton, Seoane's work on comparative legislation; García Goyena's Spanish civil code; the Chilean civil code; Freitas's draft civil code for Brazil; Savigny, Zachariae, Serrigny on administrative law; and Story on conflict of laws.[59]

The code became an influential source for other civil codes in Latin America.[60] Its drafting and the role of Vélez provide an interesting comparison to the Chilean experience with Bello's code. Codification in Argentina was delayed by the Rosas dictatorship, but shortly afterward in 1852, the new leader, General Urquiza, created a commission to begin drafting codes of civil, penal, commercial, and procedural law. The luminaries of mid-nineteenth-century Argentine law were involved in the codification effort: the civil code was led by Vélez; the criminal code by Baldomero García; the commercial code by José Gorostiaga; and the procedural and criminal codes by José Pérez.[61] Thus, in 1852 and 1853, Argentina began to appoint commissions to prepare codes addressing civil, commercial, criminal, and procedural law. The political, centralizing force of national codes was seen as a means to achieve unification of the country, and these efforts were supported in the 1853 Constitution and its 1860 reform.[62] The flurry of codification activity in the early 1850s in Argentina did not produce national codes because the nation slipped into civil war as Buenos Aires battled the rest of the country. The State of Buenos Aires adopted a civil code in 1857 drafted by Marcelo Gamboa and Marcelino Ugarte, who had earlier worked on a draft with Vélez.[63]

Vélez's code became effective in 1871, but it was not without its critics.

Vicente Fidel López criticized Vélez's work for two reasons: first, codification was such an important aspect of sovereignty that it could not be done through simple legislative bodies; and second, the form and syntax of the draft were defective.[64] Alberdi, a vehement critic of the work, asserted that a central unifying code was inconsistent with a country composed of several sovereign states. He also faulted the code for its use and imitation of foreign sources, especially the French civil code.[65] For decades after the code's enactment, students and faculty at the Buenos Aires Law School heatedly debated various aspects of the code: its refusal to secularize marriage, its strong assertion of *patria potestad*, its continuation of forced shares for family members (*legítima hereditaria*), its use of Roman law. Some criticism bought changes; marriage was secularized in Argentina in 1888.[66]

Once the general structure of a code was adopted in a country to cover a particular area of substantive or procedural law, there was, and continues to be, an almost endless opportunity to adjust the individual code provisions. Changes might reflect new government policies or exercises of power, new social conditions, or new legal needs. Drafts can be floated, discussed, and sent back to committees, in an endless search for codification perfection. While earlier codifiers sought the best way to express the place of the church in legal and economic life, to describe the family and the permanence of marriage, to determine the inheritance rights of illegitimate children, later codifiers turned to improving provisions regarding commerce and obligations, renting property, and the rights of women in law and commerce.[67]

Codification of Civil Procedure

Although the civil code was the cornerstone of the new legal systems of Latin American countries, codification was not limited to civil law. Because the Napoleonic codes came in a package of five codes, most countries also sought to codify commercial law, criminal law, civil procedure, and criminal procedure. New courts created under constitutional provisions called for new procedures, which were often individually enacted at the time of their creation. For example, José Gabriel Ocampo's set of regulations for the administration of justice for Chilean courts was a significant improvement over colonial procedure and was enacted in the early years of Chilean independence, in 1824.[68] This meant that entire new codes of civil procedure were not immediately demanded, although criticism of procedure based on colonial practices existed.

One factor leading to new codes of civil procedure was often the enactment of new codes of civil law. Thus, Mexico enacted a new code of civil procedure for the Federal District and the Territory of Baja California in 1872.[69] This followed on the heels of the new federal Civil Code of 1870. Likewise, in Argentina, the decree in 1852 began the process of codifying all areas of law along French lines, and this led to several lawyers working on drafts of procedural codes, including José Luis Domínguez, Manuel Obarrio, and Emilio Coni.[70]

Foreign models continued to be very important in drafting procedural codes in Latin America. For example, the recently available Spanish codes of the 1850s influenced Mexico's federal civil procedure Code of 1872, reformed in 1880, and also the procedural code for the state of Puebla of 1880 (*Código Béistegui*).[71] Mexico enacted new federal codes of civil procedure, again based on the Spanish model, in 1897 and 1908, the later serving until 1928.[72]

Conclusion

Codification was the most important development during the early national period of Latin American countries. Of course, in this respect, Latin America participated in a general phenomenon occurring throughout the western legal world.[73] Nonetheless, Latin American countries brought particular problems and challenges to the process. A lack of political stability, a lack of underlying political consensus of the aims of codification, a lack of adequately trained legal minds, and a lack of funding to carry through codification projects all delayed the eventual codification of private law in Latin America. Borrowing foreign codes was an essential aspect of the movement toward codification in Latin America, and the sometimes overly ready acceptance of foreign models meant that substantive reforms were a poor match to the societal, religious, economic, and commercial needs of the country. Once the dependence of national codes on foreign sources was established, these new codes led to the appropriation of foreign commentary texts on code provisions, which pulled the legal mindset of many Latin American lawyers and judges closer to their European contemporaries. Thus, while codification led to a purely national law for each country and permitted countries to assert their own national identity distinct from a colonial reliance on Spanish law, it also led to borrowing from European sources and other recent codification, which led the codified countries to a common body of secondary sources and methods of approaching private law itself.

Personal Status

REVOLUTION, independence, and the creation of new nations were ac-companied by new political, social, and as a result, legal conceptions of the individual. These events brought about foundational changes in the legal status of individuals and in society. The most significant change was the abolition of slavery, but other groups were also affected. This chapter will dis-cuss the manner in which private law developments attempted, and at times succeeded, to restructure certain aspects of society related to race, alienage, family, and sex. As revolutionary juntas made pronouncements abolishing slavery or removing certain burdens attached to Indians, Spain and its colo-nies were undergoing important social and legal changes as well. With com-munication between the colonies and Spain substantially curtailed during the first decade of the nineteenth century, many developments were independent, although concurrent.

Abolition of Slavery

The approach of the new republics toward slavery often tracked the republi-can ideas raised during independence from Spain.[1] Where not based on ideo-logical concerns, support for manumission gained urgency because of the practical concerns of war. Freedom for slaves was used on both sides to en-list the support of slaves as soldiers in battle.[2] On the level of legislation, the republics generally acted quickly to abolish or to phase out the slave trade and slavery. For example, following the lead of Great Britain, which abol-ished the slave trade in 1807, Caracas, Mexico, and Buenos Aires moved to abolish the trade in 1810 and 1811.[3] Chile enacted a law of free birth, pro-viding that the children of slaves were free, in 1811, and Argentina did the same in 1813.[4] Slavery was abolished under the Constitution of 1821 for Gran Colombia and boards of manumission were established to purchase freedom.[5] Mexican attempts to abolish slavery through the Spanish Constitution of 1812 were initially unsuccessful, but emancipation of slaves was part of Morales's plans for the country in 1813. Iturbide in the early 1820s suppressed the slave trade, and several of the Mexican states individually abolished slavery in the later 1820s. Similarly, as the republics of Central America were created in the first half of the nineteenth century, they accepted the suppression of slavery enunciated for the United Provinces of Central America in 1824.[6] Uruguay constitutionally abolished slavery in 1830.[7]

Despite constitutional or legislative provisions abolishing the slave trade, an active illegal trade continued, often with the consent of the new republics. Abolishing the slave trade did not necessarily abolish slavery. As the slave trade was disrupted, some areas experimented with slave breeding, which was uncommon before the nineteenth century, although a few examples of breeding farms were known in Argentina and the Jesuits were also known to have bred slaves, most likely for their own exploitation.[8] Private law continued to offer one avenue to freedom. Just as in colonial times, the possibility of a slave buying his or her freedom existed, was exercised, and recognized in judicial proceedings. Some *cofradías* even financed such purchases.[9]

By exerting political and economic pressure on the new republics through the first half of the nineteenth century, Great Britain was a prime mover for abolition of slavery in Latin America.[10] In the 1830s, Great Britain began to urge numerous Latin American countries to enter treaties abolishing the slave trade and to place slave trading in the legal category of piracy. Thus, in the 1830s, 1840s, and 1850s, the Latin American republics somewhat hesitantly signed these treaties and were pushed toward actively working against the slave trade and the institution of slavery itself.[11] Trafficking in slaves was made equivalent to piracy in 1825, and in 1854 the Venezuelan president abolished slavery. The Venezuelan Constitution of 1857 repeated the policy of abolition.[12] Peru abolished slavery in 1854.[13] The few Spanish possessions left in the Caribbean abolished slavery later; Puerto Rico in 1873 and nominally Cuba in 1880.[14] Brazil, dependent on slave labor for its agricultural plantations, abolished slavery in 1888.[15]

Legislated manumission met resistance not only on the state level, but often from local officials charged with carrying out laws who delayed putting the provisions into effect.[16] For example, "Venezuela decreed manumission in 1821, but around 1837 there were still almost 38,000 slaves in the country."[17] Similar states of affairs have been reported for other countries in Latin America, including Argentina, Colombia, and Paraguay.[18] As with the forced services of Indians, debt peonage replaced slavery as the main source of manual labor, and these individuals lived in a condition one scholar has described as "semi-slavery."[19] In some areas, claims were made that slaves had to continue to work to pay off accumulated debts, and such periods might extend as long as twenty years. By the mid nineteenth century the new regime of debt peonage was well established, although throughout the nineteenth century, foreign laborers were brought into countries like Peru and Cuba from the Philippines and China. For example more than eighty thousand Chinese workers entered Peru between 1850 and 1874.[20]

Citizens

Revolution and independence did not only work to change perceptions and practices of slavery. Beyond abolition, new republics sought societies of equal citizens. In 1810, Miguel Hidalgo announced a revolutionary platform that contained just three main items: the emancipation of slaves, the abolition of tribute paid by Indians and mixed races, and the substitution of regular paper for sealed paper for all judicial and legal transactions.[21] A fuller draft constitution a few years later again repeated the abolition of slavery and removed family lineage as a factor in government service. Morales's principles for a constitution drafted in 1814 contain similar language: "Slavery is forever prohibited, as well as distinctions based on race (*castas*), leaving everyone equal, and only vice and virtue will distinguish one American from another."[22] Similar developments were occurring elsewhere in Latin America. For example, in 1813, Río de la Plata abolished the use of titles of nobility and coats of arms.[23] Likewise, changes in the political structure of Spain led to change on the continent. The Spanish Constitution of 1812 (Constitution of Cádiz), which gave freeborn colonials the rights of Spaniards, had limited application in Latin America between 1812 and 1822.[24] In Mexico, it was made applicable but soon suspended by the viceroy, then a year later brought into partial application. When Ferdinand VII regained rule in Spain in 1814, the Constitution of 1812 was suspended, but then he was forced to swear his allegiance to the document in 1820. By this time, Mexico and the other countries of Latin America were well on their way to independence.[25] The Constitution of Cádiz greatly expanded the definition of citizenship to include those of Spanish decent born in the colonies as well as others born in the colonies. Freed blacks, through special procedures and under constitutionally provided standards, could request citizenship.[26] Universities began to admit blacks and *mulatos* in 1812. The legal status of Indians improved as well. New laws abolished tribute, and in 1811 Spanish authorities established new rules for distributing Indian lands. The colonial authorities abolished *mitas* and personal services from Indians in 1812. Legislation attempted to erase distinctions between Creoles and peninsulars concerning rights to undertake commerce. New laws defined the jurisdictions of the courts, limited ecclesiastical privileges, and abolished the Inquisition.[27] Some of these developments can be attributed to endemic change, others to the influence of the Spanish Constitution of 1812.

Mexico gained independence in 1821 and named Iturbide emperor shortly afterward.[28] In 1822, the Mexican Constituent Congress prohibited the description of origin of individuals following their names in public and private documents.[29] The same year, the Mexican Congress extended equal civil rights to all free inhabitants under new constitutional principles.[30]

Independence greatly affected the legal status of Indians who were usually granted citizenship under the various new constitutions. The Argentine Constitution of 1819 made Indians equal in dignity and rights to other citizens.[31] Several provisions cited above demonstrate that Mexican law from the early nineteenth century erased the separate juridical existence of Indians who were, from then on, theoretically incorporated in the citizenship of the country. Here too theory and practice were widely disparate. For example, the capital of Chiapas had separate municipal governments, one Indian and one *mestizo*, until the 1860s.[32]

A constitution, decree, or statute changing legal status might not have immediate effect in society. Indeed, illegal slave trade and slavery continued in many areas. Many of these reforms only operated on the level of aspiration. Societal practice continued to make distinctions based on race, sex, and origin.[33] Slave labor and Indian labor were replaced by a widespread system of debt peonage, which tied poor agricultural workers to land as effectively as slavery and colonial means of exploiting Indian labor. Furthermore, enlightenment values still played off firmly grounded social prejudices. For example, after significant debate concerning the scope of the franchise in Argentina during 1826, servants, day laborers, line soldiers, and criminal defendants were excluded from suffrage.[34] Thus servile status, and in some countries illiteracy, served as a basis of withholding the opportunity to vote.

Aliens

Nationhood raised questions on the other end of the economic spectrum as well, particularly as it related to the treatment of foreigners and their interests in the new countries. As newly independent states, Latin American countries had to determine what restrictions if any they would place on foreign activities and ownership of property. These rights might wash back and forth according to the political tide; at one moment a country might create policies welcoming foreign investment, and at the next, it might take a highly protectionist and nationalistic stance concerning its commercial activities and resources. Mexico provides a good example. As early as 1823, Mexico permitted aliens to be naturalized and foreigners to acquire mining rights. Rights of foreigners were extended further in 1824. By the late 1820s, such policies had changed and only Mexicans could own land, a prohibition repeated in the constitutional laws of 1836. Likewise, in 1841 the Mexican Congress prohibited foreigners from engaging in commerce, but the next year it granted them the right to own land. These back and forth provisions led to a more lasting provision in the Law on Foreigners and Nationality (*Ley sobre Extranjería y Nacionalidad*) of 1854 which, despite being formally repealed under changing political winds, probably continued to control, according to Margadant, until the *Ley Vallarta* of 1886 replaced it.[35] The regime of Porfirio Díaz encouraged foreign ownership and investment in Mexico, and by the end of his rule, U.S. interests held $650 million in Mexico, including railroads, mining, and oil.[36]

Family and the Church

Many reforms affecting the legal status of family members came close to the wider political debate concerning the place of the Catholic church in society, politics, and law. Revolution from Spain did not necessarily mean revolution from the church. The very first article of Hidalgo's platform for Mexico in 1810 states, "The Catholic religion shall be the only one, without tolerance of others."[37] Most of the early Mexican constitutions established the Roman Catholic church as the only accepted religion. Nonetheless, further debate might be had over the extent to which the church should operate in public life, guide education, control institutions, govern marriages and questions of legitimacy, and bear the responsibility for keeping records relating to births, marriages, and deaths.[38] Even in places where the power and privilege of the church had been maintained, laws limited some religious organizations, perhaps because of their assertion of power in society. For example, Colombian authorities in 1852 questioned the legal personality of the Jesuits after their expulsion from the country the year before, although the corporate identity of other religious groups was recognized. A few years later, in 1861, the society was dissolved because it had not incorporated under legislation enacted in 1855.[39]

The church and Catholic views continued to have strong sway in Latin American private law. In 1825, the English minister to Argentina asserted that under the treaty with England providing in part that English subjects would not be harmed by reason of religion, Argentina should permit marriages between Protestants and Catholics. Although such marriages were prohibited, a law of 1833 granted the government power to make dispensations.[40] For example, Vélez Sársfield's attempt to place marriage under civil authority along French lines in his Civil Code of 1871 for Argentina quickly led to church opposition and a reform continuing church control of marriage.[41] In nineteenth-century Peru, the church mostly held onto its control of marriage, family, and its special economic and political position. Indeed, in Peru the church and canon law controlled marriage until 1918.[42] Other countries, notably Mexico, secularized marriage as early as the 1850s and required a ceremony by a civil magistrate for a legally recognized marriage.[43] "Marriage is a civil contract," stated the reform law of September 25, 1873.[44] In the 1880s, Argentina, Chile, and Uruguay adopted civil marriage, but the issue remained contested into the twentieth century.[45] Within the family, the full weight of the Roman law notions of *patria potestad* was lifted in a number of countries, such as Mexico, to leave the head of the household in charge of education and raising of the rest of the family, but without the limitations on and paternal control of property that accompanied the earlier system for individuals over twenty-one years of age.[46] Similarly, as the substantive law of marriage was secularized, the use of ecclesiastical tribunals to address marital disputes declined. The nineteenth century in Latin America saw many changes in family law and familial status.[47]

Related to the issue of marriage was the status of children born out of wedlock. The harsh treatment of illegitimate children under colonial law prompted legislation in the early republics, often apart from larger civil codification projects. Colombia and Ecuador both enacted laws removing certain social or legal impediments of illegitimate children in the 1820s.[48] Rooted in the idea that the stigma or advantages one might have in society by accident of birth should be removed from the realm of law, these reforms established "vice and virtue" as determinants of an individual's fate.

Although present, but not in effect, in European models for codification, the ability of married individuals to divorce was generally not incorporated into Latin American private law in the nineteenth century. Even in countries where the power of the Catholic church had been significantly limited, such as Mexico, divorce was not permitted under the federal district Civil Code of 1884 or its antecedents.[49] Where codes spoke of divorce, it was usually in the sense of the canonically recognized separation, rather than a method by which one of the parties would be free to remarry.[50] Religious institutions provided residences (*beaterios, recogimientos de mujeres*) for wives seeking divorce and often required husbands to make support payments. Such institutions, however, isolated women from their property, and husbands might delay divorce proceedings to keep wives in them. These institutions declined during the second half of the nineteenth century.[51] Typical divorce provisions from the late 1870s provide that divorce does not dissolve the marriage, but merely suspends the common life of the spouses. Cause had to be shown, and mutual consent was not sufficient grounds. Detailed provisions addressed residence, the division of property, and the care of children. Judicial decrees of nullity of a marriage were possible, but only along rules similar to the canon law.[52]

Women

Nineteenth-century political and constitutional changes did little to affect the legal status of women after the independence period rung in a new sense of "equality." Even in Mexico after the secularization of marriage, the status of women and the legal incapacity associated with married women continued.[53] For example, although the French civil code provided a model for married women to elect out of the community property regime, only the state code of Zacatecas followed this possibility in Mexico.[54] Even in the national codification period of Mexican civil law, reforms favoring women's legal rights were not successful. Arrom observes:

> Although most reforms proposed in the early republic were incorporated into subsequent civil codes, during the heady post-independence decades when Mexicans experimented with new directions, when women were still desperately needed in the process of nation-building and had so recently shown that they could contribute to those efforts, some Mexicans were willing to consider ideas (like the remarried widow's retention of the guardianship of children and the wife's sharing of the *patria potestas*) that were rejected in the 1870 code.[55]

After studying ecclesiastical and civil records from the period, Hunefeldt makes similar observations for nineteenth-century Peru. Even though the colonial notions of law were replaced with liberal and secular bases for private law, the new system maintained the subordination of women.[56] Colonial regimes of *patria potestad* and of women's property continued even into civil codes.[57] The Peruvian civil code addressed dowries and considered them advancements on inheritance. *Arras* continued as another important type of wife's property, although also administered by the husband. A provision providing for one-quarter of the property to go to the surviving spouse on death of the other spouse reduced the importance of dowries, and the number and value of dowries declined in Peru during the nineteenth century.[58] As discussed later, improving the legal status of women in Latin America would be a battle waged more in the twentieth century and continued to today.

||||||||||||| CHAPTER 17 |||||||||||||

Land and Inheritance

WAR and the political unrest in the decades following independence provided a good opportunity for wealthy landholders to amass giant estates under their control. Colonial crown mechanisms established to curtail the political power of Creole families by restricting their ability to build giant landed estates disappeared. If independence and liberalism meant the equality of Native Americans, their lands would no longer be subject to special administrative and legal regimes developed in the colonial period.[1] There were also ideological objections to communal landholding, and governments moved to sell land to individuals.[2] In this new environment, the methods for enlarging landholdings varied. Some individuals merely needed to hold onto their large estates through independence, having aligned themselves with the winning side. Others saw civil unrest as presenting a prime opportunity to push less powerful people off land during the instability following independence. Still others amassed landed estates though the time-honored practice of dividing up the spoils of war. In some areas, farm after farm and estate after estate were brought together to give individuals ownership and authority over vast regions (*latifundios*). For example, in 1817 the Law of Dividing National Property in Venezuela gave the property formerly owned by royalists to the generals, chiefs, officials, and soldiers of the republic. Despite the numerous potential beneficiaries of the law, in fact, only a few well-placed individuals were able to take full advantage of the provision.[3] In the pulling together of massive estates, the wealth and power of the *caudillo* system developed to create an almost quasi-governmental authority in some areas. In some countries, *caudillos* rose to the top of national leadership.[4] Even where they did not rise to autocratic rule of entire countries, large landholders might organize for political and economic power. Nonetheless, large estates might coexist alongside smaller farms, and middling farmers might also press for their own political and economic benefits.[5]

During the nineteenth century landholding expanded into more rural and remote areas, often by smaller landholders with governmental encouragement. Late in the century, railroads opened up many more of these areas.[6] Independence, however, changed little for the farm laborer.[7] The continued plight of the propertyless farm laborer would later grow throughout the region into perhaps the greatest political, social, and legal question in the following centuries. Governments would struggle to provide meaningful land redistribution schemes and agrarian reform, while some workers dissatisfied with these often empty attempts would organize to form revolutionary movements.

In light of the building of large landed estates amongst the wealthy following independence, it is somewhat incongruous that colonial Spanish entailing devices, such as the *mayorazgo,* were successfully attacked and eventually abolished. *Mayorazgos* were disfavored for both political and economic reasons. Almost all holders of *mayorazgos* in the Spanish colonies were royalists, indeed the most expansive type of *mayorazgo* could only be created through royal consent. Thus, the abolition of *mayorazgos* satisfied the punitive desires of the new republican ruling elite. Entails were also seen as a hindrance to economic and social progress that was dependent on the free alienability of land. Because entails removed land from a fluid market, they did not fit into the new countries' social and legal structures. No doubt, the abolition of entails by the French Legislative Assembly in 1792 and their prohibition in the French Civil Code of 1804 lent great weight to the argument for their abolition in Latin America.[8]

Nineteenth-century Latin American constitutions and related legislation attacked entails. As part of legislation associated with the Spanish Constitution of Cádiz of 1812 that was confirmed in Mexico in 1820, *mayorazgos, vinculaciones,* and family trusts of land were suppressed.[9] Also in about 1812, the United Provinces of Río de la Plata abolished *mayorazgos.*[10] The Río de la Plata abolition was broad, extending not only to *mayorazgos* of all of one's property, but even to those created from fractions of one's estate.[11] O'Higgins unsuccessfully attempted to abolish entails in Chile in 1818.[12] Mexico modified entails in 1823.[13] Likewise, Colombia abolished *mayorazgos* in 1824.[14] The provision of the Chilean Constitution of 1828 is a typical example; it merely abolished the institution and gave little guidance for undoing entails. Article 126 of that constitution reads, in part: "*Mayorazgos* and all entails impeding the free alienation of estates are forever abolished. Their present possessors may dispose of them freely, except for the third part of their value which is reserved for the immediate successor who will dispose of them with the same liberty."[15]

Constitutional or legislative provisions abolishing entails did not necessarily put an end to their use, but began the social and legal path that led to their eventual disappearance. Clear prohibitions often led to supplemental legislation that set out ways to phase out entails or to convert them into money payments attached to the land. These money payments might be subject to a primogeniture inheritance pattern, thus continuing, to some extent, the benefit to the intended family members while freeing up the land for sale. This solution was successfully taken up by Bello as late as the mid-1850s, after Chile had debated the legal status of entails under its constitutional provisions for more than thirty years.[16]

Authorities eventually abolished or substantially limited other similar devises that tied up the alienation of land. For example, in Río de la Plata from 1810 to 1812, the *mita*, the *encomienda*, the *yanaconazgo*, and personal services by Indians were abolished.[17] In 1826, Argentina enacted legislation regulating the *enfiteusis* of public land, setting percentages and time periods for the validity of long-term leases.[18]

Nineteenth-century changes in land law were not constrained to the abolition of devices limiting alienation. Various countries throughout the period addressed the inordinate power of large landholders and the status of communal or collective land ownership. In the early part of Santa Anna's dictatorship of Mexico, Mexican authorities enacted proposals to transfer title of urban property to renters and to sell off rural ecclesiastical lands, but Santa Anna revoked these before they were put into effect.[19] Likewise, in Mexico, a number of liberal proposals followed independence. These included the free distribution of lands among the Indians and the confiscation of the large *haciendas*. The concerns the proposals expressed have been placed into five groups by Margadant: (1) collective property rights (e.g. *la dehesa*) were inconsistent with the individual property goals of liberalism; (2) unproductive large estates encroached on Indian land rights; (3) the renting of land by Indians was open to abuse; (4) families lacked land and should receive vacant waste land or land belonging to the large estates; and (5) empty, unproductive land should be opened up through colonization.[20] Despite proposals to address such concerns, governments continued to use land as political reward or special favor. For example, Mexican legislation limited the maximum grant to an individual to 96,000 acres, and yet some Mexican grants in the mid nineteenth century exceeded 1 million acres.[21] Large landholding continued, often burdened by substantial debt.

In many areas, the church continued to be an important landholder and provider of land-related financing. Such material success and wealth drew criticism and proposals for the reform of ecclesiastical land ownership. For example, Mexican legislation aimed at restricting the church's landholding backfired. In 1856 the church was legally incapacitated to receive title to land.[22] The *Ley de Desamortización* of 1856 (*Ley Lerdo*) gave anyone who worked church or Indian lands a three-month window within which to purchase the property for an amount based on the rent paid, and if the worker did not purchase the land, any third party could purchase it with the payment of an additional premium. Cash poor, and fearing excommunication if they asserted rights to former church lands, the workers did not act, and the large landholders swooped in, not only acquiring church lands but picking up communally held Indian lands as well.[23] These reforms proved to be too drastic for peaceful transition, and the country was thrust into war from 1858 to 1861. In 1859, under Juárez's reform laws, which put forth a staunchly anticlerical position, the government confiscated church lands without compensation.[24] With the defeat of the conservative forces, Juárez's more severe laws were put into effect.[25] The benefits of confiscation have been questioned; some have seen the church as more responsible farmers who at least turned some of the profits back to the community through service.[26] Large private landholding in Mexico was facilitated in 1883 by an enclosure law enacted under President Díaz that permitted private fencing and surveying to take one-third of the land surveyed as payment.[27]

The appropriate titling of land and recording of documents in notarial systems were frequently difficult and rather unsuccessful tasks. In such systems, the seller and buyer appeared before a notary who drafted a document indicating the transfer of land. The notary usually kept the original document and issued a copy to the purchaser.[28] Methods of assuring title to land through land registration gained strength during the century as countries established registries for land transactions. The appropriate sections of the civil code included such provisions; for example, the Mexican Civil Code of 1870 created a real property registry.[29]

Despite the attack against *mayorazgos* and primogeniture, inheritance provisions changed little in the decades and even the century following independence. Thus in most countries the system of *legítima* based on the provisions found in the Spanish colonial law continued, ensuring that a large portion of the estate would be reserved to close family members. Even though testators were afforded discretion in allocating the estate, they often preferred equal division to children.[30] Legislators carefully drafted these provisions into the civil law codes of the period and discussed, debated, and redrafted them more passionately than other provisions during the codification of civil law. Some drafters even favored freedom of testamentary disposition following English and American notions, and the French Civil Code of 1804 lent support for freer testamentary disposition by creating fractional shares that could be freely devised. These shares decreased according to the number of legitimate children the testator had.[31] The social and political content of inheritance was widely appreciated, and inheritance provisions provided important playing fields where the ideas of economic liberalism and traditional familial and societal notions contended for supremacy. Indeed, reforms in Latin American private law often began with attempts to change and improve inheritance provisions.[32] These ideas are perhaps best summed up in a statement by the French drafter Portalis, whose views on codification Chilean codifier Andrés Bello translated into Spanish and published in 1833. Portalis wrote and Bello translated: "It is necessary to destroy the entire system of succession, because it is of great value to create a new order of citizens for a new order of property owners."[33] Bello's own attempts to provide greater testamentary freedom in the Chilean Civil Code of 1855 met with substantial criticism, and this code's final provisions gave the testator freedom over one-quarter of the estate if he were survived by children, but the traditional colonial *mejoras* also applied even to this portion. Thus, the code carved out an additional one-quarter from this portion to a family member or members of the testator's choice.[34]

Throughout the nineteenth century, most countries continued to apply, more or less, the colonial patterns for the passage of property on death as enacted into their national civil codes. A few countries, however, moved toward greater freedom of testamentary freedom, even in the last part of the nineteenth century. For example, aiming at freer testamentary dispositions, and noting that the father's only legal duty was of support and education, the Mexican federal district Civil Code of 1884 did away with the *legítima*.[35] At least one contemporary commentator saw this change as necessitated by "modern political economy"; another however saw the change as a threat to "social order and public morality."[36]

Both landholding and inheritance demonstrate the conflict of the forces of economic liberalism, favoring freer alienation or disposition of property, and persistent colonial attitudes about the relationship of property to societal and familial structure. Wealthy families surviving the instability of the independence period used these new ideas to amass even greater tracts of land. These new ideas included the free alienability of property, the disfavored status of communally held property (both in *cabildo* and Indian hands) as hindering the property's economic movement, and in some areas, the removal of lands from church hands. Even the legislative solutions to *mayorazgos* meant that large tracts of land might be available for addition to one's estates.

Rapid change in the provisions of inheritance law did not occur during the nineteenth century. While *mayorazgos* and their associated primogeniture inheritance patterns were successfully abolished during the first part of the nineteenth century under the pressure of political and economic considerations, the general patterns of inheritance from the colonial period were left, for the most part, undisturbed.

Commercial Law

THE competing interests of liberal and conservative ideologies present at independence influenced the development of commercial law. In the colonial period, many areas of commerce were under state control or supervision. With independence, it was uncertain which aspects of commerce would be liberalized and which would remain under closer state scrutiny. Some activities were traditionally so closely related to the state and its finances that state control continued in this period. The most important example is mining. Many other areas were removed from state control, or at least saw the involvement of the state in their ambits greatly reduced.

On the structural level, attempts to incorporate the former commercial jurisdiction of the *consulados* into the newly organized ordinary jurisdiction of national courts probably did not meet the needs of the trading classes who were used to their own institutions, rules, and procedures. The idea of maintaining separate commercial tribunals, outside the general structure of the ordinary courts, did not comport with the spirit of reducing the *fueros* and the number of areas meriting special treatment under the new constitutions. The special and confined nature of commercial disputes, however, made the continuance of such tribunals quite useful.

The codification of commercial law suffered the same delays as the codification of civil law. Although new republics saw the need for new commercial law and commercial codes, other pressing political matters kept the appointed committees from the task. Commercial tribunals of the new countries continued to apply Spanish law, particularly the *Ordenanzas de Bilbao*.[1]

Commercial law, however, eventually succumbed to the pressures of codification. Areas usually addressed by a commercial code include all types of commercial transactions, contracts, insurance, the formation of business organizations and the rights and responsibilities of members of such organizations, corporations and the issuance of stock, bankruptcy, the legal aspects of the transportation of goods, and commercial paper. With the exception of corporate law, many of these aspects had been covered in extremely fine detail by colonial law, colonial merchant custom as set out in the *Ordenanzas de Bilbao,* and the popular work on commercial law by Hevia Bolaños.

Both the French Commercial Code of 1807 and Spanish Commercial Code of 1829 were available as European models, but Latin American codification of commercial law was delayed until the general codification efforts of the mid nineteenth century. Surprisingly, in some countries, discussions of and the push for codification of commercial law lagged behind similar activity surrounding civil law codification. For example, Colombia enacted its first commercial code in 1853. This code has traditionally been seen as the product of the Panamanian senator Justo Arosemena, who introduced the draft to the Colombian congress. Recent scholarship has demonstrated that although Arosemena may have modified the draft somewhat, the code was based on the earlier draft Commercial Code from 1842 and on the 1829 Spanish Commercial Code. Indeed, of 1,110 articles in the Colombian Commercial Code of 1853, only 14 cannot be traced to the Spanish Code of 1829; 995 were taken without change.[2] Although Colombia had enacted a commercial code, it apparently did not make its way into the classroom or tribunals. It was also mismatched to Colombian practices, as Robert Charles Means writes:

The Colombian draftsman deleted articles that he found objectionable, but he made no attempt to pare the code down to match the interests that produced its enactment. Formally, at least, in 1853 a commercial code reflecting a European range of concerns was imposed on commercial activity of much less than European complexity and scope. Some transactions covered by its rules seldom occurred; in other transactions parties probably often were unaware of the existence of the rules.[3]

The work of Means is highly instructive; having a code is one thing, having a code that is a good fit to the social and economic conditions and practices of the country is another. Means has accurately seen a bad fit or no fit as important indicia of legal underdevelopment.

The development of Colombian commercial law is similar to the history of Mexican civil codes outlined earlier, in which the political gains and losses of federalists and centralists can be charted in the swings of legislation reflecting the shifting power of both camps. As Colombia entered into a federal period from the late 1850s until 1885, various states of the country attempted their own commercial codes. In 1857, the state of Cundinamarca ordered a new set of codes, which were enacted in 1860. Writing in 1980, Means stated that the source of these codes had not been traced, but speculated that the source for Cundinamarca's civil code was Andrés Bello's Chilean civil code, and that the source for its commercial code was the 1853 national commercial code.[4]

Although other states of Colombia codified their procedural and substantive civil and penal law, several states such as Antioquia, Bolívar, Magdalena, and Tolima did not enact commercial codes, and it appears they used the new 1853 national commercial code by default. In 1871, Magdalena adopted a commercial code based on the national code, and the civil, penal, and procedural codes as drafted and modified by Justo Arosemena.[5]

After 1885 and a civil war, Colombian federalism was over, and new codes were once again needed for a new nation. With the federal state codes as models, the legislature had its choice of codes. In 1887, Colombian legislators saw the Panamanian Commercial Code of 1869 (based on the Chilean commercial code) as the most advanced, and enacted it for their newly unified country.[6] While several states followed the national code of 1853, the Panamanian Commercial Code of 1869 was itself drafted under the guidance of the famous jurist Justo Arosemena, who based his work on the influential Chilean Commercial Code of 1867 drafted by another luminary of nineteenth-century Latin American private law, Gabriel Ocampo.[7] The careful crafting of Ocampo led to a code that better fit the economic and commercial needs of the countries of the region, and in this way, by adopting the Ocampo code, Colombia took an important step toward "rational legal development."[8] It was, however, not a direct step, but one that had been halted and changed along the way by various model codes and numerous political turns.

As the Mexican and Colombian experiences show, the political atmosphere had to favor codification for its success. Argentina's codification of commercial law is equally instructive on this point. Attempts to draft a commercial code in Argentina date from the early 1820s. Pedro Somellera, a professor of civil law in the Department of Jurisprudence of Buenos Aires and an author of a work on civil law, drafted the portion of the code dealing with the structure of commercial tribunals. Bernardo Vélez, also an author on civil law, prepared the other portions of the draft. Typical of early republican attempts at codification, the project failed. Although praised at its time, Vélez's draft has not been found, and the congress that would have enacted the work fell apart for unrelated political reasons. Another unsuccessful push for an Argentine commercial code came in 1831 in the shadow of the 1829 Spanish commercial code. This project, under Mateo Vidal, Nicolás Anchorena, and Faustino Lezica, also produced no legislation.[9]

As had happened with a civil code under the Constitution of 1853, political events, notably the war between the Confederation and Buenos Aires, overtook attempts to draft a commercial code by José Benjamin Gorostiaga, Vicente López, and Francisco Pico. In 1856, Vélez Sársfield joined efforts with the Uruguayan Eduardo Acevedo to draft a new commercial code. Acevedo studied at the Department of Jurisprudence of the University of Buenos Aires and then in the Academy of Jurisprudence in the same city, receiving his doctorate in 1836. In 1839 he moved to Montevideo where he later served as a legal official, judge, and vice president of its Academy of Jurisprudence. In 1853 he published a draft civil code for Uruguay. In the mid-1850s, he returned to Buenos Aires where in 1855 he served as president of the Academy of Jurisprudence.[10]

This time the political atmosphere was good for the passage of the draft in Buenos Aires and despite the absence of a civil code for Buenos Aires upon which the commercial code necessarily relied, the commercial code was enacted to take effect in 1860.[11] The entire country adopted the Commercial Code in 1862 when the Confederation and Buenos Aires merged. The Eastern Republic of Uruguay also adopted it in 1865.[12] This commercial code was divided into four books with the following scheme:

Book 1 Persons in commerce
Book 2 Commercial contracts, including corporations, insurance, and commercial paper
Book 3 Navigation
Book 4 Bankruptcy[13]

Sources for their draft included the *Ordenanzas de Bilbao,* the commercial codes of France, Spain, Portugal, Holland, Brazil, and Wurtemberg, as well as many treatises on commercial law.[14]

The enactment of the code not only brought wide-ranging substantive changes in commercial law, but also directly affected the institutional structure of the courts in Argentina. Shortly after its enactment, the "Commercial Tribunal, the clearinghouse for merchant justice since 1794, closed its doors, making way for divisional courts (*Tribunales de Primera Instancia*) and special Commissary Judges chosen to handle bankruptcies."[15] The new rules and institutional tribunals were successful, and the first decision of the new Supreme Court upheld the autonomy of the commercial law and bankruptcy judges. Once the Argentine civil code was enacted, the 1,755 articles of the commercial code covering these topics were reduced to 1,611 as it was brought into agreement with the Civil Code in 1889.[16]

Like Bello's Chilean Civil Code of 1855, the Chilean Commercial Code of 1867 was a nationally important and internationally influential development in commercial law. Ocampo was born in 1799 in La Rioja (now in present-day Argentina) to a locally powerful and noble family. He studied at the Colegio Convictorio de Nuestra Señora de Monserrat and the University of Córdoba, and obtained the doctorate in law in 1818. The following year he went to stay with family in Santiago, Chile, where he matriculated into the University of

San Felipe and obtained the Chilean title of *abogado*. Over the next few years, Ocampo worked in various political and representative positions in Chile, was a member of the Constituent Congress of 1823 and later the National Congress where he served as secretary until its dissolution in 1825. In this period he drafted and saw enacted an important reform of judicial administration for Chile. Toward the end of his first long-term residence in Chile, Ocampo also taught law in the Chilean National Institute.[17]

Ocampo was in Argentina and Uruguay from 1826 to 1841 during which time he had a highly successful legal practice, taught in the Academia Teórico-Práctica de Jurisprudencia in Buenos Aires, and published in 1835 a work on the contractual, long-term mortgage loan (*enfiteusis*) in Buenos Aires. In 1841, Ocampo became a target of the powerful and autocratic governor of Buenos Aires, Juan Manuel de Rosas, and wisely set sail for Chile.[18]

Ocampo's legal career continued to flourish in Chile. He was a founding member of the University of Chile's law faculty, and was part of a small highly productive commission that undertook the final revisions of Bello's civil code. This last activity no doubt honed his drafting skills even more finely.[19]

Since 1846, Chile had been unsuccessfully attempting to begin work on a commercial code. The first commission appointed at that time, composed of jurists, politicians, and merchants, had produced no draft by 1850. A second commission composed exclusively of merchants considered the Spanish commercial code as a model to be adopted with modifications by Chile. This commission, apparently because it was expected to undertake the work out of civic responsibility rather than for payment, also produced no results. In 1852, Congress made a third attempt. It authorized the preparation of codes, the remuneration of participants, and appointed Ocampo to draft the commercial code. After success in drafting the code, Ocampo was granted Chilean citizenship, became active in establishing the Colegio de Abogados, and served as dean of the faculty of law and political sciences in Santiago. He died in 1882 at the age of eighty-four.[20]

In addition to pulling together the important sources for the undertaking such as the colonial Spanish law and the *Ordenanzas de Bilbao,* Ocampo—like a nineteenth-century Karl Llewellyn drafting the Uniform Commercial Code—sought out opinions and contemporary commercial practices through interviews, discussions, and treatise writers.[21] Like Bello's work, Ocampo's draft took many years, a total of thirteen—eight to prepare the preliminary draft, and five more for revisions before a commission. It was enacted in 1865 to become effective in 1867.[22]

The final code was similar in structure to other contemporary commercial codes. The code consisted of 1,324 articles divided into four books: Book 1 dealt with merchants and their agents, Book 2 with commercial contracts and obligations, Book 3 with maritime commerce, and Book 4 with bankruptcy. One section had preceded the total draft into effective law; the title dealing with corporations (*sociedades anónimas*) was enacted separately in 1854. As mentioned earlier the code was influential in the development of other Latin American commercial codes such as those of Argentina and Colombia and had significant impact on the commercial codes of Ecuador, El Salvador, Guatemala, Honduras, Nicaragua, and Venezuela.[23]

Mexico too relied on the *Ordenanzas de Bilbao* for many decades after independence. In the mid nineteenth century, Santa Anna turned to his minister of justice, Teodosio Lares, to draft a commercial code, which, based on the French Commercial Code of 1807 and the Spanish Code of 1829, was enacted in 1854. Santa Anna was overthrown shortly afterward, and the commercial tribunals where the code was to operate were abolished. When it was repealed in 1856, some states adopted it, while others returned to the *Ordenanzas de Bilbao*.[24]

Maximilian's imperial legislation for Mexico also considered commerce important. His laws from 1863 and 1864 touch on bills of exchange and industrial establishments, leaseholds, and the establishment of the Bank of Mexico as an issuing bank. He also reestablished the *Código Lares* in 1863 and appointed a commission to work on a new commercial code, of which the first two volumes were published in 1866. Mexico enacted a federal commercial code in 1884 (*Código Barranda*), which was this time strongly influenced by the Italian Commercial Code of 1882.[25] In 1889, the commercial code incorporated provisions for corporations (*sociedades anónimas*), which had been enacted the year before.[26] The following year, the Mexican Congress enacted a new commercial code, this time influenced by the Spanish code. Despite numerous drafts and commissions since 1890, this commercial code as amended is still in force.[27]

Every Latin American country enacted a commercial code during the mid nineteenth century. Venezuela struggled to enact a commercial code during the first decades of independence, and it was not to have such a code in effect until 1862. Once established, however, the Venezuelan commercial code, in typical fashion, was subject to revision by various committees of expert commercial lawyers in the 1870s, and then throughout the twentieth century.[28] Ecuador codified its commercial law in 1831, Bolivia in 1834, the Dominican Republic in 1845, Paraguay in 1846, Peru in 1853, Costa Rica in 1853, and El Salvador in 1855. Most of these codes were based on the Spanish Commercial Code of 1829, but Bolivia's code may have been based on the French Commercial Code of 1807.[29]

The commercial codes of the nineteenth century governed general aspects of commercial law, including who were merchants and what type of transactions were subject to the code, business association, commercial contracts, and the transportation of goods by water and land. The demands of increased trade during the period were reflected in the changing commercial law. As an example of the general changes in most Latin American countries in the period, from the late 1880s to the early 1900s, Mexico enacted legislation on negotiable instruments, banking and credit, trademarks, and patents (based on Belgian and French law). In 1903, it conformed its legislation to adhere to the 1883 Paris Convention on industrial property.[30]

Commercial legislation also responded to a need for a greater array of business entities and structures. For example, in early independence Colombia, share companies were organized to undertake particular projects or pursue certain industries, like mining or running steamboats. The Franco-Colombian Company's operations in the iron industry in the 1820s and 1830s are an early example of this type of structure.[31] These forms of business entities were limited, however, and codification responded to the growing economic needs of the countries. Following mid-nineteenth-century European lines, new codes provided a better-structured and varied array of business organizations. Commercial codes of the second half of the nineteenth century typically provide for corporations (*sociedades anónimas*), limited partnerships, general partnerships, and cooperative societies.[32] For example, the Mexican Commercial Code of 1884 provides for the five types of business entities found under the French law.[33]

One question being addressed in the mid nineteenth century was the degree to which the state should supervise the internal operations of such entities. These codes generally viewed the executive power of the state as holding the power to grant or deny corporate existence and to subject the corporation to various conditions for the privilege of obtaining a corporate identity. In addition to cautiously guarding the creation of corporations, the state also continued to watch over and monitor corporate operations. By the later nineteenth century in Europe both of these restrictions on corporate activity were being loosened. Freedom to incorporate was the first step. When a group of individuals complied with the statutory requirements, the state had to recognize their corporate existence, and there was no discretion on the part of the state.[34] "From France, freedom of incorporation spread to other continental jurisdictions; by 1882 corporations could be freely formed in nearly all of western Europe."[35] The nature of and extent to which state supervision continued after incorporation was another matter. State oversight of corporate activity was being shed by European codes, such as the French commercial code, but the idea was not immediately brought into Latin American codes. For example, just as these European commercial codes were liberating corporations from the administrative control of the state, Gabriel Ocampo's 1860 commercial code was being enacted in Chile in 1865. This influential code repeated the earlier ideas of state supervision. Considering that large state institutions continued to be difficult to fund and to staff during the nineteenth century, it is not surprising that even when commercial codes called for a state agency to supervise corporate activity, the agencies were never established. Thus, Panama adopted the Chilean commercial code, but never applied the administrative supervision provisions.[36]

Various other aspects related to commerce could weave in or out of the commercial code, depending on the time and country involved. One such area of the law is intellectual and industrial property. Along with the industrialization of the nineteenth century, and the movement toward codification generally, many countries enacted statutes protecting the rights of authors and inventors, including copyrights, patents, and trademarks. Sometimes separately enacted, these provisions found their way into the appropriate sections of the civil and commercial codes.[37]

Contracts, of course, were an essential part of commercial law but are also governed by the civil codes of most Latin American countries. Because of this characteristic civil and commercial split and because contracts were often treated only in the particular factual or business context of their creation, a unified contract law and theory were later developments. Nonetheless, new ideas of liberalism encouraged parties to reach economically rational agreements based on their wills and assumed that these ideas would be expressed in commercial codes. Still, certain aspects of formalism in formation and interpretation continued in code provisions addressing contracts.[38]

Because of the multitude of sources available to Latin American codifiers of commercial and civil law, code provisions regarding contract could vary greatly in the region. One example is the law surrounding *lesión*, which in part provides that a seller of real property may rescind if the agreed purchase price is less than five-twelfths the fair value of the property. Vélez Sársfield rejected the French code's notion of *lesión*, stressing the responsibility and free autonomy of the contracting parties. Bello, in drafting similar provisions for Chile, kept a version of this doctrine, which permitted rescission of a contract for real property when either the buyer or seller suffers "*lesión enorme.*" This occurred when the seller received less than half the just price or the buyer receives property whose just price is less than half the buyer's payment at the time of the contract.[39]

In Mexico, the Constitution of 1857 set out some general liberal guidelines for contractual agreements and only prohibited contracts in which someone lost his or her liberty. These notions were incorporated into the fuller contractual treatment of the Mexican civil codes of 1870 and 1884, as well as the commercial codes of 1884 and 1889. The civil codes of 1870 and 1884 have been viewed in particular as advancing a more general theory of contract by grouping together contractual topics such as capacity, mutual assent, licit nature and illegality, good faith, and impossibility.[40] Nonetheless, limitations placed on complete contractual freedom based on ideas of fair value, such as *lesión*, continued in these Mexican codes.[41]

Some areas of the law were just too large and complex to find a comfortable home in the existing codes. Thus, the labor contract was removed from an application of pure contractual agreement, and particular provisions for labor law were often drafted into separate labor codes in the early twentieth century. Nonetheless, the history of labor law in Latin America reveals the intense struggles of workers during the period. Similarly, the law governing railroads was too complex to fit easily into existing codes. Mexican railroads were subject to legislation through the Railroad Law of 1881 and subsequent legislation on the matter occurred in 1883, 1888, and 1899.[42]

Mining serves as a final example of an entire area of commercial law being carved out of the commercial code. Indeed, colonial mining law was always viewed as a separate area of law, and an area closely supervised by the state. As economic interests shifted from precious metals to petroleum products in the nineteenth century, so too mining law, originally focused on silver and gold, shifted in its emphasis to a broader range of natural resources. For example, Venezuelan mining law did not shift to a code until 1854 when, more or less, the colonial rules were put into a new mining code. Like other aspects of private law, mining law was subject to federalist-centralist flip-flops during the late nineteenth century.[43]

Santa Anna opened mining in Mexico to foreign investment in 1823. Mexican authorities abolished the Tribunal de la Minería by decree in 1826, and mining became subject to the individual states until a law of 1854 led to a centralized General Tribunal of Mining (Tribunal General de Minería).[44] Legislators then placed Mexican mining under federal control by constitutional amendment in 1883, which led to the Federal Mining Code of 1884.[45] The regime of Porfirio Díaz recognized private claims in perpetuity to be continued solely on payment of taxes. The Mining Code of 1892 codified this view.[46]

State and national interests also provided the background to Argentine mining law. In 1860, the Argentine Congress considered and rejected a draft mining code prepared by Domingo Oro because it deprived the provinces of their interests in existing mines in their territory. The next attempt at a mining code was in 1876 when Enrique Rodríguez, a successful mining lawyer in Chile, spent eight years preparing a new code. The draft was sent to the Argentine Congress in 1885 where again debate concerning the federal (provincial) or national ownership of mining rights called the code into question.

Manuel Sáez's critical reading of the draft in his *El Código Minería para la Confederación Argentina* (1886) led to modifications and the eventual passage of Rodríguez's code, which became effective in 1887.[47]

The commercial codes of the nineteenth century were important advances in providing legal rules and structures to match the changing economic and trade needs of the independent republics of Latin America. Although colonial rules continued to provide the rules of commercial law in the early period of independence, the French Commercial Code of 1807 and the Spanish Commercial Code of 1829 provided important models for commercial law in Latin America. Once available, the Chilean and Argentine codes were likewise influential in the region. As with civil law codification, the success of commercial codes often depended on a favorable atmosphere that included at least a temporary resolution of divisions over federal or central state structure. Commercial codes and laws were also influenced by liberal ideologies concerning the extent to which the state should help regulate and supervise economic activity. The codes governed many aspects of commercial transactions and disputes and provided a ready framework on which further advances in commercial law could be organized. Some areas dealing with commerce, such as mining or labor, were either too important or too complex to be readily incorporated into commercial codes, and these were often addressed in separate codes and subject to closer governmental scrutiny.

Part III

The Twentieth Century

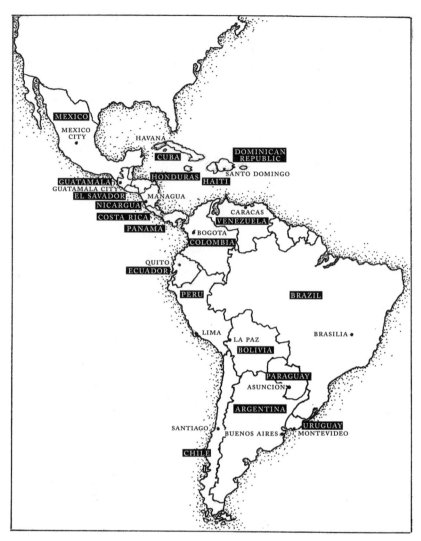

The countries of modern Latin America.

From Europe to America

I F the most important change in law in Latin America during the nineteenth century was the codification of law, constitutionalism, another tradition that had begun with independence, consumed the energies of legal
specialists in the twentieth century. Indeed, some argue that in recent times in
civil law jurisdictions, the constitution has replaced the civil code as the central text around which all law, private and public, revolves.[1] While nineteenth-
century Latin American constitutions were based mostly on French and U.S.
models, twentieth-century constitutions reflect regional and national development and innovation. For example, the Mexican Constitution of 1917 has
been called "the first really innovative Latin American Constitution."[2]

Innovation has occurred not only in constitutional law but also in private
law in the twentieth century. The most important change generally for Latin
American private law has been a turning away from the European doctrinal
literature to an indigenous doctrinal literature, although it continued to be
profoundly influenced by the European materials. Materials from other Latin
American countries became increasingly important sources in this period.
Private law ideas, solutions, and structures from the United States also gained
greater acceptance. These changes did not happen at once, but World War II
provided a watershed concerning the direction of future legal development
in private law. Latin America turned from Europe to America, from the approaches of France, Italy, and Germany to the approaches of other Latin
American countries and the United States. This may be an oversimplification.
European sources are still influential and useful tools of interpretation for private law today in Latin America. Likewise, some U.S. private law mechanisms
made their way into Latin American private law before the war. For example,
the installment sales contract of the United States led to a similar device
in Mexican civil law in the early 1920s, and the importation of the Anglo-

American trust to Latin American law dates from this period.[3] Colombia also sought the United States out as a model for law reform; for example, concerning Colombian codification efforts in the twentieth century, Dennis Lynch writes: "The first major development occurred at the beginning of the industrialization process in 1923, when the Colombian government retained a commission of American experts headed by E. W. Kemmerer to make a study and recommend legislation in the fields of finance, banking and commerce in anticipation of more United States foreign investments."[4] This led to the creation of a national bank and numerous reforms in commercial and private law, including reforms to commercial paper and corporations.[5] This is a relatively early example of countries in Latin America seeking to restructure institutions and private law to improve their systems while gaining the confidence of international investors.

Nonetheless, the general shift in perspective is apparent. Much of this shift was, of course, due to the isolation of Europe from Latin America during the war, but once the pattern of the elite young lawyers going off for graduate legal studies in Europe was broken, the readjustment of the place of European sources in Latin American law was inevitable. For example, in 1930, a young, ambitious Bogotá lawyer might look to Paris as the place to polish off his academic training in law. By 1980, that same young ambitious lawyer sought her entrance into the elite LL.M. programs of the United States. Numerous factors account for this shift, including the economic position of the United States in Latin America and the supplanting of the French by the English language as the worldwide *lingua franca* in the later part of the twentieth century. United States involvement with and engagement of Latin America increased dramatically during and since World War II, and the country's hemispheric activities have encouraged the proffering of U.S. solutions in Latin America in an often misguided or naïve attempt to "help" Latin American countries with their legal institutions and rules.[6] Thus twentieth-century private law was marked by significant indigenous legal development coupled with a long-term shift away from European continental sources toward U.S. sources as important models for borrowing.

The profound influence of European sources on the drafting and interpretation of Latin American civil codes during the nineteenth century is beyond question, and this method continued strongly into the first half of the twentieth century. In the late nineteenth century, Colombia sought the assistance and instruction of M. Edmond Champeau from France, and the French lawyers Courcelle-Seneuil and Pradier Fodéré were thought to have significantly improved Chilean law.[7] Other European countries could supply legal minds as well. Several Latin American countries benefited from the arrival of professors, jurists, and lawyers who fled Spain as Franco came to power, and the influence of this important intellectual community on their new homes has yet to be studied.

European models continued to be highly influential. For example, many countries have reexamined the traditional civil and commercial dichotomy after Italy did away with the distinction in 1942.[8] Civil law lawyers have always readily accepted foreign works as useful when based on the same general foundation, and some scholars link the greater use of foreign sources in civil law as a reflection of the civilians' perception that they are engaged in a "transnational legal science."[9]

The movement from European to American sources can be noted in a collection of reported oral histories of well-known Venezuelan practitioners conducted in the late 1970s. Lawyers recalling their studies in the 1920s and 1930s noted the use of the following as texts for legal study in Venezuela during the period: Ortolán, Petit, Pradier Fodéré, Planiol y Ripert, Demolombe, Aubry y Rau, Baudry-Lacantinerie, Colin, Capitant.[10] The sources used by Luis Felipe Urbaneja in the course of his studies, practice, and teaching is illustrative of the trend. As a law student at the Universidad Central de Venezuela from 1926 to 1934, Urbaneja recalled, "We learned by the textbook, which I estimate gave us no less than 80% of our knowledge. The texts were almost always in French or Italian, languages that we had learned to read in our *bachillerato,* above all French."[11] By the time he was teaching civil law from 1939 to 1950, Urbaneja saw his contribution as spearheading a movement away from the rhetorical tradition of the French commentators toward the use of practical cases "in the style of the North American method created at Harvard by Langdell."[12] He explained, "I did not study in the U.S. nor had I had any direct contact with this manner of teaching, but I noticed that it is necessary to complement theoretical teaching with solving cases. Case solving was introduced here before the corresponding idea of practical works (*travaux pratiques*) arose in France."[13]

Thus, after 1950, U.S. sources gained ground in offering models of private law. For example, in 1953, Mexico modeled its securities regulation law (*Ley de la Comisión Nacional de Valores*) on the U.S. Securities Exchange Commission.[14] The influence of the United States on Latin American law has not been limited to areas of civil law and commercial law. Francisco Reyes, the author of the definitive commentary on the Colombian commercial code's provisions on corporations drafted in 1995 and a chief drafter of the provisions, not only cites the Delaware Corporation Laws, but finds relevant the works of numerous U.S. authors on corporations, including Robert Clark, James Cox, Frank Easterbrook, Melvin Eisenberg, Robert Hamilton, Harry Henn, John Howell, William Klein, Bayless Manning, Alan Palmiter, Rudolf Schlesinger, Lewis Solomon, and Robert Thompson.[15] The provisions take the important step of unifying civil and commercial corporations, and Reyes finds discussions of U.S. concepts such as piercing the corporate veil, rendered accurately yet somehow less mysteriously as "la desestimación de la personalidad jurídica de la sociedad," as valuable in setting out Colombian remedies against corporations.[16]

An additional newer source for legal borrowing is international models. This trend also started in the first half of the twentieth century. For example, present Mexican negotiable instruments law dates from the 1930s and was modeled on the League of Nations Convention Providing a Uniform Law of Bills of Exchange and Promissory Notes.[17] Likewise, numerous Latin American countries have used UNCITRAL provisions as models for legislation related to e-commerce.[18] Indeed, one scholar has recently argued that the United States has used NAFTA as a means of "Americanizing" the domestic law of Mexico regarding professional and financial services, foreign investment, industrial property, labor law, and environmental protection.[19]

Several examples in the following chapters lend support to the idea that Latin American countries in the twentieth century moved away from European sources and toward their own legal development, and that when they sought outside influences they turned increasing toward U.S. models. Much work is needed to add depth to the general hypothesis expressed here. Not only could studies of particular countries and particular areas of law help substantiate or refute this general notion, but the effect of U.S. legal education on Latin American legal academics, drafters, legislators, and politicians in the decades since the law and development movement is an obvious, yet relatively unexplored, link in this process. Furthermore, the role of the Inter-American Bar Association, established in 1940, in the cross-fertilization of private law in Latin America is another question left unanswered.[20] Surely, the training Latin American lawyers received since the end of World War II in law schools throughout the United States, discussed in Chapter 21, left marks, traces, and reforms on the private law of their home countries. Exactly how, must be left for further study.

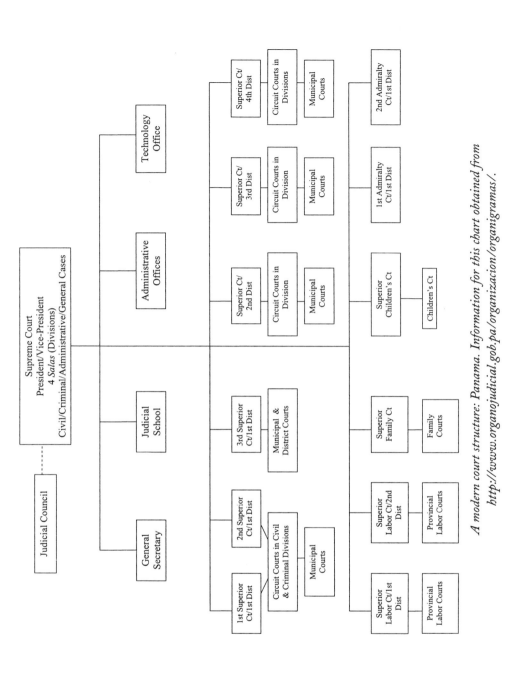

A modern court structure: Panama. Information for this chart obtained from http://www.organojudicial.gob.pa/organizacion/organigramas/.

Structures and Courts

A S in the early republic period, in the twentieth century the courts and governmental structures were the products of constitutions. After briefly describing general features for this period in Latin America, this chapter addresses judicial reform, one of the central issues concerning courts in Latin America for the past decades. Procedural aspects and institutions related to alternative dispute resolution are addressed at the end of this chapter.

This work does not attempt to deal with constitutional law, but the sources of late-nineteenth- and twentieth-century constitutionalism inform the understanding of courts in Latin American countries. Even though the twentieth century has been characterized as a century of constitutionalism, very few Latin American countries have had constitutions of long-standing existence. Indeed, in 1959, Mecham calculated that from the time of independence until that date, twenty countries in the region have had no less than 186 different constitutions.[1] This rapid turnover, however, cannot be interpreted to reflect a culture that finds it necessary to comport with constitutional provisions, and thus enacts new constitutions each time rights or institutional structures must be changed. Addressing the "discrepancies between Latin American constitutional theory and political fact," J. Busey has grouped the causes into five general areas:

1. the physical and social dissection of Latin America, which has made it difficult to agree upon the rules of the political game,
2. the intense poverty of large sectors of the Latin American population, which has deprived governments of the revenue needed for public education, communications, and general improvements,
3. the failure of leading sectors of many Latin America populations to regard government as having a social and public function,
4. the persistence of feudalistic relationships and attitudes which

emerge out of patterns of land monopoly and prevent development of a sense of public responsibility, and

5. the paucity of self-disciplined, responsible, socially conscious leaders.[2]

Therefore, the rapid turnover of constitutions really reflects the rapid turnover of successive governments in the region and the success of numerous coups d'état. Indeed, between 1930 and 1975 there were no less than ninety-four *successful* coups d'état in the Spanish-speaking countries of Latin America.[3] A new constitution is frequently a method of establishing legitimacy to a new government that came to power outside the contemplation of the former constitution.[4]

Constitutions set out the various courts, their jurisdiction, and hierarchy. Because constitutions are inherently political documents, the political unrest of many of the countries in the region has led to changing court structures and institutions. Many countries have opted for a tiered structure of courts, and where countries are federal, such as Mexico, a tiered structure of original and appellate courts exist within the states as well as the federal government. This tiered structure frequently comes from following the structure set out in the U.S. Constitution.[5] Even where the U.S. structure provides a model, further divisions of courts may follow European lines. For example, supreme courts of countries may be divided into jurisdictional divisions, panels, chambers, or *salas*. Typical divisions might correspond to criminal, civil, administrative, and labor cases. Twentieth-century Latin American constitutions typically create several highest tribunals within the hierarchy of the courts including a supreme court, a constitutional court to review constitutional aspects often limited to the constitutionality of legislation, and a council of state to review governmental administrative action.

Beyond constitutional structure, legislative enactments often deal specifically with the finer structure of the system. Legislative acts can also substantially reform institutions on their own as well. For example, in 1914, Mexican authorities reorganized the federal district courts (*Los Tribunales de Justicia Constitucionalista*) and those of the federation in 1917 (*Ley Orgánica del Poder Judicial de la Federación*).[6] The *Ley Orgánica de Tribunales de Justicia del Fuero Común del Distrito y de los Territorios Federales* reformed Mexican district courts 1932 (reformed again in 1946 and 1968).[7] Most recently, the constitutional reforms of the mid-1990s as described in the *Ley Orgánica del Poder Judicial de la Federación del 22 de noviembre de 1996* have structured Mexican courts.[8]

With a more unified system of courts, Latin American countries have generally done away with specialized commercial tribunals. Commercial jurisdiction has been placed in the hands of the ordinary courts, which may use special procedures for commercial cases.[9] Labor, agrarian reform, and tax cases, however, still often have their own tribunals. The overall movement appears to reflect a desire to streamline the court system and mainstream specialized jurisdictions.

Judicial Reform

Accompanying modifications to court structure, the judiciary has also seen substantial changes in the twentieth century.[10] For example, in the last sixty years, the judiciary, particularly in the lower courts, has become increasingly professional and legally trained. Nonetheless, considered in its entirety, the twentieth century has been a period of relative judicial weakness. Too often courts are seen as riddled with delays, backlogs, and bribes.[11] The extreme extent to which the judiciary is dependent on the executive power has hindered the development of law, and throughout the twentieth century even the supreme courts of some Latin American countries have been summarily removed and replaced by the executive or military. For example, the Supreme Court of the Dominican Republic was ousted in 1930, Ecuador's in 1970, Argentina's in 1967, and Peru's in 1969.[12] In 1989, President Menem in Argentina packed the court by expanding it from five to nine justices.[13] In 1992, Fujimori in Peru removed many judges.[14] In 1994, President Zedillo removed all of the justices of the Mexican Supreme Court and fundamentally changed the court.[15] As William Prillaman observes, "The Argentine Supreme Court has been replaced *en masse* six times this century. . . . In Bolivia, the membership of the Supreme Court has been overhauled seventeen times since 1950."[16] Substantial executive control of the judiciary is not limited to the highest levels of the courts, and these examples are listed as the extreme cases. Executive (and executive/military) control of the judiciary is a general attribute of the Latin American judiciary, but one that appears to be lessening.[17]

Many of the changes in the judiciary during the twentieth century have come about as attempts to remedy the relative weakness of the judiciary in relation to the executive power, and countries have sought to address this problem most vigorously since the 1980s. Reforms have not only sought to relocate the judiciary within the structure of governing powers but have sought to address another, equally disruptive element in some judicial systems. Just as the executive power and external threats may be perceived as enemies from without, it has become a commonplace to note the enemy from within, corruption.[18] Indeed, judicial structures, like those of government structures generally in Latin America, suffer under the burden of internal corruption.[19] Although it would be wrong to deny the existence of judicial corruption in Latin America today, many honest judges have paid with their lives or loss of personal security for their unwillingness to bend to corruption. Between 1979 and 1991 in Colombia, 515 judges were subjected to violence; more than half of these acts were assassinations or attempts to assassinate.[20] Furthermore, judiciaries have welcomed national and international attention and assistance as a way to improve both the independence and impartiality of the bench, but much improvement remains to be done.[21] Perceptive and high-quality studies of the Latin American court system and judiciary continue today, sometimes through foreign funding.[22]

Individuals are an often-overlooked aspect of judicial reform. Reform often works against vested interests and those holding such interests will actively hinder the reform process.[23] Likewise, judicial institutions and their structure may be fine, and the real weakness may be one of personnel. Those considering judicial reform "would do well to distinguish whether it is the institutional structure or merely the individuals exercising judicial authority that are in need of change."[24]

William Prillaman's study of Latin American judicial reform provides an important framework for thinking about such changes, and he suggests that three main factors must be considered: judicial independence (particularly from the executive and military), judicial efficiency in dealing with cases, and public access to the courts.[25] Often with these goals in mind, many countries have struggled to create judicial institutions that meet the demands of democratization, economic progress, international investment, and privatization, while recognizing the important function of courts in public law areas (outside the scope of this work) such as the protection of human rights and the environment, as well as the reduction of corruption.[26] The relationship of a vibrant judicial branch to the other aspects of government and the courts' place in securing meaningful democracy are the subject of much study.[27] Recent scholarship has persuasively argued that these reforms are mostly driven by the increased litigation arising from the free market economies of Latin American countries. Freer markets, more winners and losers, more debts, and more litigation all lead to a demand for more efficient and better courts.[28] Some critics warn that the general trend in judicial reform is commercialization rather than democratization.[29]

A broad-based reexamination of judicial institutions in numerous countries has developed since the 1980s; "El Salvador, Honduras, Panama, Guatemala, Paraguay, Peru, Chile, Venezuela, and Bolivia have recently changed or are discussing major changes in the laws governing the ways judges may be appointed, evaluated, held accountable, or sanctioned for their wrongdoings."[30] These changes date from the mid-1980s to the present day.[31] In the early 1990s, Costa Rica, Honduras, Panama, Chile, Colombia, and Paraguay all made significant constitutional or legislative advances to ensure the stable tenure of judges.[32] Judicial tenure is more tenuous elsewhere in the region.[33] Attention has also been given to strengthening both the power and autonomy of courts. As early as 1950, Phanor Eder suggested that courts use code provisions granting them specific performance and injunctive powers more often, as well as developing stronger powers to hold parties in contempt.[34]

Recent reforms have included establishing judiciary councils (Consejos de la Magistratura or Consejos de Poder Judicial), allocating more funds to the judiciary, improving judicial education, and cooperating with international actors to deliver justice effectively.[35] Judiciary councils are the result of constitutional reform. These councils, now to some extent active in Argentina, Colombia, Costa Rica, Ecuador, El Salvador, Panama, Paraguay, and Peru, have been established to loosen the direct control the executive has had over the courts. By 1999, Chile, Guatemala, Honduras, and Nicaragua were also reported as exploring this institution.[36] These councils, usually composed of members from all branches of government, advise on judicial appointments, efficiency, funding, resources, and legislation affecting the courts.[37] They seek to act as an essential buffer between the executive and the judiciary. Courts cannot function without the basics of decent space, lighting, filing, and office supplies. If the executive chooses to withhold funding for items, the activity of the courts can be slowed down to an insignificant trickle. A related problem is that in several countries of the region, judges spend more than half their time on administrative tasks associated with running the courts rather than on considering and deciding cases.[38]

In addition to judiciary councils with administrative oversight of the courts, another way to ensure that courts have the basics to decide cases is to allocate funds to the judiciary. Several countries have incorporated judicial funding clauses into their constitutions that guarantee a percentage of the budget to the courts. Bolivia, Costa Rica, Ecuador, El Salvador, Guatemala, Honduras, Panama, and Paraguay have all since 1990 begun to experiment with this or similar percentage budgeting for their courts.[39] A guaranteed line in the budget is one thing, actually finding the funds for the courts is another.[40] Substantial funding for reform programs has also come from international agencies, and since 1980, USAID, the World Bank, and the Inter-American Development Bank have supported judicial reform programs in Argentina, Bolivia, Chile, Colombia, Costa Rica, Honduras, Guatemala, El Salvador, Panama, Paraguay, Uruguay, and Venezuela.[41]

Programs and institutions to provide judicial education have increased dramatically. In 1930 in Venezuela, for example, only the Supreme Court, the Superior Courts, and a few courts of first instance were staffed with legally trained judges; most courts of first instance and lesser courts were staffed with lay judges, some of whom were very experienced. With the creation of a judicial school and career path, judges in Venezuela are now trained in the law.[42] Throughout the region, judicial schools have been created to train judges and generally focus on the more sophisticated side of business and commercial law that come with freer markets. Additional goals include boosting judicial independence and efficiency while lessening corruption in the courts.[43] Correa Sutil notes this development succinctly:

Some of the Latin American countries that have recently created judicial schools are as follows: Costa Rica established its judicial school in 1964, El Salvador in 1991, Guatemala in 1992, Honduras in 1991, and Panama in 1993. Bolivia created an *Instituto de Capacitación de la Judicatura y el Ministerio Público* that has not yet performed its role in a regular way. Colombia has its *Escuela Judicial*, called *Rodrigo Lara Bonilla*. In Paraguay, the Constitution of 1992 mandates its creation. In Chile, the *Academia Judicial* was created in 1995 and began functioning for preparation of judges and ongoing education of all the judicial personnel in 1996. Peru has a long-standing tradition of judicial education. It put to work a national school called *Academia de la Magistratura* in 1996. In Uruguay, the *Centro de Estudios Judiciales*, dependent on the Supreme Court, has been developing education for judges, especially to prepare them for adapting to procedural reforms.[44]

With the stated goal of creating judicial institutions that are responsive to the needs of democracy and to free-market capitalist economies and are also resistant to corruption, both individual countries and international organizations have introduced a number of attempted reforms to the judiciary in Latin American countries. The main reforms include judiciary councils, the constitutionally dictated allocation of funds to the judiciary, and judicial education programs. Some scholars have linked the failure of judicial reform to the weakening of democracy generally in countries of the region.[45] Although some advances have been made, the overall success of these and other similarly oriented reforms will, if at all, be found during the twenty-first century.

Another problem that continues today in Latin American countries is the lack of penetration of judicial institutions into peripheral areas. Thus areas may be isolated from courts because of geographic location or economic condition. Some areas are just too remote for governments with few resources to establish a full panoply of governmental services in these locations. The legal systems in Costa Rica and Uruguay have been held out as exceptions to this general description.[46]

Likewise, "the bulk of the poor live outside the market economy and penetration of the formal legal structure into rural communities is usually incomplete or nonexistent."[47] Indeed, the poor population is woefully underserved.

Of course, many countries offer clinics or legal assistance bureaus, but they seldom reach the rural poor and even the needs of the urban poor greatly outweigh the services they are able to provide.[48]

Generally, progress on judicial reforms appears to be slow despite the efforts of the international community, and the inaction and lack of dramatic change often leaves outside commentators concluding that "Latin American judiciaries have yet to show a genuine commitment to the full panoply of democratic institutions and rights."[49] Such judgments only tell part of the story; scholars must also reflect on the painful struggle of the judiciary to free itself from the bonds of corruption and intimidation.

In other countries civilian justice may take a subsidiary position. For example, in countries where military rulers have seized executive power, civil courts may be subject to military control and have dramatically less business than military tribunals.[50] Continued judicial reform will come not only from exterior trade pressure but also from within, notably from academic institutions and newly created schools for judges.[51] It appears that future successes may depend on simultaneously working on all three general factors—independence, efficiency, and access. As the works of Adelman for the nineteenth century and Prillaman for the 1990s demonstrate, making tribunals commerce friendly and accessible without ensuring their independence can backfire because commercial interests may not be willing to subject their investments to the roulette wheel of a politically controlled court system that does not independently and predictably protect property interests. Argentina's Rosas legal order and its Menem judicial reforms apparently shared this instability in the eyes of capital.[52] Chile, which has recently worked on all three aspects, is an example where judicial reform may be making progress.[53]

Procedural innovation and new remedies, such as those permitting the constitutionality of government actions to be reviewed, can have a direct impact on the structure of institutions in Latin American countries. The Mexican federal *amparo* has provided a centralizing force because of its grant of jurisdiction to review all local judicial, administrative, and legislative acts.[54] From the 1930s to the 1960s, its coverage of agrarian and labor disputes was either expanded or contracted according to certain policy goals of the executive, and courts were at times established to handle any resulting increase in work. Part of this jurisdiction led to the creation of Collegiate Tribunals of the Circuit (Tribunales Colegiados de Circuito) in 1951, which since 1967, along with the Supreme Court, can create binding case law (*jurisprudencia definida*).[55] Since the mid-1990s, the federal courts, including the Supreme Court, have focused on *amparo* cases.[56] Other Latin American countries have imported the *amparo* action into their own system as a way of reviewing judicial and other governmental action.

Procedure

During the second half of the twentieth century, courts have attempted to streamline procedure in a effort to lessen the burden of litigants. Imported customs from other civil law countries, notably Europe, have been influential in reforming Latin American civil procedure.

Following common law countries such as the United States, Latin American courts have introduced greater degrees of oral proceedings.[57] As early as 1932 the Mexican Code of Civil Procedure for the Federal District encouraged oral over written proceedings for certain aspects of trial.[58] Nonetheless, the civil methods of trial tend to predominate, including the reduction of oral testimony to written statements, the examination of witnesses by the trial judge, and minimum reporting of the analysis the court used in reaching its decision.[59] Typical procedural stages included a complaint (*demanda*) by the plaintiff (*actor*) against the defendant (*demandado*), followed by the defendant's answer (*contestación*). These, in turn, may be followed by a reply (*réplica*) and rejoinder (*dúplica*). From these documents, the process enters into an evidentiary phase during which a written record of evidence is compiled. Statements by witnesses and documentary evidence may also be added to the record. Judgments usually follow a variation on a general formulaic structure. In the "expositive" portion of the judgment, the judge summarizes the pleadings; in the "consideration" portion, the factual and legal bases of the decisions are set out; and in the "dispositive" portion, the verdict of the judge is given.[60] With substantial distrust of the judiciary, the system affords numerous appeals, with the first appeal usually before a three- to five-judge panel, which may consider new evidence. The system is criticized for being slow and, because of the imposition of administrative fees at each step of the case, costly.[61]

Appeals from a decision of the court of first instance are usually made by request to the trial judge, and if that judge denies the request, a party may petition another judge on the same court or an appellate tribunal (not necessarily the appellate tribunal for the appeal of the decision) to review the denial of appeal. The original decision is usually reviewed by a court of second instance composed of three to five judges, which may request the taking of more evidence to decide the case. Appeals usually terminate if the court of second instance affirms. If it reverses the decision of the court of first instance, an appeal may be taken to a court of *casación,* which reviews the law but will not seek additional evidence. If the court of *casación* finds that the court of second instance has incorrectly applied the law, it will remand the case for a decision consistent with its clarification of the law, but in theory, the lower court is not bound by the decision of the court of *casación*. If the lower court refuses to follow the clarified statement of law by the court of *casación,* another appeal will be permitted to the court of *casación,* which may be then empowered to direct the outcome of the case.[62] The decision of the court of *casación* is usually limited in its application to the dispute presented and does not have a general effect of universal application on the point of law clarified.[63] Some countries, like Argentina and Mexico, give some precedential effect to such cases.

As constitutions and constitutional law have grown in importance in Latin American law, new procedures have been developed in the twentieth century to permit individuals to challenge government actions on constitutional grounds. Thus appeals may also be had on constitutional grounds, even by attacking the underlying validity of legislation or government action, and a number of constitutional actions have developed in Latin American countries during mostly the twentieth century, including the Colombian popular action (*acción popular*), with similar actions available at some times during the twentieth century in Cuba, Panama, Venezuela, and El Salvador. Another well-known constitutional action is the Mexican *amparo* mentioned above.[64] The *amparo* action has been adopted in one form or another in numerous Latin American countries, including Bolivia, Costa Rica, Ecuador, El Salvador, Honduras, Guatemala, Nicaragua, Panama, and Paraguay, in the second half of the twentieth century. Some countries have experienced the suspension of constitutional rights (such as Paraguay) or the abrogation of their constitutions (such as Ecuador) since such actions were established.[65] The Colombian *tutela,* like the Argentine *amparo,* is typical of the trend to provide protection for rights established under the constitution. It reads:

Each person shall have an action of tutela to demand before the judges, at all times and places, through a preferred and summary proceedings, for himself or for whom he acts in the name of, the immediate protection of his constitutional fundamental rights, whenever these are vulnerable or threatened by the actions or the omission of any public authority.

The protection shall consist of an order for the authority in respect of the one soliciting the tutela to act or to abstain from doing something. The order which will be carried out immediately, may be challenged before a competent judge and in all cases, shall be sent to the Constitutional Court for its eventual revision.[66]

Because of the broad sweep of actions like the *amparo* and *tutela,* courts have generally been flooded with such actions, creating a substantial backlog and time delays that often effectively undercut the protective aspect of the actions.[67]

Generally, the court system is perceived as costly and slow. Alejandro Garro, in looking at these problems from the perspective of the poor litigant, notes some of the reasons these attributes are attached to procedure. He points out that the general lack of a system of precedents means that the same issue must be litigated anew for each case, instead of a particular interpretation becoming binding and thus freeing the court from a redetermination of the legal issue. He also notes the lack of a fully developed procedure for class actions that could unite multiple plaintiffs in the same action. In most Latin American countries there are significant barriers to bringing such an action. He also notes the promise of alternative dispute resolution but expresses concern that these methods of solving disputes may be reserved for the privileged and wealthy.[68]

Alternative Dispute Resolution

Although they have existed from the beginning of the colonial period, informal structures providing both rules and institutions for resolving disputes are beginning to be understood and used to a much greater degree. Within state-sanctioned activity is arbitration, and several Latin American codes since the first half of the twentieth century have recognized the validity of arbitration clauses and procedures.[69] For example, in 1945 the Cuban jurist Dr. Antonio Sánchez de Bustamante stated:

> The advantages of this procedure over litigation are self-evident. In the first place, it speeds the solution of commercial disputes which would be delayed by the complexity of the subject-matter and by process in the courts. Secondly, and for a like reason, it is less costly. And thirdly, it permits a liberal application of the rules and principles of equity which mitigate the rigors, extreme and sometimes unjust, of the strict law in a manner which the judges of the ordinary courts cannot do.[70]

Nonetheless by 1950, only Colombia had enacted full recognition of arbitration, and Phanor Eder lamented the hesitancy with which Latin American codes embraced arbitration. He also noted his own efforts since 1934 to encourage the use of arbitration through the Inter-American Commercial Arbitration Commission.[71] The situation has changed greatly since Eder wrote in 1950, and alternative dispute resolution (ADR) is presently being aggressively pursued in Latin American countries because it provides a way to avoid the overburdened courts with their slow and costly procedures. ADR in Latin America, in countries like Guatemala, Ecuador, and Mexico, has been modeled mostly on foreign methods used in the United States and France. Civil procedure codes have been amended permitting or requiring judges to refer the parties to mediation before or during trial, and commercial disputes are increasingly handled in arbitration. Mediation is beginning to take place in the family law context as well.[72] As Correa Sutil summarizes recent movement toward ADR:

In Uruguay there is a constitutional provision requiring conciliation or settlement efforts in the Peace Courts before bringing a civil suit. [A study shows it] has not reached the desired results. The constitution of Costa Rica establishes the right to arbitration. In 1993 the Supreme Court of this country, with the help of USAID, created a program in alternative dispute resolution. In Paraguay, Ecuador, El Salvador, Guatemala, Honduras, Bolivia, and Panama, there are legal provisions for encouraging arbitration and settlement of disputes during the judicial process, apparently with few effective results. In Colombia, after constitutional reform in 1991, there have been efforts to stimulate programs of alternative dispute resolution.

. . . Argentina had some failed experiments with settlement of disputes by judges, and in 1995 started a program for transferring disputes from the courts to mediation centers outside the courts before continuing the judicial procedures. Chile has a well-established tradition of arbitration, especially in commercial disputes. On the other hand, the efforts to make judges settle disputes have been quite ineffective, except in labor and family courts. There are some interesting experiences of mediation in legal aid offices and recently in family disputes.[73]

Indeed, throughout the region and especially since 1990, countries have moved toward incorporating ADR into their methods of resolving commercial disputes. The United States has been a model; for example the Argentine movement toward mediation, resulting in mandatory mediation for many federal cases since 1996, was strongly influenced by Argentine contacts with United States ADR practitioners and educators.[74] The UN Commission of International Trade Law (UNCITRAL) provisions have also been influential, for example, in Mexico's commercial arbitration law.[75] A few countries have required mediation in many cases before a suit is permitted to proceed and others are updating their provisions to encourage free markets and foreign investment.[76] Of course, one interesting aspect of ADR as it relates to national courts systems is its ability to short-circuit and bypass weak state institutions. Thus, while ADR may affect the court system's caseload and procedures, its appeal to commercial and investment interests, particularly on the international level, is its ability to abandon the court system.[77]

Another system of resolving disputes in Latin America outside of the courts are systems of "extralegal norms," created by communities to avoid anarchy where the state does not extend its power or is unwelcome by the communities, such as for workers who work outside the recognized schemes in additional cash jobs.[78] These workers on the periphery must find ways of resolving disputes that do not involve the state. Peripheral areas may not be geographically peripheral, as indicated by an important study of law and legal institutions in the barrios of Caracas by Karst, Schwartz, and Schwartz.[79] These researchers found that even where state institutions did not penetrate the community, methods of customary law and representational leadership (the barrio *junta*) stepped in to provide a noticeable degree of legal order and orderly dispute resolution surrounding property transactions and claims, rental of homes, succession, family law, and various other legal matters.[80] Indigenous tribunals usually seeking compromise between the parties exist in many countries as alternative forums for persons subject to their jurisdiction.[81] National law often permits this jurisdiction.[82] Recent shifts to cash economies in many indigenous communities have radically altered the traditional methods of resolution as well as the concern such tribunals may have had for reaching agreements and concord within the community.[83] These methods and customs are quickly disappearing. For example, respect for judges at some tribunals once included the offering and sharing of customary gifts, such as beverages. Now, however, "most town hall litigation no longer involves the proffer of liquor to calm antagonists' fears, as once it invariably did."[84]

IIIIIIIIIIII CHAPTER 21 IIIIIIIIIIII

Legal Education and Lawyers

L EGAL education in Latin America has undergone much change during the past one hundred years. In the past fifty years the region has
seen experimentation with and sometimes successful steps toward new methods of instruction, clinical education, and a wider array of institutions offering legal instruction, especially to less-privileged students. Greater access for
women to study law, an increased sense of the role of law in national politics
and society, and a recent onslaught of postgraduate courses in law have also
come about in the same period. Much, however, has remained the same since
the mid nineteenth century. Certainly the key text of the code remains the
central object of pedagogy, and exposition in class and the lecture method
predominate in instruction. Legal education continues to be closely related
to the political outlooks of the countries, which sometimes minutely regulate
the structure and subject matter of the legal curriculum.[1]

Legal Education before World War II

Before the middle of the twentieth century, legal education continued the
postcode methods of instruction established in the later nineteenth century.
The groundwork for modern legal education in Latin America was laid in the
second half of the nineteenth century, and curricular experimentation and advances continued into the early twentieth century. For example, in 1907, with
positivism, capitalism, legal science, and the "social reality" in mind, Mexican
legislation set out a curriculum for the Escuela Nacional de Leyes. Legislation removed Roman law from the curriculum and mandated the following
five-year plan of studies:

First year: Sociology, Political Economy, and Civil Law
Second year: Political Economy, Civil Law, Civil Procedure
Third year: Civil Law, Civil Procedure, Penal Law and Procedure

Fourth year: Commercial Law, Civil Law, Penal Law and Procedure
Fifth year: Constitutional Law, Administrative Law, Selected
Practical Cases, Synthesis of Law[2]

Classes were often scheduled to fill the morning hours between around 9:00 A.M. to noon, but the 1907 schedule shows two blocks of time being set for most courses, 8:00–9:00 A.M. and 3:00–4:00 P.M.[3] After passing exams and publishing a thesis, a six-month apprenticeship was required before the title of lawyer was awarded.[4]

Although the Escuela Nacional might set the model and the trend to be followed, many of the regional institutions of legal instruction continued with a more traditional curriculum. For example, the curriculum of Guanajuato in 1906 was as follows:

First year: Roman Law and Legal History, Literature of Law
Second year: Civil Law
Third year: Commercial Law, Mining Law, and Penal Law, Political
Economy, Statistics
Fourth year: Civil Procedure, Forensic Medicine
Fifth year: Constitutional Law, Federal Procedure
Sixth year: Private International Law, Legal Philosophy, Practicum[5]

Not only did the government carefully dictate the curriculum, but it also might even go so far as to approve or disapprove various texts. Thus, in Mexico in 1904, the main approved texts for courses where a code existed were the codes, perhaps supplemented by a commentary source. Although by this date Mexico and other Latin American countries had developed a substantial body of their own commentary works, sometimes the approved text continued to be a European standard work such as Ortolán on penal law, Charles Gide's work on political economy, and the ubiquitous Marcel Planiol on civil law. An increasingly prolific professorate contributed to the body of national works on law during the period, and these commentary sources were frequently used by, if not directed primarily toward, students.[6]

The narrowness of the curriculum could produce other academic and professional outlets for broader interests related to law such as the Sociedad de Estudios Sociales (Society of Social Studies) founded by law professors of the Escuela Nacional in Mexico City. The society was open to professors, students, and graduates who discussed various broader topics and encouraged broader work though talks and prizes.[7]

Because legal education carried a political component, and even at times and places a party alliance or affiliation, some law schools were established to combat the particular political outlook of existing schools. This is the origin, for example, of the Mexican Free School of Law (Escuela Libre de Derecho) founded in 1912.[8]

The curriculum and development of law schools in the region during the first half of the twentieth century are best characterized by their continuity with these aspects from the second half of the nineteenth century. While some adjustments were made to courses, content, and methods of teaching, deeper changes would not occur until the 1940s and 1950s. Similarly, the law faculties and students of the major state universities, such as the University of Mexico, the University of San Marcos (Lima), the University of Chile, and the Central University of Venezuela, formed the core of each country's legal education, and there was little international exchange of students.[9]

Legal Education after World War II

Since the 1940s, legal education has continued a democratic and inclusive trend, losing much of its elitist elements so prevalent in its colonial and early republic period.[10] Nonetheless, even in the 1950s, when class sizes had greatly increased, a woman law student was a rarity.[11] From the 1960s to the present, the number of women law students in Latin America has become substantial, sometimes exceeding half the student population in some law faculties. There appear to be no studies of the racial composition of law students in Spanish-speaking Latin America.[12]

At the same time, faculties of law throughout Latin America have increased dramatically. For example, today Mexico has several law faculties in the capital, including UNAM, the Escuela Libre, and the Universidad Iberoamericana, as well as regional centers such as Guanajuato, Guadalajara, Veracruz, Michoacán, and Chihuahua.[13] Private universities, religious and secular, have contributed greatly to the number of law faculties in the region, especially in the last twenty years.[14]

Some universities now grant the title of *abogado* to signify that the graduate is ready to practice the profession, although often in regular parlance the lawyer may carry the title of *doctor* or *licenciado*.[15] Law is typically a five-year undergraduate course of study in Latin America, and thus law students often enter business, politics, and public service, in addition to the expected professions of lawyer, notary, or judge.[16]

The curriculum has generally moved away from the broader political education to settle more on topics of private law with an increasing emphasis being placed on practice-oriented studies.[17] Despite subject-matter changes in the legal curriculum during the late nineteenth and early twentieth century, the lecture teaching method predominates.[18] Full-time law professors are rare, and most law professors in Latin America continue to work part-time on instruction and research, often coupling these duties with practice.[19]

Examinations may be oral or written, but the required undergraduate theses may serve better to familiarize the student with the literature rather than to advance the body of knowledge in a particular field.[20] "Student theses tend to be in the scissors and paste tradition—back-to-back quotations from German, French, Italian, and Spanish authors."[21] Law faculties in Latin America have a growing interest in more active forms of learning based on case studies and clinical activities. Successful passage of the university exams and graduation are the typical requirements for the practice of law, without an additional state-run bar exam.[22] Some countries, such as Chile, Colombia, and Venezuela, require a period of public service, usually under a year, before a license to practice is granted to the student.[23]

The shift away from European influences as the most important foreign influence can be seen in legal education as well. Writing in 1950 one U.S. law professor described the lecture method in Latin American law schools this way, "All the schools have been influenced by the formal lecture methods of the continental law schools, particularly those of Spain, France and Italy where until recent years many students and professors went for special or post-graduate study."[24] Charting out their own futures, Latin American law schools met in Mexico City in 1959 and issued a joint "Statement of Principles on the Teaching of Law" that addressed pedagogy, the professorate, and other aspects of Latin America legal education. The principles did not put forth major changes. For example, part-time teaching positions were considered favorable to full-time positions, unless the professor actively conducted research. The joint statement of principles encouraged curricular flexibility based on the country and the inclusion of regional Latin American courses. The preferred method of instruction was lecture and discussion.[25]

Legal Education and the Cold War: United States and Latin America

Since World War II, U.S. law schools have demonstrated intermittent interest in Latin American law and legal education, often in response to international events. The interest has usually led to a flurry of activity and programs, which subside with a change in seasons and the loss of funding. For example, in 1947, the year of the Treaty of Rio leading to the Organization of American States, New York University (NYU) began the Inter-American Law Institute when Dean Vanderbilt convinced "United States corporations having substantial interests in Latin America [to] make it possible for outstanding young lawyers from the countries to the south to spend an academic year in the United States to study the Anglo-American legal system by financing a program of fellowship awards which would cover not only the high tuition fee required for this instruction but also a reasonable allowance for living and travel expenses." United Fruit, Standard Oil, the Texas Company, Shell, Squibb, Eli

Lilly, RCA, and Pan Am, among others leapt in.[26] The program appears to have been particularly active in the late 1940s and early 1950s.

The influx of refugees to Miami after the Cuban Revolution was a similar stimulus for the University of Miami. Its Program for Latin American Law Students and Lawyers grew out of a nondegree ten-month course for Cuban refugee lawyers in the early 1960s. Under its auspices, John C. Chommie prepared a three-volume introduction to American law in Spanish.[27] By 1969, two Miami students were able to describe optimistically a slew of degree and nondegree programs dealing with inter-American law, including an LL.M. and M.C.L., courses on the common law presented in Spanish, a planned series of books on the topic, faculty and student exchange programs, institutes, and conferences all leading to the hopes that the "institute for Inter-American Legal Studies at the University of Miami will, in due time, become a clearing house or center for the exchange and supply of legal materials and information in the Western Hemisphere."[28] These hopes were expressed in 1969 in the first volume of *Lawyer of the Americas,* which continues today as the highly regarded specialty law journal, the *University of Miami Inter-American Law Review,* an enduring fixture emanating from the 1960s and early 1970s. Many of these projects and the journal were the work of Rafael C. Benitez who successfully coached numerous Latin American lawyers through Miami programs. On retirement he left these programs in the expert hands of Keith S. Rosenn, who, in enumerating all the programs and activities left him on Benitez's retirements, jokingly remarked, "He may also have left me the Inter-American Institute for Legal Studies, but I have never been able to find it."[29]

The activities of NYU and Miami are just two examples of the way United States law schools responded to Latin America during the postwar and cold war period. By the mid-1960s, the United States became actively involved in attempting to reform Latin American legal education. As in all countries of the world, Latin American countries periodically experience proposals for the reform of legal education. It is somewhat unusual that proposals during the 1960s and early 1970s were not the product of internal desires to restructure legal education, but came along with a host of other suggestions from the United States as part of the law and development movement.[30]

With the idealism of the times, and with significant funding resulting from the cold war interest in foreign aid, lawyers sought to take an active role in development alongside of economists, engineers, and other professionals.[31] Law professors quickly took the lead and, with funding from USAID, the Ford Foundation, and the Ford Foundation's International Legal Center created in 1966, focused efforts on the reform of legal education in developing countries, including Latin America.[32] The legal reform project took place on four fronts:

(1) methodological, the American case and Socratic method of teaching law; (2) educational, the basic American model and structure of legal education; (3) professional, the American model of the law as a pragmatic problem-solver and social engineer; and (4) jurisprudential, the antiformal "rule-skeptical," and "instrumental" vision of law drawn largely from American legal realism.[33]

In the 1960s, Costa Rica, Brazil, Chile, Colombia, and Peru were all recipients of international attention concerning their systems of legal education.[34] Institutes for legal education and research were created in Brazil, Chile, and Colombia, as well as in the United States. Stanford, with funding from the Ford Foundation administered through the International Legal Center, created the Chile Law Program in 1971.[35] Then law professor Derek Bok made a tour of Colombian law schools, and in 1969 five Colombian law schools with USAID and Ford Foundation funding created an Association for the Reform of Legal Education. The Universidad de los Andes in Bogotá "found[ed] a Law School in 1968 with some assistance from the Agency for International Development and the Ford Foundation. During the first few years the school was controlled by a group of Colombian lawyers who had completed postgraduate training in U.S. law faculties. They tried to adapt the U.S. model of legal education to the Colombian context with limited success."[36]

Professors were flown around and law school deans met.[37] Yale got $1 million in 1969 for a program in law and modernization, and Stanford got $750,000 in 1971 to study law and development in Latin America.[38] These legal educational reforms not only were the product of the U.S. law and development movement but also reflected Latin American law professors' concerns about the lowering status of the bar and the lack of legal skills training offered by law faculties.[39] As Dennis Lynch observes, "The actual motivations of the reform movement's leaders and participants are somewhat obscure."[40] Despite opaque motivations, the movement brought in the best and the brightest from some of the most prestigious institutions in the United States.

One aim was to increase the number of full-time law professors, but this goal was hindered by funds to employ them, an underappreciation of the importance of the part-time law professor in the professional and social patronage system of the bar, and in some instances the overly politically left leanings of full-time faculties assembled. Dennis Lynch mentions two situations in which this third aspect led to poor results: the first where the full-time faculty took up students' grievances, which undermined their authority with the local practicing elite, and the other where the imported Socratic method so annoyed the powerful elite part-time professors that institutional reputation was undermined, and the dean promoting such changes "was replaced by an older French trained attorney" who returned the faculty to its established order.[41]

It is not clear that the ideas of reforming legal education in Latin America introduced in the late 1960s were completely unsuccessful in affecting the course of legal education and its function in Latin America. Certainly, the ideas that law might be closely tied to social and economic progress were influential, and the ties created in this brief flurry of U.S. involvement served to further the institutional and personal links between Latin American and U.S. legal academics. In retrospect, some Latin American participants recall the experience as being valuable.[42] Additionally, it is likely that the skills-training component of U.S. law school curricula have led to emulation in many Latin American law faculties as seen by the establishment of legal clinics that provide some legal assistance to the poor and some practice experience for law students.[43] Furthermore, it is likely the movement stimulated and paralleled endemic debate about legal education in Latin America.[44]

Even outside the law and development sphere, such links were felt in Latin America. In Argentina, Julio Cueto Rua, who took an LL.M. from and taught at Southern Methodist University in the mid-1950s has been seen as "a pioneer in the post-war in linking Argentine lawyers with legal education in the United States."[45] After some earlier positions of importance in the public sphere, Cueto Rua split his time between Louisiana State University and the University of Buenos Aires until 1990.[46] He "became a broker for the shift in focus from Europe to the United States," and in 1998, he was "active in promoting alternative dispute resolution" in Argentina.[47] Similarly, the links between Carlos Nino, Owen Fiss, the "so-called 'Nino boys (and girls)'" (Yale graduate law students, many of whom have returned to Argentina to academic and other positions of great import), and the University of Palermo, continue to affect legal education both in the United States and Argentina. Indeed, the influence can also be seen in Chile with Jorge Correa, a Yale graduate who, when dean at the University of Diego Portales, established similar and participating activities.[48]

Improvements have also been made in increasing law faculty autonomy in relationship to the government and its political party. For example in 1950, "Legal education [was] largely in control of the state in many Latin-American countries with the government exercising more or less control over appointments, particularly of administrative officers and sometimes of professors."[49] Most law faculties in Latin America are now free from such direct government intervention, and some countries have moved to European-style competitions, *concursos,* to fill faculty positions. There is some interest in augmenting the number of full-time faculty members, who are increasingly drawn not only from their countries' elite law schools but also from further postgraduate legal studies in the United States. Professors who undertake research and scholarship may find facilities and funding through research institutes affiliated with law schools. For professional reasons not necessarily related to scholarship and for funding opportunities, research often addresses current analysis, problems, and proposed solutions.[50]

While individuals involved with law and development discussed legal reform with a number of elite law schools in Latin America, another transformation in legal education in the region was occurring, an even greater widening of the access to legal education for the more middling sort of student on both economic and perhaps academic levels. Night law schools were opening to provide legal education to students underrepresented in the traditional elite law schools. Because, for example, in Colombia, the requirement to practice was a law degree, new law schools began to emerge to provide new lawyers who would serve clients and cases further down the economic scale. The established bar responded with concern about the quality of the profession (and perhaps about increased economic competition) and was successful in enacting legislation that placed quality controls on the newer institutions in the early 1970s.[51]

The professional course for law students today in Latin America is typically a five-year program, which has a number of required courses and some flexibility to permit students to select a number of more specialized courses. A number of faculties now offer postgraduate study leading to a specialization (*especialización*) or masters degree (*maestría*) after a year or two of full-time or part-time study. These are usually a set of required courses in a particular area of law such as tax, banking, or commercial law. Such courses of study give added depth to a student's legal education and provide a competitive advantage in the job market.[52] Some countries have begun to see a U.S. LL.M. as a requisite to the elite firms that deal with international and large national businesses. For such firms in Argentina, for example, "the source of their foreign legitimacy and expertise is the U.S. much more than the Continental legal world. Foreign study in the United States is practically required for a career in these firms."[53]

Legal Practice

In the last half of the twentieth century, the number of lawyers has increased significantly in relation to the total population of Latin America.[54] Those law school graduates entering a legal career in Latin America typically enter private practice, a government legal position, or the judiciary. Generally, recent graduates choose one path or the other and this decision determines the remainder of the career of the lawyer. Some countries offer somewhat greater movement between the positions, such as Colombia, where a lower-level judge may enter practice and then return to government position later in his or her career.[55] Top lawyers in other countries are also able to move in and out of the public and private sectors of practice. For most lawyers such moves are, however, the exception, and to accomplish this, lawyers would necessarily rely on carefully assembled networks of support, often constructed through family ties and law school bonds.[56]

The opening up of legal education has led to a more diversified bar. Depending on the country's economic and commercial successes, the bar has expanded into a number of new methods and areas of practice. The bar is geographically more dispersed in most countries as a result both of more lawyers per population than before and of better professional prospects in outlying areas that have new opportunities stemming from economic growth. In the main commercial centers, lawyers have found new forms of practice in legal departments of businesses (*consultorías jurídicas*), and larger U.S.-style law firms.[57] In recent decades, foreign firms have seen the necessity and profitability of establishing offices in Latin America, and some firms have established themselves as experts in serving foreign interests and specialized practice in a global legal environment.[58]

Although somewhat less so than in the past, law schools and the bar continue to be a main source for the political elite of Latin American countries, and lawyers continue to constitute a large portion of those in all branches of government.[59] The way lawyers have supported or opposed dictatorships, regimes, or the military in various countries has not been the subject of much study.

As legal practice has become more diverse in the last fifty years, countries have established codes of professional ethics to regulate the profession. Countries have also sought to regulate the bar more closely though legislation concerning training and qualifications, as well as through bar associations that may or may not be responsible for disciplinary proceedings against lawyers.[60] The supreme or an appellate court often formally grants the title of *abogado*.[61] Most countries now require practicing lawyers to be members of either the local or national bar (*colegio de abogados*).

Despite the opening of the bar to a wider range of society, lawyers still represent the repressive hand of power and the state to many. Indigenous communities have particular reason to be wary. "Lawyers, as far as Indians are concerned, are the ones who connect literacy and law to the power that ladinos [non-indigenous Spanish speakers] hold over Indians."[62] Similarly, access to legal services for the poor continues to be a significant and, for the most part, unaddressed problem throughout the region.[63]

Judges

Judges in Latin America continue to be relatively poorly paid and lack the social prestige they enjoy in other, particularly common law, countries.[64] The pay and status of Latin American judges are in part reflections of the place of judges in civil law systems with their limited function within the government.[65] The Latin American judiciary in the twentieth century continued to be politically subordinate to the executive. Survival through political turmoil may depend on limiting the scope of judicial action and being perceived as a "good technician."[66]

The position of the courts in written constitutions is often equivalent to the other powers.[67] In practice—and this is one area where recent scholarship has gone beyond the positive, written law—judges often function at the mercy of the executive. Two main reasons account for this subsidiary position of the judiciary. First, the executive branch, to maintain centralized power, has often stepped in as the main forum for disputes of national importance on the economic and business level, leaving the courts to deal with smaller, less important, and often administrative matters such as debt collection. Second, the courts are often financially, and even politically, dependent on the executive, from small items such as the payment of office supplies and electric bills, to larger items such as training and salaries, all the way to the mere pleasure of the executive as to whether one may stay on the bench. Courts as institutions and their personnel come and go with constitutions, which, depending on the country, have a much more frequent rate of change than those in Europe or in the United States. The diminution in actual power opens the door to low judicial prestige, questionable exercises of influencing decisions, outright corruption, and the possible improper delegation of decision-making powers to judicial clerks, *actuarios*. Nonetheless, many judges, remaining honest, face violent retribution and death from unhappy parties. Recent steps toward strengthening the judiciary, as discussed earlier, have come not only from international pressure, but also from within.[68]

Sources

I N 1950, one famous civil law professor and reviser of Argentina's Vélez code could assert that for Latin America "French law has not lost its primacy, be it in its norms, or in its commentaries."[1] He was looking back as a new wave of foreign influences was rushing in. As described earlier, World War II effectively ended the period of strong European influence on Latin American law, although, of course, some influence continues today. From the 1950s to the present day, Latin American private law has been influenced more by internal legal developments, the private law of the United States, and various international sources.

The second half of the nineteenth century was the period for setting out the basic element of private law in Latin America through a set of relatively comprehensive and self-referring codes in the European style. These codes continue to be updated and reformed to the present day, but the general structure they provided in the last century has endured. The codes provide the backbone structure of legal practice and legal education. More recent decades may be characterized as a period of "decodification" in which important changes and additions to law are not brought about in the codes, but rather arise outside the traditional codes as their own legislation and even as their own independent subject-matter codes.[2] Private law has even developed through judicial decisions, as the Latin America law of civil responsibility, paralleling Anglo-American torts, demonstrates.[3] Although the traditional codes and newer codes continue as important sources of law in Latin America, other sources of law have in certain circumstances begun to dominate. Constitutions have become sources of guiding legal rules that must be adhered to, particularly in areas traditionally thought of as public law, but most constitutions also touch on subjects related to private law, such as the ownership, use, and transfer of property. Far from constitutional guarantees, where the executive branch has seized control of all aspects of government function, executive decrees have become increasingly important as a source that is capable of completely and rapidly rewriting entire areas of private law.

Decrees establishing rules in both the private and public legal order were common in the twentieth century. Executive decrees issued in the normal course of an executive officeholder's duties are, of course, frequent and necessary. Where executive power is de facto much greater than legislative or judicial power regardless of the constitutional provisions, such decrees frequently have a greater depth of coverage and importance than in countries where legislatures undertake the law-giving function. A second kind of decree, the legislative decree, or decree law, should also be noted because of its prevalence and importance in many countries of the region. These laws, enacted by executive fiat are often considered to be legally equivalent to legislative acts.[4] Decree laws frequently arise after a coup d'état in which the new military government asserts its power to provide new laws. They may also arise in the constitutional context of laws decreed by the executive during a constitutionally declared "state of siege" or "state of emergency" in which the executive is given broad-ranging powers to remedy a particularly difficult situation for the government. Because of the wide executive powers constitutionally granted during such states and the seemingly unending political, economic, social, and natural conditions that can give rise to such declarations, some countries have become quite used to living under an almost perpetual succession of states of siege or emergency.[5] Especially where the military and executive powers have combined, countries can be governed for years and even decades through decree laws, such as Chile for many years after the overthrow of Allende. Peru's opening of markets has been almost entirely the product of decree laws enacted by Fujimori in the 1990s.[6] Likewise, Menem's market reforms for Argentina in the 1990s were based on such decrees.[7]

Despite the rise of decree laws in some countries, codes continue today as the most important general source of private law in Latin America. Indeed, there is nothing to prevent decrees from being codified in the appropriate place in a commercial or civil code, or even establishing an entire new code effected through decree law. The development and turns of the various codes of civil, commercial, and procedural law of each country are beyond the scope of this study. Some examples, here taken from Mexican law, give some idea of the complex changes that might occur in codes during the twentieth century. For example, Mexico adopted a new District Civil Code in 1928. Since then, however, various areas traditionally thought to be within the ambit of civil or commercial law have been splitting away, with their own legislation apart from the code, including agrarian matters and copyright.[8]

Indeed, with so much country-specific legislation, anything more than broad generalizations at this point are not possible. Even within the same country, especially federal countries, there is no guarantee of uniformity between the states. Regional variations between the Mexican states have created a number of jurisdictions where the civil code no longer follows the 1928 model: Tlaxcala, Sonora, Morelos, Tamaulipas, Zacatecas, Puebla and Guanajuato.[9]

Some general trends in civil law can be observed. Changes in society and new ideas about property have led to numerous amendments in Latin American civil codes in the twentieth century. The provisions of the Mexican district civil code have been amended over time to note certain changes in the family, the equality of the sexes, and new methods of alienating and mortgaging land.[10] These changes in the Mexican civil code can be traced to the 1928 code for the Federal District and Territories, enacted after the important changes brought about by the 1917 Constitution.[11] But almost all Latin American civil codes have seen similar amendments during the course of the twentieth century. As Karst and Rosenn summarize changes in private law during the twentieth century:

Moderate social limitations of the use of private property, protection of the obviously weaker party in certain bargaining situations, workmen's compensation for injuries without regard to fault, and an expanded protection of the rights of illegitimate children and women reflect the extensive supplementary legislation and code revisions modifying the civil codes of most Latin American nations.[12]

Likewise, the Argentine civil code has been amended to extend civil rights to women, to provide adoption, to recognize horizontal property rights, and to create liability without fault for dangerous instrumentalities.[13]

Similarly, complex development can be seen in the procedural codes of Mexico. In 1942, Mexico enacted a new Federal Code of Civil Procedure based on the work of Adolfo Maldonado, who helped draft the Guanajuato Code of Civil Procedure of 1934 and who was highly influenced by Italian civil procedure. Matching the right substantive and procedural law in Mexico appears to have its difficulties. For example, writing in 1990, Margadant noted that special federal procedures are linked to the Commercial Code of 1889, the Bankruptcy Code uses district civil procedure, and the Law of General Means of Communication uses the Federal Code of Civil Procedure. The state of district civil procedure in Mexico is even worse if one looks for uniformity. Using one of the two main competing drafts available in the early 1930s, a draft commissioned by the bar and the Superior Court of Justice of the Federal District, three lawyers worked to remove the slowness and complexity present in the 1884 code. Their product became the new Code of Civil Procedure for the district and federal territories in 1932 whose improvements included greater orality and the possibility of forced arbitration. Since 1932, the code has been amended to divide work between judges, expand the justice of peace jurisdiction, and increase orality. This code has served as a model for the states, but there are numerous exceptions giving a multiplicity of district procedural codes. Sonora (1949) and Morelos (1954) have adopted civil procedure codes based on a draft prepared in 1948; Guanajuato and Tlaxcala kept to older codifications, as did Zacatecas until it adopted a new code in 1965. This situation gave birth to professional organizations that study procedural problems in Mexico.[14]

This possible divergence in specific provisions can be seen as an indication of a more mature legal development in which changes in private law are brought about to address particular needs of individual countries.[15] Doctrinal writings continue to be the main source for interpretation of code provisions. In the first half of the twentieth century, law students, professors, practitioners, and judges used mature doctrinal sources of the private law. For example, in Mexico, with the new District Civil Code of 1928, lawyers moved away from the earlier commentaries of Aubry y Rau (French, 1839) and Laurent (Belgian, 1869) to more modern studies such as Planiol (French, *Traité élémentaire* 1899-1901, *Traité pratique* 1925-1934).[16] The period also saw the development of indigenous treatises, many with European roots but growing into distinct species in Latin America. For example, in Colombia, Arturo Valencia Zea's *Derecho civil* (1957) picked up from Vélez's treatise on civil law. In the 1930s, Miguel Moreno Jaramillo published a five-volume work on corporations.[17] Doctrinal writings by acknowledged experts interpreting areas of law continue to be a key source of law in every Latin American country today.[18]

Another possible source or interpretation is custom and judicial decisions. As a general rule in Latin American courts, cases do not create binding law of general application beyond the particular cases they decide. This view of case law has its roots in the Code Napoleon and can be traced into the nineteenth century codes of civil law drafted for Chile and Colombia, for example.[19] When a court of *casación* overturns points of law in a particular case, the decision of the higher court will be implemented by the lower courts, but in the theory of civil law jurisdictions there is debate about whether the higher court's interpretation is binding on the lower court. Generally, it is not binding on other courts or on similar issues, even in the same lower court.

Mexico presents an exception to the prohibition of law created by cases. A binding precedent that may be introduced in another proceeding may be created from case law where the Mexican Supreme Court gives five final decisions on a question of law. The five decisions must all be by a vote of seven or more of the eleven justices and there must not be any decision to the contrary during the course of the five decisions. If these conditions are met, the

Supreme Court has established binding precedent (*jurisprudencia*).[20] Even setting the possibility of binding precedent in Mexico aside, important cases in other countries, especially of the supreme or constitutional courts, can settle, for practical purposes, certain questions of law, even to the point of declaring legislation unconstitutional.[21] Court precedents in Argentina also have some binding effect.[22] Alejandro Garro, citing the work of others, indicates that Colombia has had a statute since 1896 that "encourages judges to apply the doctrine affirmed by three uniform decisions of the Supreme Court." The statute seems never to have been put into use.[23]

Despite the slight importance of case law in establishing rules of law, decisions or opinions of the supreme courts of Latin American countries are routinely printed in judicial gazettes of the particular court.[24] Argentina has several case reporters, and in Mexico, where case law may rise to the level of establishing law, cases are reported in the *Seminario judicial de la federación*, which has been in print since 1917.[25] Likewise, civil lawyers today in Colombia still speak with pride of the Colombian "Corte de Oro," the civil division of Colombia's highest court in the 1930s, for both its rigorously intelligent approaches and socially and economically progressive decisions.[26]

Custom continues to be a disfavored source of law and is usually permitted only when the statutory text allows its introduction. Merchants have always relied on customary practices and modern Latin American commercial codes may recognize this practice. Thus the following provision of the Chilean commercial code is typical for this exception: "Commercial customs are supplementary in cases where the law is silent, when the facts that make it up are uniform, public, generally executed within the Republic or in a determined locality and have taken place over a long period of time, a fact that will be appreciated by the commercial courts."[27] In addition to commercial law, other areas of law may also invoke custom when needed, including industry practices, land reform, and mining law.[28]

An important source of new law is international conventions and agreements. In 1928, the sixth Pan-American Congress of Law approved a draft code of private international law by Antonio Sánchez de Bustamante y Sirven that consisted of four books: international civil law, international commercial law, international criminal law, and international procedural law. The Bustamante Code has been ratified by fifteen nations of Latin American; Argentina, Colombia, Mexico, Paraguay, and Uruguay have not ratified the code, and the United States has also not signed the code. In theory, the Bustamante Code was expected to work side by side with domestic legislation. Although the code has not been as influential in the ratifying countries as was hoped, it does mark a first and early example of an attempt to coordinate internationally the direction of private law.[29] Similarly, with earlier commercial cooperative agreements and the military insecurity of the region from World War II as a backdrop, nations of the Western Hemisphere founded the Organization of American States 1948.[30] Created to address concerns about national security, the organization later took up issues of mutual economic benefit and international trade. In recent decades there has been a great rush toward incorporating international conventions into domestic law, and international cooperation is viewed as an important aspect of private law today.[31]

From the mid nineteenth century, legal periodicals became important sources of legal developments and speculative thinking. These publications provided forums for lawyers, judges, and politicians to debate various aspects of legal development. These newspapers, many originating in the late nineteenth century and running into the present day, were popular in Mexico and numerous other countries in the region.[32] Regardless of the source of legal provisions, Latin American countries have official reports or bulletins in which new laws are published.

Sources of law continued much the same from the mid nineteenth century. Codes predominated as the most important source, and doctrinal works interpreting code provisions took an important second place. As the century progressed, reliance on European models and scholarship decreased but did not disappear. Indigenous developments and models drawn from a wider range of sources became particularly important after the Second World War. As they expanded, various areas of law were removed from their original place in the traditional structure of codes and established as separate codes addressing discrete areas. Concurrently, in the 1980s and 1990s, the substance of private law within these sources both expanded and changed drastically, reflecting new national and international economic and political demands.[33] In countries governed by executive or military autocracies, decrees supplanted much if not all legislation as a means of bringing new law into effect. New technology and especially computers have greatly expanded the accessibility of sources both through official and unofficial websites. Several countries have moved toward making their official bulletins available on the internet, fundamentally changing the ability to access and to search this information.[34]

Personal Status

ALTHOUGH nineteenth-century constitutions in Latin America made progress in reducing privileges in society, many advances in social and legal equality had to wait until the twentieth century. Twentieth-century constitutions expanded the ambit of protection. For example, under the Bolivian Constitution of 1967, "constitutional guarantees of individual liberties were broadly expanded, and the inviolability of individual dignity and freedom was linked with guarantees against discrimination based upon race, color, sex, language, origin, political creed, economic or social status, or 'any other reason.'"[1] Numerous other Latin American constitutions contain similar aspirations.[2] Of course, such language all too often operated only on a symbolic plane. At times, many such important constitutional provisions could be ignored in the exigencies of political strife and military rule. The characteristic lack of penetration of legal institutions and rules meant that many segments of society were, and are, not beneficiaries of such constitutional promises. Nonetheless, a general change in attitudes and in the legal protection afforded less powerful groups in society is noticeable during the period.

Many of the substantial changes in personal status can be attributed to the shifting power of the church as a political actor to shape law during the period.[3] The secularization of marriage and of public records related to birth, marriage, and death meant that secular authorities took control of these areas of law from the church. Many countries introduced divorce, beyond the previously accepted ecclesiastical separation, during the period. Likewise, new statutes improved the legal status of women and indigenous peoples. Countries began to consider the treatment of children and put significant social welfare programs into place.[4]

In most Latin American countries marriage has become a civil act performed by civil officials who keep an official record of the act in a public registry, and only this civil marriage is recognized in law. Some countries, like

Argentina and Nicaragua, permit a religious ceremony only after the civil requirements have been fulfilled, and a few, such as Guatemala and Venezuela, permit priests and ministers to perform a ceremony that takes civil effect. Other countries such as Colombia, the Dominican Republic, and Peru give the Catholic church more active involvement in marriage and its dissolution.[5]

Marriage has significant effects on property, and generally the marital property scheme in Latin America is community property (*bienes comunes, comunidad de gananciales*). This treatment often extends to property brought into the marriage during the marriage, as well as to property owned by the spouses individually before the marriage. Some countries treat the individual property of the spouses as separate property and may even treat as separate property some types of property obtained during the marriage, such as property individually received as a bequest, gift, or inheritance.[6] With this in mind, some countries require engaged couples to declare the manner in which they will hold property after the marriage, singularly or as community property (*sociedad conyugal*).[7] Other countries substantially curtail or prohibit agreements contrary to the national scheme of marital property.[8] Some Central American countries provide for separate property schemes without an agreement otherwise.[9]

Some couples who live in countries with civil marriage requirements may not be validly married. This may result from resistance to the secularization of marriage or from ignorance of the law requiring a civil ceremony. A relatively substantial body of law had to be developed to address the property rights of those not validly married for these and other causes, as well as for "concubines" and illegitimate children.[10] Mexico recognizes claims through concubinage and has developed complex rules addressing the rights of the partner and children of such unions.[11] Other countries had different ways of addressing the same problem, for example, the Guatemala Constitution of 1945 recognized the legal status of a "common law" or de facto marriage.[12] Thus, by legally recognizing a permanent relationship between two individuals as a marriage, Guatemalan law extended the body of law related to marriage to these couples.

Same sex unions are not legally recognized in Latin America, and the advancement of legal and civil rights for gays and lesbians will most likely belong to the twenty-first century. In December 2002, Buenos Aires enacted laws to extend certain civil rights to same sex couples, such as health and pension benefits. It is the first city in Latin America to do so.[13]

Marriage also determines the legitimacy of children. By the 1950s, most countries had enacted legislation to improve the claims of illegitimate children to the property of their parents. For example, in 1954, Argentine legislation expanded the rights of extramatrimonial children.[14] Likewise, most countries now have provisions for adoption, but some countries require a minimum age of the adopting parents that may be ten or even close to twenty years older than the age of majority.[15]

The availability of divorce in Latin American countries in this period reflects the region's overwhelming Catholicism and particular countries' relationship to the church. Where the church had and has a strong influence on the government, divorce with right to remarry is limited. Several countries' experiences are illustrative of this important aspect of the interaction of religion and private law. The Mexican Revolution brought substantial changes in family legislation. Divorce was introduced through a separate law of 1914 and several other individual changes, including the legal equality of husband and wife within the home, led to the sweeping changes found in the Family Relations Law of 1917 later incorporated into the District Civil Code of 1928.[16] Mexico has been seen as having a particularly permissive divorce law. For example, among the numerous grounds for divorce exists simple "mutual consent."[17]

Somewhat more conservative is the present Colombian civil code, which permits the dissolution of civil marriages, but leaves the dissolution of religious marriages in the hands of the ecclesiastical authorities. A civil decree of divorce also acts over the civil aspects of a religious marriage.[18] Some countries experimented with divorce legislation and then, with a shift of the political winds, repealed it. For example, in 1954 Argentina enacted a provision by which a divorce could be had by either party after a one-year period of judicial separation. This was but a small piece of Perón's rift with the church in 1954 and 1955. After Perón's fall, the provision was suspended.[19] Another, more recent example, also from Argentina, is the *Sejean* case of 1986, where the Supreme Court found that the civil law provision prohibiting divorce was based on a religious belief and therefore violated the constitution.[20]

Most separation and divorce laws in Latin America require either cause or mutual consent combined with a waiting period of a few years. Many countries also require a waiting period of gestation before the wife is permitted to remarry. Under some circumstances, the judge is required to have the parties seek reconciliation, especially when the divorce is sought without cause.[21] At the writing of this book, Chile does not permit divorce.[22] It provides for judicial separation with cause, but legislation permitting divorce is pending in the Chilean legislature. Some countries will recognize a recorded judgment of annulment of an ecclesiastical court as having civil effect.[23]

The legal status of women and minorities in Latin America also changed dramatically in the twentieth century. In 1950, one author could note with accuracy the "subordination of the married woman to the husband" found in Latin American law, while also observing the recent extension of "absolute divorce (formerly unknown)" and "the autonomy of the married woman."[24] The ownership and management of property, divorce, labor conditions, access to education, and suffrage were issues commonly affecting women. In several countries, the legal and economic autonomy of women and the well-being of children was advanced by nascent socialist and feminist organizations.[25] Activities by such groups led, for example, to the improved legal status of women under the Argentine Civil Code of 1926.[26] In early-twentieth-century Peru, women workers were protected under new labor laws and universities granted admission to women.[27]

Gains in political status usually accompanied other gains in economic and legal status. Women won the right to vote in Argentina in 1947 and in Chile in 1949.[28] In Mexico, women were enfranchised in the 1950s and given juridical equality with men in 1969 and again in 1974.[29] In 1955, the Venezuelan commercial code was amended to eliminate the need for a married woman to have her husband's consent to exercise commerce.[30] Most Latin American countries have removed legal disabilities formerly imposed on married women, and throughout the second half of the twentieth century, women generally have gained substantial legal rights to function as autonomous persons in the civil law.[31] As with divorce law, the question of legalizing abortion reflects the political power of the church within the government. In 1991, about one-third of Latin American countries permitted abortions under certain circumstances.[32] International law and conventions have guided countries to recognize political, economic, and social rights for women in recent decades.[33]

In the early republic period, Indians and free blacks were quickly oppressed into systems of debt peonage. In several countries where legislation prohibited debt peonage, authorities used antivagrancy laws to require Indians and others to demonstrate they had worked a minimum number of days per year. For example, after the abolition of debt peonage in Guatemala in 1934, antivagrancy laws required workers to carry documents showing they had worked between 100 and 150 days. El Salvador had a similar act dating from the 1880s.[34]

Protection for workers under labor laws was unknown in the early republic period, other than the specific protections offered in mining law. From the late 1920s, however, Venezuela enacted more general labor laws, which were expanded greatly in the mid-1930s. Broadly based labor laws, touching all aspects of work, contracting, safety, and rights were then brought into force in the mid-1940s in Venezuela.[35]

Despite such constitutional and legislative change concerning the status of workers in the early part of the twentieth century, little had changed since the days of the Spanish colonies; debt or lack of opportunity elsewhere tied agricultural workers to the land. As Tannenbaum observed in 1963:

They cannot leave because they may be in debt, or because there is no place to go, for this is home and every other place is foreign. And here too their fathers and grand-fathers were born and buried. If the place changes hands, they change with it. In 1948 the leading newspaper of La Paz, Bolivia, carried an advertisement offering for sale on the main highway a half hour from the capital of the country a hacienda with five hundred acres of land, fifty sheep, much water and *twenty peons*. And similar advertisements have appeared even more recently in Ecuador and Chile.[36]

It is unlikely that one would find such advertisements in the later half of the twentieth century anywhere in Latin America and yet such poor agricultural workers continue to live similar existences to those of their ancestors. In recent decades, the strictures of debt and poverty no longer hold agricultural workers to rural areas. Many have left rural poverty for the cities in search of better wages and better personal security. Many have found only urban poverty.

Racism and racial discrimination continue in Latin America.[37] Despite the constitutional prohibitions against racism noted above, most Latin American countries do not have specific legislation on the topic or agencies to carry out enforcement.[38]

Indigenous tribunals continue to settle disputes in civil and criminal law matters between members of their communities. These tribunals often attempt and succeed in reaching compromises between the parties based on informal dispute resolution methods. Litigants frequently have a choice of law and choice of forum, with non-Indian institutions and legal rules as alternate means of seeking relief. Rules governing property ownership and inheritance rights are frequently different from those of the state or federal government covering the areas where these populations live.[39] Indians continue to be subject to special, often well-intentioned legislation to protect their interests, autonomy, and living environment. The applicability and effectiveness of such special rules often tend to fall short.[40]

Land and Inheritance

TWENTIETH-CENTURY Latin American constitutions generally assert the constitutional protection of private property. Several of these constitutions have qualified the protection of private property by stating that, as in the Bolivian Constitution of 1967, its use must be consistent with the national interest, or that, as in the Venezuelan Constitution of 1961, property has a social function.[1] For some countries, this social theory of property dates to the late nineteenth century. For example, the Colombian Constitution of 1886 declared, "Property is a social function that implies obligations."[2] Many of these constitutional provisions reflect the Catholic church's recognition of private property as a means of combating Marxist attacks on property. The papal encyclical *Rerum Novarum* of 1891 affirmed the right to private property, but noted that owners of property and employers had to be fair with their workers.[3] Thus the constitutional principle that property or ownership has a social function is common throughout the region.[4] This provides a notable limitation on private property; thus one may have the right to use and to enjoy property, but one may not have the right not to use it, and these provisions have been central to the land reform acts discussed in Chapter 26.

Land continued to be tied to political change and unrest in Latin America after World War II, and land reform and redistribution has been a centerpiece for guerrilla movements and the call for political democratization.[5] Revolutionary guerrilla movements might stimulate land reform directly by seizing land and political power or by instituting legislative schemes to carry out redistribution, such as the Sandinista government of Nicaragua attempted during the 1980s with lands formerly held by the Somoza family.[6] Guerrilla movements might also bring about land reform indirectly by providing sufficient pressure on governments to force them into accommodating peasant needs through more or less effective legislative schemes, such as the Venezuelan land redistribution in the 1960s.[7]

After the Mexican Revolution, legislation by Luis Cabrera in 1915 moved toward restoring lands that had been reallocated under earlier settlement regimes to communities and farmers. This required some expropriations from large estates. These goals were incorporated into Article 27 of the Mexican Constitution of 1917, and Mexico began the region's first widespread agrarian or land reform program.[8] The constitution not only took on the large landholders, but also the mining companies by removing their subsoil rights. Venustiano Carranza placated these powerful interests by letting them know he would not enforce the provisions.[9] Article 27 was softened even further under Alvaro Obregón, who through the Treaty of Bucareli with the United States agreed to not apply the provision retroactively and to provide compensation for lands taken.[10] The Mexican Revolution brought about other changes in land law as well. For example, in 1917, Mexico abolished the resale contract (a method of securing credit) and provided new laws for mortgages.[11]

Although Article 27 may prohibit foreign ownership of land in certain areas of the country, notably within a certain distance from the coast and international borders, Karst and Rosenn have observed the manner in which legal formalism is used to defeat the application of this provision. Ironically, a trust may be established with foreign beneficiaries enjoying possessory rights to the land.[12] Indeed, the use of such trusts is now consistent with Mexican constitutional provisions.[13]

In many countries, the sweeping effects and uncertainty created by land reform legislation and movements have created real concern over the actual ownership of land. Redistribution that is overly successful from a revolutionary standpoint has been a contributing factor to U.S. intervention. For example, in 1954 the U.S.-backed coup of Colonel Carlos Castillo Armas in Guatemala led to the United Fruit Company getting all of the land that had been seized and redistributed under legislation enacted by President Arbenz in 1952.[14]

Such uncertainties are often seen as a factor hindering internal economic growth and foreign direct investment. Governments of countries where land reform and rereform have swung with the political pendula of their recent history are actively searching for legislative means to provide certainty to land titles, offer fair restitution for seized lands, and improve the mechanical aspects of registration of title.

Most land in Latin America is not subject to doubts of ownership resulting from land reform. Generally, the civil code governs questions about land. Throughout the region, interests and transfers of land are often recorded in public registries, *registros públicos*, which are supported by recording systems of variable reliability and utility.[15] Like deeds, real property mortgages are

THE TWENTIETH CENTURY

considered public instruments requiring proper recording to be fully effective.[16] Security of title is promoted by the general requirement that title documents must be recorded to be effective.[17] The Dominican Republic uses the Torrens land registration system.[18] Such advances in the legal recognition of property rights have been seen as essential steps to improve economic stability and growth in the region.[19]

New methods for conducting commercial transactions dealing with land have evolved during the period, and countries have created new legal institutions and methods of holding and using land. The creation of *fideicomisos* (trusts), usually through state-regulated institutions serving as trustee, has enabled complicated projects to succeed by memorializing and clarifying the various duties of owners, builders, financiers, bankers, and other parties.[20] The interposition of an institutional trustee reduces possible corruption or dishonesty in the transaction. Complex methods of creating security interests and mortgages in property have aided in the circulation of capital and the marketability of land.[21]

Twentieth-century codes continue the independence notions of promoting the alienability of property. Thus, in the mid twentieth century, both Argentina and Mexico had provisions limiting the duration of leasehold interests in land to a number of years — in the case of Mexico, from ten to twenty years depending on the use of the land. Other Latin American codes did not contain these limitations. Likewise, the possibility of creating future interests in land is substantially limited, sometimes by setting out a maximum number of years, such as thirty, that alienation might be suspended.[22] Some countries hinder alienation by prohibiting certain classes of purchasers. Bolivia, Mexico, and Nicaragua continue to have prohibitions of foreign ownership of land within certain distances from international borders or coastal areas.[23]

New interests in land have been legislatively recognized in this period. For example, Mexico legislated for condominiums (*propiedad por piso*) in 1954 and then again in 1974, and other countries such as Honduras, Panama, and Paraguay have similar provisions.[24] A new state civil code in Mexico, of Quintana Roo, influenced by the German civil code, also has provisions for time sharing (*tiempo compartido*).[25] These forms of ownership have become more common in Latin America in recent decades.

Inheritance rights have generally followed European models. Intestate succession usually divides property equally among living descendants with right of representation for those who predeceased the property owner. A share is frequently provided for the surviving spouse, or in the case of some countries like Costa Rica and Mexico, the surviving partner, although not married to the decedent.[26]

Where the property owner leaves a will, the freedom of testation is usually limited by statutory requirements that certain portions be devised to family members.[27] For example, in Argentina four-fifths of the estate is to go to the children per capita, with the surviving spouse taking a child's share. If there are no children or ascendants living, the surviving spouse takes one-half of the estate, the other half being distributed to more distant family members. The other one-fifth is distributed according to the wishes of the testator. The provisions of Bolivia and Paraguay are similar.[28] In Chile, one-half is for the descendants or ascendants of the decedent (as *legítima*), one-quarter (as *mejora*) is to a family member or members selected by the decedent, and one-quarter subject to free disposition. This pattern is similar to that in Colombia.[29] Other South American countries have variations on these patterns, which depend on the nature and number of surviving family members.[30]

Although most countries continue to have forced shares for family members (*legítima*), even by 1950 some countries had moved toward testamentary freedom, as can be seen in Mexico, Panama, and Nicaragua.[31] Indeed, greater testamentary freedom is generally found in Mexico and Central American countries, where the testator may devise all his property subject to some restrictions that are less onerous than the full *legítima/mejora* regime. One common restriction is that the surviving spouse must be adequately supported, and some countries, such as Costa Rica, cap gifts to religious organizations at a percentage of the total estate, such as 10 percent.[32]

The form of testaments is governed by the civil code, and most countries provide for various types of valid testaments, the most common being either open or closed, the latter preserving the secrecy of the content of the document until after the death of the testator while maintaining its authenticity as the genuine document. Both require the participation of a notary and a recording in the protocol. Countries may also have various other forms of valid testaments including holographic testaments, those in the handwriting of the testator, and privileged testaments, those executed under certain unusual conditions, such as military service as a soldier or sailor.[33] Bolivia has a certain class of privileged testaments for Indians.[34]

Although trusts are common vehicles for commercial transactions, they are disfavored as a method to provide for the intergenerational transfer of wealth. Testamentary trusts are forbidden in some countries, such as Bolivia and the Dominican Republic, or are severely restricted in scope and duration.[35] Countries permitting trusts usually limit their term to some fixed period of twenty to thirty years, and often limit the power to serve as a trustee or fiduciary to institutional trustees such as banks.[36] Other restrictions may also impede the flexibility of trusts in Latin America. For example, Costa Rica prohibits successive beneficiaries, and Mexico permits them, but they must be lives in being at the settlor's death.[37] Venezuela has a similar perpetuities period.[38] Panama has enacted legislation in the twentieth century incorporating many aspects of the common-law trust into to private law system, and Mexico too has adopted many common-law aspects of trust law.[39]

Commercial Law

COMMERCIAL law in Latin America in the twentieth century continued to be governed by commercial codes, many dating from the middle and late nineteenth century. In light of the rapid and recent economic changes in Latin America and the desire for greater international investment, many of the older commercial codes have been criticized as stifling economic development.[1] Response to such concerns has been swift in the past few decades. In some areas, such as business organizations and their regulation, legislation has grown so much that some express concerns that overregulation is hindering efficiency.[2] Furthermore, even the simplest forms of establishing businesses within the existing legal framework are often prohibited by the cost and delay of formalism, bureaucracy, and corruption.[3]

Various forms of modern business entities were developed in or imported into Latin American legal systems during the twentieth century, and all countries now have a well-developed panoply of possible institutions for commercial enterprises. Thus, for example, the 1930s was an active period in Mexico for legislation on business organizations, including the *sociedad mercantil,* the *sociedad de responsabilidad limitada de interés público,* and the *sociedad cooperativa.*[4] Today, most Latin American countries provide for corporations, joint stock companies, joint ventures, general partnerships, and limited partnerships. The rise of limited liability companies (L.L.C.) in other parts of the world has led several countries to provide for this form of enterprise as well.[5]

Corporate law in many countries has remained bifurcated between corporations created under the civil code and those under the commercial code, although commercial code provisions govern most for-profit corporations. Some countries, such as Colombia in the mid-1990s, have unified their corporate law under a single code.[6] Government regulatory agencies, which often serve not only to track the issuance and trading of securities but also to keep a watchful eye on other corporate activities, commonly monitor the corporations. Standards for disclosure and authentication of information of traded securities of corporations are much less stringent than U.S. or European requirements. Nonetheless, as companies seek outside financing, particularly through listing American depository receipts on a U.S. exchange, they are forced to comply with U.S. requirements. This has, in turn, given those securities a premium on the domestic market. Latin American countries are moving toward greater requirements for publicly traded companies, and Chile has been recognized as a leader in the field.[7]

In addition to business entities and securities, another area of importance, especially as it relates to the opening of markets and international trade, is the protection of copyright, patents, trademarks, and commercial names. These were the subject of new Mexican legislation in the first half of the twentieth century. Mexico enacted a new law concerning technology transfers, trademarks, and patents in 1972, which was replaced by even newer legislation on the same topics in 1982 that some view as overly bureaucratic. In 1987, a law established a fourteen-year period for the protection of inventions after earlier legislation placed it at fifteen then ten years. Again in 1987, a law permitted private complaints to protect inventions. Copyright law falls under mercantile law and is federal in Mexico, which adhered to the American Convention on Literary and Artistic Property in 1963 and the Bern Convention in 1968. In 1982 the protection period for authors was extended from twenty to fifty years.[8] Many countries have substantially redrafted this area of law in recent years, and even countries with developed law in these areas have moved toward improving their intellectual property provisions since 1990 to help attract foreign investment and to become more active participants in regional and world trade. For example, Mexico's most recent legislation in this area dates from the 1990s. Many countries have looked toward international conventions in reworking these areas of the law.

In addition to business enterprises and intellectual property, Latin American countries typically have a wide range of developed legislation in commercial areas. Debts are created, secured, and collected; commercial paper and negotiable instruments are exchanged; companies are created, reorganized, dissolved, and liquidated.[9] All of these items have particular legislation in each country.

Another structure important to civil law that became well-entrenched during the twentieth century was the notarial system of publicly recorded documents. Specially trained lawyers, notaries prepare and either store or abstract original documents and produce copies for individuals. Latin American countries today usually have a series of public notaries and public registries or protocols dedicated to particular types of documents. Common registries may include those for real property, civil status (births, marriages, deaths), and commerce. Some countries have other specialized registries, for example, those for mining, industry, testaments, security interests, or foreign investment. Almost all important civil and commercial transactions or property rights require notarial drafting and recording to have full legal effect.[10]

One important development in early-twentieth-century Latin American law that one might not expect was the importation of the Anglo-American trust. In 1950, one of New York University's first comparative law professors looking at Latin American law wrote that the

practical utility of the trust in solving unlimited family and business problems of every kind has awakened the universal admiration of jurists, and an attempt has been made to transplant the express trust to Latin America. The chief propagandist for this movement has been Dr. Ricardo J. Alfaro, author of the Panama Law of 1925 (amended in 1941), and his work facilitated the introduction of the trust into Mexico in 1926, extended by the present Law of 1932, and the banking laws. The banking laws of some other countries, adopted under the aegis of Dr. Kemmerer by authorizing banks to open trust departments have given a slight nod of recognition to the trust. The Chilean Law No. 4827 gives banks the practical equivalent of some trust powers under the name of *comisiones de confianza.*[11]

Thus, in an early attempt to transplant private law ideas from the common law and following the suggestions of the Panamanian jurist Ricardo J. Alfaro, Mexico created banks that would have trust or fiduciary powers (*bancos de fideicomiso*). This occurred in 1926 with hopes that its economy could make use of these institutions. Mexico adopted the legal device of the trust (*fideicomiso*) in legislation in 1932.[12] The range of uses of the common law trust was and continues to be much greater than the traditional civil law *fideicomiso*, which was adopted throughout Latin American in civil codes.[13] Indeed, the trust and government-regulated fiduciary company are common elements in business transactions in Latin America today. Nonetheless, Latin American trusts are not as flexible as devices in the common law world. They are typically limited to a maximum duration of twenty to thirty years and often the only trustee permitted under the laws of Latin America is an institutional trustee. Time limitations in some countries do not apply to trusts for charitable or public purposes.[14]

In addition to the aspects noted above, during the first half of the twentieth century Latin American countries enacted legislation in many of the general areas of commercial law, often with state intervention or regulation in mind. For example, in this period Mexico enacted legislation concerning interior aspects of commerce such as communications, transportation and the railroads, antitrust, agriculture, bankruptcy, and insurance.[15] In the 1970s and 1980s, Mexico's commercial legislation addressed exterior commerce, fishing, and *maquiladoras*. Industry and manufacturing groups have also grown in this period.[16] More recently, countries have enacted or revised provisions for open market economies with less state intervention in economic activity and have been working on establishing effective competition or antitrust regimes.[17]

Aware of the link between commercial law and successful commerce, some countries have sought to keep their commercial codes as current as possible. Commercial codes were subject to periodic examination and revisions during the period. For example, in Colombia a 1929 proposal by the Bogotá Cámara de Comercio to examine the commercial code for changes led, in Robert Means's view, to new steps in "autonomous legal development" because law reform responded to contemporary practice.[18] Tentatively linking the failure of this project to a lack of commercial treatises and literature in Colombia, Means notes that the next effort in the mid-1950s coincided with an important treatise of José Gabino Pinzón.[19] Another effort succeeded in the early 1970s, and a new code was enacted in 1972. Likewise the 1977 Colombian Commercial Code was the first in that country to be a product of its own country rather than principally a borrowed code from another country.[20]

Numerous other areas of commerce developed their own provisions, which were codified as separate ancillary codes to the major civil and commercial codes. During the twentieth century in Mexico, for example, as a result of their increasing complexity, the areas of mercantile companies, bankruptcy, banking, and industrial property have all left their positions in the commercial code, to become the subject of separate codes.[21] Some other areas have always been seen as separate, yet ancillary areas, of law related to commerce, such as mining and labor law. These areas have also been some of the most subject to change according to political power and philosophy. Several countries like Argentina, Bolivia, Chile, and Mexico have all had these areas substantially changed as political parties and figures move in and out of power. The case of Mexico is illustrative of this process.

The great attention paid to mining law in the colonial and independence periods continued in the twentieth century. In Mexico, the Mining Law of 1904, which linked mining rights with surface ownership, did away with the earlier requirement of active exploitation to assert a mining claim.[22] In the same period, the Mexican Petroleum Law followed the liberal regime of the mining legislation.[23] The Mexican Revolution brought different views on the ownership of mines and oil. The Mexican Constitution of 1917, in its famous Article 27, removed the mining companies' rights to the subsoil, but the provision was not immediately put into effect.[24] In the early 1920s, oil companies in the United States sought assurances that the provisions would not be applied retroactively, and after a heated legal and diplomatic battle, the Mexican Supreme Court determined that where the company had engaged in "positive acts" to exploit the resources, the provision would not apply. In 1923, an agreement was reached that in return for Mexico's upholding the "positive acts" doctrine, the United States would reestablish diplomatic relations. By 1925, relations were again strained when President Calles enacted new provisions requiring the confirmation of oil companies' claims and a fifty-year limit on their exploitation. The Mexican Supreme Court again reached a decision both sides could abide by: confirmations were necessary, the doctrine of "positive acts" continued to apply, and there would be no fifty-year limit on the interest held by the companies.[25] Oil drilling and production continued to be at the center of Mexican and U.S. relations. Nonetheless, in 1937, Cárdenas expropriated the property of the seventeen largest oil companies and created PEMEX to run the industry for the state in 1938.[26] With World War II, relations between Mexico and the United States were resumed in 1942.[27]

Similar swings in policy affected the general mining law. In 1926 Mexican law moved from permanent grants to temporary licenses for mining, and the 1930 Mining Law followed this method. Article 27 of the constitution was further implemented through the Mineral Resources law of 1961, and in 1962 Mexico decided to grant mineral rights to companies that had majority Mexican ownership. New mining laws were enacted in 1966 and 1975.[28]

Since the creation of PEMEX, petroleum production was regulated by a series of state agencies during the 1930s and 1940s in Mexico. In implementing Article 27 of the constitution in 1940, Mexico moved to favor Mexican nationals in the related areas of refineries and pipelines. In 1960, Mexico decided to end granting further licenses for oil and all hydrocarbons, using them exclusively for the state. The petrochemical industry was subjected to extensive regulation in 1971 and PEMEX also got a new set of laws that year.[29] New major legislation dates from the 1990s.[30]

Numerous other countries sorted out their mining laws in the first half of the twentieth century, and as oil and gas became more important, codes were amended to deal with these resources. In 1914, Argentine Joaquín V. González, appointed the first chair of mining legislation in 1894, made various proposals for changes to the 1887 code, which with modification were enacted in 1917.[31] In 1935, Argentina enacted new laws for oil and hydrocarbons, which became part of the National Mining Code.[32] Argentina entertained often short-lived experiments to nationalize these resources. For example, in 1949, Argentina under Perón made minerals and energy sources national property. This action was annulled on Perón's fall in 1955.[33] Venezuela's modern regime of mining law with a focus on oil and coal was initiated with its Mining Law of 1920, which formed the basis for its modern legislation.[34]

Another area that quickly broke away from the provisions of the general codes during the twentieth century was labor law. As expected, it is also subject to great fluctuations according to political viewpoints. After the Mexican Revolution, numerous laws affecting labor were enacted, including those touching on minimum salaries, workers' debts, and working hours. Margadant points to the legislation enacted on the state level (Jalisco, Veracruz, and Yucatán) of the socialist Salvador Alvarado whose five codes, called the "five sisters" (*cinco hermanas*) addressed farm land, finances, property registration, municipal government, and labor. With the establishment of federal panels of conciliation and arbitration in the late 1920s and under Article 123 of the constitution, Mexico enacted a Federal Labor Law in 1931. Various reforms have ensured the right to strike and the protection of constitutional rights of public service workers and state employees. A new Federal Labor Law was enacted in 1970 with procedural reforms added in 1980. Workers in banks and universities are governed by separate regimes.[35]

Since the 1930s most countries have created some sort of labor code or provisions. These deal with working conditions, wages, leaves, vacations, collective bargaining, strikes, and often include protection for women and children who work. Perhaps because the provisions themselves are often quite progressive, employers often side-step and work around the provisions to frustrate their application. Enforcement of such provisions is also a regionwide problem.[36]

Another area touching on commercial activity and conduct is tort law, which has substantially developed outside the framework of extended carefully drafted code provisions. Latin American codes contain few provisions related to civil liability outside contracts and other obligations. Indeed, tort recovery in Latin American countries is usually pegged to a very general provision stating that someone who acts or omits to act, negligently or with fault, and causes harm to another has the obligation to repair the harm suffered.[37] In some countries the collection of civil damages for conduct was tied directly to criminal guilt until the second half of the twentieth century.[38] Some civil codes, no doubt in response to an increasingly industrial and mechanized society, created areas of liability for the use of dangerous items. For example, in 1950 the applicable provision of the Mexican civil code read:

Whenever a person makes use of machinery, instruments, apparatus, or materials which are *per se* dangerous, by reason of their velocity, their inflammable or explosive nature, by the electric current they transmit or for other analogous causes, he is liable for the damage that he may cause, even though he does not act unlawfully, unless he proves that the damage was due to the fault or inexcusable negligence of the victim.[39]

Likewise, provisions specifically address areas of nuisance by enumerating offending items or conduct.[40] Furthermore, some types of tortlike liability may arise from illicit acts or contractual obligations.[41] The illicit act provision for

Mexico reads: "He who acting illegally or against good customs causes damage to another, is obliged to repair it, unless he proves that the damage occurred in consequence of the fault or inexplicable negligence of the victim."[42]

With such brief statements, systems of civil liability for negligence in Latin American countries are the product of a few broadly worded individual code provisions, along the European model. Thus, tracing the development of tort law, particularly with the general lack of substantive reported decisions of cases, has not yet been undertaken. Other aspects may have lessened the need for a developed system of tort law in Latin America. For example, responsible parties may automatically assume the payment of certain damages and expenses, and recovery may be limited to the analogous provisions of the labor codes for injuries.[43] Some countries, such as Mexico, with few exceptions limit damages to actual damages without compensation for pain and suffering, or limit punitive-type damages to a particular fraction of actual damages. Nonetheless, the past few decades have witnessed the recognition of moral damages, *daños morales*, or damages to compensate feelings, honor, reputation, and the like. These damages have been used to increase recovery beyond actual damages.[44] By code provision, strict liability may be imposed for a defendant's use of dangerous instrumentalities, lessening the plaintiff's burden.[45] Under such a collection of provisions leading to liability for negligence, the contributory negligence of the plaintiff often serves as a complete bar to recovery, as it does in Mexico.[46] Certain aspects of vicarious responsibility, *respondeat superior*, and joint liability, are recognized, but not, of course, under these common law terms.[47]

As a result, in many Latin American countries the Anglo-American notion of a separate area of law called "torts" simply does not exists. "From a theoretical perspective, Mexico, unlike the United States, has not constructed a legal doctrine to explain the functions, goals and justifications of tort law, or to describe the evolutions of tort concepts and remedies mainly because of socioeconomic reasons."[48] Nonetheless, there is a growing body of law under the general topic of extracontractual liability, *obligaciones extracontractuales*, applied when a defendant has created a risk that harms the plaintiff.[49] Furthermore, Vargas makes the interesting observation that a case law of Mexican torts principles may be under development in U.S. courts where injured parties seek redress for actions arising in Mexico under Mexican law.[50]

Contractual obligations continue to be dictated by the code provisions and categories.[51] The area of law in Latin America is seldom unified, but rather split between treatment in the civil code and commercial code, depending on the nature of the contract. Thus a commercial contract will be governed by the commercial code, and contract for the purchase of residential real property will be governed by the civil code. Even where code provisions proved to be inflexible in light of economic conditions, lawyers skillfully crafted provisions to adapt to the situation presented. For example, in light of rampant inflation and, at times, hyperinflation, loans and financing continued to be possible through clever contractual provisions, escalator clauses, and foreign currency clauses to adjust for rapidly declining currency values. Likewise, various methods have been used to structure transactions to avoid prohibitions on usury.[52]

Although the idea of unifying civil and mercantile obligations under one system had much appeal in the region, since the 1920s, in Mexico, it was realized that coordinating the state-level civil codes with the federal commercial code was not feasible.[53] Greater coordination is possible where federalism does not create such a large divide between the two areas of law. Furthermore, recodifying many areas now dealt with apart from the commercial code has remained an elusive goal.[54]

Emiliano Zapata.

Land Reform

INDEPENDENCE did little to change the daily existence of the agricultural laborer, and working on the estate of a royal landholder in the colonial period was much like working on the estates of a *latifundista*. The social tension of such great inequalities in wealth and of widespread rural poverty continues to plague Latin America today. Countries of the region historically and presently exhibit very unequal distribution of land, with a wealthy, small percentage of the population owning most of the land.[1] Attempting to ease the tensions resulting from this inequality, some governments have undertaken land, or agrarian, reform. Where revolutions have succeeded, land reform has often followed as a centerpiece of the promised changes. Nonetheless, land reform has been used facilely for the purely political ends of granting boons to friends, garnering votes, quelling peasant unrest, instilling counterinsurgency measures, and establishing stability for a favorable (foreign) investment climate.[2] Furthermore, the term *land reform* does not have one meaning: "In Latin America the expression 'land reform' has sometimes been used to describe such diverse policies as the colonization of desert and jungle lands, the regulation of labor contracts or the introduction of new seeds and fertilizers."[3]

The Mexican experience with land reform was the first and served as a model for the efforts of other countries that were to follow.[4] Although initially not strictly land reform as we think of it today, Mexico, like most of the newly independent republics, had laws governing the occupation or colonization of unoccupied or waste lands. Thus, in the mid-1850s various laws attempted to deal with the settling of uncultivated lands, leading to a slightly more lasting law of 1857, and an additional law giving the Mexican government the power to establish the boundaries of such lands. The distribution of large estates became a revolutionary platform as early as 1849, when a group sought under the *Plan de Sierra Gorda* to transform *haciendas* into towns. There were similar early land-based uprisings of the rural poor in Yucatán, San Luis Potosí, and

Guerrero, but these uprisings only prefigured the Mexican Revolution that was to take hold in 1910. Before then, legislation focused on unoccupied land. In 1863, the Law on the Occupation and Alienation of Uncultivated Lands gave the owner twenty-five-hundred hectares, dividing the balance among those who worked it.[5] In the mid-1860s, Maximilian also tried his hand at redistributing land: he hoped to transfer ownership to occupants in a manner that would favor the poor, the married, and those with families, and he attempted to create ways to continue communal landholding.[6]

In the 1870s and 1880s, the Porfirio Díaz regime turned to settlement laws that provided that boundary companies should survey the land to determine where clear title was lacking, often including, again, Indian lands and communal lands. Uncultivated lands were defined by statute during the period. These lands would then be opened up to settlement in maximum plats of twenty-five-hundred hectares and the companies would receive a third of the applicable land as compensation. This again only served to increase the large landed estates because there was a lack of settlers, and in 1894, Mexico confirmed the rights of the companies, leaving about twenty-four large landowners to divide the 12 million hectares of compensation.[7] These survey and settlement laws were often the pretext for ousting the rural poor and indigenous communities who were then excluded permanently because they lacked documentation establishing their claims.

By 1910, more than half the rural population of Mexico lived and worked on these large estates.[8] Although historians differ about the relative importance of factors leading to the Mexican Revolution, the control of these lands and their usurpation under Díaz was one of the main problems igniting the period of unrest.[9] Emiliano Zapata, who led the revolution in the south of Mexico, made the restoration of the lands seized under Díaz the political core of his action. His *Plan de Ayala* of 1911 demanded that "the lands, woods, and water that the landlords, *científicos,* or bosses have usurped will be immediately restored to the villages or citizens who hold the corresponding titles to them. The usurpers who believe they have a right to those properties may present their claims to a special court that will be established on the triumph of the Revolution."[10]

Even with Díaz's removal from power and a new president in office, the reforms were not brought about quickly or fully enough for Zapata, and during the first half of the 1910s, Mexico was caught up in regional and civil wars with Zapata in the south and Pancho Villa in the north.[11] By 1916, Venustiano Carranza had consolidated enough power to call a constitutional convention, and he chose to ensure that dissenting voices such as Zapata and Pancho Villa were not represented.[12] Although Carranza did not go far enough in the eyes of Zapata, the Constitution of 1917 directly addressed land reform following Carranza's Agrarian Law of 1915.[13] Article 27 of the Constitution of 1917 required the breaking up of large estates and substituting a communal system of ownership, the *ejido,* with rights to participation in land spread over the population working it.[14] The Constitution of 1917 permitted contracts and concessions related to land disputes to be examined back to the beginning Díaz's regime, 1876, recognizing the inequity of these distributions.[15] It also made provisions for communities or owners who could not meet the strict burdens of proof to establish legal claim to land seized during the Díaz regime.[16]

Instead of launching into widespread distributions under the new constitution, Carranza and the presidents immediately following him, who were either owners of large estates or supported by such owners, were slow to parcel out land.[17] Zapata continued his criticism until his assassination in 1919. When lands were distributed, they were given to defuse politically dangerous situations or to reward political friends. Lands were usually given in communal ownership, with the beneficial effect of isolating any particular peasant landholder from undue pressure to sell. At the same time, this method of ownership limited ability to sell, inherit, rent, mortgage, or lease the property concerned. A boom in distributions under the presidency of Lázaro Cárdenas, 1934–1940, with more than 49 million acres distributed during the period, meant that by the end of his presidency about a third of the Mexican population had directly benefited from land reform. Even Cárdenas used the powers of land reform for political purposes, but the extent of the distributions meant that the overwhelming control of the large estates in rural Mexico had been abated. In the 1940s, a shift toward private, individual grants away from communal grants occurred during the presidency of Ávila Camacho who distributed more than 12 million acres.[18] Land reform slowed to a standstill during World War II until the late 1950s, as land reform was cooled to ensure support of the landowners during the war.[19] From 1958 to 1964, however, President López Mateos initiated distributions once again, allocating around 30 million acres during his presidency.[20] During the 1960s the government distributed more land than had been given out by Cárdenas during the 1930s, but only about 10 percent of it was arable.[21] Even by the 1970s, however, the economics of the *ejido* system were being questioned.[22]

The government's policy toward land reform changed drastically under the presidency of Carlos Salinas de Gortari. Assessing land reform in light of its comparative low production and economic inefficiency rather than its social and political successes, Salinas stated, "In the past, land distribution was a path of justice, today it is unproductive and impoverishing."[23] A radical change in policy followed. It was a course eased by changes in national demographics. By the 1990s, many rural workers had left for the cities.

Salinas focused on converting the communally held *ejido* lands into lands held in individual private ownership.[24] Article 27 was rewritten in 1992 to end the constitutional requirement of redistribution, ensure that improved lands would not be subject to expropriation, and create agrarian tribunals appointed by the president to settle land reform disputes. It also permitted holders of *ejido* lands to rent, sharecrop, or mortgage their lands and to sell them with approval of the *ejido* assembly. The new language also permitted ownership rights in *ejido* lands without personal work on the land. Other changes to Article 27 continued to enforce maximum landholding amounts and allowed holders of *ejido* lands to enter into joint ventures with others in the use of the property.[25] On the eve of these changes, "about half the farmland in Mexico is occupied by 23,000 *ejidos*. Most are 'parceled *ejidos*,' that is, they are divided into individual family-farmed plots, often with some land, usually forest or pasture, held in common."[26] The ability to pledge and alienate these lands was a significant change. Nonetheless, scholars have pointed out that on the practical level, it was unlikely that many holders of *ejido* lands would be able to sell. Impediments to alienation included poor legal descriptions of the *ejido* tracts, the poor quality of the land itself, a disincentive for holders to sell, and a market not packed with potential purchasers.[27]

Salinas's rejection of the underpinnings of the Mexican Revolution was, perhaps, politically a poor move. It certainly provided fuel to the fire of a nascent antigovernment military movement in the south. The leader of the Zapatista Army of National Liberation (Ejército Zapatista de Liberación Nacional) stated:

The government really screwed us, now that they destroyed Article 27, for which Zapata and his Revolution fought. Salinas de Gortari arrived on the scene with his lackeys, and his groups, and in a flash they destroyed it. We and our families have been sold down the river, or you could say that they stole our pants and sold them. What can we do? We did everything legal that we could so far as elections and organizations were concerned, and to no avail.[28]

Following Salinas, President Zedillo did little to further land reform in Mexico.[29] The party of Mexico's most recent president, Vicente Fox (2000), the National Action Party, has the abolition of land reform as a founding plank of its platform. Despite its uneven successes and recent end, Mexican land reform has served as a model throughout Latin America.[30]

Most other Latin American countries had laws from the early republic period addressing the settlement of unoccupied lands. Some even had early laws addressing some forms of land redistribution. For example, early attempts at land redistribution in 1830 and 1864 failed in Venezuela, and a worker uprising in 1859 led to the short-lived *Guerra Federal*, but little progress was made on the legislative front for almost a century in Venezuela. The Venezuelan government enacted agrarian laws in 1945, 1948, and 1949, but brought about no significant change.[31]

Most Latin American countries enacted land reform statutes when co-operating with John F. Kennedy's Alliance for Progress. In 1961, in response to the Cuban Revolution and the Cold War, the alliance encouraged the signatories to undertake meaningful land reform.[32] The Charter of Punta del Este creating the alliance led to land reform provisions in nineteen Latin American and Caribbean countries.[33]

This initiative has been seen as underestimating the power of those interests already possessing land as well as not fully taking into account the way landholding is tied to almost all aspects of civil, social, and religious life.[34] Nonetheless, with U.S. support dependent on a showing of land reform, countries moved ahead. Some countries, like Colombia, Venezuela, or Paraguay made only "minimal" reforms. The Dominican Republic, Ecuador, and Honduras made more heartfelt efforts; and Chile and Peru experienced true change in the process of land reform.[35] Indeed, it appears that only Argentina, which has a historical tradition of mid-sized farms; Paraguay; and Uruguay have never undertaken significant land reform programs.[36]

From the 1960s to the present, land reform legislation in most of the countries has changed over time. Different institutions, legal methods, and instruments have been put to use at different times.[37] Questions concerning the necessity and adequacy of compensation to landholders abound.[38] Land reform might work region-by-region, as in the Bolivian legislation of the 1950s, or as in Ecuador during the 1960s and 1970s.[39] Another method is to begin with the largest estates and subject the next smaller sized estates to reform provisions on a stepped scale, as in Nicaragua, El Salvador, and Guatemala.[40] Where land subject to reform was based on the size or underutilization of the parcels, owners quickly moved to divide parcels among family members or to put land under production to avoid expropriation.[41]

As a general rule, lands granted into communal or cooperative ownership, such as the *ejido,* could not be sold, rented or mortgaged, but those holding such property have exercised such rights over the property in practice.[42] Additionally, inheritance rights have been asserted and informally recognized on *ejido* parcels.[43] Some countries have created special banks, such as Mexico's *Banrural,* to extend credit against *ejido* parcels.[44]

In recent decades reform efforts have shifted toward privatization of communally held agricultural lands distributed through land reform. These changes have been justified on the grounds that they reward the work of the individual, increase the individual's ability to manage the resource, maximize the family's ability to share in the work and benefit of the work, and pass the improved land on to family members. One trend in the past few decades has been to change the nature of ownership from communally or cooperatively held lands to individual private ownership. This has been undertaken in Bolivia, Chile, the Dominican Republic, Mexico, and Peru.[45] Mexico, Peru, Honduras, and the Dominican Republic have also put forth official policies of encouraging an open land market.[46] Sandinistas in Nicaragua moved to private ownership by rural workers, reasoning that they would protect their interests more effectively against the *contras* if they owned the land individually.[47] In the mid-1980s, El Salvador moved toward individual ownership in land grants for similar reasons.[48] Such shifts to privatize completely communal lands have been resisted in Cuba where communally held production cooperatives continue.[49] Even Castro's government, though, initially increased private landholding and has recently shifted from state-owned farms to cooperative forms of farming.[50]

As the discussion of Mexican land reform above has shown, the process of land distribution has a deeply political content, and there may be wide variation between the written legislation and the actual undertakings by any individual government over time. As would be expected, socialist and populist leaders have historically put land reform near the top of their agendas; significant land reformers include Castro in Cuba and the Sandinistas in Nicaragua.[51] For example, in Chile, "the Allende government, from 1970 to 1973, used the same basic legal framework that had been established under the Frei government, but it greatly accelerated the pace of expropriation and reform."[52] After the 1973 coup in Chile, only a little more than half the lands distributed remained in the possession of those receiving the lands either cooperatively or individually.[53] Pinochet sought to place land in Chile into the free-market.[54] The Sandinistas started with the lands formerly held by the Somozas, about one-fifth of Nicaragua's farmland, as the pool from which to begin distributions.[55] "It should be noted that populism does not need to include land reform; it surely did not under Perón in Argentina and under Vargas in Brazil after 1945."[56] Likewise in some countries, the political aspects of land reform and its connection to leftist thought can make it a prohibited topic. In Guatemala, "in the 1960s and 1970s, it was considered subversive to even speak of land reform."[57] Other on-again, off-again patterns of land reform depending on the political climate occurred in Bolivia during its revolution in the 1950s, Venezuela,[58] Guatemala,[59] Chile,[60] and El Salvador.[61] Most recently, President Hugo Chávez of Venezuela has promised substantial land reform.

Where land reform stemmed from political revolution, the extent of expropriated land was the greatest. For example, in Bolivia and Cuba, about four-fifths of agricultural lands were expropriated. At the height of land reform efforts in Mexico, Chile, Peru, and Nicaragua, about one-half the land was expropriated. Countries in which governments expropriated about one-quarter or less of the land include Colombia, Costa Rica, the Dominican Republic, Ecuador, El Salvador, Honduras, Panama, Venezuela, and Uruguay.[62]

Opposition to land reform need not attack the basic legislation. Legal barriers can be thrown up in side areas that effectively halt distribution. For example, procedures can be slow or lack specific criteria for a taking. Mandating cash payment for expropriated land can slow redistribution through fiscal constraints. Those selecting lands may pass over the most productive and better lands. The legal machinery for distribution may be extremely complex, and funding for the agencies charged with redistribution may be cut.[63] Where distributed land is of very poor quality, those granted it will abandon it. For example, by 1985 in Honduras, one-fifth of those granted land had left it.[64] Staff members of land reform agencies who work too hard can be transferred, and agencies can be saddled with charges of improperly using funds.[65] Merely making land reform dependent on a worker's filing a claim may be sufficient to reduce greatly the amount of land distributed.[66] Land reform centered on converting tenancy contracts into ownership rights for occupants have also backfired as landowners in Argentina, Colombia, and Peru summarily evicted rural workers from land before such legislation took effect.[67] Funding, of course, is also crucial to the success of a program. Colombia's program of land reform has been stifled by lack of funds.[68] Government revenues from oil supported Venezuela's system.[69] Chile's land reforms were held up due to a constitutional provision, later amended, that required payment in cash.[70] Indeed, concerning land reform, Karst and Rosenn caution, "but it must be remembered that these laws are approved with the tacit agreement that they will not be vigorously enforced."[71] When they are enforced, owners can attack the decisions in court.[72]

Adequate legal institutions are also needed to make land reform programs successful. Land reform is usually carried out by an administrative agency, usually termed an institute.[73] In addition to an overarching authority to conduct the process, other needed legal institutions include recording or registration systems, a rapid and reliable method of issuing certificates or confirmations of landholding, simple and intelligible administrative steps for obtaining and recording documents, and inexpensive filing fees.[74]

Despite such efforts, land reform is easily foiled. For example, certain areas of Mexico have been plagued with slow, overly burdensome bureaucratic procedures, with checks and reviews on both the state and federal level.[75] In Mexico, "according to one study, land claims involved some twenty-two different government groups and public agencies and a twenty-seven-step process requiring almost two years of bureaucratic effort, *if the claim is unop-*

posed."[76] In Bolivia, the process included twenty-nine steps with three or four years for the simplest cases and up to ten years for disputed cases.[77] Even when lands were allocated, governments might be slow to issue final certificates of title; for example, in Mexico where *ejido* holders might under certain circumstances elect to divide the land into individual parcels, as many as 90 percent of the individual parcel recipients never received official title to the parcel.[78] Likewise, the Sandinista government, perhaps thinking itself impervious to democratic ouster, left an administrative nightmare for the Chamorro government, which had to establish special commissions to address the problem of "the fact that 70 percent of redistributed land was neither retitled nor reregistered to reflect new ownership."[79] Delays in granting certificates may not be purely a matter of institutional inefficiency, and Karst and Clement have persuasively argued that "insecurity of land tenure performs an important political function" by maintaining the party and national loyalty of those yet to have their claims certified beyond question.[80]

Vague statutory language defining different types of land has led to administrative inconsistency and opportunities for legal challenges.[81] Because of the specialized nature of these claims, legislation may create special agrarian courts for disputes under land reform.[82] Some countries, such as Chile and Bolivia, have at times, established special agrarian courts.[83] Land financing mechanisms, mortgages, and institutions that issue them are needed to permit the small and middle-sized landowner to participate in a more fluid land market.[84] It appears that there is great room for improvement in these areas.

In response to the many intentional and unintentional roadblocks along the way to making an effective claim under land reform provisions, land invasion and squatting have become methods of establishing de facto possession of land, which, according to the land reform legislation of the particular country, may ripen into a legally recognized claim.[85] Such actions, of course, may lead to the use of force by others claiming the land.[86] Some countries have also witnessed legislation specifically prohibiting this form of seizure.[87] Rural workers seeking land or land reform may also resort to marches or protests, such as the twenty-five-hundred-member march of Amazonian Indians into Ecuador's capital in 1992, that reawaken dormant programs of redistribution.[88] In recent decades, land reform protests have occurred in Bolivia, as well.[89]

Many observers doubt the long-term significance of land reform. Many of the goals sought by land reform, such as increased agricultural production, greater income distribution, and the alleviation of rural poverty, have not been achieved.[90] Recent studies have revealed that both historically and in the present, land reform programs have perpetuated gender inequalities by excluding women.[91] Even the shift to an industrial economy means that the economic value of land has been declining in its relationship to capital and technology.[92] If an information and electronic economy washes over land-based and industrial economies, then the search for economic opportunity based on landholding is even further removed from the contemporary sources of wealth. Advances in agricultural sciences and mechanization in farming techniques also challenge some of the underlying principles of land reform. With the shift to neoliberal policies in most Latin American countries today, the era of state-supported land reform has most likely ended. Efforts today are centered on "privatization, decollectivization, land registration, titling and land tax issues."[93] Indeed, the World Bank and nongovernmental agencies have funded land registration and titling programs in the region furthering this new view of land in society, and the World Bank continues to include land reform as part of its programs for economic and social improvement.[94] Likewise, recent work has focused on ways to improve the transactional and financial aspects of land dealings through new types of land information systems and cadastres and to incorporate communally held property into liberal economies.[95]

Thus land reform has been an important feature of Latin American property law. Long-term land reform and distribution of land has changed the political and social makeup of some countries such as Mexico and, of course, Cuba. In some countries the movement for land reform sprang from internal inequalities of distribution of land, while in others, land reform was the product of U.S. desires to ease perceived mounting revolutionary pressure throughout the region. The procedures and problems of land reform in many ways demonstrate some of the larger challenges presented to Latin American systems of property law. Self-interest and lukewarm commitments by governments, coupled with many systemic and procedural opportunities to foil redistribution, have led to mixed results. Additionally, policy shifts toward international open markets, domestic privatization, and individual ownership indicate that land reform is not a priority for most Latin American countries at present.

Development, Investment, Globalization, and an Exception

ALTHOUGH economic development and social progress are universal goals of independent modern countries, the pressures of the Cold War during the 1960s and 1970s resulted in various U.S. influences on Latin American legal development with these aims in sight. Both the land reform efforts brought about by the Alliance for Progress and the attempts to reform Latin American legal education can be seen as examples of projects and initiatives to strengthen legal institutions and the rule of law in Latin America during this period. The hopes were that changes in law and legal education could create an environment conducive to positive social and economic change. While the aim of the law and development movement was to improve the economic and social reality of Latin American countries, it met with little success. Some scholars have sought to understand the failure of the movement in theoretical or jurisprudential terms.[1] A postmortem of the law and development movement concluded that further research on the way law plays itself out in society was needed for the law and development agenda to proceed.[2] While recognizing the need for background doctrinal studies to frame investigation, the committee "was in general agreement that research on law would make a greater contribution to development if it went beyond purely doctrinal study and examined the social origins and functions of law, explored the relationship between legal rules and institutions and specific developmental efforts, and examined the actual and potential impact of law on developmental goals."[3] Indeed, without assessing changes brought about in society, law can be "an obstacle to development while hiding behind the face of change and legal equality."[4]

Perhaps the law and development movement was not a complete failure. Certainly the cross-fertilization of ideas about law and legal education has left important traces in those countries exposed to its attempts. Furthermore, the experiments of the movement provide important data for both legal historians and those interested in pursuing more successful cooperation for legal, social, and economic development today.[5] On the academic level, it also helped to advance present thinking on law and society.

Investment and Globalization

For much of the twentieth century, Latin American countries attempted to stimulate economic growth through protective tariffs and domestic production to substitute for imports. Restrictions on foreign ownership of property were often associated with these methods. Indeed, Mexico's severe prohibitions on foreign ownership resulted from popular reaction to a perception that too much of the country and its lands were in foreign hands. Some sectors in some countries are almost completely closed to foreign ownership such as oil and some lands in Mexico.[6]

For the most part, a complete change in policy has occurred in recent decades, as Latin American countries embrace freer trade and more open markets. This has been accompanied by active encouragement of foreign investment. Many countries have sought to reform laws related to property ownership, commerce, and banking to entice foreign investment. Even Cuba has had provisions protecting foreign investment since 1995.[7] Autocratic regimes such as Fujimori's Peru have established numerous changes in private law to encourage an open market economy and foreign investment.[8] Some of the most dramatic changes have been in Mexico during the 1990s, both in preparation for and in response to NAFTA.[9]

NAFTA and the possibility of a Free Trade Area of the Americas (FTAA) have important precursors in other regional agreements on both private law and international economic law. Early in the twentieth century, Latin American countries sought international means to unify and harmonize their private law systems. Ideas of Pan-Americanism and internationalism produced numerous efforts in the area of private law, particularly with uniformity as a goal. For example, in the 1920s, the Inter-American High Commission examined these questions as well as the Inter-American Council of Jurists.[10] Since its creation in 1948, the Organization of American States has included amongst its many aims the improvement of juridical problems between the states.[11]

Along with domestic changes to private law to stimulate free markets and foreign investment, Latin American countries have entered into numerous bilateral and regional trade agreements in recent decades. The early agreements sought to continue the import substitution policies while opening trade within defined limits. Legal integration and harmonization has been far down on the list of priorities for Latin American countries, even where economic cooperation has been seen as essential to the prosperity and development of the region. Thus in 1960 the Central American Common Market (CACM) and the Latin American Free Trade Association (LAFTA, ALALC) were created to reduce tariffs between members and further import substitution policies through a regionwide approach. Likewise, in 1969 the Andean Common Market linked Bolivia, Chile, Colombia, Ecuador, and Peru.[12] In 1960, the Treaty of Montevideo created the Latin American Free Trade Zone, which was to be phased in over twelve years. This attempt was unsuccessful, and the project was transformed into the Asociación Latinoamericana de Integración (ALADI) in 1981.[13]

In the past few decades, Latin American governments have turned from protectionist, import-substitution models of economic development toward a broad-based opening of markets, goods, and services to foreign investment, without regard to the different political persuasions of the governments effecting such changes. The pace of these changes was significantly accelerated by the economic debt crisis of the early 1980s.[14] Although dates of entry vary, most of the countries studied here entered GATT, and all are now WTO members.[15] From the unfulfilled hopes of LAFTA and ALADI, Mercosur was created in 1991 through the Treaty of Asunción, which united Argentina, Brazil, Paraguay, and Uruguay for trade activity.[16] NAFTA came into force in 1994 and dramatically changed Mexican domestic and international law and economic activity.[17] Such regional agreements and organizations have different aims and procedures.[18] Likewise, there appears to be a trend to incorporate or link nontrade issues, such as labor and the environment, to such trade agreements.[19] Proponents of the FTAA hope that hemispheric free trade will be obtained beginning early in the twenty-first century.[20]

This opening has been coupled with the conversion of state-run industries into privately held businesses, or privatization, with general goals of increasing competitiveness and efficiency in industry and liquidity in governments. Public-private partnerships are also possible under more recent reforms.[21]

In addition to reducing requirements related to foreign ownership, further related reforms have included easing requirements for doing business and moving capital in and out of countries, streamlining financial institutions, and providing new or revamped institutions for resolving business disputes.[22] Nonetheless, some areas require further change to encourage a full breadth of commercial activity by foreign companies and investors. For example, some companies may hold back high tech production or licenses, fearing that the domestic law of the country does not offer sufficient substantive or institutional protection of intellectual property rights.[23]

These dramatic shifts have required numerous changes in both domestic law and international arrangements. Countries have acted to bring about legislative, and sometimes constitutional, changes to foreign ownership requirements and the structure of financial institutions.[24] For example, the Fujimori administration in Peru that came to power in 1990 was instrumental in replacing the 1979 socialist constitution with the 1993 capitalist one.[25] Many countries have recently undertaken substantive reform in areas of corporate law and bankruptcy, which can also create environments that are favorably viewed by foreign investors.[26] An independent, speedy, transparent, and trustworthy judiciary for business is viewed as a central aspect of these reforms.[27]

Movement toward a global trading economy has ushered in changes to institutions and the law of property. Freer trade has been linked to freer democracy, the battling of corruption, and the protection of human rights by a number of international agencies proposing legal reform in Latin America, including the World Bank, the Agency for International Development (AID), the Inter-American Development Bank (IDB), and the United Nations Development Program (UNDP).[28] This link is not, however, necessary; autocratic regimes throughout Latin American history and in the present have provided exceptionally welcome environments for big business.

Joseph Thome suggests that the proper assessment of present law-related economic and development agendas is best viewed from a critical, unbiased examination of the law and development movement of the 1960s and 1970s. He importantly asks what conditions have changed so that law-based development will work today when it failed yesterday.[29] Just as reliable institutions have been linked to economic development, so have the rules of private law. Thome quotes the president of the World Bank addressing the area of private law, stating that "without the protection of human and property rights and a comprehensive framework of laws, no equitable development is possible. A government must ensure that it has effective systems of property, contract, labor, bankruptcy, commercial codes, personal rights laws, and other elements of a comprehensive legal system."[30] It is not clear that this internationalization formula for economic success and social progress will produce the hoped-for results. Indeed, without effective enforcement mechanisms in the courts, some even see the approach as potentially harmful to good legal development.[31]

New forms of investment and commerce, such as electronic and internet services and products, are making substantial inroads in Latin America as well. Advances in these areas provide new challenges for legal institutions and substantive law.[32] Too much freedom in economic activity has also led to problems at times. For example, when Chile privatized its banks the first time, lack of regulation and careless action sent many of the institutions into bankruptcy.[33]

Likewise, international agreements in various forms are clearly driving many of these internal reforms. These agreements include both bilateral trade agreements and regional agreement, or a combination of both such as the recent Mexican–European Union trade agreement.[34] Along with increased international business, international corruption and, in return, legal responses to such corruption have arisen.[35] Indeed, concern for the proper control of corrupt practices and money laundering from illegal dealings is an essential, if not dominant, aspect of Latin American trade today.

International pressure has certainly led to recent and substantial reforms in private law. Latin American countries in the twentieth century have striven to improve their economies and social conditions. These goals have been sought through development, investment, and trade both nationally and internationally. On the national level, private law is the mechanism by which these activities are undertaken, and as a result, numerous changes to national private law systems both anticipated and followed attempts to open markets and commerce. Privatization means that one must have the private law mechanisms to convert state-held property into private ownership, and in an effort to make all such activities successful, countries have made drastic changes to private law dealing with corporations, securities, and transactions in the closing decade of the twentieth century. The process of transferring state controlled businesses to the private sector is also rife with possibilities for inside dealing and corrupt profit-making; reliable private law mechanisms and judicial institutions can do much to decrease such abuses.[36]

Cuba: An Exception

An exception to many of these general trends is Cuba. Because of Cuba's unique status in Latin American law, this section addresses its legal system and private law separately. The Cuban Revolution of 1959 and the creation of a socialist state by Fidel Castro meant drastic changes in the law's recognition of private property.[37] Indeed, his first major law was the Agrarian Reform Law of May 17, 1959, discussed in Chapter 26.[38] In the first five years of the revolution, private ownership of dwellings was prohibited except for habitation, permitted private agricultural holdings were reduced in size, and most rental real estate and commercial property was expropriated.[39] Small farmers were permitted to continue on their land, and houses were redistributed for individual and family occupancy.[40] Nonetheless, in recent decades, particularly since 1989, Cuba has made certain concessions toward private ownership to encourage tourism and foreign investment.[41]

In the early 1960s the court system was restructured to create popular courts with lay judges and revolutionary courts to try antirevolutionaries. This structure was replaced in 1973 with a tiered system of courts: base, district, provincial, and supreme.[42] The Supreme Court contains six *salas:* criminal, civil and administrative, labor, state security, military, and economic. Panels composed of two lay and one professional judge hear lower court cases.[43] Since

1990, the intermediate tribunals have been reduced from mixed lay and professional panels of five to three, and lay judges make up the vast majority of the Cuban judiciary.[44] Labor councils, composed exclusively of laypeople, handle labor disputes.[45] From 1977 to 1991, disputes between state enterprises were handled through arbitration, but a new division of the provincial and supreme courts now has this jurisdiction.[46]

From the revolution until 1976, the Cuban Council of Ministers enacted legislation, but since the latter date, a law passed by the council places the power to enact laws in the hands of the National Assembly of the People's Power and the executive. The Council of State holds the power to declare decree-laws, and the Council of Ministers has the power to declare decrees.[47] In recognition of the way legal rules can reshape society, much legislation is aimed at promoting socialist economic and societal values. The Family Code of 1975, which attempted to raise the social and familial position of women, is perhaps the best-known example.[48]

Cuba continued as a Spanish colony until the very end of the nineteenth century and developed law faculties and bar associations to train and regulate the profession. Until 1959, the Cuban legal profession was quite similar in its education and organization to the profession in other Latin American countries. Castro, a law graduate from the University of Havana, continued to see law and lawyers as—provisionally at least—an important part of his system of government.[49] Despite this view, the number of law students fell off sharply in the mid-1960s, and by the mid-1970s, exclusively night classes were offered in the law faculties of the country: Havana, Camagüey, Las Villas, and Oriente. These night schools were dismantled at the end of the 1970s when a shift in policy recognized the importance of legal education and lawyers.[50] Cuba's law schools have recently turned from a more traditional civil law approach based on the substantive rules as set out in codes and decrees toward a more hands-on approach, which includes several cycles of apprenticeships.[51] The University of Havana has been designated the governing center of Cuban legal education.[52] The course is five years in duration and covers, in addition to standard legal topics, politics and economics.[53] Writing in 1994, Marjorie Zatz indicated that students with the highest marks write an honors thesis and are admitted to the bar without a separate examination. Other students must sit the bar exam.[54] Writing in 2000, Gerard Clark stated that the National Organization of *Bufetes Colectivos*, the ONBC, admits lawyers to practice, and a legal education is the only prerequisite to practice.[55] Until the disintegration of the Soviet Union, some particularly well-qualified individuals were selected for graduate legal studies in that country.[56] Since 1983, new law graduates are required to perform three years of social service. Placements for these positions are based on national need and student qualifications.[57]

In the mid-1960s, lawyers were organized into collective legal offices (*bufetes colectivos*), and the private practice of law was eliminated.[58] Since 1974, legal practice in service of the socialist state is coordinated by the ONBC, which provides legal services to Cubans in mostly criminal and family law matters.[59] There are specialized offices charged with representing indigents and with bringing appeals; another office, the Consultoría Nacional, established in 1991, handles legal matters for foreign investors.[60] Various governmental ministries, which seek experts whose practice focuses on the administrative aspects of their organizations, employ a significant number of lawyers.[61]

Even independence and the revolution did not completely sever the ties of Spanish law. "Indeed, the Spanish Civil Code of 1889 was retained in Cuba, with some modifications, until 1987."[62] As of 1994, the Commercial Code of 1956 was still in force.[63] Significant changes to the institutional structure and legal sources were based on the Constitution of 1976 and the related attempt to "institutionalize" the revolution.[64] Many important modifications deal with private property. For example, interests in homes are sometimes exchanged through notarial documents based on the needs of the individuals. Furthering the social interest in housing, inheritance rules are weighted in favor of occupants.[65] Likewise, under Cuban law, Cubans who have "abandoned" the country may not take by intestacy or will.[66] Like other Latin American countries, Cuba has often looked outside its borders to find useful sources of law. The main foreign influences for Cuban laws have been the former Soviet Union, other socialist countries, and other Latin American countries.[67]

The Gap

E VEN in the most smoothly running and politically stable countries of
Latin American a wide gap exists between the law as written and the
law as practiced. The gap between the law and the fact, rhyming smartly in
Spanish as *el derecho y el hecho,* has been a perplexing problem for historians
of Latin American law and continues to be a frustrating reality for citizens,
businesses, lawyers, and judges today. This brief chapter examines some of
the viewpoints about this gap.

In the colonial period, with its highly structured bureaucracy, minute reporting requirements, and the lack of the peninsular *fueros* that guarded regional autonomy, judicial and government structures would appear to be extremely compliant with the orders of the crown. Although the question is
predominantly in the arena of public law, noncompliance by colonial officials
is a well-known, if not well-studied, aspect of colonial government. It is worth
examining here because, of course, high-level noncompliance shapes the attitudes and expectations of all actors in the legal and governmental sphere.

Where royal decrees arrived to colonial officials who considered them impossible or impolitic to effect, the official might respond to the crown with
the phrase "I obey but do not carry it out" (*acato pero no cumplo* or *se respeta,
pero no se cumple* or *se acataban pero no se cumplían*). Thus, a governing official
might substitute his judgment for that of the crown given certain changed circumstances resulting from local conditions, delay in communication, or other
unexpected events. It was most likely, at first, a means of sending the order
back to the crown for reconsideration, but nevertheless, it created a breach
in the law as written and the law as carried out. Colonial officials frequently
disregarded royal orders and exerted more or less autonomous control, relying
on distance, poor communication, and time to cushion their noncompliance.[1]

For the colonial era, Ots Capdequí saw this split rooted in the drafting of
legislation. He stated that theologians and moralists, rather than jurists and

politicians, were responsible for the tone of colonial legislation and that such elevated goals could not function in colonial society. Thus, for example, laws protecting Indians only slightly touched the realities of the *encomienda*. He viewed the response "I obey but do not execute" as a means of sending back royal orders for review and changes to have them fit better the social condition of the colonies.[2] Emphasizing the nature of suspending the enforcement of the order and the flexibility this provided in serious situations to avoid injustice, Ots Capdequí saw this response as a beneficial and infrequently used tool of colonial power as it related to the crown.[3]

Examining the gap in the same period, Phelan argued that the multiplicity of conflicting laws on any particular topic provided not only flexibility, but also a force for centralizing authority. By selective enforcement, the crown could decide when and how to guide its colonial officials.[4] On a larger scale, the gap was the product of two incompatible goals in the Indies, extracting wealth and converting native inhabitants.[5]

Such avoidance of laws was not limited to special royal commands, but also rules of general application, and some historians have observed that this led to a "disrespect for law" generally.[6] Ricardo Levene has noted that this freedom created such problems. "This unobservance of the law was a liberating factor in the life of the colonists, when it was a question of eluding the enforcement of absurd prescriptions regarding commerce, the exchequer, the admittance of foreigners, and the publication and diffusion of books; but it was deplorable in so far as it perverted the organization of justice and corrupted the administration and government of the Indians."[7] Phelan has also noted a positive side to this gap in colonial administration:

The wide gap between the two was not a flaw, as has been traditionally assumed. On the contrary, the distance between observance and nonobservance was a necessary component of the system. Given the ambiguity of the goals and the conflict among the standards, all the laws could not be enforced simultaneously. The very conflict among the standards, which prevented a subordinate from meeting all the standards at once, gave subordinates a voice in decision making without jeopardizing the control of their superiors over the whole system.[8]

In the early independence period, Means saw the gap between formal legal rules and social and economic reality as being caused, in part, by "legal underdevelopment" and "legal borrowing" not based in rational decisions.[9] Because legal sources and legal education, what he calls "cognitive legal institutions," did not adequately track practitioners' assumptions, legal change occurred in the wake of this failure.[10] In his presentation of this quandary, Means distinguishes between "enforcement unreality," where rules overtax the ability of institutions, and "legislative unreality" where those enacting laws do not take account of the social conditions in which the rules must operate, particularly evident when foreign codes were imported to Latin America.[11]

Summarizing the place of law in Latin America in the nineteenth and twentieth centuries, noted historian Charles Gibson writes that "law leads a life of its own, much as historical scholarship in the United States. It is an academic subject, separated from reality by the continuing assumption that its significance and application are in doubt."[12] The roots of this gap in Gibson's view are not a fundamental lawlessness in Latin American society, but rather its appeal to natural law as a higher set of rules through which to conduct and transact business.[13]

The unwillingness to recognize the extent of this gap has led to numerous difficulties and failures, some of which have been mentioned in this book. This aspect of Latin American law has substantially hampered land reform, law and development, and judicial reform.[14] Similarly, innumerable individual personal and business transactions have been and are subject to the gap.[15] Just as Phelan observed some benefits to the gap in the colonial period, some have argued that the gap in present-day Latin America is to be studied and recognized, but should not be the subject of prescriptive projects to close it. Instead, it is to be worked with to undertake incremental transformations.[16] Others, as expected, see the closing of such gaps as a positive development to be sought through reform.[17]

The gap continues today. Therefore, this book is at most one-half of the picture of Latin American private law today. Thome sees the present-day gap as a product of a "socio-political context which has a direct impact on the norms, processes, institutional structures, and cultures of a given legal system," which for Latin America has been, in his view, the subordination of the judiciary to the executive.[18] Karst and Rosenn likewise see the gap arising from the history and culture of the region and identify five factors that characterize Latin American law.

Much of the explanation for this wide disparity between the law on the books and actual practice lies in a complex of historical and cultural factors that have conditioned Latin American attitudes towards law. Five of the most important of these factors are idealism, paternalism, legalism, formalism, and lack of penetration.[19]

Another approach to the gap between written and practiced law has been to recognize it as a feature of all legal systems. "We have the rules, and then we have our way of doing things," an overly savvy international lawyer once told me. The rules, then, become a body of normative, aspirational principles that function on a symbolic rather than practical plane.[20] "To our friends, everything; to our enemies, the law," as the saying goes.[21] Thus the gap in Latin America may be more evident, but it is not unique to Latin America. Indeed, as Jorge Esquirol has persuasively argued, the gap as a theoretical device to advance legal change in Latin America has been a lasting and little-understood legacy of the law and development movement.[22]

Corruption and crime only exacerbate the gap. Corruption continues to hinder many aspects of the rule of law in Latin American countries.[23] It enters both private business relationships and public institutions, such as courts. While some countries have managed to control corruption, other countries today have been so infiltrated with corruption that according to some, private law systems and international obligations are blocked from effective operation.[24] Sociologists and political scientists debate the question of whether the rule of law exists in Latin American countries.[25]

High criminality, especially crime associated with the illegal trafficking of drugs and the associated crime of money laundering, greatly impacts private law and the economies in which private law operates. Administrative and regulatory steps that require numerous bureaucratic actions at each step along the way impede fluid economic transactions. The goals of freer and open trade and battling crime and corruption point in opposite directions. Better monitoring of criminal activity slows trade, and faster and more active trade means fewer opportunities to monitor crime.

|||||||||||||||||||||||||||||||||||||||||||||||||

Conclusion

THE UNFINISHED BUSINESS OF
LATIN AMERICAN PRIVATE LAW

PRIVATE law in Latin America has tracked the social and economic needs of those in power throughout its history. In the colonial period, it provided the rules for the passage of property and economic transactions that enabled Spain to exploit economically its colonies, to construct a Spanish society in the New World, to accommodate new legal objects, to create cost effective sources of labor, and to provide a basis of religious evangelization. Immediately on independence, private law rules changed little, with the exception of those rules related to the new republican values brought in by revolution. New private law rules came about in the middle of the nineteenth century when the pressures of commerce, trade, and nation building pushed countries to adopt codes based on European models. The earliest of the attempts demonstrate a lack of legal development, in that the borrowing undertaken was often a poor match to the society adopting it. Twentieth-century developments have been varied, particularly as the needs of commerce and international trade have led countries to more open economies. Legal systems have had to respond. In the most recent century, various social advances have led to the legal adjustment of the status of women and illegitimate children. Marriage and divorce laws have been secularized. On the economic side, laws relating to business entities, trade, and commerce have been greatly enhanced and have grown in sophistication as countries have entered into a period of legal development driven by their own needs. Likewise, the models for private law have shifted in the twentieth century, from the almost purely European, and especially French, influences of the early twentieth century to the increased importance of domestic legal developments supplemented with international and U.S. models.

Many basic ideas, structures, and developments have been set out in this book. Nonetheless, within the scope of this work, private law in Spanish Latin American countries, these pages serve merely as an introduction to the topic.

Numerous areas have been slighted or not mentioned at all. Some were considered entirely beyond the scope of this study, such as constitutional or criminal law. Similarly, the influence of and interaction with Brazilian law are not addressed, although there are presently available excellent English-language works of Brazilian law.[1] Puerto Rico is part of Spanish America, and yet its status and history have for the most part placed it outside the general scope of the work.[2] Other aspects should be here, but are not, and it is hoped that these omissions reflect the lack of available secondary sources in English or Spanish, rather than the lack of diligence and care of the author. For example, I have only touched on the development of tort law and have not addressed the relationship of taxation to private law arrangements. The development of national legal systems in the twentieth century has unfortunately made only the most superficial observations possible, but it is hoped that with this brief introduction to contemporary private law concerns and developments, researchers will at least find some guiding stars to navigate present legal developments. From the historian's point of view, the contextualization of legal developments with social and economic changes has been attempted only quite generally, but such studies are best left for more focused presentations rather than those attempting to give a broad overview.[3]

One will marvel that, despite the gap, private law rules and institutions are capable of operating successfully even in the midst of great political unrest and turmoil. From the time of national independence, many countries have experienced wide swings in political stability, and yet very often, even in near crisis, the sectors dependent on private law—property owners, commercial enterprises, miners, growers, and traders—have been able to function with little disturbance. Thus economies continue to run and private law transactions are completed today even in the midst of what others might conceive of as crippling political instability and corruption. One reason for this phenomenon is that in some areas private law is relatively independent of the state. The ability of private law to function in modern-day Argentina, for example, has been linked to its dependence on a "very strong and profitable private sphere organized around domestic family and social networks and international connections."[4] Private law, however, is not immune from the difficulties created by weak states, as the case of land titles demonstrates.

A deep, nuanced scholarship in the history of Latin American law has arisen in recent decades. Recent studies have addressed the spread of the *ius commune* in Latin America and Mexico, the development of commercial law in Argentina, and the social history of bar and lawyers in Colombia.[5] Academics are only just beginning to apply new critical scholarship to the changes in private law in Latin America. Some have undertaken a reexamination of fundamental assumptions concerning Latin American law, such as its assumed, essential "Europeanness" and the importance of the "gap."[6] Others have sought to examine the needs of the poor and subordinate populations in Latin America.[7] There is a growing body of work on the social history of law, particularly criminal law.[8] At the writing of this book the U.S. LatCrit movement is less than a decade old and has only just begun to consider how its methods of scholarship may apply to the study of law in Latin America.[9]

If this work provides a general foundation for further research and scholarship it has served its purpose. Like so many works of its kind, it perhaps raises more questions than it answers. It is hoped that these pages may aid in the better understanding of Latin American legal systems and lead to better social, political, and economic relations between the English- and Spanish-speaking worlds. It is also hoped that this work may contribute to an understanding of the legal mechanisms that have too often served the powerful and have placed the weak on the periphery of law.

Introduction

1. A recent bibliography of *derecho indiano* exceeds four hundred pages. Dagrossa (2000).

Prologue

1. Offner (1983); Widener (1999).
2. Margadant S. (1990), 13, 25.
3. Offner (1983), 17, 37, 88–98.
4. Ibid., 148–50.
5. Ibid., 59.
6. Ibid., 59.
7. Ibid., 151.
8. Ibid., 150, 156, 158.
9. Ibid., 65–66.
10. Ibid., 158–162.
11. Ibid., 222–224.
12. Ibid., 251.
13. Ibid., 250.
14. Ibid., 254.
15. Ibid., 255.
16. Ibid., 253.
17. Ibid., 253.
18. Ibid., 77, 79, 112, 137, 253.
19. Ibid., 47, 51, 66, 79, 282.
20. Ibid., 65.
21. Ibid., 205–206; Socolow (2000), 21.
22. Kellogg (1995), 93. Margadant S. (1990), 28, states that in matters of inheritance the male line excluded the female.
23. Margadant S. (1990), 26–27.
24. Ibid., 27.
25. Offner (1983), 140.
26. Ibid., 141.
27. Ibid., 173–174, 203, 257–266.
28. Margadant S. (1990), 28.
29. Offner (1983), 22, 48–49.
30. Cline (1984); Gibson (1964), 257–299.
31. Offner (1983), 134.
32. Ibid., 134–39, 168.
33. Ibid., 135.
34. Ibid., 217.
35. Ibid., 114.
36. Kellogg (1995), 123–124, 170–171; Socolow (2000), 21.
37. Offner (1983), 204, 209.

38. Ibid., 208.

39. Ibid., 206–208.

40. Margadant S. (1990), 26.

41. Socolow (2000), 23.

42. Offner (1983), 280.

43. Moore (1958), 1.

44. Ibid., 99–125.

45. Ibid., 74–75, 92–97.

46. Ibid., 33–34, 57, 109.

47. Ibid., 79, 97.

48. Ibid., 108.

49. Ibid., 78–79, 92, 108, 170.

50. Ibid., 20, 22, 23.

51. Ibid., 27–38, 93.

52. Ibid., 93–98.

53. Kellogg (1995), xxii.

54. Levene (1985), 36; Burkholder and Johnson (1998), 21.

55. Margadant S. (1990), 32.

56. Ibid., 32, citing *Leyes de las Indias,* Book 2, Title 1, Law 4; Book 5, Title 2, Law 22.

Chapter 1

1. Pagden (1995); Zavala (1971).

2. Kellogg (1995), 36, 213–219.

3. Cutter (1999), 8; Gibson (1966), 90–111; Kagan (1981), 123–24, 150–160; Malagón-Barceló (1961); Stern (1993), 114–137.

4. Bello Lozano (1983), 231–232.

5. Kagan (1981), 2–20.

6. Ibid., 145.

7. Greenblatt (1991), 52–85.

8. *Inter caetera* (May 4, 1493), *Examiae devotionis* (May 4, 1493), and *Dudum siquidem* (September 26, 1493). Levene (1985), 55. Bello Lozano (1983), 222–227; Gibson (1966), 14–19.

9. Levene (1985), 55.

10. Margadant S. (1990), 110–118.

11. Levene (1985), 58–59.

12. Schwaller (1987); Schwaller (2000). The royal patronage was set out in laws of June 1, 1574, by Philip II, which were incorporated into the *Recopilación* of 1680 in Book I, Title VI, Law 1. Levene (1985), 61.

13. Levene (1985), 45–46, 64.

14. Hanke (1949); Hanke (1974); Ots Capdequí (1952), 59–64.

15. Bello Lozano (1983), 252–53.

16. Soberanes Fernández (1998), 47.

17. Karst and Rosenn (1975), 33. The text of the *Requerimiento* in English may be found at Karst and Rosenn (1975), 31–33. See also Hanke (1949), 31–36; and Seed (1995), 69–99 for possible Islamic influences in its text.

18. Ots Capdequí (1952), 62–63.

19. Ibid., 54–59; Bello Lozano (1983), 254–256.

20. Ots Capdequí (1952), 99.

21. Levene (1985), 49.

22. Ibid., 143, n.1.

23. González Hernández (1992), 48–52; Ots Capdequí (1952), 33–34.

24. The most important of these sources are: the *Fuero Juzgo* (654); the *Fuero Real* (1255); the *Siete Partidas* (1265); the *Espéculo* (1290); the *Leyes de Estilo* (1310); the *Ordenamiento de Alcalá* (1348); the *Fuero Viejo de Castilla* (1356); the *Ordenanzas Reales de Castilla* (1485); the *Ordenamiento Real* (1490); the *Leyes de Toro* (1505); the *Nueva Recopilación de Castilla* (1567); and, toward the very end of the colonial period, the *Novísima Recopilacíon de Castilla* (1805). This list is taken and modified from Clagett and Valderrama (1973), 387 and Van Kleffens (1968), 235, with approximate dates from Pérez-Prendes (1986), 573; Van Kleffens (1968), 75, 168, 188, 215, 222.

25. García Gallo (1964), 57; Margadant S. (1990), 35.

26. García Gallo (1964), 58; Van Kleffens (1968), 74–80.

27. Margadant S. (1990), 36–37.

28. Van Kleffens (1968), 94–113.

29. Ibid., 124–135.

30. García Gallo (1964), 90; Margadant S. (1990), 37; Pérez-Prendes (1986), 573.

31. Kagan (1981), 141.

32. García Gallo (1964), 386–394; Van Kleffens (1968), 171–214.

33. Margadant S. (1990), 39.

34. Kagan (1981), 24–25.

35. García Gallo (1964), 398; Margadant S. (1990), 39.

36. García Gallo (1964), 394–395; Margadant S. (1990), 39; for the text, translated into English, see Van Kleffens (1968), 232–234.

37. Margadant S. (1990), 41.

38. García Gallo (1964), 399; Margadant S. (1990), 41.

39. Pérez-Prendes (1986), 850–851.

40. García Gallo (1964), 88; Margadant S. (1990), 40.

41. Gibson (1966), 78–87; Salinas Araneda and García y García (1994).

42. García Gallo (1964), 396–397; Margadant S. (1990), 42.

43. Ots Capdequí (1952), 41.

44. Margadant S. (1990), 42.

Chapter 2

1. Margadant S. (1990), 47.

2. Benton (2000).

3. Ots Capdequí (1952), 103.

4. Haring (1975), 14.

5. Karst and Rosenn (1975), 37.

6. Phelan (1960), 47–48.

7. Ibid.

8. Karst and Rosenn (1975), 42.

9. Because these two institutions dealt specifically with the Indies and trade, few cases touching these important topics found their way to what was otherwise the most important civil appellate tribunal in Castile in the sixteenth and seventeenth centuries, the *Chancillería de Valladolid*. Kagan (1981), 92–97.

10. Ots Capdequí (1952), 119.

11. Bello Lozano (1983), 287–288.

12. Cutter (1995), 49.
13. Levene (1985), 78.
14. Ibid., 79.
15. Ots Capdequí (1959), 304.
16. León Pinelo (1892), 1–13.
17. Levene (1985), 80.
18. Cutter (1995), 49.
19. Ibid., 52.
20. Ots Capdequí (1952), 116.
21. Levene (1985), 80.
22. Ots Capdequí (1952), 116.
23. Haring (1975), 107–109.
24. Levene (1985), 74.
25. Ibid., 75.
26. Ots Capdequí (1952), 115.
27. Haring (1975), 299.
28. Ots Capdequí (1952), 116.
29. Margadant S. (1990), 62–63.
30. Haring (1975), 117.
31. Margadant S. (1990), 62–63.
32. Ots Capdequí (1952), 111.
33. Haring (1975), 118–119.
34. Levene (1985), 118.
35. Haring (1975), 122.
36. Cutter (1995), 70.
37. Margadant S. (1990), 65.
38. Parry (1948), 6. See also Levaggi (1987), vol. 2, 16–24.
39. Haring (1975), 15.
40. Kellogg (1995), 9.
41. Haring (1975), 125.
42. Cutter (1999), 15.
43. Soberanes Fernández (1980b), 30.
44. Cutter (1995), 52–53.
45. Kellogg (1995), 9; Parry (1948), 55–83.
46. Cutter (1995), 52.
47. Haring (1975), 69–93.
48. Ots Capdequi (1952), 111; Haring (1975), 69–93.
49. Soberanes Fernández (1980b), 20–21. For the late colonial period see Lynch (1969), 237–261.
50. Burkholder and Chandler (1977), 3; Phelan (1967), 132–135.
51. Parry (1948), 133.
52. Soberanes Fernández (1980b), 49–59.
53. Levene (1985), 116; Soberanes Fernández (1980b), 70–72.
54. Levene (1985), 199–200.
55. Soberanes Fernández (1980b), 42–45.
56. Levene (1985), 199–200.
57. Margadant S. (1990), 63–64.
58. Soberanes Fernández (1980b), 72.

59. Levene (1985), 115.

60. Ibid., 118.

61. Ibid., 119.

62. Ibid., 115.

63. Bello Lozano (1983), 316.

64. Ibid., 304.

65. Soberanes Fernández (1980b), 62–63.

66. Borah (1993), 4.

67. Bello Lozano (1983), 305–306.

68. Ibid., 308–309; Lynch (1969), 52–56.

69. Lynch (1969), 65.

70. Ibid., 83–84.

71. Clagett and Valderrama (1973), 209; Gibson (1966), 166–178.

72. Levaggi (1987), vol. 2, 26–28; Margadant S. (1990), 66–68; Ots Capdequí (1959), 279–287.

73. De Estrada (1978), 83.

74. Haring (1975), 151.

75. Levene (1985), 88.

76. Lynch (1969), 201–236.

77. De Estrada (1978), 59, 104–105. The city *cabildo* should be distinguished from the larger ad hoc open *cabildo* (*cabildo abierto*) composed of the important members of the community to address a problem of particular concern. De Estrada (1978), 59. Open *cabildos* functioned only at the initial phases of colonization and then again in the years leading up to independence. Ots Capdequí (1952), 114. Peru saw some open *cabildos* in the mid sixteenth century during a time of regional civil war. Levene (1985), 90.

78. De Estrada (1978), 58. The method for sale of positions and the type of positions sold are addressed in Haring (1975), 271–273.

79. Haring (1975), 154–156.

80. Bello Lozano (1983), 340.

81. De Estrada (1978), 59.

82. Bello Lozano (1983), 332–333.

83. Ibid., 341.

84. Levene (1985), 222.

85. Ibid., 221. For an example of an illiterate *alcalde* see Cutter (1995), 97.

86. Cutter (1995), 82.

87. Levene (1985), 232.

88. Ibid., 221; Ots Capdequí (1959), 281–282.

89. Bello Lozano (1983), 448; Partida 3, Title 2, Law 41.

90. Borah (1996), 223; Partida 3, Titles 10 and 14.

91. Kellogg (1995), 10.

92. Borah (1996), 223.

93. Ibid., 223.

94. Alonso Romero y Garriga Acosta (1998), 81.

95. Ots Capdequí (1952), 30.

96. Alonso Romero y Garriga Acosta (1998), 84.

97. Kagan (1981), 27.

98. Borah (1996), 222.

99. Ibid., 222.

100. Ibid., 222.

101. Phelan (1967), 147–176.

102. Ots Capdequí (1952), 95.

103. Bello Lozano (1983), 451–452.

104. Levene (1985), 119.

105. Ibid., 60.

106. Levaggi (1987), vol. 2, 34–35; Levene (1985), 121.

107. Soberanes Fernández (1980a), 148–49, 159–160.

108. Levene (1985), 60.

109. Ibid., 121.

110. Esquivel Obregón (1980), 205–229; Lewin (1962), 139–230.

111. Burkholder and Johnson (1998), 102.

112. Greenleaf (1969), 174–182; Haring (1975), 190.

113. Hevia Bolaños (1980), 123–141.

114. Bello Lozano (1983), 283–284.

115. Levaggi (1987), vol. 2, 32–33; Levene (1985), 122.

116. Kagan (1981), 18.

117. Margadant S. (1990), 69.

118. Means (1980), 8, n. 13.

119. De Estrada (1978), 57.

120. Haring (1975), 301.

121. Levene (1985), 239.

122. Ibid., 239.

123. Ibid., 122–123.

124. Ibid., 239.

125. Haring (1975), 279.

126. Ibid., 282–283.

127. Howe (1949).

128. Levene (1985), 111. See also Moreno de los Arcos (1980), 267–280.

129. Levene (1985), 111. See also McAlister, "Militares" in Soberanes Fernández (1980a), 247–265; Jesús Fébles (1980), 281–291; Madrazo (1980), 333–364.

130. MacLachlan (1980), 85–122.

131. Levene (1985), 120; Haring (1975), 123; Miranda (1980b), 231.

132. Levene (1985), 124–125.

133. Kellogg (1995), xxviii.

134. Ibid., 21.

135. Borah (1996), 232–234.

136. Miranda (1980a), 170–171.

137. The jurisdiction, procedure, and review of judgments of these courts are found in *Leyes de las Indias*, Book 5, Titles 9–15.

138. Cutter (1995), 6.

139. Ibid., 68.

140. Ibid., 36.

141. Borah (1996), 218–220; Partida 3, Title 4, Laws 23–35.

142. Eder (1950), 66–67.

143. Borah (1996), 229–230.

144. Cutter (1995), 9–10, 40–43.

145. Gutiérrez Sarmiento (1992), 180–181.

146. Lynch (1969), 116–132; Margadant S. (1990), 104–109; Sánchez Bella (1980), 293–331; *Leyes de las Indias*, Book 8.

147. Lynch (1969), 120.

148. De Estrada (1978), 62; Ots Capdequí (1952), 117.

149. Burkholder and Chandler (1977), 18–22; Ots Capdequí (1952), 100; Phelan (1967), 143–145.

150. Lynch (1969), Ots Capdequí (1952), 120.

151. Levene (1985), 231; Lynch (1969), 81.

Chapter 3

1. Icaza Dufour (1998), 48–53.

2. Margadant S. (1990), 98.

3. Mendieta y Núñez (1975), 36.

4. González González (1988), 455–477.

5. Pérez Perdomo (2002), 31–33.

6. Uribe-Uran (2000), 11, 23.

7. Ibid., 35.

8. Mendieta y Núñez (1975), 111–113.

9. Ibid., 57–62.

10. González Echenique (1954), 113; Parra Márquez (1952), 79–88.

11. González Echenique (1954), 112.

12. Pérez Perdomo (2002), 33.

13. Barrientos Grandón (1993), 38–39.

14. Ibid., 41.

15. Ibid., 130–132.

16. González Echenique (1954), 139–142; Pérez Perdomo (2002), 34.

17. Mendieta y Núñez (1975), 65–71. The term *prima* was associated with those important subjects traditionally taught in the mornings. González Echenique (1954), 42.

18. Mendieta y Núñez (1975), 73–75. Mendieta y Núñez sets out a detailed plan of reading covering five years for colonial law students in Mexico at 77–81.

19. Barrientos Grandón (1993), 39.

20. Mendieta y Núñez (1975), 91. This would comport with the existence of such possibilities at Salamanca. González Echenique (1954), 34–35.

21. Mendieta y Núñez (1975), 53, 93.

22. Ibid., 93–96.

23. Barrientos Grandón (1993), 43.

24. Ibid.; González Echenique (1954), 187–212.

25. Barrientos Grandón (1993), 39–51.

26. Levene (1949), 36, 32.

27. Means (1980), 48–49.

28. Barrientos Grandón (1993), 136–139; González Echenique (1954), 52–56, 98.

29. Uribe-Uran (2000), 103.

30. Ibid., 103.

31. Gutiérrez Sarmiento (1992), 169.

32. Means (1980), 50.

33. Uribe-Uran (2000), 104.

34. Ibid., 26–28.

35. Barrientos Grandón (1993), 46–49; González Echenique (1954), 176–185.

36. Barrientos Grandón y Rodríguez Torres (1991), 293.

37. Icaza Dufour (1998), 111–115; Levene (1949), 16, 26–27.

38. Parra Márquez (1952), 241–257.

39. Alonso Romero y Garriga Acosta (1998), 51–65; Icaza Dufour (1998), 60–66. See generally Navas (1996).

40. Kagan (1981), 71.

41. Alonso Romero y Garriga Acosta (1998), 64–69; González Echenique (1954), 223–227; Kagan (1981), 66.

42. Barrientos Grandón (1993), 46–49.

43. Alonso Romero y Garriga Acosta (1998), 51–65; González Echenique (1954), 228–233; Gutiérrez Sarmiento (1992), 169–176. For clerics practicing as *abogados* see González Echenique (1954), 241–242.

44. Pérez Perdomo (2002), 45.

45. Alonso Romero y Garriga Acosta (1998), 71–75. For a description of an *abogado's* oral practice before an *audiencia* see González Echenique (1954), 266–270.

46. Alonso Romero y Garriga Acosta (1998), 86–98; González Echenique (1954), 275–289, 299–306.

47. Alonso Romero y Garriga Acosta (1998), 98–108. González Echenique (1954), 271–275. A list of duties and prohibitions for colonial *abogados* is found in Sagaón Infante (1984), 631–640.

48. Alonso Romero y Garriga Acosta (1998), 108–113.

49. Pérez Perdomo (2002), 51.

50. Haring (1975), 9.

51. Pérez Perdomo (1981), 44.

52. Kagan (1981), 19.

53. González Echenique (1954), 253–256; Levene (1985), 177.

54. Ibid., 217–264.

55. González Echenique (1954), 22–28; Pérez Perdomo (2002), 37.

56. Levene (1985), 214.

57. Cutter (1995), 4–6.

58. Kicza (1984) in Spores and Hassig, 127–144.

59. Baade (1984), 119–128; Baade (1981), 242–243; Baade (1981b).

60. Pérez Perdomo (1981a), 72.

61. Cutter (1995), 100–101.

62. Pérez Perdomo (2002), 41–44.

63. Icaza Dufour (1998), 83–111; Kicza (1984) and Hassig, 127–144.

64. Parra Márquez (1952), 124–160. A facsimile of the college's statutes and a list of members, as well as a list of colonial law graduates from the University of Mexico are found in Icaza Dufour (1998), 163–217.

65. Parra Márquez (1952), 182–192.

66. Armstrong (1989), 20.

67. Pérez Perdomo (1981), 75–80.

68. Pérez Perdomo (2002), 49–51. For the dress required of *abogados* in the *audiencia* see González Echenique (1954), 265–266.

69. Pérez Perdomo (2002), 48.

70. Uribe-Uran (1999), 46, 38–39. See also Levene (1959).

71. Alonso Romero y Garriga Acosta (1998), 78–80.

72. Kellogg (1995), 15.

73. Borah (1996), 221–222; Pérez Perdomo (2002), 47.

74. Gonzalbo Aizpuru (1989), 77–93; Herzog (1996).

75. Barrientos Grandón (2000a); Barrientos Grandón (2000b); Burkholder (1980); Burkholder and Chandler (1977); Herzog (1995); Lohmann Villena (1974); López Bohórquez (1984); Mayorga García (1991); Parry (1948); Phelan (1967); Polanco Alcántara (1992); Restrepo Sáenz (1952); Suárez (1989); Vigil (1987).

76. Kagan (1981), 158–159.

77. Kellogg (1995), 11.

78. Margadant S. (1990), 66; Soberanes Fernández (1980b), 48; Phelan (1967), 151–153.

79. Burkholder and Chandler (1977), 41, 110–114.

80. Levene (1985), 117. Many of these requirements are set out in the first eight chapters of Book 5 of the *Recopilación* of 1680.

81. Kellogg (1995), 12.

82. Chevalier (1963), 160–165, 172–173; Vigil (1987), 49–50.

83. Burkholder and Chandler (1977).

84. Ibid., 35.

85. Carter (1971); Vigil (1987).

86. Burkholder (1980); Phelan (1967), 128.

87. Burkholder and Chandler (1977), 145.

88. Phelan (1967), 136.

89. Vigil (1987).

90. Burkholder and Chandler (1977), 18–22.

91. Ibid., 18–22.

92. Levene (1985), 119.

93. Ibid., 119.

Chapter 4

1. Pérez-Prendes (1989), 170. See also González Hernández (1992), 54–67.

2. Soberanes Fernández (1998), 60–61. The later *cédulas* beginning with 1679 have been edited and compiled. Muro Orejón (1956).

3. Cutter (1995), 32.

4. Kagan (1981), 28–30.

5. Margadant S. (1990), 51.

6. Phelan (1960).

7. Ots Capdequí (1952), 91.

8. Levene (1985), 151.

9. Ots Capdequí (1952), 91; Bernal (1984); Vigil (1987).

10. Margadant S. (1990), 52; Ots Capdequí (1952), 91.

11. Ots Capdequí (1952), 91.

12. Levene (1985), 154.

13. Ibid., 154–155.

14. Ots Capdequí (1952), 91–92.

15. Ibid., 92.

16. Ibid., 92.

17. The sources used as models were the *Siete Partidas* (1265) and the *Nueva recopi-*

lación de las leyes de Castilla (1567). Ots Capdequí (1952), 92. This work was later edited by Montemayor in 1678 and incorporated into Eusebio Bentura Beleña's *Recopilación sumaria* in 1787. Margadant S. (1990), 51–52.

18. Ots Capdequí (1952), 92.

19. Levene (1985), 26.

20. Margadant S. (1990), 51–52.

21. Ibid., 51–52.

22. A facsimile of the work and numerous excellent introductory essays are found in Icaza Dufour (1987).

23. Levene (1985), 173.

24. Ots Capdequí (1952), 93; Soberanes Fernández (1998), 73–77.

25. Levene (1985), 174.

26. Ots Capdequí (1952), 93.

27. Ibid., 93.

28. Margadant S. (1990), 52–53; Icaza Dufour (1987).

29. Margadant S. (1990), 53.

30. Ibid., 55.

31. Levene (1985), 196.

32. Ibid., 196–197.

33. Ibid., 197.

34. Ibid., 198–199.

35. Ibid., 156.

36. Ibid., 161–162.

37. Ots Capdequí (1952), 34. For an examination of the difficulty of determining applicable law in the colonial period see Werner (2000).

38. English translations are available. *Las Siete Partidas* (2001); *The Laws of Las Siete Partidas* (1978).

39. Levene (1985), 192.

40. *Las Siete Partidas* (2001).

41. Ots Capdequí (1952), 38.

42. Ibid., 39.

43. Ibid., 39; Martínez Cárdos (1960).

44. Means (1980), 51–52.

45. Levene (1948).

46. Solórzano y Pereyra (1972). See also Scafidi (2003).

47. Ochoa Brun (1972); Ots Capdequí (1952), 95–96; Parry (1948), 7.

48. Ots Capdequí (1952), 97.

49. Ibid., 95.

50. Kagan (1981), 21.

51. Ots Capdequí (1952), 95; Hevia Bolaños (1652).

52. Levene (1985), 197.

53. Ibid., 197.

54. Means (1980), 57; Kagan (1981), 149; Ots Capdequí (1952), 95.

55. Hevia Bolaños (1652).

56. Means (1980), 8.

57. Levaggi (1986), vol. 1, 153–155.

58. Margadant S. (1990), 55–56.

59. Bello Lozano (1983), 507.

60. Haring (1975), 101.

61. Ibid., 101.

62. Kellogg (1995), xxviii, 7.

63. González (1981), 42.

64. Gutiérrez Sarmiento (1992), 53, 57, 61, 64, 66, 71, 72, 80, 82, 91, 95, 97, 98, 101, 103, 104, 117, 126, 127, 132, 144.

65. Ibid., 59, 92, 96, 97, 101, 102, 103, 105, 106, 117, 126, 127, 130, 133, 134, 135, 136.

66. Ibid., 130.

67. Barrientos Grandón (1993), 229–272.

68. Oddo (1981), 35–37.

69. Kagan (1981), 21, 70.

70. Cutter (1995), 36; see also Kagan (1981), 27.

71. Cutter (1995), 30, 34, 39.

72. Ibid., 37.

73. Ibid., 37; McKnight (1989).

74. Levene (1985), 190, n. 1.

Chapter 5

1. There is a large, complex body of work on the sociolegal history of these distinctions. For example, see Arrom (1985a); Benton (2002); Chevalier (1963); Cutter (2000); Gutiérrez (1991); Hanke (1949); Herzog (2002); Kellogg (1995); Kellogg and Restall (1998); Konetzke (1953); Rípodas Ardanaz (1977); Seed (1988); Socolow (2000); Stern (1993); Twinam (1999); Uribe-Uran (2000); Zavala (1971); Zavala (1984). This chapter can only touch on some of the basic aspects of this subject.

2. Vera Estañol (1994), 8–10.

3. Levene (1985), 138, 140, 165–166.

4. Armstrong (1989), 6–7.

5. Haring (1975), 199.

6. Margadant S. (1990), 74.

7. Ots Capdequí (1952), 64–67.

8. Levene (1985), 138.

9. Haring (1975), 26.

10. Levene (1985), 164–65.

11. Cottrol (2001), 31–34; Cutter (1995), 25; Rípodas Ardanaz (1977), 25–35.

12. Vera Estañol (1994), 31.

13. Lavrin and Couturier (1979); Ots Capdequí (1952), 23–24.

14. Lavrin and Couturier (1979), 288–291.

15. Arrom (1985a), 62, 68.

16. Margadant S. (1990), 124.

17. Ots Capdequí (1952), 122.

18. Levene (1985), 143, 179.

19. Cook and Cook (1991).

20. Bello Lozano (1983), 377–378.

21. Levene (1985), 44, 142. See generally Socolow (2000), 32–51.

22. Margadant S. (1990), 124; Rípodas Ardanaz (1977), 63–101, 155–222.

23. Kellogg (1995), 202; Rípodas Ardanaz (1977), 103–153.

24. Levene (1985), 144.

25. Kellogg (1995), 203.

26. Levene (1985), 200–201; Rípodas Ardanaz (1977), 259–315.

27. Bello Lozano (1983), 378.

28. Levene (1985), 201–202.

29. Mellafe (1975), 123.

30. Ibid., 112.

31. Borah (1996), 228, 231–233, 235.

32. Ibid., 237.

33. Ibid., 225–226.

34. Levene (1985), 127, 145.

35. Ots Capdequí (1952), 71. See generally Twinam (1999).

36. Bello Lozano (1983), 379.

37. Arrom (1985a), 71–81.

38. Ibid., 56–70; Levene (1985), 143; Socolow (2000), 9.

39. Kellogg (1995), 106 citing Arrom (1985a), 61.

40. Bello Lozano (1983), 380; Vera Estañol (1994), 31.

41. Kellogg (1995), 107.

42. Lavrin and Couturier (1979), 300–302.

43. Kellogg (1995), 104–105.

44. Gutiérrez Sarmiento (1992), 162–163.

Chapter 6

1. Taylor (1972), 195.

2. Ibid., vii.

3. Ibid., 142. Mortgages encumbering land in the colonial period were so common, that by the end of the period, to lessen litigation over land titles and mortgages, recording offices for mortgages were established in the 1780s in some areas. Vera Estañol (1994), 45.

4. *Leyes de las Indias,* Book 4, Title 12, Law 6; Armstrong (1989), 3; Mariluz Urquijo (1978), 25–32; Seed (2001), 83–90.

5. Ots Capdequí (1952), 81.

6. Margadant S. (1990), 85; Ots Capdequí (1952), 81.

7. Margadant S. (1990), 85 citing *Leyes de las Indias,* Book 4, Title 12, Law 14; Mariluz Urquijo (1978), 58–63.

8. Ots Capdequí (1952), 81.

9. Ibid., 81.

10. Chevalier (1963), 268.

11. Armstrong (1989), 3.

12. Margadant S. (1990), 86.

13. Ibid., 86.

14. Ots Capdequí (1952), 82.

15. Levene (1985), 96. Book 4, Title 12, of the *Recopilación* of 1680 collects many of these.

16. Haring (1975), 240.

17. Lynch (1969), 166–167.

18. Haring (1975), 240.

19. Ebright (1994), 18, 25.

20. Taylor (1972), 161.

21. Ebright (1994), 24.

22. Ibid., 24.

23. Ibid., 87, 105; Margadant S. (1990), 86. For *montes* see Mariluz Urquijo (1978), 97–137.

24. Harris (1975), 5; Mariluz Urquijo (1978), 97–137; Van Young (1981), 297–307.

25. Chevalier (1963), 134–147.

26. Ibid., 211–212.

27. Taylor (1972), 132.

28. Chevalier (1963), 132.

29. Harris (1975), 20–22; Van Young (1981), 107–269, 315–342.

30. Ramírez (1986), 144–145.

31. Ebright (1994), 19; Harris (1975), 1–144; Ramírez (1986), 99–120; Tutino (1976); Van Young (1981), 295–314.

32. Taylor (1972), 122.

33. Gutiérrez Sarmiento (1992), 74, 78.

34. Taylor (1972), 134.

35. Ots Capdequí (1952), 43.

36. Ibid., 123. A summary of its provisions is found at Soberanes Fernández (1998), 55–56.

37. Amunátegui Solar (1901, 1902, 1904); Clavero (1974); De Montagut (1993), 221–222; Donoso (1967) 90–93; Fernández de Recas (1965); Gutiérrez Ramos (1998); Mariluz Urquijo (1978), 141–173. *Mayorazgos* were scarce in Rio de la Plata. Mariluz Urquijo (1978), 75–76, 152. Although the *mayorazgo* was the main legal device for establishing entailed estates that passed in a primogeniture inheritance pattern, other interests in property could also be made subject to this pattern. *Encomiendas* were also subject to a primogeniture scheme and are discussed in Chapter 9. It should be noted here, however, that although it may seem tempting to see the *encomienda* system as a lineal ascendant of many of the large estates of the late colonial and republic period, this is not the case. Phelan (1967), 60.

38. Ots Capdequí (1952), 43.

39. Ibid., 43–44.

40. Gutiérrez Sarmiento (1992), 110.

41. Margadant S. (1990), 126.

42. Mirow (2001), 317, note 164; Ots Capdequí (1952), 45.

43. Taylor (1972), 154; Chevalier (1963), 255.

44. Ramírez (1986), 166–167, 211–240.

45. Taylor (1972), 162. *Mayorazgos* have been shown to insulate large estates from sale during economically hard times and to keep these estates in the intended families rather than subjecting them to sale. Van Young (1981), 114–138.

46. Margadant S. (1990), 127.

47. Armstrong (1989), 9–10; Gibson (1966), 83–85; Haring (1975), 178; Margadant S. (1990), 120; Mariluz Urquijo (1978), 70–71; Van Young (1981), 168–172, 182–191.

48. Margadant S. (1990), 120–121.

49. Taylor (1972), 193.

50. Ibid., 194.

51. Schwaller (1985), 111–128; Van Young (1981), 183. Similarly, if the chantry was established with a principal sum or other property to provide these services, the income was, in turn, often invested in other estates and might be returned to the owner with

the understanding that the owner would make the payments to the church. Ramírez (1986), 108; Schwaller (1985), 114. Such liens creating the income stream were called *censos.* Schwaller (1985), 114.

52. Ramírez, (1986), 108; Schwaller (1985), 115, 121.

53. Taylor (1972), 169–170, 186.

54. Chevalier (1963), 234.

55. Margadant S. (1990), 42.

56. Ibid., 118.

57. Ibid., 109.

58. Abercrombie (1998), 249–250; Cline (1998), 13–18; Erie (1995); Kellogg (1995), 130–132.

59. Cline (1998), 16.

60. Kellogg (1995), 135–136.

61. De Montagut (1993), 202. Women often served as executors of their husbands' wills. Lavrin and Couturier (1979), 287.

62. De Montagut (1993), 201–202; Levene (1985), 147. The *Leyes de Toro* provided certain modifications concerning the types of children who were able to inherit, testaments by proxy (*comisario*), and other areas related to testaments. Pacheco Caballero (1993), 242–243, 251–254.

63. Ots Capdequí (1952), 24.

64. Arrom (1985a), 63.

65. Gutiérrez Sarmiento (1992), 107. For illegitimacy and inheritance see Twinam (1999), 216–240.

66. Pacheco Caballero (1993), 242–246.

67. Vera Estañol (1994), 32. A daughter might be disinherited for marrying against her father's wishes. Arrom (1985a), 69.

68. Kellogg (1995), 104–105; Lavrin and Couturier (1979), 286–287. Indeed, "after the death of the husband, the wife was entitled to half of the wealth accumulated during the marriage, her dowry, and whatever property she may have owned separately." Lavrin and Couturier (1979), 287. If a wife predeceased her husband, the dowry was given to her children or returned to her parents. Arrom (1985a), 67. See also Korth and Flusche (1987).

69. Kellogg (1995), 106.

70. Abercrombie (1998), 251. The required distribution to heirs, apart from the *mayorazgo* or similar device, meant that landed estates might be divided among several children, thereby fragmenting larger holdings. Van Young (1981), 308–309.

71. Pacheco Caballero (1993), 229–234.

72. Ibid., 254–256.

73. Ibid., 246–247.

74. Gutiérrez Sarmiento (1992), 117–118.

75. Margadant S. (1990), 125.

76. Book 6, Title 1, Law 32 and Book 1, Title 13, Law 9 of *Recopilación* of 1680. Levene (1985), 147.

77. Kellogg (1995), 158–159. For Indian testaments see Kellogg and Restall (1998).

78. Ots Capdequí (1952), 126.

79. Taylor (1972), 140.

80. Kellogg (1995), 128–129.

81. Gutiérrez Sarmiento (1992), 43–88.

Chapter 7

1. The exploitation of slave and native labor is discussed in the following chapters.
2. Bello Lozano (1983), 359.
3. Stein and Stein (2000).
4. Margadant S. (1990), 91.
5. Levene (1985), 76.
6. Margadant S. (1990), 91.
7. Werner (2002).
8. Haring (1975), 262.
9. Ibid., 306; Bello Lozano (1983), 360.
10. Margadant S. (1990), 92–92; Stein and Stein (2000), 136–144.
11. Brading (1984), 413.
12. Stein and Stein (2000), 200–230.
13. Brading (1984), 413; Margadant S. (1990), 92–93.
14. Brading (1984), 413–426; Gibson (1966), 169.
15. Margadant S. (1990), 90 citing *Partida* 2, Title 15, Law 15.
16. De Estrada (1978), 171.
17. Haring (1975), 245.
18. Margadant S. (1990), 90; Levene (1985), 103.
19. Margadant S. (1990), 90.
20. Levene (1985), 104; Haring (1975) 247.
21. Haring (1975), 248; Howe (1949), 62–77.
22. Haring (1975), 259.
23. Bello Lozano (1983), 353–354.
24. Mellafe (1975), 24.
25. Ots Capdequí (1952), 83–84.
26. Haring (1975), 247.
27. Levene (1985), 103.
28. Margadant S. (1990), 90. Levene (1983), 104, puts the date at 1779. Howe provides a chapter on the organization of the Tribunal from 1770 to 1777. Howe (1949), 27–77.
29. Howe (1949), 261–300, 288.
30. Ibid., 65.
31. Margadant S. (1990), 88.
32. Ots Capdequí (1952), 127. See generally Levaggi (1987), vol. 2, 161–189.
33. Bello Lozano (1983), 382.
34. Ots Capdequí (1952), 127.
35. *Partida* 5, Title 11.
36. *Partida* 6, Titles 5 and 6.
37. Vera Estañol (1994), 57.
38. Levene (1985), 145.
39. Levaggi (1987), vol. 2, 178.
40. Ots Capdequí (1952), 48.
41. Ibid., 48–49.
42. Ibid., 49.
43. Ibid., 49.
44. Armstrong (1989), 9–10.

45. Margadant S. (1990), 53; Werner (2002).

46. Ibid., 43.

47. Clagett and Valderrama (1973), 127.

48. De Estrada (1978), 38.

49. Gutiérrez Sarmiento (1992), 124–146.

50. Ibid., 128–138.

51. Ots Capdequí (1952), 23.

52. *Partida* 5, Title 10.

53. Means (1980), 5.

54. Ibid., 12.

55. Gutiérrez Sarmiento (1992), 148–50; Levaggi (1991), vol. 3, 142–148.

56. Levaggi (1991), vol. 3, 148–150; Means (1980), 19–20.

57. Haring (1975), 301.

58. Levene (1985), 101; *Leyes de las Indias,* Book 5, Title 3, Law 17; Hevia Bolaños (1652). For the Roman and canon law origins of "just price" see Berman (1983), 247–248 and works cited there.

59. Levene (1985), 101; *Leyes de las Indias,* Book 5, Title 3, Law 17.

60. Levaggi (1991), vol. 3, 156–165.

61. Vera Estañol (1994), 46–47.

Chapter 8

1. Mellafe (1975), 2.

2. Bowser (1984), 358.

3. Klein (1986).

4. Mellafe (1975), 14–16, 24, 27–29, 109.

5. Ibid., 16, 19, 31.

6. Haring (1975) 203–205.

7. Mellafe (1975), 73.

8. Ibid., 23.

9. Haring (1975) 203–205.

10. Mellafe (1975), 39.

11. There are numerous studies and descriptions of the international dimension of the slave trade. See, for example, Blackburn (1997); Eltis (1987); Thomas (1997).

12. Mellafe (1975), 40, 42–43.

13. Ibid., 64.

14. Ibid., 65, 75.

15. Ibid., 45.

16. Ibid., 48–49, 70–71.

17. Ibid., 54–57, 60–62.

18. Ibid., 63.

19. Ibid., 88–96.

20. Cottrol (2001), 29–30; Mellafe (1975), 10; Watson (1989), 42–46.

21. *Leyes de las Indias,* Book 8, Title 18.

22. Lucena Salmoral (1996); its provisions are summarized in Watson (1989), 59–62.

23. Mellafe (1975), 104.

24. Levene (1985), 176; *Leyes de las Indias,* Book 1, Title 1, Law 13.

25. Mellafe (1975), 100.

26. Ibid., 101. These are summarized well in Watson (1989), 42–50. See also, Knight (1970), 124.

27. Watson (1989), 44–45.

28. Bowser (1984), 375–376.

29. Mellafe (1975), 106.

30. Bowser (1984), 374.

31. Bergad et al. (1995), 122.

32. Watson (1989), 50–56.

33. Bergad et al. (1995), 122–142; Knight (1970), 130–131; Scott (1985), 13–14.

34. Mellafe (1975), 117, 118. For enslaved women see Socolow (2000), 130–146.

35. Watson (1989), 48.

36. Bowser (1984), 369; Knight (1970), 125–126; Watson (1989), 49–50, 57–58.

37. Gutiérrez Sarmiento (1992), 94.

38. Mellafe (1975), 63, 97–99.

39. Ibid., 122; Lucena Salmoral (1996), 295. For a description of the Slave Code of 1842 see Knight (1970), 126–136.

40. Burkholder and Johnson (1998), 60.

41. Margadant S. (1990), 76–77.

42. Vigil (1987), 83–160.

43. Margadant S. (1990), 53.

Chapter 9

1. Benton (2002), 81–82; Parry (1977), 52–58; Zavala (1971), 54–63.

2. Burkholder and Johnson (1998), 108–113.

3. Miranda (1980a), 165.

4. Ibid., 166.

5. Gibson (1984), 388–395.

6. Levene (1985), 65.

7. Margadant S. (1990), 58.

8. Haring (1975), 40.

9. Levene (1985), 67. See also Scafidi (2003).

10. Burkholder and Johnson (1998), 69. "Theological debates about the legal status of Indians influenced crown policy deeply in the first decade of rule and have been amply treated by historians." Benton (2000), 32, citing Colin M. MacLachlan, *Spain's Empire in the New World: The Role of Ideas in Institutional and Social Change* (Berkeley: University of California Press, 1988); and Robert A. Williams, *The American Indian in Western Legal Thought: The Discourse of Conquest* (New York: Oxford University Press, 1990). See also, Hanke (1949); Zavala (1971), 260–318.

11. González (1981), 18.

12. Bello Lozano (1983), 366; Zavala (1935), 15–20.

13. Benton (2002), 82; Esquivel Obregón (1980), 228.

14. Margadant S. (1990), 58–59; Ots Capdequí (1952), 74; Zavala (1935), 88–177.

15. Levene (1985), 69.

16. Burkholder and Johnson (1998), 57.

17. Haring (1975), 51.

18. Levene (1985), 70.

19. Ibid., 218–219.

20. Book 6, Title 17.

21. Levene (1985), 220.

22. Taylor (1972), 198.

23. Gibson (1984), 399–401; Miranda (1952); Ots Capdequí (1952), 76–77.

24. Burkholder and Johnson (1998), 95.

25. Chevalier (1963), 196.

26. For Mexico see generally Zavala (1984–1987).

27. Gibson (1966), 48–67; Gibson (1984), 386–388. The grant of an *encomienda* did not carry with it a concomitant grant of land where the *encomienda* Indians lived. Although by other means, *encomenderos* often acquired property in or near the *encomienda*. Zavala (1940), 20, 29, 47, 81. The institution is treated in many contemporary sources including Solórzano's *Política Indiana* and the *Recopilación* of 1680. Zavala (1935), 254–293 describes this topic in these sources.

28. Margadant S. (1990), 78–79.

29. Ibid., 58–59; Ots Capdequí (1952), 74.

30. Haring (1975), 41.

31. Burkholder and Johnson (1998), 117–118.

32. Margadant S. (1990), 79.

33. Ibid., 79–80.

34. Haring (1975), 51–52.

35. Ots Capdequí (1952), 73–74; Zavala (1935), 110–113, 177–179. For contemporary debate concerning the duration of *encomiendas* see Zavala (1935), 183–269.

36. Burkholder and Johnson (1998), 120.

37. Ibid., 120.

38. Ots Capdequí (1952), 73.

39. Ibid., 74.

40. Levene (1985), 146.

41. Ots Capdequí (1952), 124.

42. Ibid., 124–125.

43. De Estrada (1978), 89–90.

44. Zavala (1935), 330–333.

45. Ebright (1994), 22.

46. Ots Capdequí (1952), 74; Zavala (1935), 334–343.

47. Zavala (1935), 344–345.

48. Phelan (1967), 60.

49. Ibid., 62. *Alcaldes* of Indian municipalities could also force Indians to buy products at profitable prices under a system of *repartimiento de mercancías*, not to be confused with the *repartimiento* of Indians discussed here. Armstrong (1989), 12; Gibson (1984), 415.

50. Gibson (1984), 386. On the overlap of these two terms see Gibson (1966), 49, 143.

51. Chevalier (1963), 279.

52. Taylor (1972), 145–146.

53. Armstrong (1989), 21.

54. Margadant S. (1990), 81–82; Chevalier (1963), 277–288.

55. Taylor (1972), 148–150.

56. Ibid., 152.

57. Margadant S. (1990), 82 citing *Leyes de las Indias,* Book 6, Title 5.

58. Ots Capdequí (1952), 77–78.

59. Ibid., 78; *Leyes de las Indias,* Book 6, Title 15.

60. Armstrong (1989), 16.

61. Phelan (1967), 70–71.

62. Gutiérrez Sarmiento (1992), 160–161.

63. Gibson (1984), 387, 409–410; Ots Capdequí (1952), 75.

64. Margadant S. (1990), 83.

65. Ibid., 60.

66. Ibid., 83 citing *Leyes de las Indias,* Book 7, Title 3.

67. Ots Capdequí (1952), 76.

68. Margadant S. (1990), 83 citing *Leyes de las Indias,* Book 6, Title 3, Law 15.

69. Ibid., 84.

70. Ots Capdequí (1952), 75. Similarly, *encomiendas* that reverted to the crown became *corregimientos.* Gibson (1984), 387; Zavala (1935), 64–65.

71. Ots Capdequí (1952), 75–76.

72. Book 6, Title 3.

73. Haring (1975), 180.

74. Ots Capdequí (1952), 79.

75. Haring (1975), 185.

76. Ibid., 186.

77. Ibid., 57.

78. Ibid., 62.

79. Phelan (1967), 63.

80. Margadant S. (1990), 86.

81. Taylor (1972), 4.

82. Ibid., 7–8.

83. Ibid., 78.

84. Ibid., 35–36.

85. Ibid., 38–45.

86. Ibid., 55–65.

87. Ibid., 65–66.

88. Ots Capdequí (1952), 125.

89. Taylor (1972), 48–49.

90. Ibid., 68–78.

91. Zavala (1940), 50–57, 81.

92. Chevalier (1963), 217.

93. Lira (1980), 199–202.

94. Ibid., 202.

95. Kellogg (1995), 30.

96. Borah (1996), 227–228, citing Hipólito Vallarroel, *Enfermedades políticas,* 3d ed. (Mexico City: Miguel Angel Porrúa, 1979), 53.

97. Kellogg (1995), 7; Miranda (1980a), 173.

98. Taylor (1972), 83–84.

99. Stern (1993), 115, 132–133.

100. Kellogg (1995), 40.

101. Ibid., 35.

102. Ibid., 32–33.

103. Ibid., 54–56.

104. Mellafe (1975), 95.

105. Kellogg (1995) 60–63.
106. Ibid., 73, 81.
107. Stern (1993), 114–137.
108. Margadant S. (1990), 86.

Chapter 10

1. Jaksić (2001), 156; Means (1980), 143.
2. Bolívar, *Discurso ante el Congreso de Angostura* as translated by Mirow (2000a), 91–92.
3. Ibid., 93.
4. Mirow (2000a), 107–109; Mirow (2001).
5. Bellomo (1995), 2.
6. Ibid., 2.
7. Mirow (2000a).
8. Varga (1991), 334.
9. Vanderlinden (1967), 223–225, 243.
10. Adelman (1999). See generally Lynch (1992).
11. Adekman (1999), 115.
12. Ibid., 112.
13. Ibid., 34–36, 125, 128–130.
14. Ibid., 132.
15. Ibid., 145–150, 165–166, 237.
16. Ibid., 239–240, 245.
17. Ibid., 245–246.
18. Ibid., 281.
19. Jaksić (1998), 17–20.
20. Jaksić (2001), 156–157.
21. Jaksić (1998), 25–26.
22. See generally, Jaksić, (2001), 156–181.
23. Jaksić (1998), 22–23, 31–32.
24. Jaksić (1997), 263 as quoted in Jaksić (2001), 177–178.
25. Mirow (2001).
26. Jaksić (2001), 164; Mirow (2001).
27. Mirow (2001).

Chapter 11

1. See generally, Bushnell and Macaulay (1994); Peloso and Tenenbaum (1996).
2. González (1981), 20; Bello Lozano (1983), 427–432.
3. Jaksić (2001), 156–181; Zimmermann (1999b), 1.
4. Karst and Rosenn (1975), 43.
5. González (1981), 21.
6. Ibid., 44; Soberanes Fernández (1998), 111, 115–163.
7. Miller (1997a). For Bentham see Mirow (2000a), 97–100; Williford (1980), 15–30. Codification is addressed in Chapter 15.
8. Levene (1985), 406.
9. Pérez Perdomo (1981), 80–94.
10. Zimmermann (1999b), 6.

Chapter 12

1. Constitutions are political documents, and each country has a different constitutional history. A good summary of the relevant aspects is found at Pérez Perdomo (2002), 64–71.

2. Mirow (2000a), 103–104. For a general description of Bolívar's laws for tribunals and their functions see Polanco Alcántara (1983), 21–47.

3. See, for example, Chile's legislation of 1875. Stabili (2000), 236–238.

4. De Estrada (1978), 110, 128.

5. Levene (1985), 263.

6. Ibid., 238, 251.

7. Polanco Alcántara (1962), 9–59.

8. Levene (1985), 271.

9. De Estrada (1978), 130.

10. Levene (1985), 281.

11. Ibid., 282–283.

12. Clark (1975), 413–416; Golbert and Nun (1982), 40–42.

13. Miller (1997a), 1494–1495.

14. Levene (1985), 267.

15. Stabili (2000), 238, 252.

16. Uribe-Uran (1999), 44.

17. Clagett and Valderrama (1973), 210–211, 215.

18. Ibid., 216–221.

19. Arnold (1988), 56–80.

20. Uribe-Uran (1999), 42–45; Barreneche (1999), 91; Stabili (2000); Zimmermann (1999c), 106–108.

21. Levene (1985), 284.

22. Ibid., 285–286, 309.

23. Polanco Alcántara (1983), 49–50.

24. Stabili (2000), 230–232.

25. Levene (1985), 380–381.

26. Ibid., 386.

27. Ibid., 382–383.

28. Bliss (2000), 268, 271, 282; Levene (1985), 317–322; Stabili (2000), 237.

29. Bliss (2000), 268; Levene (1985), 317–322.

30. Miller (1997a), 1497–1522.

31. Levene (1985), 420–421; Miller (1997a), 1501.

32. Miller (1997a), 1493–1534, 1554; Miller (1997b), 238–244.

33. Bliss (2000), 266–267.

34. Levene (1985), 358. See also Piccirilli (1942).

35. Ibid., 359–362.

36. Stabili (2000), 239.

37. Arnold (1988), 62.

38. Armstrong (1989), 20, 24–26; Arnold (1988), 56–80; Arnold (1996), 20–22; Soberanes Fernández (1980b), 36–37. See generally, Benson (1966).

39. Tena Ramírez (1998), 186–190.

40. Arnold (1996), 49.

41. Ibid., 67–70, 77; Ibid., 48–62.

42. Ibid., 71–97.

43. Armstrong (1989), 27.

44. Margadant S. (1990), 150.

45. Tena Ramírez (1998), 423–425.

46. Arnold (1996), 134–141.

47. Ibid., 143–158.

48. Ibid., 158–159.

49. Ibid., 162.

50. Armstrong (1989), 30, 42–43.

51. Margadant S. (1990), 180.

52. Ibid., 183.

53. See, for instance, the discussion of Morales, Mexico, in Bliss (2000), 269–283.

54. Arnold (1988), 62–63; Vera Estañol (1994), 19–20. For Chile see Stabili (2000), 240.

55. Arnold (1999), 49–61.

56. Lira (1980), 189–197.

57. Means (1980), 147.

58. Vera Estañol (1994), 22.

59. Esquivel Obregón (1980), 229.

60. Levene (1985), 292.

61. Ibid., 294.

62. Ibid., 372–377.

63. Margadant S. (1990), 165; Vera Estañol (1994), 33.

64. Serrano (2000); Traffano (2000).

65. Bello Lozano (1983), 451.

66. Ibid., 453.

67. Ibid., 454–455.

68. Margadant S. (1990), 166, 182–183.

69. Stabili (2000), 233.

70. Arnold (1996), 118–119.

71. Levene (1985), 272.

72. Gibson (1948), 63; Article 175.

73. Vera Estañol (1994), 85–86.

74. Gutiérrez Sarmiento (1992), 180–181.

75. Ebright (1994), 62–64.

Chapter 13

1. De Trazegnies (1979), 221–256; Tau Anzoátegui (1977a), 71–123.

2. Uribe-Uran (2000), 76–79. See also Pérez Perdomo (2002), 95.

3. Uribe-Uran (2000), 106–107.

4. Ibid., 115.

5. Mendieta y Núñez (1975), 123–130.

6. Pérez Perdomo (2002), 82–83.

7. Mendieta y Núñez (1975), 128.

8. Ibid., 132–133.

9. Ibid., 133.

10. Ibid., 140–141.

11. Levene (1985), 335.

12. Ibid., 336.

13. Ibid., 336–338.

14. Ibid., 338–339.

15. Ibid., 340.

16. Miller (1997c), 108–110.

17. Levene (1985), 224.

18. Ibid., 429.

19. Mirow (2000a), 97–100; Uribe-Uran (2000), 108–113.

20. Levene (1985), 366–367.

21. Means (1980), 116; Pérez Perdomo (2002), 84.

22. Means (1980), 119–120.

23. Uribe-Uran (2000), 115–116.

24. Means (1980), 117.

25. Ibid., 120–121.

26. Ibid., 122–123.

27. Ibid., 167–168.

28. Ibid., 169.

29. Ibid., 173.

30. Ibid., 169.

31. Ibid., 173.

32. Ibid., 175–176. Similar courses of study with early emphasis on Roman and canon law later adapting to more modern trends such as national law and legislation are found for Venezuela and Chile. Pérez Perdomo (2002), 83, 85. For San Marcos, Lima, Peru, see Ugarte del Pino (1968), 44, 94–99, 125–128. For Chile and postindependence legal education at the *Instituto Nacional* see De Ávila Martel (2000), 38–54; Bravo Lira (1999), 83–85, 94–96; Dougnac Rodríguez (1999); Hanisch Espíndola (2000).

33. Pérez Perdomo (1981), 110–119; Pérez Perdomo (2002), 86–88.

34. De Marco (1973), 126–130.

35. Levene (1985), 258.

36. Uribe-Uran (1999), 39.

37. Ibid., 45–46.

38. Barreneche (1999), 90–96.

39. Means (1980), 144.

40. Uribe-Uran (2000), 1, 6.

41. Levene (1985), 258.

42. Uribe-Uran (2000), 65.

43. See generally, Pérez Perdomo (2002), 53–60.

44. Uribe-Uran (2000), 5–6.

45. Ibid., 45–59.

46. Ibid., 46, 49.

47. Ibid., 156.

48. Ibid., 67–69.

49. Ibid., 71.

50. Pérez Perdomo (1981), 134; Pérez Perdomo (2002), 97; Uribe-Uran (2000), 78.

51. Uribe-Uran (2000), 140.

52. Pérez Perdomo (1981), 160–161.

53. Adelman (1999).

54. Pérez Perdomo (2002), 101–110.
55. Zimmermann (1999a), 108.
56. De Marco (1973), 133–143.
57. Ibid., 72–87.
58. Ibid., 86.

Chapter 14

1. Gibson (1948), 30.
2. Ibid., 65.
3. Guzmán Brito (2000a), 122–124; Tena Ramírez (1998), 158.
4. González (1981), chart between 30 and 31.
5. Ibid., 31, 36, 41.
6. Ibid., 46.
7. Margadant S. (1990), 150 (23.v.1837).
8. Clagett and Valderrama (1973), 136.
9. Cordova (1956), 66–69.
10. Arnold (1996), 44–45.
11. Pérez Perdomo (2002), 79–80.
12. Means (1980), 141, n. 9.
13. Ebright (1994), 27, 61, 67.
14. Levene (1985), 364.
15. Ibid., 363.
16. Margadant S. (1990), 147.
17. Means (1980), 115.
18. Guzmán Brito (1996); Ramos Núñez (1997), 217–238.
19. Clagett and Valderrama (1973), 119–120, 130, 133, 138; Guzmán Brito (1992).
20. Zimmermann (1999c), 117.
21. De Marco (1973), 141–142. An excellent introduction to these sources is Halpérin (1996).
22. Means (1980), 58.
23. Levene (1985), 432.
24. Margadant S. (1990), 149. See also Cruz Barney (1999), 591–604.
25. Ibid., 177.
26. Levene (1985), 455.
27. Means (1980), 115, n. 218.
28. Ibid., 278.
29. An interesting body of English translations of colonial Spanish and Mexican legislation was published for use in the United States Court of Private Land Claims resulting from the Treaty of Guadalupe Hidalgo. See Ebright (1994); Reynolds (1895). See also Schmidt (1851).
30. Margadant S. (1990), 177.
31. Miller (1997b), 242, 247.
32. Margadant S. (1990), 178.
33. Merryman (1985), 24, 144.
34. Arnold (1996), 176–177.
35. Means (1980), 278; Miller (1997b), 250.
36. Margadant S. (1990), 170.

Chapter 15

1. Guzmán Brito (2000a), 160–164; Jaksić (2001), 156–181; Levene (1985), 444; Mirow (2000a); Ramos Núñez (1997), 22–23.

2. Guzmán Brito (1979); Guzmán Brito (2000a), 124–129, 147–151.

3. Means (1980), 272.

4. González (1981), 28, 75, 80–82; Guzmán (2000), 147, 164–168; Ramos Núñez (1997), 43–69; Tau Anzoátegui (1977b), 19–31, 65–218, 253–308.

5. Gibson (1948), 86.

6. Means (1980), 142, n. 13.

7. Levene (1985), 296.

8. González (1981), 29. Several other examples are listed at Guzmán Brito (2000a), 156–160. See also Tau Anzoátegui (1977b),309–352.

9. Guzmán Brito (2000a), 136–137.

10. González (1981), 28.

11. Córdova (1956), 85–93; Bello Lozano (1983), 437–438.

12. Córdova (1956), 92. The Ecuadorian draft was based on the Bolivian Civil Code of 1830. Córdova (1956), 86.

13. Bolívar, *Decretos del Libertador,* vol. 1 (1961), 356, as quoted in Mirow (2000a), 101–102.

14. Guzmán Brito (2000a), 138; Mirow (2000a), 115.

15. Means (1980), 144.

16. Ibid., 145; Mirow (2000a), 115.

17. Guzmán Brito (2000a), 145–146, 151–153; Ramos Núñez (1987), 148–153. This Bolivian civil code is also known as the Santa Cruz Civil Code. Guzmán Brito (2000a), 200–208.

18. Levene (1985), 384.

19. Code Napoleon (1960).

20. Guzmán Brito (2000a), 140, 215–228; Ramos Núñez (1997), 160–179.

21. The most recent and extensive study, with excellent diagrams, is Guzmán Brito (2000a). See also, Ramos Núñez (1997), 132–211.

22. Guzmán Brito (2000a), 153–156; Williford (1980). See also Scholfield (1995); Scholfield and Harris (1998).

23. Zimmermann (1999c), 121, 123; Mirow (2000a).

24. González (1981), 89–92; Guzmán Brito (2000a), 197–199; Ramos Núñez (1997), 141–145.

25. Ortiz-Urquidi (1974); Soberanes Fernández (1998), 170.

26. González (1981), 95.

27. Ibid., 100–102.

28. Ibid., 106.

29. Ibid., 106.

30. Ibid., 107.

31. Margadant S. (1990), 173–174.

32. González (1981), 109.

33. Margadant S. (1990), 174, n. 20.

34. González (1981), 110–111.

35. Arrom (1985a); González (1981), 112–113.

36. See generally Guzmán Brito (1982); Guzmán Brito (2000a), 229–282.

37. Córdova (1956), 183–191, 363–370; Guzmán Brito (2000a), 141–142.

38. Bello Lozano (1983), 438.

39. Mirow (2001).

40. Jaksić (1997); Jaksić (2001), Mirow (2001).

41. See generally, Guzmán Brito (1982), Bello (1955).

42. Clagett and Valderrama (1973), 64.

43. Bello Lozano (1983), 439, 486.

44. Ibid., 440.

45. Clagett and Valderrama (1973), 104, 106–107.

46. See generally Cháneton (1938); Guzmán Brito (2000a), 293–303; Miller (1997c), 105–110.

47. Levene (1985), 427.

48. Ibid., 433.

49. Ibid., 426–429.

50. Ibid., 430–431.

51. Ibid., 433.

52. Ibid., 434.

53. Ibid., 436. For Acevedo's draft civil code see Guzmán Brito (2000a), 305–307; Ramos Núñez (1997), 189–193.

54. Levene (1985), 437.

55. Ibid., 437.

56. Cháneton (1938), vol. 2, 159–227; Miller (1997c), 105–107.

57. Karst and Rosenn (1975), 46.

58. Ibid., 46.

59. Levene (1985), 440, 443.

60. Guzmán Brito (2000b).

61. Levene (1985), 426.

62. De Estrada (1978), 166–167.

63. Levene (1985), 426.

64. Ibid., 438.

65. Ibid., 439–441. The texts of Alberdi's criticism and Vélez's response are reproduced in Ramos Núñez (1997), 305–359.

66. Cháneton (1938), vol. 2, 131–156; Tau Anzoátegui (1977b), 365–408; Zimmermann (1999c), 118–120.

67. Bello Lozano (1983), 444–445; Clagett and Valderrama (1973), 131.

68. Braun Menéndez (1951), 16.

69. Margadant S. (1990), 174.

70. Levene (1985), 455.

71. Margadant S. (1990), 183.

72. Ibid., 183.

73. Bellomo (1995), 1–33. The Spanish code was made applicable to Cuba and Puerto Rico in 1889. Guzmán Brito (2000a), 143.

Chapter 16

1. Klein (1986), 243–271.

2. Blackburn (1988), 341–360; Hunefeldt (1994), 22–27, 86–88.

3. Mellafe (1975), 129.

4. Blackburn (1988), 351, 354; De Estrada (1978), 91.

5. Blackburn (1988), 349, 362; De Estrada (1978), 91; Mellafe (1975), 130-134, 140-141; See also, Bello Lozano (1983), 421; Blackburn (1988), 363-365.

6. Blackburn (1988), 368-372.

7. Ibid., 367.

8. Mellafe (1975), 130-132, 140-141.

9. Hunefeldt (1994), 24, 63-79, 97-106, 169-170.

10. Eltis (1987), 3-28.

11. Ibid., 85-88.

12. Bello Lozano (1983), 472.

13. Hunefeldt (1994), 3, 5.

14. Mellafe (1975), 135; Scott (1985), xi. Some sources give 1886 as the date of final abolition of slavery for these colonies. Bowser (1984), 379; Evenson (1994), 109. Indeed, Scott's authoritative study documents a process of gradual emancipation in Cuba from 1870, with the Moret Law, to 1886. Scott (1985).

15. Mellafe (1975), 136-137.

16. Blackburn (1988), 362; Mellafe (1975), 139.

17. Mellafe (1975), 134.

18. Blackburn (1988), 365-368.

19. Mellafe (1975), 138. Similarly, the Cuban *patronato* system in the 1880s justified its labor practices as providing a transitional period from slave to free status for workers. Scott (1985), 127-144.

20. Hunefeldt (2000), 51; Mellafe (1975), 140, 145.

21. Tena Ramírez (1998), 22.

22. Ibid., 30.

23. Levene (1985), 293.

24. Armstrong (1989), 21-22.

25. Tena Ramírez (1998), 59.

26. Ibid., 60-63.

27. Margadant S. (1990), 136.

28. Ibid., 137.

29. González (1981), 22.

30. Armstrong (1989), 38; Tena Ramírez (1998), 124.

31. Levene (1985), 462.

32. González (1981), 26-27. See also Clavero (2002).

33. Hunefeldt (2000), 54-56.

34. Levene (1985), 348.

35. Margadant S. (1990), 153-154.

36. Ibid., 179.

37. Tena Ramírez (1998), 24.

38. For the persistence of church control over these aspects in Peru during the nineteenth century see Hunefeldt (2000), 83-88. For an example of citizens caught between religious and civil systems in Mexico see Traffano (2000).

39. Means (1980), 202.

40. Levene (1985), 378.

41. De Estrada (1978), 170.

42. Hunefeldt (2000), 79-85. For marital requirements, impediments, and dispensations see Hunefeldt (2000), 94-146.

43. Herget and Camil (1978), 37.
44. Vera Estañol (1994), 34.
45. Hunefeldt (2000), 85.
46. Vera Estañol (1994), 35.
47. For the unique developments in Mexico see Arrom (1985a); Arrom (1985b).
48. Córdova (1956), 68, 77–78.
49. Margadant S. (1990), 180.
50. Hunefeldt (2000), 13.
51. Ibid., 147–176.
52. *Los doce códigos del estado soberano de Cundinamarca* (1878), vol. 2, 20–27.
53. Vera Estañol (1994), 34–35, 40–41.
54. Arrom (1985a), 91.
55. Ibid., 97.
56. Hunefeldt (2000), 14–15.
57. Guy (2000), 108–121.
58. Hunefeldt (2000), 224–272.

Chapter 17

1. Seed (2001), 152.
2. De Trazegnies Granda (1979), 48–51, 185–193.
3. Bello Lozano (1983), 520.
4. Lynch (1992).
5. Hora (2001), 13–35.
6. Adelman (1994), 63–97; Hora (2001), 41–42; LeGrand (1986), 1–90; Tovar Pinzón (1995).
7. Bello Lozano (1983), 521.
8. Mirow (2001), 316–321.
9. Margadant S. (1990), 136, n. 5; Vera Estañol (1994), 21.
10. De Estrada (1978), 131.
11. Levene (1985), 293.
12. Collier and Sater (1996), 36.
13. Armstrong (1989), 23.
14. Córdova (1956), 68. For Peru see De Trazegnies Granda (1979), 188.
15. Donoso (1967), 103.
16. Mirow (2001), 320.
17. Levene (1985), 292.
18. Ibid., 351.
19. Margadant S. (1990), 144.
20. Ibid., 138.
21. Ebright (1994), 27.
22. Margadant S. (1990), 167. For similar developments in the Dominican Republic see Clausner (1973), 116–117.
23. Armstrong (1989), 44–45.
24. Margadant S. (1990), 165.
25. Vera Estañol (1994), 24–25.
26. Margadant S. (1990), 164–165.
27. Armstrong (1989), 59.
28. Clausner (1973), 118–124.

29. Vera Estañol (1994), 49.

30. Lamar (1994).

31. Mirow (2001), 323–324.

32. Mirow (2000a); Mirow (2001).

33. Portalis, "Lejislación, Discurso preliminar del proyecto de código civil de Francia por Mr Portalis," *El Aruacano*, August 17, 1833, at 2 (No. 153, trans. A. Bello into Spanish).

34. Mirow (2001), 324.

35. Arrom (1985b), 313–315; Margadant S. (1990), 180; Vera Estañol (1994), 38.

36. Armstrong (1989), 64–65.

Chapter 18

1. Bello Lozano (1983), 459; De Trazegnies Granda (1979), 201.

2. Means (1980), 145–164.

3. Ibid., 163.

4. Ibid., 184, 185.

5. Ibid., 187–191.

6. Ibid., 187–191, 262.

7. Ibid., 190–194.

8. Ibid., 182.

9. Levene (1985), 324–328.

10. Ibid., 447–448.

11. Adelman (1999), 245–246.

12. Levene (1985), 450.

13. De Estrada (1978), 167–168.

14. Levene (1985), 449.

15. Adelman (1999), 246.

16. Ibid., 246–248. See also Levaggi (1991), vol. 3, 189–197.

17. Braun Menéndez (1951), 13–17.

18. Ibid., 18–21.

19. Ibid., 24–26.

20. Ibid., 26–27, 31–34.

21. Ibid., 27–29; Mirow (1997), 427–429.

22. Braun Menéndez (1951), 27–30.

23. Ibid., 30–31; Karst and Rosenn (1975), 49.

24. Margadant S. (1990), 150, 170–171.

25. Ibid., 170–171, 180.

26. Armstrong (1989), 60; Margadant S. (1990), 180.

27. Margadant S. (1990), 180.

28. Bello Lozano (1983), 460–461.

29. Means (1980), 185, n. 151. For the Peruvian commercial code see De Trazegnies Granda (1979), 201–205.

30. Margadant S. (1990), 181.

31. Means (1980), 62–98.

32. Clagett and Valderrama (1973), 146.

33. Vera Estañol (1994), 61–62.

34. Means (1980), 191–192. See, for example, for Peru, De Trazegnies Granda (1979), 202–205.

35. Means (1980), 192.
36. Ibid., 194, 196, 262.
37. Vera Estañol (1994), 47–48.
38. De Trazegnies Granda (1979), 202.
39. Karst and Rosenn (1975), 477.
40. Vera Estañol (1994), 59–61.
41. Armstrong (1989), 34–35, 50–51.
42. Margadant S. (1990), 183, 188.
43. Bello Lozano (1983), 509–510.
44. Margadant S. (1990), 151.
45. Ibid., 182.
46. Clagett and Valderrama (1973), 274.
47. Levene (1985), 450, 452.

Chapter 19

1. Merryman (1985), 151.
2. Karst and Rosenn (1975), 44.
3. Eder (1950), 71, 87.
4. Lynch (1981), 25. See also Aguilera (1965), 309–317.
5. Aguilera (1965), 310–311.
6. Gardner (1980).
7. Aguilera (1965), 414.
8. Karst and Rosenn (1975), 50.
9. Means (1980), 281.
10. Pérez Perdomo (1981), 359, 377, 389.
11. Ibid., 376.
12. Ibid., 379.
13. Ibid., 379.
14. Margadant S. (1990), 253, n. 71.
15. Reyes Villamizar (1996), 661–666. See also Reyes Villamizar (2002).
16. Ibid., 44–48.
17. Eddington (1998), 322.
18. Nagle (2001), 920–922, 926.
19. Zamora (1993).
20. Dahlgren (1969).

Chapter 20

1. Karst and Rosenn (1975), 79. Most would view Argentina and Chile, with long-standing constitutions, as exceptions.
2. Ibid., 86–87 quoting J. Busey, "Observations on Latin American Constitutionalism," *The Americas* 24 (1967): 40–60.
3. Ibid., 185.
4. Ibid., 187, 192.
5. Golbert and Nun (1982), 40–41; Herget and Camil (1978), 71–72; Miller (1997a).
6. Margadant S. (1990), 195.
7. Ibid., 237.
8. Vargas (1998), vol. 1, 24–27.
9. Karst and Rosenn (1975), 50.

10. Pérez Perdomo (2002), 144–146.

11. Buscaglia (1998), 16.

12. Karst and Rosenn (1975), 93.

13. Dezalay and Garth (1998), 83.

14. Correa Sutil (1999), 266.

15. Meyer et al. (1999), 676; Vargas (1996).

16. Prillaman (2000), 20.

17. Rico and Salas (1990), 14–20.

18. Ibid., 34–38.

19. Buscaglia (1998), 23; Karst and Rosenn (1975), 637–639; Prillaman (2000), 25–26.

20. Prillaman (2000), 21.

21. Domingo and Sieder (2001); Rosenn (1987). On the recent judicial reform activities of the World Bank, the Instituto de Cooperación Iberoamericana, the USAID, the UNDP, and the IDB see Jarquín and Carrillo (1998), 117–154.

22. For example, the Ford Foundation aided in publishing Correa Sutil (1993) and the British Council in publishing Faundez (1997). See also, for example, for Bolivia, Gamarra (1991); for Ecuador, Chinchilla and Schodt (1993); for Nicaragua, Solís and Wilson (1991); for Peru, Hammergren (1998); for women judges in Central America, Rivera Bustamante (1991).

23. Buscaglia (1998), 26–28; Prillaman (2000), 167.

24. Prillaman (2000), 171.

25. Ibid., 6.

26. Dakolias (1995); Sáez García (1998); Sherwood (1998), 31; Yamin and Noriega García (1999).

27. Prillaman (2000); O'Donnell (1999); Stotzky (1993).

28. Correa Sutil (1999), 261–263, 268.

29. Correa Sutil (1999), 268; O'Donnell (1999), 320.

30. Correa Sutil (1999), 260.

31. Ibid., 272–273.

32. Ibid., 275. See also Rico and Salas (1990), 27–31.

33. Prillaman (2000), 19.

34. Eder (1950), 151–156.

35. Correa Sutil (1999), 255–277.

36. Ibid., 255.

37. Ibid., 260–261.

38. Buscaglia (1998), 19.

39. Correa Sutil (1999), 255, 272.

40. Rico and Salas (1990), 32–34.

41. Correa Sutil (1999), 256. See also Domingo and Sieder (2001).

42. Pérez Perdomo (1981), 212.

43. Correa Sutil (1999), 264–266. See also Salas and Rico (1990), 24–29.

44. Correa Sutil (1999), 273.

45. Prillaman (2000), 60 (El Salvador), 129 (Argentina).

46. O'Donnell (1999), 311, 322.

47. Garro (1999), 281.

48. Ibid.; Horack (1950), 289; O'Donnell (1999), 311–313; Samway (1996); Selinger (1995).

49. Thome (2000), 700.

50. Buscaglia (1998), 21.

51. Thome (2000), 708–709.

52. Adelman (1999), 132; Prillaman (2000), 113, 127–128.

53. Prillaman (2000), 151.

54. Margadant S. (1990), 208.

55. Ibid., 236–237.

56. Vargas (1998), vol. 1, 24–27.

57. Clagett and Valderrama (1973), 114–115. The trend is mostly for criminal actions, but these ideas are making their way into some civil aspects as well.

58. Ibid., 104.

59. Herget and Camil (1978), 74–77; Thome (2000), 702, 709.

60. Golbert and Nun (1982), 21–31; Karst and Rosenn (1975), 51–53.

61. Karst and Rosenn (1975), 54.

62. Golbert and Nun (1982), 32.

63. Merryman (1985), 40–41, 120–121.

64. Karst and Rosenn (1975), 125–160.

65. Ibid., 160–183.

66. Constitución Política de Colombia (1991), Article 86.

67. Vargas (1998), vol. 1, 26.

68. Garro (1999), 288–290.

69. Eder (1950), 67.

70. Ibid., 138.

71. Ibid., 138–139.

72. Correa Sutil (1999), 263–264.

73. Ibid., 276–277.

74. Dezalay and Garth (1998), 91–94.

75. Vargas (1998), vol. 2, 2–3.

76. Martindale-Hubbell (2002), Arg-8, Bol-4, Cr-5, Ecu-5, Gua-4-5, Mex-10, Nic-4, Per-6, Uru-5, Ven-5.

77. Dezalay and Garth (1998), 93–95.

78. Dorner (1992), 67. See also De Soto (1989).

79. Karst et al. (1973). This view has been questioned by Pérez Perdomo and Nikken (1982).

80. Karst and Rosenn (1975), 574–628.

81. Collier (1973); Nader (1990).

82. Collier (1994), 57.

83. Ibid., 136–137.

84. Ibid., 137.

Chapter 21

1. Lynch (1981), 119; Wilson (1989), 382–384.

2. Mendieta y Núñez (1975), 149–150. Similar plans of study from the beginning of the twentieth century are listed for Argentina, Chile, and Venezuela in Pérez Perdomo (2002), 89.

3. Mendieta y Núñez (1975), 172–174.

4. Ibid., 149, 154–161.

5. Ibid., chart 2, following 198.

6. Ibid., 138, 162–168, 197.

7. Ibid., 142.

8. Margadant S. (1990), 195.

9. Pérez Perdomo (2002), 92.

10. Ibid., 119.

11. Ibid., 96–97.

12. Ibid., 119–120.

13. Margadant S. (1990), 239.

14. Pérez Perdomo (2002), 122–123.

15. In Venezuela, for example, this change occurred in 1957. Pérez Perdomo (1981), 203.

16. Herget and Camil (1978), 89–98. The number of law students at different times and in different countries is listed in Pérez Perdomo (2002), 118.

17. Pérez Perdomo (1981), 196–197.

18. For a discussion of teaching methods see Wilson (1989).

19. Pérez Perdomo (2002), 114–117.

20. Karst and Rosenn (1975), 66.

21. Ibid., 67. See also Dezalay and Garth (1998), 33.

22. Karst and Rosenn (1975), 67–68.

23. Garro (1999), 298, n. 32; Law 446 of 1998 (Colombia).

24. Horack (1950), 288.

25. "First Conference on Latin-American Law Schools." *Inter-American Law Review* 1 (1959): 241–249. Four more conferences were held until 1965. The second conference, in Lima, emphasized "active" teaching methods. Wilson (1989), 393–394.

26. Eder (1950), xi.

27. Chommie (1963).

28. Polen and Thomas (1969), 48.

29. Rosenn (2000), 10.

30. Gardner (1980), 6–15, 56; Research Advisory Committee on Law and Development (1974). See generally Gardner (1980).

31. Merillat (1966), 72.

32. Gardner (1980), 48.

33. Snyder (1982), 382, citing Gardner (1980), 4.

34. Gardner (1980), 7.

35. Ibid., 126–190; Merryman (2000a); Snyder (1982), 378.

36. Lynch (1981), 37. See also, Gardner (1980), 191–210.

37. Lynch (1981), 111–113.

38. Trubek and Galanter (1974), 1066–1067. See also Merryman (2000b).

39. Lynch (1981), 111–113.

40. Ibid., 113.

41. Ibid., 116.

42. Merryman (2000a).

43. Garro (1999), 285; Wilson (2002).

44. Pérez Perdomo (2002), 124 citing Witker (1976). See also Wilson (1989), 402.

45. Dezalay and Garth (1998), 12.

46. Ibid., 13.

47. Ibid., 13, 17.

48. Ibid., 80–81, 98–100. In the 1970s, Peruvian legal educators spoke of the "Wisconsin boys." Pérez Perdomo (2002), 125.

49. Horack (1950), 289.

50. Pérez Perdomo (2002), 116.

51. Lynch (1981), 91.

52. Pérez Perdomo (2002), 125-126.

53. Dezalay and Garth (1998), 96. See also Pérez Perdomo (2002), 131-138.

54. Pérez Perdomo (2002), 128-131.

55. Lynch (1981).

56. Lomnitz and Salazar (2002).

57. Pérez Perdomo (1981), 215-216, 227-235.

58. Pérez Perdomo (2002), 147-151.

59. Pérez Perdomo (1981), 244-255.

60. Bello Lozano (1983), 400-401.

61. Pérez Perdomo (2002), 97-98.

62. Collier (1994), 136.

63. Lynch (1981), 101-105; Garro (1999).

64. Lynch (1981), 123.

65. Merryman (1985), 102-103; Pérez Perdomo (2002), 138. For the number of judges in Latin American countries see Pérez Perdomo (2002), 138-140. For efforts at establishing a judicial career path in Latin America see Salas and Rico (1990).

66. Dezalay and Garth (1998), 31; Pérez Perdomo (2002), 140-141. Only in the last twenty years have willful ignorance or inaction by Latin American judges in the face of executive or military abuses of power and human rights violations become the subject of study. Pérez Perdomo (2002), 141-144.

67. Conference of Supreme Courts of the Americas (1996), 1319-1549.

68. Thome (2000), 702-703. See also Pérez Perdomo (2002), 143-151.

Chapter 22

1. Lafaille (1959), 33.

2. See, for example, the synopsis of Mexican legislation related to business, trade, and investment in Vargas (1998), vol. 2, 429-452.

3. Merryman (1985), 151-156; Miller (1985).

4. Prillaman (2000), 114.

5. Golbert and Nun (1982), 10-11; Karst and Rosenn (1975), 223-240.

6. Ortiz de Zevallos (1994), 1-13.

7. Prillaman (2000), 123.

8. Margadant S. (1990), 237, 249.

9. Ibid., 250.

10. Ibid., 250.

11. Karst and Rosenn (1975), 47.

12. Ibid., 47.

13. De Estrada (1978), 170. Civil Code of Argentina, Art. 1113. I thank Jonathan Miller for the last of these examples. See also González Hernández (1992), 158-162.

14. Margadant S. (1990), 235-238.

15. Means (1980), 274-276.

16. Margadant S. (1990), 249. Dates for Belgian and French sources are from Halpérin (1996), 65, 69, 184-185.

17. Means (1980), 278-279.

18. See, for example, the list of such authors for Mexico in Vargas (1998), vol. 1, 7.

19. Eder (1950), 13–14.

20. Ibid., 15; Karst and Rosenn (1975), 137–139.

21. Nagle (1995), 77–78, 82–90.

22. Miller (1985), 614.

23. Garro (1999), 300, n. 42.

24. Golbert and Nun (1982), 13.

25. Margadant S. (1990), 236.

26. A comparative study of this court, similar well-respected Latin American courts of the period, and the United States New Deal court may reveal unnoticed important international threads in judicial approach and in resolution of similar social and economic problems.

27. Golbert and Nun (1982), 15.

28. Ibid., 15.

29. Bello Lozano (1983), 490–495. A Spanish-English edition of the code is available. Bustamante (1996).

30. De Vries and Rodriguez-Novás (1965), 3–33.

31. Margadant S. (1990), 268. See, for example, Nagle (2001); Sheppard (2001).

32. Mendieta y Núñez (1975), 169.

33. Pérez Perdomo (2002), 113.

34. Websites are listed in the bibliography.

Chapter 23

1. Golbert and Nun (1982), 50.

2. Hernández (2002), 1128.

3. The legal aspects of Mexico's anticlerical policies during the second half of the nineteenth and the twentieth centuries, as well as a discussion of its more tolerant legislation passed in 1981 and 1992 is found in Capseta Castellà (1997). One scholar has recently reassessed the church's legal and political position in Mexico during the twentieth century, finding that despite official anticlericalism, the Mexican government has, in fact, closely cooperated with the church in postrevolutionary Mexico. Reich (1995).

4. Guy (2000), 33–71.

5. Martindale-Hubbell (2002), Arg-11, Bol-5, Chl-7–8, Col-9, Dr-5–6, Ecu-7, Es-7, Gua-6, Hon-5, Mex-13–14, Nic-6, Pan-15, Per-8, Uru-7, Ven-8.

6. Martindale-Hubbell (2002), Arg-11.

7. Herget and Camil (1978), 38; Martindale-Hubbell (2002), Ecu-6–7, Es-7, Gua-6, Mex-14, Pan-14, Ven-7.

8. Martindale-Hubbell (2002), Bol-5, Par-7.

9. Ibid., Hon-5, Nic-5.

10. Herget and Camil (1978), 37–38.

11. Herrerías Sordo (1998).

12. Eder (1950), 123; Evenson (1994), 134–136 (Cuba).

13. *Houston Chronicle,* December 14, 2002, p. 33.

14. Levene (1985), 464.

15. Evenson (1994), 136, 144, n. 83.

16. Margadant S. (1990), 194. See also Macías (1978).

17. Herget and Camil (1978), 39.

18. Colombian Civil Code, Art. 152, 154.

19. Levene (1985), 464; Rock (1987), 314–318.

20. Miller (2000), 391.

21. Martindale-Hubbell (2002), Nic-5, Uru-7, Ven-7.

22. Ibid., Chl-7.

23. Ibid., Dr-5.

24. Eder (1950), 120, 121.

25. See, for example, Guy (2000), 54–71; Macías (1978); Tuñón Pablos (1999), 93–103.

26. Little (1978), 242–249.

27. Hunefeldt (2000), 348–349.

28. Rock (1987), 287; Collier and Sater (1996), 287.

29. Margadant S. (1990), 202, 208, 217.

30. Bello Lozano (1983), 461.

31. For the capacity of married women to act in commerce in Latin America at mid twentieth century see Ramírez B. (1944), 572–578.

32. Hernandez (1991), 354–355.

33. Inter-American Development Bank (1995), 103–107, 152–170.

34. Thiesenhusen (1995), 73, 141.

35. Bello Lozano (1983), 483–484.

36. Karst and Rosenn (1975), 248 quoting F. Tannenbaum, "Toward an Appreciation of Latin America" in H. Matthews, ed., *The United States and Latin America,* 33–39, 2nd ed. (1963).

37. Cottrol (2001).

38. Hernández (2002), 1128–1129.

39. Collier (1973).

40. Margadant S. (1990), 206.

Chapter 24

1. Golbert and Nun (1982), 49, 67.

2. Ibid., 55.

3. Reich (1995), 148 n. 41. See also Corrin (2002), 73–76; Curran (2002), 174–179.

4. Karst and Rosenn (1975), 286–292, 353 (Chile).

5. Bird (1994), 42.

6. Ibid., 101–125.

7. Ibid., 53–59.

8. Margadant S. (1990), 194; Clagett and Valderrama (1973), 14.

9. Margadant S. (1990), 197.

10. Ibid., 198.

11. Ibid., 194.

12. Karst and Rosenn (1975), 64.

13. Vargas (1998), vol. 1, 387–388.

14. Bird (1994), 77–80.

15. Herget and Camil (1978), 53–56.

16. Martindale-Hubbell (2002), Arg-14, Bol-7, Chl-9, Col-11, Cr-9–10, Dr-7–8, Ecu-9, Es-8, Gua-8, Hon-7, Mex-17, Nic-7, Pan-17, Ven-10.

17. Eder (1950), 126–127.

18. Clausner (1973), 194–210; Martindale-Hubbell (2002), Dr-8.

19. De Soto (1998), 73–78.

20. Herget and Camil (1978), 52–53.

21. Ibid., 48–52.

22. Eder (1950), 112–115.

23. Martindale-Hubbell (2002), Bol-7, Nic-7.

24. Margadant S. (1990), 250; Martindale-Hubbell (2002), Hon-7, Pan-17, Par-11.

25. Margadant S. (1990), 270.

26. Herget and Camil (1978), 59; Martindale-Hubbell (2002), Cr-6, Mex-12.

27. Herget and Camil (1978), 57–58.

28. Martindale-Hubbell (2002), Arg-9–10; Bol-5, Par-6.

29. Ibid., Chl-6; Col-7–8.

30. Ibid., Dr-5, Ecu-6, Per-7, Uru-6, Ven-6–7.

31. Eder (1950), 128.

32. Martindale-Hubbell (2002), Cr-7, Es-6, Gua-6, Hon-5, Mex-12–13, Nic-5, Pan-14. See also Deere and León (2001), 262–291.

33. Ibid., Arg-10–11, Chl-6–7, Col-8, Mex-12–13.

34. Ibid., Bol-5.

35. Herget and Camil (1978), 58; Eder (1950), 89; Martindale-Hubbell (2002), Bol-5, Dr-5.

36. Martindale-Hubbell (2002), Arg-10, Col-8, Ecu-6, Es-6, Gua-5–6, Hon-5, Mex-12, Per-7.

37. Ibid., Cr-7, Mex-12.

38. Ibid., Ven-7.

39. Ibid., Mex-12, Pan-12; Vargas (1998), vol. 1, 351–391.

Chapter 25

1. Karst and Rosenn (1975), 51; Kozolchyk (1972).

2. Martínez (1998), 6.

3. De Soto (1989), 131–187. Suggested solutions include simplification, decentralization, and deregulation. De Soto (1989), 247–252.

4. Margadant S. (1990), 253.

5. Martindale-Hubbell (2002), Bol-1, Col-2, Cr-2, Ecu-2, Es-2, Gua-1, Hon-2, Mex-3, Pan-7, Par-1, Per-2, Uru-2.

6. Reyes Villamizar (1996), 59–67.

7. Glade (1998), 64–65.

8. Margadant S. (1990), 224–225, 252–254, 270.

9. For recent advances in secured transactions see Sheppard (2001).

10. Martindale-Hubbell (2002), Arg-8–9, Bol-4, Chl-5, Col-7, Cr-6, Dr-4, Ecu-5, Es-5, Gua-5, Hon-4, Mex-10–11, Nic-4, Pan-12, Par-4–5, Per-6, Uru-5–6, Ven-5–6. See also Malavet (1996); Malavet (1997); Malavet (1998); Vargas (1998), vol. 1, 15–17.

11. Eder (1950), 87–88.

12. Margadant S. (1990), 253.

13. Eder (1950), 88–90.

14. Martindale-Hubbell (2002), Hon-4.

15. Margadant S. (1990), 218–221; Clagett and Valderrama (1973), 160, 162.

16. Armstrong (1989), 103–117; Margadant S. (1990), 222.

17. Rowat (1997), 165–188.

18. Means (1980), 274–275.

19. Ibid., 275.

20. Ibid., xvi.

21. Vargas (1998), vol. 2, 429–452.

22. Margadant S. (1990), 182.

23. Ibid., 182.

24. Ibid., 197.

25. Meyer et al. (1999), 558, 566.

26. Margadant S. (1990), 200.

27. Ibid., 201.

28. Ibid., 213.

29. Ibid., 213–214.

30. See generally Vargas (1998), vol. 2, 97–159.

31. Levene (1985), 452. For this code with annotations to European and other Latin American sources, see Cano (1944).

32. De Estrada (1978), 172.

33. Ibid., 157; Rock (1987), 289, 320.

34. Bello Lozano (1983), 510.

35. Margadant S. (1990), 193, 246–248. See generally, Vargas (1998), vol. 1, 151–189.

36. Karst and Rosenn (1975), 57.

37. Eder (1950), 53. For a discussion of Colombian tort law see Bartels and Madden (2001).

38. Eder (1950), 43–50.

39. Ibid., 51 (Article 1913).

40. Ibid., 58.

41. Vargas (1998), vol. 2, 211.

42. Ibid., vol. 2, 222. The use of the plaintiff's contributory negligence as a complete bar to recovery is noteworthy. Ibid., vol. 2, 227.

43. Ibid., vol. 2, 214–215.

44. Ibid., vol. 2, 238.

45. Herget and Camil (1978), 44–45.

46. Vargas (1998), vol. 2, 221.

47. Ibid., vol. 2, 232.

48. Ibid., vol. 2, 216.

49. Ibid., vol. 2, 217.

50. Ibid., vol. 2, 233.

51. Eder (1950), 133.

52. Karst and Rosenn (1975), 421–538.

53. Margadant S. (1990), 252.

54. Ibid., 255.

Chapter 26

1. Thiesenhusen (1995), 54 (Bolivia), 89 (Chile).

2. Ibid., 160, 162, 172.

3. Karst and Rosenn (1975), 241.

4. See generally Armstrong (1989), 71–101.

5. Margadant S. (1990), 151, 163, 165, 172.

6. Ibid., 171. Juárez revoked the legislation in 1867. Margadant S. (1990), 172.

7. Ibid., 184–85.

8. Meyer et al. (1999), 444; Thiesenhusen (1995), 30.

9. Thiesenhusen (1995), 32.

10. *Plan de Ayala* as quoted, edited, and translated in Meyer et al. (1999), 496; see also Karst and Rosenn (1975), 279 for selections from the Plan in English.

11. Meyer et al. (1999), 516–522.

12. Ibid., 523.

13. The law is translated into English in Karst and Rosenn (1975), 280–283.

14. Herget and Camil (1978), 29–30.

15. Margadant S. (1990), 184–185.

16. Meyer et al. (1999), 525.

17. Thiesenhusen (1995), 35.

18. Meyer et al. (1999), 528–530, 556, 563, 571, 577, 584–585, 606.

19. Thiesenhusen (1995), 37.

20. Meyer et al. (1999), 628.

21. Dorner (1992), 40.

22. Herget and Camil (1978), 29–30.

23. Meyer et al. (1999), 672, quoting Salinas's third state of the nation message.

24. Ibid., 672; Collier (1994), 124.

25. Thiesenhusen (1995), 46–47.

26. Ibid., 40.

27. Ibid., 48.

28. As translated and quoted in Collier (1994), 45.

29. Meyer et al. (1999), 683.

30. Thiesenhusen (1995), 29.

31. Bello Lozano (1983), 523–524.

32. Dorner (1992), 11; Kay (1998), 11.

33. Dorner (1992), 33.

34. Ibid., 11–12, 18.

35. Thiesenhusen (1995), 87. For a discussion of the Dominican Republic see Clausner (1973), 230–265.

36. Kay (1998), 15.

37. Dorner (1992), 33–34.

38. Karst and Rosenn (1975), 336–366.

39. Thiesenhusen (1995), 61; Dorner (1992), 35–36.

40. Dorner (1992), 44, 45; Thiesenhusen (1995), 76.

41. Kay (1998), 15.

42. Thiesenhusen (1995), 39, 62; Karst and Rosenn (1975), 400–401, 406.

43. Thiesenhusen (1995), 39. See also Hamilton (2002)

44. Thiesenhusen (1995), 42; Kay (1998), 26.

45. Dorner (1992), 37, 41, 49, 52; Thiesenhusen (1995), 67–68, 174.

46. Thiesenhusen (1995), 174.

47. Ibid., 130.

48. Ibid., 152.

49. Dorner (1992), 52.

50. Kay (1998), 19, 27.

51. Dorner (1992), 34; Thiesenhusen (1995), 125–131.

52. Dorner (1992), 33; Thiesenhusen (1995), 103–109.

53. Dorner (1992), 39.

54. Karst and Rosenn (1975), 396.

55. Dorner (1992), 45.

56. Thiesenhusen (1995), 178.

57. Ibid., 85.

58. Dorner (1992), 47, 49; Thiesenhusen (1995), 58–67.

59. Thiesenhusen (1995), 69, 75–76, 79–80.

60. Ibid., 97.

61. Ibid., 148–158.

62. Kay (1998), 17.

63. Dorner (1992), 35.

64. Ibid., 43.

65. Karst and Rosenn (1975), 275.

66. Thiesenhusen (1995), 61.

67. Karst and Rosenn (1975), 269.

68. Dorner (1992), 46.

69. Ibid., 48.

70. Thiesenhusen (1995), 96.

71. Karst and Rosenn (1975), 269.

72. A translated record of such a proceedings can be found in Karst and Rosenn (1975), 294–304.

73. Ibid., 367.

74. Dorner (1992), 76–77.

75. Collier (1994), 46.

76. Ibid., 47.

77. Thiesenhusen (1995), 62–63. Similarly, for housing on state land in Peru, see De Soto (1989), 136–142.

78. Thiesenhusen (1995), 38.

79. Ibid., 136, 137.

80. Karst and Rosenn (1975), 399–400, citing K. Karst and N. Clement, "Legal Institutions and Development: Lessons from the Mexican Ejido," *U.C.L.A. Law Review* 16 (1969): 281, 293–297.

81. Thiesenhusen (1995), 61.

82. Ibid., 67 (Bolivia), 98 (Chile), 130 (Nicaragua).

83. Karst and Rosenn (1975), 369–371.

84. Dorner (1992), 80–85.

85. De Soto (1989), 17–57; Dorner (1992), 46, 48; Collier (1994), 48; Thiesenhusen (1995), 59–60, 78 (Guatemala); 101, 106 (Chile); Kay (1998), 18 (Colombia, Ecuador, Mexico, Chile, Peru).

86. Collier (1994), 78; Thiesenhusen (1995), 56.

87. Collier (1994), 127.

88. Thiesenhusen (1995), 6.

89. Ibid., 66.

90. Kay (1998), 20–23.

91. Deere and León (2001), 330–350; Kay (1998).

92. Dorner (1992), 22.

93. Kay (1998), 9, 10.

94. Ibid., 25; Thome (2000), 699.

95. Riddell (2000), 1–11.

Chapter 27

1. Trubek (1972); Trubek and Galanter (1974).
2. Research Advisory Committee on Law and Development (1974), 27–28, 36–38, 47–50, 74.
3. Ibid., 20.
4. Thome (2000), 711. See De Soto (1989).
5. Thome (2000), 710–711.
6. Margadant S. (1990), 222–224.
7. http://www.geo.unipr.it/~davide/cuba/economy/LAW95.
8. Boza (1994).
9. Vargas (1998), vol 1, xi–xii, 5.
10. Clagett and Valderrama (1973), 170.
11. Karst and Rosenn (1975), 69–70.
12. Ibid., 72–73.
13. Margadant S. (1990), 240.
14. Glade (1998), 58–59.
15. See membership lists at http://www.wto.org.
16. Roett (1999), 1.
17. Vargas (1998), vol. 2, 383–400; Vargas (2001), vol. 4, 1–51.
18. Taylor (1997).
19. Taylor (1998).
20. Valls Pereira (1999), 15.
21. Erim et al. (1998).
22. Von Mehren (1997), xv–25; Ortiz de Zevallos (1994), 1–13.
23. Glade (1998), 61.
24. Technical Working Group on Trade, Reconstruction and Transformation of Central America; "Foreign Investment Regulations" (1999); Glade (1998).
25. De los Hero (1994), 15–22.
26. Reyes Villamizar (1996); Reyes Villamizar (1998).
27. Thome (2000), 696–699.
28. Ibid., 696.
29. Ibid., 710.
30. Ibid., 699.
31. Adelman and Centeno (2002), 140–142, 154–159.
32. Nagle (2001); Symposium: Responding to the Legal Obstacles to Electronic Commerce in Latin America.
33. Glade (1998), 68.
34. Vega (1994).
35. Symposium: The Role of Legal Institutions in the Economic Development of the Americas; Tulchin and Espach (2000).
36. Prillaman (2000), 125. On such changes, see generally Dezalay and Garth (2002).
37. Peñalver (2000), 122–134.
38. Skidmore and Smith (2001), 274.
39. Carro (1985), 90–91; Evenson (1994), 177–194.
40. Evenson (1994), 178, 182–183; Peñalver (2000), 129–133.
41. Clark (2000), 414–415; Evenson (1994), 212–214.
42. Evenson (1994), 71.

43. Clark (2000), 423–424; Carro (1985), 92; Zatz (1994), 72–90.
44. Evenson (1994), 75–80; Zatz (1994), 88, 163–184.
45. Zatz (1994), 185–202.
46. Evenson (1994), 73, 205–211.
47. Zatz (1994), 55–57.
48. Evenson (1994), 126–140; Zatz (1994), 90–96.
49. Pérez Perdomo (1981), 277; Clark (2000), 418.
50. Evenson (1994), 2, 8, 41–43; Zatz (1994), 110–115.
51. Clark (2000), 427; Evenson (1994), 54–57; Zatz (1994), 129–132.
52. Zatz (1994), 115.
53. Carro (1985), 118–120.
54. Zatz (1994), 119.
55. Clark (2000), 431.
56. Carro (1985), 109; Zatz (1994), 134.
57. Zatz (1994), 128–129.
58. Carro (1985), 100–105.
59. Clark (2000), 418, 426; Evenson (1994), 41–53.
60. Evenson (1994), 49, 54.
61. Carro (1985), 107–09.
62. Zatz (1994), 140; Evenson (1994), 9.
63. Evenson (1994), 205, 210–211.
64. Ibid., 2.
65. Ibid., 182–83, 192.
66. Ibid., 187.
67. Zatz (1994), 139–159.

Chapter 28

1. Bello Lozano (1983), 296, 410; Karst and Rosenn (1975), 40; Ots Capdequí (1952), 90; Phelan (1960), 59–60.
2. Ots Capdequí (1952), 90.
3. Ibid., 108–109.
4. Phelan (1960), 49–50.
5. Ibid., 54–55.
6. Haring (1975), 114.
7. Ibid., 103 (quoting Levene).
8. Phelan (1960), 64.
9. Means (1980), xiii.
10. Means (1980), 45.
11. Ibid., 151–152.
12. Gibson (1966), 212.
13. Ibid., 213.
14. For law and development see Burg (1977), 511–512.
15. De Soto (1989).
16. Wiarda (1971), 460–463.
17. See, for example, Clausner (1973); De Soto (1989).
18. Thome (2000), 702.
19. Karst and Rosenn (1975), 58.
20. García Villegas (1993).

21. Thome (2000), 704.
22. Esquirol (2003).
23. Tulchin and Espach (2000).
24. Nagle (2000), 1235, 1281–1294.
25. O'Donnell (1999), 315–319.

Conclusion

1. See, for example, Dolinger and Rosenn (1992); Lewin (2003a); Lewin (2003b).
2. Concerning the status of Puerto Rico see Román and Simmons (2002).
3. Means (1980); Adelman (1999).
4. Dezalay and Garth (1998), 29.
5. Barrientos Grandón (1993), Adelman (1999), Uribe-Uran (2000).
6. Esquirol (1997); Esquirol (2003).
7. Méndez et al. (1999).
8. See, for example, Salvatore et al. (2001).
9. http://personal.law.miami.edu/~fvaldes/latcrit/.

GLOSSARY

A similar list with references to various sources for terms may
be found at Mirow (2000b).

abogado—university-trained lawyer, an advocate, a lawyer who argues in court or
  prepares legal arguments, *letrado*

abrevadero—water source with public access

acequia—irrigation ditch

Acordada—see *Santa Hermandad, Tribunal de la Acordada*

acuerdo—administrative session of an *audiencia*

adelantado—title granted to a leader of an expedition to discover and settle new lands

afuerino—landless, migratory, or seasonal agricultural worker

albacea—executor

albedrío—customary law, legal custom

alcabala—sales tax

alcalde—*cabildo* official

alcalde de barrio—municipal official charged with police supervision in a subdivision of
  a large city

alcalde de crimen—judge of the *audiencia* with criminal jurisdiction

alcalde de la hermandad—police magistrate for a rural district

alcalde de la mesta—police magistrate for a rural district

alcalde ordinario—town magistrate

alcaldía mayor—local jurisdiction, run by an *alcalde mayor*

alférez real—*cabildo* member, herald or municipal standard bearer

alguacil mayor—*audiencia* official charged with enforcing the orders of the *audiencia*

almojarifazgo—duty on exported or imported goods

alvedriador—mediator

alzada—appeal

Antiguo Cuaderno—collection of mining regulations enacted by Philip II, 1563

arancel—published, official tariff for fees related to filing a legal action

arbitrios—municipal taxes

arrendero—agricultural worker who resides on the estate

arriendo—borrowed plot of land under a *colonato*

asentamiento—temporary form of production cooperative

asesor—legal advisor to a governing official

asiento—exclusive right to import a certain number of slaves for a period of years;
  contract or written memorial

atarque—dam

audiencia—governmental body with administrative and judicial functions, usually the
  highest level appellate body located in a geographic area governed by a viceroy
  or other royal official

auto—legal document

auto acordado—administrative decision of an *audiencia*

Autos Acordados—supplement to the *Nueva Recopilación de Castilla* of 1567, separately
  compiled in the 1770s

avería—convoy tax collected by the *Casa de Contratación*

ayuntamiento—town council

balanza—shipping tax based on amount of cargo

baldías—*tierras baldías,* vacant public lands held by crown

bozal—slave unfamiliar with Spanish language

caballería—unit of land of about 105 acres

cabildo—local or municipal council

cabildo abierto—open *cabildo,* a broader municipal meeting than the regular *cabildo* to
  address matters of great importance

cacicazgo—estate of a native chieftain, often held in similar manner as a *mayorazgo*

cacique—indigenous chief

caja de comunidad—Indian municipality's community fund

Caja de Consolidación—Consolidation Treasury, royal institution created as receiver of
  church lands, 1799

Capitán General—regional royal official with military and civil powers

capitulación—contract between crown and *adelantado* setting out the grant of wealth,
  powers, and honors to be given on successful discovery or settlement of new
  territories

careo—judicially supervised face-to-face meeting of the parties to a legal dispute

carimba—a brand burned into a slave indicating that the slave entered the colonies
  legally and that duties had been paid

carta de poder—power of attorney, often used to permit lawyer to represent client

Casa de Contratación—the Royal Board of Trade located in Seville and later Cádiz,
  governed all aspects of trade with the colonies, 1503-1790

casa de fundación—royal smeltery

Casa de las Indias—see *Consulado de Mercaderes*

Casa de Océano—see *Consulado de Mercaderes*

casos de Corte—form of original jurisdiction for *audiencias* based on questions
  concerning *encomiendas* of Indians

casta—racial origin, often applied to shipments of slaves

Cátedra de Clementinas—law professor who lectured on the *Clementines, Decretales
  Clementinae,* a collection of canon law containing the constitutions of the
  Council of Vienne and the decretals of Clement V from 1305 to 1314

Cátedra de Decreto—law professor who lectured on Gratian's *Decretum, Concordia*

Discordantium Canonum, a foundational work of the canon law dating from the mid twelfth century

Cátedra de Prima de Cánones—law professor who lectured on Gregory IX's *Decretals,* a foundational work of canon law from the mid-thirteenth century

Cátedra de Sexto—law professor who lectured on the *Sexto, Liber Sextus,* a foundational work of canon law promulgated at the end of the thirteenth century

cédula—legal document

Cedulario de Vasco de Puga—chronological collection of royal decrees affecting New Spain, compiled in 1563

censo—contractual form of mortgage annuity

censo al quitar—a loan in the form of a sale

censo consignativo—purchase of an annual pension for a cash payment secured by land

censo enfitéutico—contractual, long-term mortgage loan

censo perpetuo—contractual grant of land, reserving a fixed annual rent out of the land

censo reservatio—reserving an annual pension of fruits or money from land

certificado de inafectabilidad—certificate exempting lands from expropriation of land reform

chacra—lands worked collectively by *inquilinos* for their own benefit

chanciller—*audiencia* official charged with keeping the royal seal

Chancillería de Valladolid—most important civil appellate tribunal in Castile in the sixteenth and seventeenth centuries

chorrillo—small *obraje,* with 10–20 workers

cimarrón—runaway slave

cinco hermanas—"five sisters" or five codes of Mexican Salvador Alvarado: farm land, finances, property registration, municipal government, and labor

coartación—ability of a slave to purchase freedom by him- or herself or through another

cobos—tax of 1½ percent applied for essaying metal, originally a grant by Charles V to Francisco Cobos, but later allocated to the treasury

Código de 1550—see *Ordenanzas de Minería de 1550 para la Nueva Galicia*

Código Andrés Bello—Chilean Civil Code of 1855

Código Arandino—Venezuelan code of civil procedure drafted by Francisco Aranda, 1836

Código Arosemena—Colombian Commercial Code of 1853, drafting by Justo Arosemena is disputed; Panamanian state commercial code of 1869

Código Barranda—Mexican federal commercial code, 1884

Código Béistegui—procedural code for Puebla, Mexico, 1880

Código de Bustamante—code of private international law drafted by Cuban jurist Antonio Sánchez de Bustamante y Sirven, 1928

Código Negro—set of laws addressing the treatment and obligations of slaves

Código Justo Sierra—draft civil code for Mexico, late 1850s

Código Lares—Mexican commercial code, 1854; repealed, 1855; reestablished, 1863

Código Ocampo—Chilean commercial code, enacted 1865

Código Vélez Sársfield—Argentine civil code, enacted 1869

collera—judicial punishment of forced labor usually imposed on Indians

colonato—system of agricultural production where land is exchanged for the work of an agricultural laborer on a large estate

colono—agricultural worker who resides on the estate

composición de tierra—governmental confirmation or legalization of land title

concegiles—*tierras concegiles*, public lands held by municipality

conciliación—informal dispute resolution

Consejo de las Indias—Council of the Indies, charged with royal oversight of the Spanish colonies

consulado—commercial tribunal

Consulado de Mercaderes—a commercial tribunal established in Seville to handle disputes arising from colonial trade

contador—comptroller, one of the *oficiales reales*

contratación—business or commercial contract

cordel—rope for measuring land, varying from fifty to a hundred *varas*

corregidor de indios—official charged with collecting Indian tribute, judicial and political official over a *corregimiento de indios*

corregimiento—a local jurisdiction, theoretically, but not practically, of a smaller area than an *alcaldía mayor;* in Spain the *corregidor* was usually a university-trained lawyer, but not in Latin America

costumbre—custom

criollo—person of Spanish descent born in the colonies

cruzada—ecclesiastical tax based on the Bulls of the Crusade, a type of indulgence; after mid eighteenth century, administered by royal officials and usually collected every two years

Cuadernillo de Gutiérrez—see *Prontuario de los Juicios, su Orden, Sustanciación e Incidencias*

Curia Philipica—work on court procedure and commercial law by Juan de Hevia Bolaños, perhaps first published in Lima, 1603, but with many subsequent editions

dádiva—loan or gift of money

dehesa—lands held as a municipal enclosed pasture

demasías—surplus lands between granted plots

depositario general—member of the *cabildo* who serves as public trustee

derecho de unión de armas—mid-seventeenth-century sales tax to provide a fleet to protect Atlantic shipping

derecho indiano—laws applicable to the Indies, or Spanish colonies

derecho vulgar—term used to describe the body of customary law applied by peripheral courts *diezmo*—tithe, a tax on products coming from land, such as mining and agriculture, mostly expended for ecclesiastical purposes

ejidatario—a holder or beneficiary of *ejido* lands

ejido—lands held as a municipal commons; municipally held common lands used for several purposes including threshing, dumping garbage, or keeping stray animals; lands vested in a peasant community through land reform; also "*exido*"

encomienda—a grant of services of inhabitants to an *encomendero* based on a duty to Christianize and defend the inhabitants. In return, the *encomendero* received the inhabitants' tribute payments or labor.

esclavo—slave

escribano—scribe, notary

escribano de cámara—scribe for an *audiencia*

escribano público de número—public scribe

escritura de compromiso—an agreement compromising or settling a dispute

Espéculo—mid-thirteenth-century work on law under Alfonso X

esquina de provincia—see *Juzgado de Provincia*

estancia—common unit of land for the raising of livestock in New Spain; a large farm

estancia de ganado mayor—unit of agricultural land of about 6.7 square miles

estatuto—law governing a group or body with sufficient legal autonomy to govern its internal life

exido—see *ejido*

expediente—documentation of a land grant; a case file in a legal proceeding

factor—business manager, one of the *oficiales reales*

fiel ejecutor—member of the *cabildo* charged with inspecting weights and measures, ensuring the supply of foodstuffs, and adjusting market prices

finca de mozo—serf farm

fiscal—crown attorney; prosecutor; *audiencia* official charged with defending the interests of the royal fisc

fuero—grant of special rights and privileges through a charter; a collection of such laws

Fuero Juzgo—mid-seventh-century Visigothic law code

Fuero Real—collection of royal laws drafted to provide uniformity under Alfonso X, 1255

fundo—subdivision of a *hacienda*

gañán—native worker who hired himself out voluntarily

gobernación—geographical area covered by a civil jurisdiction

gobernador—head of a *gobernación*

gobernador intendente—head of an *intendencia*

gobierno—local jurisdiction originating in an *adelantado's* jurisdiction or in an outlying area

Gobierno del Perú—work of Juan de Matienzo, a sixteenth-century jurist who was *oidor* of the *audiencia* of Charcas

golondrina—landless, migratory, or seasonal agricultural worker

gracias al sacar—proceeding to change legal status

hacienda—large agricultural estate

hacienda de beneficio—large landed estate for mining

hacienda de ganado—large landed estate for raising livestock

hacienda de labor—large landed estate for raising crops

Hacienda Real—Treasury

hato—private grazing land

hijuela—deed; a plot, possibly divided land into several tracts; a subdivision of a *fundo*

honorario—fee paid to lawyer for services

huasipungero—agricultural worker who resides on the estate

Ilustración del derecho real de España—work by Juan Sala on Spanish law published in 1803, widely used in the colonial and early republic period; Mexican editions often use a derivative title of *Sala Mexicano*

indultos—blanket fines assessed against ships to offset loss of royal revenue from customs evasion

información de derecho—legal brief stating client's argument

inquilino—agricultural worker who resides on the estate

Inquisición—*Tribunal del Santo Oficio de la Inquisición,* the Inquisition

instrucción—instructions to an official stating how to exercise the office

Instrucción de lo que deben observar los regentes de las reales Audiencias de América—royal legislation from 1776 appointing regents to colonial *audiencias*

intendencia—Bourbon government administrative unit, replacing *corregimientos, gobiernos,* and *alcaldías mayores*

interrogatorio—written questions to be answered by witnesses

juez—judge

juez arbitro arbitrador y amigable compendidor—designated *abogado* to serve as an arbitrator of a dispute

juez cuadrillero—judge of the *Santa Hermandad*

juez de comisión—investigating judge appointed by viceroy, president, or *audiencia*

juez de competencias—jurisdictional arbitrator

juez de menores—*alcalde ordinario* charged with protecting the interests of children

juez de residencia—commissioned judge charged with conducting an investigation of an official at the end of the official's term, usually one of the *audiencia's oidores*

juez pesquisidor—special investigator, *visitador-general, juez de residencia juicio plenario*—full legal proceeding

juicio sumario—summary legal proceeding

junta de diezmos—tithe collection agency under the intendancy system

Junta Superior de Real Hacienda—council of finance, Bourbon supervisory council for *intendentes*

jurisprudencia definida—binding case law

juro—annuity

justicia mayor—deputy of the governor or *corregidor* appointed to preside in the *cabildo* of towns within the jurisdiction of the governor or *corregidor*

Juzgado de Bienes de Difuntos—*oidor* of an *audiencia* serving as a probate judge

Juzgado de Provincia—court of original civil and criminal jurisdiction sitting in the city of the *audiencia*

Juzgado General de Indios de la Nueva España—General Indian Court of New Spain with a jurisdiction over Indian disputes

Juzgados de Alzadas—appellate tribunal for mining disputes in New Spain during the eighteenth and early nineteenth centuries

labor—farm, small rural estate

ladino—in the slave trade, a black person born in Africa, but who had adopted the Spanish language and customs; in Mexico, a nonindigenous Mexican in the south of the country; in Guatemala, a person of Creole and Indian descent

latifundio—large landed estate consisting of several *haciendas*

letrado—university-trained lawyer, see *abogado*

ley—law

Ley Lerdo—*Ley de Desamortización* of 1856, Mexico; gave those who worked church or Indian lands the opportunity to buy them

Ley Vallarta—Mexican Law of Aliens, 1886

Leyes de Burgos—laws requiring the humane treatment of Indians forced to work under the *encomienda* system, 1512

Leyes de Estilo—fourteenth-century collection of Castilian procedural law, explaining the *Fuero Real*

Leyes de Toro—collection of Castilian law addressing private law and the order of precedence of extant laws, 1505

Leyes hechas . . . por la brevedad y orden de los pleitos—a collection of Castilian procedural law, 1499

Leyes Nuevas—set of laws protecting Indians from poor treatment, establishing their legal status, and reorganizing the administrative structure of the Indies, 1542

libros de acuerdo—records of an *audiencia's* administrative session

limosna de la Santa Bula de Cruzada—see *Santa Cruzada*

limpieza de sangre—purity of blood

manzana—unit of land of approximately 1.75 acres

mayor—adjective added to office to imply powers of patronage

mayorazgo—entailed estate of land passing in primogeniture inheritance pattern

mayordomo—manager of a large landed estate; when used in the context of municipal government, a custodian of civic property

media anata—Hapsburg-period tribute exaction from *encomenderos* equivalent to one-half annual income; one-half annual income paid to crown for taking an office; replaced *mesada* for royal officials in 1631; after 1754, applied to higher ecclesiastical offices

mediero—sharecropper

mejora—portion of the testator's estate that can be freely devised to family members selected by the testator, between one-fifth and one-third of the estate

merced—a grant of land or water

meritorio—unpaid apprentice in colonial bureaucracy

mesada—one month's income of new royal or ecclesiastical official paid to crown

Mesta—guild of ranchers raising livestock that maintained a jurisdiction in related disputes

minifundio—agricultural holding too small to maintain its owner

ministro—minister in governmental service

mita—periodic conscription of Indian laborers in Peru

monte—municipally held public lands used for gathering wood and low-quality pasturing

montepío—charitable fund for incapacitated members of a group or guild, or for their widows and orphans

mulecón—slave child between the ages of twelve and sixteen

muleque—slave child between the ages of seven and twelve

mulequillo—slave child up to the age of seven

novenos—payment to the crown in recognition of the Royal Patronage equivalent to two-ninths of half the tithes collected

Novísima Recopilación—compilation of Castilian laws, 1805

Nueva Recopilacíon—compilation of Castilian laws, compiled under Philip II, 1567

Nuevo Cuaderno—collection of mining laws amending the *Antiguo Cuaderno*, 1584; later annotated by Francisco Javier de Gamboa

obraje—textile plant

oficial real—exchequer official, royal revenue collector

oficial real de hacienda—see *oficial real*

oidor—judge belonging to an *audiencia*

Ordenamiento de Alcalá—collection of Castilian laws confirming prior laws, giving new provisions on private law and the nobility, and stating the order of precedence of existing laws, 1348

ordenamientos—collection of laws

ordenanzas—collection of laws on a particular topic

Ordenanzas de Alfaro—early-seventeenth-century set of laws regulating reductions of Indians written by Francisco de Alfaro

Ordenanzas de Aranjuez—see *Ordenanzas de Minería de Nueva España*

Ordenanzas de Bilbao—set of commercial rules dating from the mid fifteenth century and reaffirmed as authority in commercial matters in 1737

Ordenanzas de Minería de 1550—mining laws for Zacatecas and New Galicia

Ordenanzas de Minería de Nueva España—mining laws established by Charles III in 1783

Ordenanzas de Montalvo—see *Ordenanzas Reales de Castilla*

Ordenanzas de Población—laws setting out method for establishing new settlements enacted by Philip II in 1573

Ordenanzas de Toledo—collection of laws governing mining law established by Viceroy Francisco de Toledo

Ordenanzas del Patronazgo—royal laws setting out the powers and limitations of the secular and religious clergy in the colonies, 1574

Ordenanzas del Perú—expanded version of the *Ordenanzas de Toledo* put into effect throughout the colonies in 1683

Ordenanzas Reales de Castilla—collection of laws updating the *Siete Partidas* and glossing the *Fuero Real* drafted by Alfonso Díaz de Montalvo (1405-1499), also known as *Ordenanzas Reales* or *Ordenanzas de Montalvo*, 1485

palenque—community of runaway slaves

palmeo—measuring each slave to determine the *piezas* in a shipment

papel sellado—paper sealed with a mark indicating that payment has been made to royal or state officials, used for all types of legal transactions and relationships between individuals

paraje—boundary marker

partido—in mining law, right of worker to one-half of ore extracted beyond daily quota

penas de cámara—local judicial fines; court costs

peón acasillado—agricultural worker who resides on the estate

perito—expert

pesquisa—investigation

pieza de Indias—measurement for slaves in a shipment; one *pieza* was equal to a slave measuring at least 5 feet, 7 inches tall

Plan de Ayala—Zapata's revolutionary platform for land reform, Mexico, 1911

plenario—phase of a legal proceeding in which evidence is evaluated and final sentence given

pliego de mortaja—sealed letter of a viceroy stating who should temporarily fill his position on his death, eighteenth century

Política indiana—work describing colonial institutions by Juan de Solórzano Pereira, a famous jurist specializing in the law of the Indies, 1647

práctico—legal practitioner without formal legal training

prado—municipally held public lands used as high-quality pasture, often irrigated

pragmática—royal law addressing areas of general interest and concern or major aspects of judicial system

pregón—public announcement, often required for sale of Indian lands

Prima de Cánones—university lectures on Canon law, see *Cátedra de Prima de Cánones*

Prima de Instituta—university lectures on Justinian's *Institutes*

Prima de Leyes—university lectures on Roman law

primitivo patrimonio—Indian lands with legal claim dating from preconquest period

procesillo—determination of applicant's racial, religious, family, and economic background when applying to *colegio mayor*

procurador—solicitor; an expert in the procedural aspects of the lawsuit

procurador de número—municipal lawyers who assisted *vecinos* in legal actions

procurador de pobres—lawyer appointed by an *audiencia* to assist the poor

Procurador del Cabildo—see *Procurador General*

Procurador General—lawyer charged with representing a municipality

promesa de dote—dowry agreement

Prontuario de los Juicios, su Orden, Sustanciación e Incidencias—early work on procedure by Bolivian Francisco Gutiérrez

propios del consejo—municipal lands rented to individuals for gardens and other purposes

Protomedicato—judicial and administrative tribunal to regulate public health and health professions

Protomédico—official charged with protecting the health by examining and licensing those involved with health care

provincia—geographic subdivision of governmental administration

provisión—law addressing a particular concern or problem, or legislative act in general

prueba—presentation of evidence at a trial

querella—complaint

quilombo—community of runaway slaves

quinto—a fifth, portion reserved to the crown from precious metals, by mid eighteenth century became a tenth, *diezmo*

quinto de azogue—5 percent tax on mercury

quita—remission of a debt

quitación—income, profit, or salary

Real Academia Carolina de Leyes y Práctica Forense—institute established in 1779 in Chile to teach royal law

Real Hacienda—see *Hacienda Real*

Real Ordenanza para el Establecimiento de Intendentes de Ejército y Provincia en el Reino de Nueva España—Royal ordinance establishing the intendency system in New Spain, 1786

Real Patronato—Patronato Real, Royal patronage of the Catholic church that gave the crown substantial control over church government and revenue in the colonies

Real y Supremo Consejo de las Indias—see *Consejo de las Indias*

realengas—tierras realengas, public lands owned by crown

rebeldía—failure to answer in a legal proceeding

receptor de penas—cabildo member charged with collecting judicial fines

receptor de penas de cámara, gastos de estrado y justicia—audiencia official charged with collecting judicial fines

reconvención—countercomplaint

Recopilación de Leyes de los Reinos de las Indias—compilation of law concerning the Indies enacted by Charles II in 1680 addressing mostly public law aspects of the colonies, often abbreviated as "L.I." or "R.I."

Recopilación Granadina—collection of Colombian laws and decrees, 1845

recurso de fuerza—see *via de fuerza*

recusación—complaint of improper conduct on part of a legal official

reducción—Indians gathered into a municipality under their own *alcalde* and *alguaciles*, and later called a *corregimiento*, usually under the supervision of regular clerics

regente—regent

regidor—alderman, town councillor, a *cabildo* member with right to speak and vote

Reglamento de Comercio Libre de España e Indias—law of 1778 opening all peninsular ports to trade directly with ports in the Indies

relator—reporter; *audiencia* official charged with preparing summaries of litigation documents for the court and determining whether the documents have satisfied the formalities for proceeding with the case

remate—forced seizure and sale of property, usually as a remedy for debt

repartimiento—general term for division, partition, or distribution of something; a division of lands

repartimiento de bienes—distribution of goods, monopoly of selling goods to Indians in Indian municipalities; sale of goods to Indians by *corregidores*

repartimiento de indios—assignment of Indians for tasks as required by the colonial community; the group of laborers itself; granted by viceroy or *audiencia*, or in New Spain by the *juzgados de indios;* abolished by decree in some areas in 1601

requerimiento—statement read to indigenous populations before military action requesting that they surrender and accept the authority of the Spanish crown and Christianity, used as a justification for aggression against these populations

resguardo—lands belonging to a *reducción*

residencia—judicial review of an official's conduct, sent to Council of the Indies

residenciado—official under investigation at the close of term of his office

Sala Mexicana—see *Ilustración del derecho real de España*

saneamiento—obligation to make good a hidden defect in a thing sold

Santa Cruzada—royal tax originating the church's practice of selling indulgences and ecclesiastical privileges attached to the *Bula de la Santa Cruzada;* a specialized tribunal with this name determined the rights of those exercising such ecclesiastical privileges

Santa Hermandad—organization that kept the highways free from banditry, acted against violent crime, and prohibited liquors

Santo Oficio—see *Inquisición*

sementera—communally owned cultivated land

sentencia—decision of the court in a dispute

sentencia fundada—written explanation of a judge's decision

servicio—payment by Indians in addition to tribute

Siete Partidas—legal code with broad coverage of topics used as a practical source of private law in Castile and colonial Latin America; drafted under Alfonso X; greatly influenced by Roman law, 1265

síndico—lawyer charged with representing a municipality

sisa—excise tax on food stuffs

sitio—unit of grazing land equal to eighteen *caballerías,* or about 780 hectares

sitio de ganado mayor—unit of grazing land for cattle; in Mexico, about four thousand acres

sitio de ganado menor—unit of grazing land for sheep; in Mexico, about two thousand acres

solar de casa—building lot in a municipality

suerte—garden plot in a municipality

Suma de tratos y contratos—work by Fray Tomás de Mercado, a sixteenth-century commercial lawyer

sumaria—phase of a legal proceeding in which evidence is collected and the case presented

superintendente general—superior of *intendentes* in the capital city

tacha—disqualification of a witness

tasación—tribute rate; tax rate

tasador repartidor—*audiencia* official charged with dividing court filings between the scribes and *relatores*

teniente—deputy of a local official, needed to be approved by the *audiencia* or the Council of the Indies

terrasguerro—native laborer occupying *cacicazgo* lands

tesorero—treasurer, one of the *oficiales reales*

testimonio—grantee's copy of the *expediente*

tienda del raya—company or *hacienda* store

tinterillo—legal practitioner without formal legal training

tonelada—tonnage of a ship; in slaving one ton was equivalent to one slave, but in practice it could be up to 7 slaves; a royal tax based on tonnage

Tratado de confirmaciones reales, encomiendas, oficios y casos en que se requiren para las Indias—treatise on law of the Indies by Antonio de León Pinelo

tribunal de alzadas—appellate tribunal

tribunal de cuentas—tax courts created in 1605 in Mexico, Lima, and Bogotá

Tribunal de la Acordada—court to investigate and try crimes concerning the safety of roads, the production of prohibited drink, as well as theft, physical violence, homicide, robbery and the like in villages and rural areas

Tribunal de Minería—late-eighteenth and early-nineteenth-century judicial and administrative guildlike body handling disputes related to mining in New Spain

tributo de indios—tribute payment or tax placed on Indians as royal subjects

unión de armas—sales tax

Universidad de Mercaderes—see *Consulado de Mercaderes*

vara—unit of measurement of approximately thirty-three inches; staff of authority

vecindad—allotment to a settler of a town carrying the title of *vecino*, and usually consisting of a building lot in the town, a garden, one or two *caballerías*, and a sheep pasture

veedor—inspector; one of the *oficiales reales*

vía de fuerza—procedure for removing or appealing a case from an ecclesiastical to a royal court

vinculación—entail or family trust of property

Virrey—Viceroy

visita—secret judicial investigation of an official at any time during his tenure in office

visita general—broadly based *visita* usually investigating an entire *audiencia* and revenue officials

visitador—inspector-general

visitador-general—judge selected by the Council of the Indies to conduct a *visita*

Víspera de Cánones—university lectures on canon law, see also *Cátedra de Prima de Cánones*

Víspera de Decreto—university lectures on Gratian's *Decretum*, see also *Cátedra de Decreto*

vista—initial hearing

vista de ojos—judicial survey of land

yanacona—special class of natives in viceroyalty of Peru, originally bound to estates

Abercrombie, Thomas A. 1998. "Tributes to Bad Conscience: Charity, Restitution, and Inheritance in Cacique and Encomendero Testaments of Sixteenth-Century Charcas." In Kellogg and Restall (1998), 249–289.

Adelman, Jeremy. 1994. *Frontier Development: Land, Labor, and Capital on the Wheatlands of Argentina and Canada, 1890–1914.* Oxford: Oxford University Press.

———. 1999. *Republic of Capital: Buenos Aires and the Legal Transformation of the Atlantic World.* Stanford: Stanford University Press.

Adelman, Jeremy, and Miguel Angel Centeno. 2002. "Between Liberalism and Neoliberalism: Law's Dilemma in Latin America." In Dezalay and Garth (2002), 139–161.

Aguilera, Miguel. 1965. *La legislación y el derecho en Colombia.* Bogotá: Lerner.

Aguirre, Carlos. 1993. *Agentes de su propia libertad. Los esclavos de Lima y la desintegración de la esclavitud, 1821–1854.* Lima: Pontificia Universidad Católica del Perú.

Alonso Romero, Paz, and Carlos Garriga Acosta. 1998. "El régimen jurídico de la abogacía en Castilla (siglos XIII–XVIII)." *Recueils de la société Jean Bodin pour l'histoire comparative des institutions.* 65 (4):51–75.

Amunátegui Solar, Domingo. 1901, 1902, 1904. *La sociedad chilena del siglo XVIII: mayorazgos i titulos de Castilla.* 3 vols. Santiago de Chile, Imprenta Barcelona.

Andrés-Gallego, José, coord. 2000. *Nuevas aportaciones a la historia jurídica de Iberoamérica.* Madrid: Digibus.

Armstrong, Jr., George M. 1989. *Law and Market Society in Mexico.* New York: Praeger.

Arnold, Linda. 1988. *Bureaucracy and Bureaucrats in Mexico City 1742–1835.* Tucson: University of Arizona Press.

———. 1996. *Política y justicia: la Suprema Corte mexicana 1824–1855.* Mexico: Universidad Nacional Autónoma de México.

———. 1999. "Privileged Justice? The *Fuero Militar* in Early National Mexico." In Zimmermann (1999a).

Arrom, Silvia Marina. 1985a. *The Women of Mexico City, 1790–1857.* Stanford: Stanford University Press.

———. 1985b "Changes in Mexican Family Law in the Nineteenth Century: The Civil Codes of 1870 and 1884." *Journal of Family History* 10(3): 305–317.

Baade, Hans W. 1978. "The Formalities of Private Real Estate Transactions in Spanish North America. A Report on Some Recent Discoveries." *Louisiana Law Review* 38: 655–745.

———. 1981a. "Law and Lawyers in Pre-Independence Texas." In *Centennial History of the Texas Bar 1882–1982.* Burnet, Texas: Eakin Press, 1981, 240–255.

———. 1981b. "Rare Books and Rare Lawyers in Eighteenth-Century Texas." In Roy M. Mersky, *Collecting and Managing Rare Law Books.* Dobbs Ferry, N.Y.: Glanville Publishers, 1981, 293–316.

———. 1984. "Número de abogados y escribanos en la Nueva España, la Provincia de Texas y la Luisiana." In Soberanes Fernández (1984) 119–128.

Backus, Richard C., and Phanor J. Eder. 1943. *A Guide to the Law and Legal Literature of Colombia.* Washington, D.C.: Library of Congress.

Barreneche, Osvaldo. 1999. "Criminal Justice and State Formation in Early Nineteenth-Century Buenos Aires." In Zimmermann (1999a), 86–103.

Barrientos Grandón, Javier. 1993. *La cultura jurídica en la Nueva España.* Mexico: Universidad Nacional Autónoma de México.

———. 2000a. *La Real Audiencia de Santiago de Chile (1605–1817): la institución y sus hombres.* In Andrés-Gallego (2000).

———. 2000b. *Guía prosopográfica de la judicatura letrada indiana (1503–1898).* In Andrés-Gallego (2000).

Barrientos Grandón, Javier, and Javier Rodríguez Torres. 1991. "La biblioteca jurídica antigua de la facultad de derecho de la universidad de Chile." *Revista de estudios histórico-jurídicos* 14:291–334.

Bartels, Natalia M., and M. Stuart Madden. 2001 "A Comparative Analysis of United States and Colombian Tort Law: Duty, Breach, and Damages." *Pace International Law Review* 13: 59–92.

Bello, Andrés. 1955. *Código civil de la República de Chile.* In Andrés Bello, *Obras completas de Andrés Bello.* Vols. 12, 13. Caracas: Ministerio de Educación.

Bello Lozano, Humberto. 1983. *Historia de las fuentes e instituciones jurídicas venezolanas.* 6a ed. Caracas: Librería La Logica.

Bellomo, Manlio. 1995. *The Common Legal Past of Europe 1000–1800.* Trans. Lydia G. Cochrane. 2d ed. Washington: Catholic University of America Press.

Benson, Nettie Lee, ed. 1966. *Mexico and the Spanish Cortes, 1810–1822.* Austin: University of Texas Press, 1966.

Benton, Lauren. 2000. "The Legal Regime of the South Atlantic World, 1400–1750: Jurisdictional Complexity as Order." *Journal of World History* 11:27–56.

———. 2002. *Law and Colonial Cultures: Legal Regimes in World History, 1400–1900.* Cambridge: Cambridge University Press.

Bergad, Laird W., Fe Iglesia García, and María del Carmen Barcia. 1995. *The Cuban Slave Market 1790–1880.* Cambridge: Cambridge University Press.

Berman, Harold J. 1983. *Law and Revolution: The Formation of the Western Legal Tradition.* Cambridge: Harvard University Press.

Bernal, Beatriz. 1984. "La colección de leyes de Alonso de Zorita: avance del libro primero." In Soberanes Fernández (1984), 163–176.

———, coord. 1988. *Memoria del IV congreso de historia del derecho mexicano.* 2 vols. Mexico: Universidad Nacional Autónoma de México.

Bird, Shawn L. 1994. "Hollow Promises: Land Redistribution and Democratization in Latin America." Master's thesis, University of Colorado.

Blackburn, Robin. 1988. *The Overthrow of Colonial Slavery 1776–1848.* London: Verso.

———. 1997. *The Making of New World Slavery: From the Baroque to the Modern 1492–1800.* London: Verso.

Bliss, Santiago Rex. 2000. "La administración de la justicia y el orden liberal. Tucumán, 1850–1860." In Carmagnani (2000), 259–286.

Borah, Woodrow. 1983. *Justice by Insurance: The General Indian Court of Colonial Mexico and the Legal Aides of the Half-Real.* Berkeley, University of California Press, 1983.

———. 1996. "Assistance in Conflict Resolution for the Poor and Indians in Colonial Mexico." *Recueils de la société Jean Bodin pour l'histoire comparative des institutions* 63: 217–237.

Bowser, Frederick P. 1984. "Africans in Spanish American Colonial Society." In *The*

Cambridge History of Latin America. Vol. 2. Edited by Leslie Bethell. Cambridge: Cambridge University Press, 357-379.

Boza, Beatriz, ed. 1994. *Doing Business in Peru: The New Legal Framework.* 2d ed. Lima: PromPerú.

Brading, D. A. 1984. "Bourbon Spain and Its American Empire." In *The Cambridge History of Latin America.* Vol. 1. Edited by Leslie Bethell. Cambridge: Cambridge University Press, 389-439.

Braun Menéndez, Armando. 1951. *José Gabriel Ocampo y el Código de Comercio de Chile.* Buenos Aires: Instituto de Historia del Derecho.

Bravo Lira, Bernardino. 1999. "Los abogados y el estado en Chile: del estado modernizador al estado subsidario, 1758-1998." In Dougnac Rodríguez and Eyzaguirre (1999), vol. 1, 77-105.

Burg, Elliot M. 1977. "Law and Development: A Review of the Literature and a Critique of 'Scholars in Self-Estrangement.'" *American Journal of Comparative Law* 25: 492-530.

Burkholder, Mark A. 1980. *Politics of a Colonial Career: José Baquíjano and the Audiencia of Lima.* Albuquerque: University of New Mexico Press.

Burkholder, Mark A., and D. S. Chandler. 1977. *From Impotence to Authority: The Spanish Crown and the American Audiencias, 1687-1808.* Columbia, Mo.: University of Missouri Press.

———. 1982. *Biographical Dictionary of Audiencia Ministers in the Americas, 1687-1821.* Westport, Conn.: Greenwood Press.

Burkholder, Mark A., and Lyman L. Johnson. 1998. *Colonial Latin America.* 3d ed. New York: Oxford University Press.

Buscaglia, Edgardo. 1998. "Obstacles to Judicial Reform in Latin America." In Jarquín and Carrillo (1998), 15-30.

Bushnell, David and Neill Macaulay. 1994. *The Emergence of Latin America in the Nineteenth Century.* 2d ed. New York: Oxford University Press.

Bustamante, Antonio. 1996. *The Bustamante Code.* Baton Rouge: Lawrence Publishing.

Cano, Guillermo J. 1944. *Código de minería de la República Argentina anotado con sus fuentes.* 2 vols. Buenos Aires: Guillermo Kraft.

Capseta Castellà, Joan. 1997. *Personalidad jurídica y régimen patrimonial de las asociaciones religiosas en México.* México: Instituto Mexicano de Doctrina Social Cristiana.

Carmagnani, Marcello, Coordinador. 2000. *Constitucionalismo y orden liberal: América Latina, 1850-1920.* Torino: Otto Editore.

Carro, John. 1985. "The Structure of Legal Education and the Practice of Law in Cuba." *Revista de derecho puertorriqueño* 25:89-127.

Carter, Constance. 1971. "Law and Society in Colonial Mexico: *Audiencia* Judges in Mexican Society from the Tello de Sandoval *Visita General,* 1543-1547." Ph.D. diss., Columbia University.

Cháneton, Abel. 1938. *Historia de Vélez Sársfield.* 2d ed. 2 vols. Buenos Aires: Bernabé.

Chevalier, François. 1963. *Land and Society in Colonial Mexico: The Great Hacienda.* Trans. Alvin Eustis. Berkeley: University of California Press.

Chinchilla, Laura, and David Schodt. 1993. *The Administration of Justice in Ecuador.* San José, Costa Rica: CAJ.

Chommie, John C. 1963. *El derecho de los Estados Unidos.* 3 vols. Coral Gables: University of Miami Faculty of Law.

Clagett, Helen L., and David M. Valderrama. 1973. *A Revised Guide to the Law and Legal Literature of Mexico.* Washington: Library of Congress.

Clark, David S. 1975. "Judicial Protection of the Constitution in Latin America." *Hastings Constitutional Law Quarterly* 2:405–442.

Clark, Gerard J. 2000. "The Legal Profession in Cuba." *Suffolk Transnational Law Review* 23:413–436.

Clausner, Marlin D. 1973. *Rural Santo Domingo: Settled, Unsettled, and Resettled.* Philadelphia: Temple University Press.

Clavero, Bartolomé. 1974. *Mayorazgo: propiedad feudal in Castilla.* Madrid: Siglo Veintiuno Editores.

———. 2002. "Culture versus Rights: Indian Law and *Derecho indiano.*" In Kirshner and Mayali (2002), 227–297.

Cline, Sarah L. 1984. "Land Tenure and Land Inheritance in Late-Sixteenth-Century Culhuacan." In Harvey and Prem (1984), 277–309.

———. 1998. "Fray Alonso de Molina's Model Testament and Antecedents to Indigenous Wills in Spanish America." In Kellogg and Restall (1998), 13–33.

Code Napoleon. 1960. Trans. George Spence. Baton Rouge: Claitor's.

Los códigos españoles concordados y anotados. 1872–1873. 2d ed. Madrid: Antonio de San Martin.

Collier, Jane F. 1973. *Law and Social Change in Zinacantan.* Stanford: Stanford University Press.

Collier, George A., with E. L. Quaratiello. 1994. *Basta! Land and the Zapatista Rebellion in Chiapas.* Oakland: Food First.

Collier, Simon, and William F. Sater. 1996. *A History of Chile, 1808–1994.* Cambridge: Cambridge University Press.

Conference of Supreme Courts of the Americas. 1996. *Saint Louis University Law Journal* 40:1–1549.

Constitución Política de Colombia. 1991. Bogotá: Panamericana.

Cook, Alexandra Parma, and Noble David Cook. 1991. *Good Faith and Truthful Ignorance: A Case of Transatlantic Bigamy.* Durham, N.C.: Duke University Press.

Córdova, Andres F. 1956. *Derecho civil ecuatoriano.* Vol. 1. Quito: Casa de la Cultura.

Correa Sutil, Jorge, ed. 1993. *Situación y políticas judiciales en América Latina.* Santiago: Universidad Diego Portales.

———. 1999. "Judicial Reform in Latin America: Good News for the Underprivileged?" In Méndez et al. (1999), 255–277.

Corrin, Jay P. 2002. *Catholic Intellectuals and the Challenge of Democracy.* Notre Dame: University of Notre Dame Press.

Costeloe, Michael P. 1967. *Church Wealth in Mexico: A Study of the 'Juzgado de Capellanías' in the Archbishopric of Mexico 1800–1857.* Cambridge: Cambridge University Press.

Cottrol, Robert J. 2001. "The Long Lingering Shadow: Law, Liberalism, and Cultures of Racial Hierarchy and Identity in the Americas." *Tulane Law Review* 76:11–79.

Cruz Barney, Oscar. 1999. *Historia del derecho en Mexico.* Mexico: Oxford University Press.

Curran, Charles E. 2002. *Catholic Social Teaching 1891–Present: A Historical, Theological, and Ethical Analysis.* Washington: Georgetown University Press.

Cutter, Charles R. 1995. *The Legal Culture of Northern New Spain, 1700–1810*. Albuquerque: University of New Mexico Press.

———. 1999. "The Legal Culture of Spanish America on the Eve of Independence." In Zimmermann (1999a), 8–24.

———. 2000. "The Legal System as a Touchstone of Identity in Colonial New Mexico." In Roniger and Herzog (2000), 57–70.

Dagrossa, Norberto C. 2000. *Bibliografía de historia del derecho indiano*. In Andrés-Gallego (2000).

Dahlgren, John O. 1969. "Inter-American Bar Association." *Lawyer of the Americas* 1:113–119.

Dakolias, María. 1995. "A Strategy for Judicial Reform: The Experience of Latin America." *Virginia Journal of International Law* 36:167–231.

———. 1999. "Court Performance Around the World: A Comparative Perspective." *Yale Human Rights and Development Law Journal* 2:87–142.

De Ávila Martel, Alamiro. 2000. "La enseñanza del derecho romano en Chile, desde sus orígenes hasta el siglo XIX." In Dougnac Rodríguez and Eyzaguirre (2000), vol. 1, 339–342.

Deere, Carmen Diana, and Magdalena León. 2001. *Empowering Women: Land and Property Rights in Latin America*. Pittsburgh: University of Pittsburgh Press.

De Estrada, Liniers. 1978. *Manual de historia del derecho*. Buenos Aires: Abeledo-Perrot.

De los Hero, Alfonso. 1994. "The Constitutional Reform." In Boza (1994), 15–26.

De Marco, Miguel Angel. 1973. *Abogados, escribanos y obras de derecho en el Rosario del siglo XIX*. Rosario, Argentina: Facultad de Derecho y Ciencias Sociales.

De Montagut, Tomás. 1993. "Los actos a causa de muerte en los derechos ibéricos medievales." *Recueils de la Société Jean Bodin* 60(2):185–226.

De Soto, Hernando. 1989. *The Other Path: The Invisible Revolution in the Third World*. Trans. June Abbott. New York: Harper and Row.

———. 1998. "Protection of Property Rights and Civil Society." In Jarquín and Carrillo (1998), 73–82.

De Trazegnies Granda, Fernando. 1979. *La idea de derecho en el Perú republicano del siglo XIX*. Lima: Pontificia Universidad Católica del Perú.

De Vries, Henry P., and José Rodriguez-Novás. 1965. *The Law of the Americas: An Introduction to the Legal Systems of the American Republics*. Dobbs Ferry: Oceana.

Dezalay, Yves, and Bryant Garth. 1998. *Argentina: Law at the Periphery and Law in Dependencies: Political and Economic Crisis and the Instrumentalization and Fragmentation of Law*. Working Paper 9708. Chicago: American Bar Foundation.

———. Eds. 2002. *Global Prescriptions: The Production, Exportation, and Importation of Legal Orthodoxy*. Ann Arbor: University of Michigan Press.

Los doce códigos del estado soberano de Cundinamarca. 1878. 3 vol. Paris, L.R.G.

Dolinger, Jacob, and Keith S. Rosenn, eds. 1992. *A Panorama of Brazilian Law*. Coral Gables: University of Miami North-South Center.

Domingo, Pilar, and Rachel Sieder, eds. 2001. *Rule of Law in Latin America: The International Promotion of Judicial Reform*. London: Institute of Latin American Studies.

Donoso, Ricardo. 1967. *Las ideas políticas en Chile*. 2d ed. Santiago: Facultad de Filosofía y Educación, Universidad de Chile.

Dorner, Peter. 1992. *Latin American Land Reforms in Theory and Practice*. Madison: University of Wisconsin Press.

Dougnac Rodríguez, Antonio. 1999. "Dos cátedras universitarias con historia (1758–1998)." In Dougnac Rodríguez and Eyzaguirre (1999), vol. 1, 27–46.

Dougnac Rodríguez, Antonio, and Felipe Vicencio Eyzaguirre, eds. 1999–2000. *La escuela chilena de historiadores del derecho y los estudios jurídicos en Chile.* 2 vols. Santiago: Universidad Central de Chile.

Ebright, Malcolm, ed. 1989. *Spanish and Mexican Land Grants and the Law.* Manhattan: Sunflower University Press, 1989.

———. 1994. *Land Grants and Lawsuits in Northern New Mexico.* Albuquerque: University of New Mexico Press.

Eddington, Jeffrey S. 1998. "Mexican Negotiable Instruments." In Vargas (1998), vol. 1, 321–350.

Eder, Phanor J. 1950. *A Comparative Survey of Anglo-American and Latin-American Law.* New York: New York University Press.

Eltis, David. 1987. *Economic Growth and the Ending of the Transatlantic Slave Trade.* New York: Oxford University Press.

———. 2000. *The Rise of African Slavery in the Americas.* Cambridge: Cambridge University Press.

Erie, Carlos M. N. 1995. *From Madrid to Purgatory: The Art and Craft of Dying in Sixteenth Century Spain.* Cambridge: Cambridge University Press.

Erim, Martin, et al. 1998. "Financing Sources for Trade and Investment in Latin America." *American University International Law Review* 13:815–855.

Escriche y Martín, Joaquín. 1837. *Diccionario razonado de legislación.* Mégico: Galvan.

Esquirol, Jorge L. 1997. "The Fictions of Latin American Law (Part I)." *Utah Law Review* 1997:425–470.

———. 2003. "Continuing Fictions of Latin American Law." *Florida Law Review* 55: 41–114.

Esquivel Obregón, Toribio. 1980. "Inquisición." In Soberanes Fernández (1980a), 205–229.

Evenson, Debra. 1994. *Revolution in the Balance: Law and Society in Contemporary Cuba.* Boulder: Westview Press.

Faundez, Julio, ed. 1997. *Good Government and Law: Legal and Institutional Reform in Developing Countries.* London: Macmillan Press.

Febrero, José. 1806–1808. *Febrero adicionado ó librería de escribanos: instrucción teórico práctica para principiantes.* 7 vols. Madrid: Imp. de Don Josef del Collado.

Fernández de Recas, Guillermo S. 1965. *Mayorazgos de la Nueva España.* Mexico: Instituto Bibliográfico Mexicano.

"Foreign Investment Regulations." 2000. *Business Latin America.* Feb. 7, 2000. Economist Intelligence Unit Ltd.

Gamarra, Eduardo A. 1991. *The System of Justice in Bolivia: An Institutional Analysis.* San José, Costa Rica: CAJ.

García Gallo, Alfonso. 1945. *Cedulario indiano recopilado por Diego de Encinas.* Madrid: Ediciones Cultura Hispánica.

———. 1964. *Manual de historia del derecho español.* 2d ed. Madrid: Artes Gráficas y Ediciones.

García Goyena, Florencia, and Joaquín Aguirre. 1852. *Febrero ó librería de jueces, abogados y escribanos, comprensiva de los códigos civil, criminal y administrativo.* 6 vols. 4th ed. Madrid: Gaspar y Roig.

García Villegas, Mauricio. 1993. *La eficacia simbólica del derecho.* Bogotá: Uniandes.

Gardner, James A. 1980. *Legal Imperialism: American Lawyers and Foreign Aid in Latin America*. Madison: University of Wisconsin Press.

Garro, Alejandro M. 1999. "Access to Justice for the Poor in Latin America." In Méndez et al. (1999), 278–302.

Gibson, Charles. 1964. *The Aztecs under Spanish Rule*. Stanford: Stanford University Press.

———. 1966. *Spain in America*. New York: Harper and Row.

———. 1984. "Indian Societies under Spanish Rule." In *The Cambridge History of Latin America*. Vol. 2. Edited by Leslie Bethell. Cambridge: Cambridge University Press, 381–419.

Gibson, William Marion. 1948. *The Constitutions of Colombia*. Durham, N.C.: Duke University Press.

Glade, William. 1998. "Current Trends and Problems in Foreign Investment in Latin America." *NAFTA: Law and Business Review of the Americas* 4:57–76.

Golbert, Albert S. and Yenny Nun. 1982. *Latin American Law and Institutions*. New York: Praeger.

Gonzalbo Aizpuru, Pilar. 1989. "De Escrituras y Escribanos." *Anuario mexicano de historia del derecho* 1:77–93.

González, María del Refugio. 1981. *Estudios sobre la historia del derecho civil en México durante el siglo XIX*. Mexico: Universidad Nacional Autónoma de México.

———. 1996. *Ordenanzas de la minería de la Nueva España formadas y propuestas por su real tribunal*. Mexico: Universidad Nacional Autónoma de México.

González Echenique, Javier. 1954. *Los estudios jurídicos y la abogacía en el reino de Chile*. Santiago de Chile: Imprenta Universitaria.

González González, Enrique. 1988. "Oidores contra canónigos. El primer capítulo de la pugna en torno a los estatutos de la Real Universidad de México (1553–1570)." In *Memoria del IV congreso de historia del derecho mexicano*, Vol. 1, 455–477.

González Hernández, Juan Carlos. 1992. *Influencia del derecho español en América*. Madrid: Editorial Mapfre.

Greenblatt, Stephen J. 1991. *Marvelous Possessions: The Wonder of the New World*. Chicago: University of Chicago Press.

Greenleaf, Richard E. 1969. *The Mexican Inquisition of the Sixteenth Century*. Albuquerque: University of New Mexico Press.

Gutiérrez, Ramon. 1991. *When Jesus Came, the Corn Mothers Went Away: Marriage, Sexuality, and Power in New Mexico, 1500–1846*. Stanford: Stanford University Press.

Gutiérrez Ramos, Jairo. 1998. *El mayorazgo de Bogotá y el marquesado de San Jorge: riqueza, linaje, poder y honor en Santa Fé, 1538–1824*. Bogotá: Instituto Colombiano de Cultura Hispánica.

Gutiérrez Sarmiento, Humberto. 1992. *El derecho civil en la conformación de América*. Bogotá: Ecoe ediciones.

Guy, Donna J. 2000. *White Slavery and Mothers Alive and Dead: The Troubled Meeting of Sex, Gender, Public Heath, and Progress in Latin America*. Lincoln: University of Nebraska Press.

Guzmán Brito, Alejandro. 1979. "Crítica del derecho patrio y proyectos para su fijación." *Revista de Derecho* (Universidad Católica de Valparaiso) 3:67–94.

———. 1982. *Andrés Bello codificador: historia de la fijación y codificación del derecho civil en Chile*. 2 vols. Santiago: Universidad de Chile.

———. 1992. "El código civil de Chile y sus primeros intérpretes." *Revista chilena de derecho* 19(1):81–88.

———. 1993. "La cirulation du modéle juridique français: Chili." *Travaux de l'asociation Henri Capitant des amis de la culture juridique française* 44: 141–152.

———. 1996. "Mos latinoamericanus iura legendi." *Roma e America: dritto romano comune* 1:15–20.

———. 2000a. *Historia de la codificación civil en Iberoamérica.* Madrid: Fundación Histórico Tavera.

———. 2000b. "La influencia del código civil de Vélez Sársfield en las codificaciones de Iberoamérica hasta principios del siglo XX." In *Homenaje a Dalmacio Vélez Sársfield.* Vol. 5. Córdoba: Academia Nacional de Derecho y Ciencias Sociales de Córdoba, 235–254.

Halpérin, Jean-Louis. 1996. *Histoire du droit privé français depuis 1804.* Paris: Presses Universitaires de France.

Hamilton, Sarah. 2002. "Neoliberalism, Gender, and Property Rights in Rural Mexico." *Latin American Research Review* 37: 119–143.

Hammergren, Linn A. 1998. *The Politics of Justice and Justice Reform in Latin America: The Peruvian Experience in Comparative Perspective.* Boulder: Westview Press.

Hanisch Espíndola, Hugo. 2000. "Los ochenta años de influencia de Andrés Bello en la enseñanza de derecho romano en Chile." In Dougnac Rodríguez and Eyzaguirre (2000), vol. 2, 55–105.

Hanke, Lewis. 1949. *The Spanish Struggle for Justice in the Conquest of America.* Philadelphia: University of Pennsylvania Press.

———. 1974. *El prejuicio racial en el nuevo mundo.* México: Sep/Setenta.

Haring, C. H. 1975. *The Spanish Empire in America.* San Diego: Harcourt Brace Jovanovich.

Harris, Charles H., III. 1975. *A Mexican Family Empire: The Latifundo of the Sánchez Navarros, 1765–1867.* Austin: University of Texas Press.

Harvey, H. R., and Hanns J. Prem, eds. 1984. *Explorations in Ethnohistory: Indians of Central Mexico in the Sixteenth Century.* Albuquerque: University of New Mexico Press.

Herget, James E., and Jorge Camil. 1978. *An Introduction to the Mexican Legal System.* Buffalo: Hein.

Hernandez, Berta E. 1991. "To Bear or Not to Bear: Reproductive Freedom as an International Human Right." *Brooklyn Journal of International Law* 17:309–358.

Hernández, Tanya Katerí. 2002. "Multiracial Matrix: The Role of Race Ideology in the Enforcement of Antidiscrimination Laws, A United States—Latin American Comparison." *Cornell Law Review* 87:1093–1176.

Herrerías Sordo, María del Mar. 1998. *El concubinato: análisis histórico jurídico y su problemática en la práctica.* México: Porrúa.

Herzog, Tamar. 1995. *Los ministros de la audiencia de Quito (1650–1750).* Bogotá: Libri-Mundi.

———. 1996. *Mediación, archivos, y ejercicio: los escribanos de Quito (siglo XVII).* Frankfurt am Main: Vittorio Klostermann.

———. 2002. "Citizenship and Empire: Communal Definition in Eighteenth-Century Spain and Spanish America." In Kirshner and Mayali (2002), 147–167.

Hevia Bolaños, Juan de. 1652. *Primera y segunda parte de la curia filipica.* Madrid: Melchor Sanchez.

————. 1980. "Consulado." In Soberanes Fernández (1980a), 123–141.

Hora, Roy. 2001. *The Landowners of the Argentine Pampas: A Social and Political History, 1860–1945*. Oxford: Oxford University Press.

Horack, H. Claude. 1950. "Legal Education in Latin-American Republics." *Journal of Legal Education* 2:287–297.

Howe, Walter. 1968. *The Mining Guild of New Spain and its Tribunal General*. Cambridge: Harvard University Press, 1949. Reprint. New York: Greenwood Press.

Hunefeldt, Christine. 1994. *Paying the Price of Freedom: Family and Labor among Lima's Slaves 1800–1854*. Berkeley: University of California Press.

————. 2000. *Liberalism in the Bedroom: Quarreling Spouses in Nineteenth-Century Lima*. University Park: Pennsylvania State University Press.

Icaza Dufour, Francisco de, coord. 1987. *Recopilación de leyes de los reynos de las Indias*. 5 vols. México: Porrúa.

————. 1998. *La Abogacía en el Reino de Nueva España 1521–1821*. México: Porrúa.

Inter-American Development Bank. 1995. *Women in the Americas: Bridging the Gender Gap*. Baltimore: Johns Hopkins University Press.

Jaksić, Iván, ed. 1997. *Selected Writings of Andrés Bello*. Trans. Frances M. López-Morillas. New York: Oxford University Press.

————. 1998. "Andrés Bello and the Problem of Order in Post-Independence Spanish America." Working Paper 97/98-1. David Rockefeller Center for Latin American Studies, Harvard University.

————. 2001. *Andrés Bello: Scholarship and Nation-Building in Nineteenth-Century Latin America*. Cambridge: Cambridge University Press.

Jarquín, Edmundo, and Fernando Carrillo, eds. 1998. *Justice Delayed: Judicial Reform in Latin America*. Washington: Inter-American Development Bank.

Jesús Fébles, Manuel de. 1980. "Protomedicato." In Soberanes Fernández (1980a), 281–291.

Kagan, Richard L. 1981. *Law Suits and Litigants in Castile, 1500–1700*. Chapel Hill: University of North Carolina Press.

Karst, Kenneth L., and Keith S. Rosenn. 1975. *Law and Development in Latin America: A Case Book*. Berkeley: University of California Press.

Karst, Kenneth L., Murray L. Schwartz, and Audrey James Schwartz. 1973. *The Evolution of Law in the Barrios of Caracas*. Los Angeles: Latin American Center, University of California.

Kay, Cristóbal. 1998. "Latin America's Agrarian Reform: Lights and Shadows." *Land Reform* 1998(2):8–31.

Kellogg, Susan. 1995. *Law and the Transformation of Aztec Culture, 1500–1800*. Norman: University of Oklahoma Press.

Kellogg, Susan, and Matthew Restall, eds. 1998. *Dead Giveaway: Indigenous Testaments of Colonial Mesoamerica and the Andes*. Salt Lake City: University of Utah Press.

Kicza, John. 1984. "The Legal Community in Late Colonial Mexico: Social Composition and Career Patterns." In Spores and Hassig (1984), 127–144.

Kirshner, Julius, and Laurent Mayali, eds. 2002. *Privileges and Rights of Citizenship: Law and the Juridical Construction of Civil Society*. Berkeley: Robbins Collection.

Klein, Herbert S. 1986. *African Slavery in Latin America and the Caribbean*. New York: Oxford University Press.

Knight, Franklin W. 1970. *Slave Society in Cuba during the Nineteenth Century*. Madison: University of Wisconsin Press.

Konetzke, Richard. 1953. *Colección de documentos para la historia de la formación social de Hispanoamérica, 1493–1810*. 3 vols. Madrid: Consejo Superior de Investigaciones Científicas.

Korth, Eugene H., and Della M. Flusche. 1987. "Dowery and Inheritance in Colonial Spanish America: Peninsular Law and Chilean Practices." *The Americas* 43:395–410.

Kozolchyk, Boris. 1972. "Commercial Law Recodification and Economic Development in Latin America." *Lawyer of the Americas* 4:189–205.

Lafaille, Hector. 1959. *Fuentes del derecho civil en América Latina*. Buenos Aires: Abeledo-Perrot.

Lamar, Marti. 1994. "'Choosing' Partible Inheritance: Chilean Merchant Families, 1795–1825." *Journal of Social History* 28(1): 125–145.

Lavrin, Asunción, ed. 1978. *Latin American Women: Historical Perspectives*. Westport, Conn.: Greenwood, 1978.

Lavrin, Asunción, and Edith Couturier. 1979. "Dowries and Wills: A View of Women's Socioeconomic Role in Colonial Guadalajara and Puebla, 1640–1790." *Hispanic American Historical Review* 59(2):280–304.

The Laws of Las Siete Partidas. 1978. Trans. L. Moreau-Lilet and Henry Carleton. New Orleans: James McKaraher, 1820. Reprint. Baton Rouge: Claitor's.

Lawyers Committee for Human Rights et al. 1996. *Halfway to Reform: The World Bank and the Venezuelan Justice System*. New York: Lawyers Committee for Human Rights.

LeGrand, Catherine. 1986. *Frontier Expansion and Peasant Protest in Colombia*. Albuquerque: University of New Mexico Press.

León Pinelo, Antonio de. 1892. *Tablas cronológicas de los reales consejos supremo y de la cámara de las Indias Occidentales*. 2d ed. Madrid: Impresor de la Real Casa.

Levaggi, Abelardo. 1969. *Dalmacio Vélez Sársfield y el derecho eclesiástico*. Buenos Aires: Perrot.

———. 1986, 1987, 1991. *Manual de historia del derecho argentino*. 3 vols. Buenos Aires: Depalma.

Levene, Ricardo. 1948. *En el tercer centenario de "política indiana" de Juan de Solórzano Pereira*. Vol. 20. Conferencías y Comunicaciones, Insituto de Historia del Derecho, Argentina. Buenos Aires: Imprenta de la Universidad.

———. 1949. *Antecedentes históricos sobre la enseñanza de la jurisprudencia y de la historia del derecho patrio en la Argentina*. Buenos Aires: Instituto de Historia del Derecho.

———. 1959. "Notas para la historia de los abogados en Indias." *Revista chilena de historia del derecho* 1:9–12.

———. 1985. *Manual de historia del derecho argentino*. 5th ed. Buenos Aires: Depalma.

Lewin, Boleslao. 1962. *La inquisición en Hispanoamérica*. Buenos Aires: Editorial Proyección.

Lewin, Linda. 2003a. *Surprise Heirs I: Illegitimacy, Patrimonial Rights, and Legal Nationalism in Luso-Brazilian Inheritance, 1750–1821*. Stanford, Calif: Stanford University Press.

———. 2003b. *Surprise Heirs II: Illegitimacy, Inheritance Rights, and Public Power in the Formation of Imperial Brazil, 1822–1889*. Stanford, Calif.: Stanford University Press.

Lira, Andrés. 1980. "Indios." In Soberanes Fernández (1980a), 189–203.

Little, Cynthia Jefress. 1978. "Education, Philanthropy, and Feminism: Components of Argentine Womanhood, 1860–1926." In Lavrin (1978), 235–253.

Lohmann Villena, Guillermo. 1974. *Los ministros de la Audiencia de Lima en el reinado de los Borbones (1700–1821)*. Sevilla: EEHA.

Lomnitz, Larissa Adler, and Rodrigo Salazar. 2002. "Cultural Elements in the Practice of Law in Mexico: Informal Networks in a Formal System." In Dezalay and Garth (2002), 209–248.

López Bohórquez, Alí Enrique. 1984. *Los ministros de la Audiencia de Caracas (1786–1810)*. Caracas: Academia Nacional de la Historia, 1984.

Lucena Salmoral, Manuel. 1996. *Los códigos negros de la América Española*. Alcalá: UNESCO.

Lynch, Dennis O. 1981. *Legal Roles in Colombia*. Uppsala: Scandinavian Institute of African Studies.

Lynch, John. 1969. *Spanish Colonial Administration, 1782–1810*. New York: Greenwood.

————. 1992. *Caudillos in Spanish America 1800–1850*. Oxford: Clarendon Press.

Macías, Anna. 1978. "Felipe Carrillo Puerto and Women's Liberation in Mexico." In Lavrin (1978), 286–301.

MacLachlan, Colin. 1974. *Criminal Justice in Eighteenth-Century Mexico: A Study of the Tribunal of the Acordada*. Berkeley: University of California Press.

————. 1980. "Acordada." In Soberanes Fernández (1980a), 85–122.

Madrazo, Jorge. 1980. "Universitario." In Soberanes Fernández (1980a), 333–364.

Maier, Julio, et al. 1993. *Reformas procesales en América Latina: La oralidad en los procesos*. Santiago de Chile, CPU.

Malagón-Barceló, Javier. 1961–1962. "The Role of the *Letrado* in the Colonization of America." *Americas* 18:1–17.

Malavet, Pedro A. 1996. "Counsel for the Situation: The Latin Notary, a Historical and Comparative Model." *Hastings International and Comparative Law Review* 19:389–488.

————. 1997. "The Non-Adversarial, Extra-Judicial Search for Legality and Truth: Foreign Notarial Transactions as an Inexpensive and Reliable Model for a Market Driven System of Informed Contracting and Fact-Determination." *Wisconsin International Law Journal* 16:1–60.

————. 1998. "The Foreign Notarial Legal Services Monopoly: Why Should We Care?" *John Marshall Law Review* 31:945–970.

Margadant S., Guillermo Floris. 1990. *Introducción a la historia del derecho mexicano*. 9th ed. Naucalpan: Editorial Esfinge.

Mariluz Urquijo, José M. 1978. *El régimen de la tierra en el derecho indiano*. Buenos Aires: Perrot.

Martindale-Hubbell International Law Digest. 2002. New Providence, N.J.: Martindale-Hubbell. Curtis, Mallet-Prevost, Colt & Mosle, New York, New York revise most Latin American entries. The Mexican entry is revised by Noriega y Escobedo, A.C., Mexico City. Icaza, Gozalez-Ruiz & Aleman, Panama revise the Panamanian entry. Peroni, Sosa, Tellechea, Burt & Narvaja, Asunción revise the Paraguayan entry.

Martínez, Néstor Humberto. 1998. "Rule of Law and Economic Efficiency." In Jarquín and Carrillo (1998), 3–13.

Martínez Cárdos, José. 1960. *Gregorio López, Consejero de Indias, Glosador de las Partidas (1496–1560)*. Madrid: Instituto Gonzalo Fernández de Oviedo.

Mayorga García, Fernando. 1991. *La Audiencia de Santa Fé en los siglos XVI y XVII*. Bogotá: Instituto Colombiano de Cultura Hispánica.

McAlister, Lyle N. 1980. "Militares." In Soberanes Fernández (1980a), 249–265.

McKnight, Joseph W. 1981. "Tracings of Legal History: Breaking Ties and Borrowing Traditions." In *Centennial History of the Texas Bar 1882–1982*. Burnet, Texas: Eakin Press, 256–275.

———. 1989. "Law Books on the Hispanic Frontier." In Ebright (1989), 74–84.

Means, Robert Charles. 1980. *Underdevelopment and the Development of Law: Corporations and Corporation Law in Nineteenth-Century Colombia*. Chapel Hill: University of North Carolina.

Mellafe, Rolando. 1975. *Negro Slavery in Latin America*. Trans. J. W. S. Judge. Berkeley: University of California Press.

Méndez, Juan E., Guillermo O'Donnell, and Paulo Sérgio Pinheiro, eds. 1999. *The (Un)Rule of Law and the Underprivileged in Latin America*. Notre Dame: University of Notre Dame Press.

Mendieta y Núñez, Lucio. 1975. *Historia de la facultad de derecho*. 2d ed. México: Universidad Nacional Autónoma de México.

Merillat, H. C. L. 1966. "Law and Developing Countries." *American Journal of International Law* 60: 71–80.

Merryman, John Henry. 1977. "Comparative Law and Social Change: On the Origins, Style, Decline and Revival of the Law and Development Movement." *American Journal of Comparative Law* 25:457–491.

———. 1985. *The Civil Law Tradition: An Introduction to the Legal Systems of Western Europe and Latin America*. 2d ed. Stanford: Stanford University Press.

———. 2000a. "Law and Development Memoirs, I: The Chile Law Program." *American Journal of Comparative Law* 48:481–499.

———. 2000b. "Law and Development Memoirs, II: SLADE." *American Journal of Comparative Law* 48:713–727.

Merryman, John Henry, David S. Clark, and Lawrence M. Friedman. 1979. *Law and Social Change in Mediterranean Europe and Latin America: A Handbook of Legal and Social Indicators for Comparative Study*. Stanford: Stanford Law School.

Meyer, Michael C., William L. Sherman, and Susan M. Deeds. 1999. *The Course of Mexican History*. 6th ed. New York: Oxford University Press.

Miller, Jonathan. 1985. "Products Liability in Argentina." *American Journal of Comparative Law* 33:611–636.

———. 1997a. "The Authority of a Foreign Talisman: A Study of U.S. Constitutional Practice as Authority in Nineteenth-Century Argentina and the Argentine Elite's Leap of Faith." *American University Law Review* 46:1483–1572.

———. 1997b. "Courts and the Creation of a 'Spirit of Moderation': Judicial Protection of Revolutionaries in Argentina, 1863–1929." *Hastings International and Comparative Law Review* 20:231–329.

———. 1997c. "Judicial Review and Constitutional Stability: A Sociology of the U.S. Model and its Collapse in Argentina." *Hastings International and Comparative Law Review* 21:77–176.

———. 2000. "Evaluating the Argentine Supreme Court under Presidents Alfonsín and Menem (1983–1999)." *Southwestern Journal of Law and Trade in the Americas* 7:369–433.

Miranda, José. 1952. *El tributo indígena en la Nueva España durante el siglo XVI.* México: El Colegio de México.

———. 1980a. "Indios." In Soberanes Fernández (1980a), 165–174.

———. 1980b. "Mesta." In Soberanes Fernández (1980a), 231–248.

Mirow, M. C. 1997. "La codificación del derecho commercial en los estados unidos." In Jaime Alberto Arrubla Paucar, *Evolución del Derecho Comercial.* Medellín: Biblioteca Jurídica Diké, 419–430.

———. 2000a. "The Power of Codification in Latin America: Simón Bolívar and the *Code Napoléon.*" *Tulane Journal of International and Comparative Law* 8:83–116.

———. 2000b. "Latin American Legal History: Some Essential Spanish Terms." *La Raza Law Review* 11:43–86.

———. 2001. "Borrowing Private Law in Latin America: Andrés Bello's Use of the *Code Napoléon* in Drafting the Chilean Civil Code." *Louisiana Law Review* 61:291–329.

Monslave, J. D. 1924. *Estudios jurídicos y de la historia de la legislación colombiana.* Bogotá: Imprenta Nacional.

Moore, Sally Falk. 1958. *Power and Property in Inca Peru.* New York: Columbia University Press.

Moreno de los Arcos, Roberto. 1980. "Minería." In Soberanes Fernández (1980a), 267–280.

Muñiz, Jorge. 1994. "Private Investment Regime." In Boza (1994), 53–63.

Muro Orejón, Antonio. 1945. *Las leyes nuevas, 1542–1543.* Sevilla: Escuela de Estudios Hispano-Americanos.

———. 1956. *Cedulario Americano de Siglo XVIII.* Sevilla: Escuela de Estudios Hispano-Americanos.

Nader, Laura. 1990. *Harmony Ideology: Justice and Control in a Zapotec Mountain Village.* Stanford: Stanford University Press.

Nagle, Luz E. 1995. "Evolution of the Colombian Judiciary and the Constitutional Court." *Indiana International and Comparative Law Review* 6:59–90.

———. 2000. "U.S. Mutual Assistance to Colombia: Vague Promises and Diminishing Returns." *Fordham International Law Journal* 23:1235–1294.

———. 2001. "E-Commerce in Latin America: Legal and Business Challenges for Developing Enterprise." *American University Law Review* 50:859–936.

Navas, José Manuel. 1996. *La abogacía en el siglo de oro.* Madrid: Ilustre Colegio de Abogados de Madrid.

Ochoa Brun, Miguel Angel. 1972. "Estudio preliminar." In Solórzano y Pereyra (1972), vol. 1, xi–lxiv.

Oddo, Vicente. 1981. *Abogados de Santiago del Estero durante el primer siglo de existencia de la ciudad (1553–1663).* Santiago del Estero, Argentina: Herca.

O'Donnell, Guillermo. 1999. "Polyarchies and the (Un)Rule of Law in Latin America: A Partial Conclusion." In Méndez et al. (1999), 303–337.

Offner, Jerome A. 1983. *Law and Politics in Aztec Texcoco.* Cambridge: Cambridge University Press.

Ortiz de Zevallos, Felipe. 1994. "Reforms for a Better Future." In Boza (1994), 1–13.

Ortiz-Urquidi, Raúl. 1974. *Oaxaca, cuna de la codificación iberoamericana.* México: Editorial Porrúa.

Ots Capdequí, José María. 1952. *España en América.* 2d ed. Bogotá: Universidad Nacional de Colombia.

————. 1959. *Instituciones.* Vol. 14. *Historia de América y de los pueblos americanos.* Barcelona: Salvat.

Pacheco Caballero, Francisco Luis. 1993. "El acto *mortis causa* en los derechos hispánicos durante la edad moderna (notas sobre sucesión testamentaria)." *Recueils de la société Jean Bodin pour l'histoire comparative des institutions* 60(2):227–256.

Pagden, Anthony. 1995. *Lords of All the World: Ideologies of Empire in Spain, Britain, and France c. 1500–1800.* New Haven: Yale University Press.

Parra Márquez, Hector. 1952. *Historia de colegio de abogados de Caracas.* Vol. 1. Caracas: Imprenta Nacional.

Parry, J. H. 1968. *The Audiencia of New Galicia in the Sixteenth Century: A Study in Spanish Colonial Government.* Cambridge: Cambridge University Press, 1948. Reprint.

————. 1977. *The Spanish Seaborne Empire.* New York: Knopf.

Peloso, Vincent C., and Barbara A. Tenenbaum, eds. 1996. *Liberals, Politics, and Power: State Formation in Nineteenth-Century Latin America.* Athens: University of Georgia Press.

Peñalver, Eduardo Moisés. 2000. "Redistributing Property: Natural Law, International Norms, and the Property Reforms of the Cuban Revolution." *Florida Law Review* 52:107–217.

Pérez Perdomo, Rogelio. 1981. *Los abogados en Venezuela: estudio de una elite intelectual y política 1780–1980.* Caracas: Monte Avila Editores.

————. 2002. *Lawyers of Latin America: A Historical Introduction.* Santiago: Santiago de Chile Press, forthcoming (as downloaded from http://lawschool.stanford.edu/library/perezperdomo/lla.html).

Pérez Perdomo, Rogelio, and Pedro Nikken with the assistance of Elizabeth Fassano and Marcos Vilera. 1982. "The Law and Home Ownership in the *Barrios* of Caracas." In Alan Gilbert in association with Jorge E. Hardoy and Ronaldo Ramírez, eds., *Urbanization in Contemporary Latin America: Critical Approaches to the Analysis of Urban Issues.* New York: Wiley, 205–229.

Pérez-Prendes y Muñoz de Arracó, José Manuel. 1986. *Curso de historia del derecho español.* Vol. 1. Madrid: Universidad Cumplutense de Madrid.

————. 1989. *La monarquía indiana y el estado de derecho.* El Puig, Valencia: Asociación Francisco López de Gomara.

Phelan, John Leddy. 1960. "Authority and Flexibility in the Spanish Imperial Bureaucracy." *Administrative Science Quarterly* 5:47–65.

————. 1967. *The Kingdom of Quito in the Seventeenth Century: Bureaucratic Politics in the Spanish Empire.* Madison: University of Wisconsin Press.

Piccirilli, Ricardo. 1942. *Guret Bellemare, los trabajos de un jurisconsulto francés en Buenos Aires.* Buenos Aires: Instituto de Historia del Derecho Argentino y Americano.

Polanco Alcántara, Tomás. 1962. *Las formas jurídicas de la independencía.* Caracas: U.C.V.

————. 1983. *Bolívar: la justicia, primera necesidad del estado.* Caracas: Lagoven.

————. 1992. *Las reales audiencias en las provincias americanas de España.* Madrid: Mapfre.

Polen, M. E., and J. A. Thomas. 1969. "Inter-American Legal Studies at the University of Miami." *Lawyer of the Americas* 1: 42–49.

Prillaman, William C. 2000. *The Judiciary and Democratic Decay in Latin America: Declining Confidence in the Rule of Law.* Westport, Conn.: Praeger.

Ramírez, Susan E. 1986. *Provincial Patriarchs: Land Tenure and the Economics of Power in Colonial Peru.* Albuquerque: University of New Mexico Press.

Ramírez B., Luis M. 1944. "Capacity in Inter-American Law." *Michigan Law Review* 43:559–590.

Ramos Núñez, Carlos. 1997. *El código Napoleónico y su recepción en América Latina.* Lima: Pontificia Universidad Católica del Perú.

Reich, Peter Lester. 1995. *Mexico's Hidden Revolution: The Catholic Church in Law and Politics since 1929.* Notre Dame: University of Notre Dame Press.

Research Advisory Committee on Law and Development, International Legal Center. 1974. *Law and Development: The Future of Law and Development Research.* New York: International Legal Center.

Restrepo Sáenz, José María. 1952. *Biografías de los mandatarios y ministros de la real audiencia.* Bogotá: Cromos.

Reyes Villamizar, Francisco. 1996. *Reforma al régimen de sociedades y concursos.* Bogotá: Cámara de Comercio de Bogotá.

———. 1998. *Disolución y liquidación de sociedades.* 3d ed. Bogotá: Doctrina y Ley.

———. 2002. *Derecho Societario.* 2 vols. Bogotá: Temis.

Reynolds, Matthew Givens. 1895. *Spanish and Mexican Land Laws: New Spain and Mexico.* St. Louis, Mo.: Buxton and Skinner.

Rico, José Maria, and Luis Salas. 1990. *Independencia judicial en América Latina: replanteamiento de un tema tradicional.* San José, Costa Rica: CAJ.

Riddell, James C. 2000. "Emerging Trends in Land Tenure Reform: Progress towards a Unified Theory." Posted June 20, 2000 at <http://www.fao.org/waicent/faoinfo/sustdev/Ltdirect/LTan0038.htm>.

Rípodas Ardanaz, Daisy. 1977. *El matrimonio en Indias: realidad social y regulación jurídica.* Buenos Aires: Fundación para la Educación, la Ciencia y la Cultura.

Rivera Bustamante, Tirza, ed. 1991. *Las Juezas en Centro América y Panamá.* San José, Costa Rica: CAJ.

Rock, David. 1987. *Argentina 1516–1987: From Spanish Colonization to Alfonsín.* Berkeley: University of California Press.

Roett, Riordan, ed. 1999. *Mercosur: Regional Integration, World Markets.* Boulder, Colo.: Lynne Rienner.

Román, Ediberto, and Theron Simmons. 2002. "Membership Denied: Subordination and Subjugation under United States Expansionism." *San Diego Law Review* 39:437–518.

Roniger, Luis, and Tamar Herzog. 2000. *The Collective and the Public in Latin America: Cultural Identities and Political Order.* Brighton: Sussex Academic Press.

Rosenn, Keith S. 1987. "The Protection of Judicial Independence in Latin America." *University of Miami Law Review* 19: 1–35.

———. 2000. "In Memoriam: Rafael C. Benítez." *University of Miami Inter-American Law Review* 31:9–11.

Rowat, Malcolm D. 1997. "Competition Policy in Latin America: Legal and Institutional Issues." In Faundez (1997), 163–188.

Sáez García, Felipe. 1998. "The Nature of Judicial Reform in Latin America and Some Strategic Considerations." *American University International Law Review* 13: 1267–1325.

Sagaón Infante, Raquel. 1984. "Historia de la abogacía." In Soberanes Fernández (1984), 631–640.

Sala, Juan. 1803, 1820. *Ilustración del derecho real de España.* 2 vols. 1st ed. Valencia, Imprenta de Joseph de Orga, 1803; 2d ed., Madrid: J. del Collado, 1820.

———. 1845. *Sala mexicano, o sea: la ilustración del derecho real de España*. Mexico: Libreria del Portal de Mercaderes.

Salas, Luis, and José María Rico. 1990. *Carrera Judicial en América Latina*. San José, Costa Rica: CAJ, 1990.

Salinas Araneda, C., and A. García y García. 1994. "Una década de bibliografía sobre el derecho canónico indiano." *Revista española de derecho canónico* 51:671–727.

Salvatore, Ricardo D., Carlos Aguirre, and Gilbert Joseph, eds. 2001. *Crime and Punishment in Latin America: Law and Society since Late Colonial Times*. Durham, N.C.: Duke University Press.

Samway, Michael A. 1996. "Access to Justice: A Study of Legal Assistance Programs for the Poor in Santiago, Chile." *Duke Journal of Comparative and International Law* 6:347–369.

Sánchez Bella, Ismael. 1980. "Real hacienda." In Soberanes Fernández (1980a), 293–331.

Scafidi, Susan. 2003. "Old Law in the New World: Solórzano and the Analogical Construction of Legal Identity." *Florida Law Review* 55:191–204.

Schmidt, Gustavus. 1851. *The Civil Law of Spain and Mexico*. New Orleans: Thomas Rea.

Scholfield, Philip, ed. 1995. *Jeremy Bentham, Colonies, Commerce and Constitutional Law: Rid Yourselves of Ultramaria and Other Writings on Spain and Spanish America*. New York: Oxford University Press.

Scholfield, Philip, and Jonathan Harris, eds. 1998. *Jeremy Bentham, 'Legislator of the World': Writings on Codification, Law, and Education*. New York: Oxford University Press.

Schwaller, John F. 1985. *Origins of Church Wealth in Mexico: Ecclesiastical Revenues and Church Finances, 1523–1600*. Albuquerque: University of New Mexico Press.

———. 1987. *The Church and Clergy in Sixteenth Century Mexico*. Albuquerque: University of New Mexico Press, 1987.

———. 2000. "The Ordenanzas del Patronazgo in New Spain, 1574–1600." In John F. Schwaller, ed. *The Church in Colonial Latin America*. Wilmington, Del.: SR Books, 49–69.

Scott, Rebecca J. 1985. *Slave Emancipation in Cuba: The Transition to Free Labor, 1860–1899*. Princeton: Princeton University Press.

Seed, Patricia. 1988. *To Love, Honor, and Obey in Colonial Mexico: Conflicts over Marriage Choice, 1574–1821*. Stanford: Stanford University Press.

———. 1995. *Ceremonies of Possession in Europe's Conquest of the New World*. New York: Cambridge University Press.

———. 2001. *American Pentimento: The Invention of Indians and the Pursuit of Riches*. Minneapolis: University of Minnesota Press.

Selinger, Carl M. 1995. "Public Interest Lawyering in Mexico and the United States." *University of Miami Inter-American Law Review* 27:343–360.

Serrano, Sol. 2000. "La estrategia conservadora y la consolidación del orden liberal en Chile, 1860–1890." In Carmagnani (2000) 121–154.

Sheppard, Hale E. 2001. "Overcoming Apathetic Internationalism to Generate Hemispheric Benefits: Analysis of and Arguments For Recent Secured Transactions Laws in Mexico." *Journal of Transnational Law and Policy* 10:133–181.

Sherwood, Robert. 1998. "Judicial Systems and National Economic Performance." In Jarquín and Carrillo (1998), 31–37.

Las Siete Partidas. 2001. Trans. Samuel Parsons Scott. Ed. Robert I. Burns. 5 vols. Philadelphia: University of Pennsylvania Press.

Skidmore, Thomas E., and Peter H. Smith. 2001. *Modern Latin America.* 5th ed. New York: Oxford University Press, 2001.

Snyder, Francis G. 1982. "The Failure of 'Law and Development.'" *Wisconsin Law Review* 1982:373–396.

Soberanes Fernández, José Luis. 1980a. *Los tribunales de la Nueva España.* México: Universidad Nacional Autónoma de México.

———. 1980b. "Tribunales ordinarios." In Soberanes Fernández (1980a), 19–83.

———. 1980c. "Eclesiásticos." In Soberanes Fernández (1980a), 143–163 (selections from the *Curia Filípica Mexicana*).

———, coord. 1984. *Memoria del III congreso de historia del derecho mexicano.* Mexico: Universidad Nacional Autónoma de México.

———. 1998. *Historia del derecho mexicano.* 6th ed. México: Porrúa.

Socolow, Susan Midgen. 2000. *The Women of Colonial Latin America.* Cambridge: Cambridge University Press.

Solís, Luis G., and Richard J. Wilson. 1991. *Political Transition and the Administration of Justice.* San José, Costa Rica: CAJ.

Solórzano y Pereyra, Juan de. 1972. *Política Indiana.* Vol. 1–5. Reprinted in Biblioteca de Autores Españoles. Vols. 252–256. Madrid: Atlas.

Spores, Ronald, and Ross Hassig, eds. 1984. *Five Centuries of Law and Politics in Central Mexico.* Nashville: Vanderbilt University Publications in Anthropology.

Stabili, Maria Rosaria. 2000. "Jueces y justicia en el Chile liberal." In Carmagnani (2000) 227–258.

Stein, Stanley J., and Barbara H. Stein. 2000. *Silver, Trade, and War: Spain and America in the Making of Early Modern Europe.* Baltimore, Md.: The Johns Hopkins University Press.

Stern, Steve J. 1993. *Peru's Indian Peoples and the Challenges of Spanish Conquest: Huamanga to 1640.* 2d ed. Madison: University of Wisconsin Press.

Stotzky, Irwin P., ed. 1993. *Transition to Democracy in Latin America: The Role of the Judiciary.* Boulder, Colo.: Westview.

Suárez, Santiago-Gerardo. 1989. *Las reales audiencias indianas: fuentes y bibliografía.* Caracas: Academia Nacional de la Historia.

Symposium: Responding to the Legal Obstacles to Electronic Commerce in Latin America. 2000. *Arizona Journal of International and Comparative Law* 17:1–255.

Symposium: The Role of Legal Institutions in the Economic Development of the Americas. 1999. "Panel Three: The Law, Expectation and Reality in the Marketplace: The Problems of and Responses to Corruption." *Law and Policy in International Business* 30:196–210.

Tau Anzoátegui, Victor. 1977a. *Las ideas jurídicas en la Argentina (siglos XIX–XX).* Buenos Aires: Perrot.

———. 1977b. *La codificación en la Argentina, 1810–1870: mentalidad social e ideas jurídicas.* Buenos Aires: Impr. de la Universidad.

Taylor, C. O'Neal. 1997. "Dispute Resolution as a Catalyst for Economic Integration and an Agent for Deepening Integration: NAFTA and MERCOSUR." *Northwestern Journal of International Law and Business* 17:850–899.

———. 1998. "Linkage and Rulemaking: Observations on Trade and Investment and

Trade and Labor." *University of Pennsylvania Journal of International Economic Law* 19:639–696.

Taylor, William B. 1972. *Landlord and Peasant in Colonial Oaxaca.* Stanford: Stanford University Press.

Technical Working Group on Trade. 1999. Consultative Group meeting for the Reconstruction and Transformation of Central America. Stockholm, Sweden, 25–28 May 1999. http://www.eadb.org/regions/re2/consultative_group/groups/trade.htm. Visited March 7, 2000.

Tena Ramírez, Felipe. 1998. *Leyes Fundamentales de México 1808–1998.* 21st ed. México: Porrúa.

Thiesenhusen, William C. 1995. *Broken Promises: Agrarian Reform and the Latin American Campesino.* Boulder, Colo.: Westview Press.

Thomas, Hugh. 1997. *The Slave Trade: The Story of the Atlantic Slave Trade: 1440–1870.* New York: Simon and Schuster.

Thome, Joseph R. 2000. "Heading South but Looking North: Globalization and Law Reform in Latin America." *Wisconsin Law Review* 2000:691–712.

Tovar Pinzón, Hermes. 1995. *Que nos tengan en cuenta: colonos, empresarios y aldeas: Colombia 1800–1900.* Bogota: Tercer Mundo.

Traffano, Daniela. 2000. "'Y el Registro Civil no es más que un engaño del gobierno . . .' sociedad civil y iglesia frente a un nuevo registro de los datos vitales: Oaxaca en la segunda mitad del siglo XIX." In Carmagnani (2000), 201–225.

Trubek, David. 1972. "Toward a Social Theory of Law: An Essay on the Study of Law and Development." *Yale Law Journal* 82: 1–50.

Trubek, David, and Marc Galanter. 1974. "Scholars in Self-Estrangement: Some Reflections on the Crisis in Law and Development." *Wisconsin Law Review* 1974: 1062–1102.

Tulchin, Joseph S., and Ralph H. Espach, eds. 2000. *Combating Corruption in Latin America.* Washington: Woodrow Wilson Center Press.

Tuñón Pablos, Julia. 1999. *Women in Mexico: A Past Unveiled.* Trans. Alan Hynds. Austin: University of Texas Press.

Tutino, John Mark. 1976. "Creole Mexico: Spanish Elites, Haciendas, and Indian Towns, 1750–1810." Ph.D. diss., University of Texas.

Twinam, Ann. 1999. *Public Lives, Private Secrets: Gender, Honor, and Sexuality, and Illegitimacy in Colonial Spanish America.* Stanford: Stanford University Press.

Ugarte del Pino, Juan Vicente. 1968. *Historia de la Facultad de Derecho.* Lima: Universidad Nacional Mayor de San Marcos.

Uribe-Uran, Victor M. 1999. "Colonial Lawyers, Republican Lawyers, and the Administration of Justice in Spanish America." In Zimmermann (1999a), 25–48.

———. 2000. *Honorable Lives: Lawyers, Family, and Politics in Colombia, 1780–1850.* Pittsburgh: University of Pittsburgh Press.

Valls Pereira, Lia. 1999. "Toward the Common Market of the South: Mercosur's Origins, Evolution, and Challenges." In Roett (1999), 7–24.

Vance, John. 1943. *The Background of Hispanic-American Law.* New York: Central Book.

Vanderlinden, Jacques. 1967. *Le concept de code en Europe Occidentale du XIIIe au XIXe siècle, essai de définition.* Bruxelles: Éditions de l'Institut de Sociologie de l'Université Libre de Bruxelles.

Van Kleffens, E. N. 1968. *Hispanic Law until the End of the Middle Ages.* Edinburgh: Edinburgh University Press.

Van Young, Eric. 1981. *Hacienda and Market in Eighteenth-Century Mexico: The Rural Economy of the Guadalajara Region, 1675–1820.* Berkeley: University of California Press.

Varga, Csaba. 1991. *Codification as a Socio-Historical Phenomenon.* Trans. Sándor Eszenyi et al. Budapest: Akadémiai Kiadó.

Vargas, Jorge A. 1996. "The Rebirth of the Supreme Court of Mexico: An Appraisal of President Zedillo's Judicial Reform of 1995." *American University Journal of International Law and Policy* 11:295–340.

———. 1998–2001. *Mexican Law: A Treatise for Legal Practitioners and International Investors.* 4 vols. St. Paul: West.

Vega, María del Carmen. 1994. "Bilateral Investment Treaties." In Boza (1994), 65–82.

Vera Estañol, Jorge. 1994. *La evolución jurídica.* Reprint of 1900 edition. Mexico: Universidad Nacional Autónoma de México.

Vigil, Ralph. 1987. *Alonso Zorita: Royal Judge and Christian Humanist, 1512–1585.* Norman: University of Oklahoma Press.

Von Mehren, Philip T. 1997. *Cross Border Trade and Investment with Mexico: NAFTA's New Rules of the Game.* Irvington-on-Hudson, New York: Transnational.

Watson, Alan. 1989. *Slave Law in the Americas.* Athens: University of Georgia Press.

Werner, Patrick S. 2000. "Sources of Law in Nicaragua during the Colonial Period." *Nicaraguan Academic Journal* 1:71–101.

———. 2002. "El régimen legal de actividad marítima del Imperio Hispánico: el libro nuevo de la Recopilación." *Nicaraguan Academic Journal* 3:39–62.

Wiarda, Howard J. 1971. "Law and Political Development in Latin America: Toward a Framework for Analysis." *American Journal of Comparative Law* 19:434–463.

Widener, Mike. 1999. "Resources on Aztec and Mayan Law." Updated 10/7/1999 at <http://www.law.utexas.edu/rare/aztec.htm>.

Williford, Mariam. 1980. *Jeremy Bentham on Spanish America: An Account of his Letters and Proposals to the New World.* Baton Rouge: Louisiana State University Press.

Wilson, Richard J. 1989. "New Legal Education in North and South America." *Stanford Journal of International Law* 25:375–465.

———. 2002. "Three Law School Clinics in Chile, 1970–2000: Innovation, Resistance, and Conformity in the Global South." *Clinical Law Review* 8:515–582.

Witker, Jorge V., ed. 1976. *Antología de estudios sobre enseñanza del derecho.* Mexico: Universidad Nacional Autónoma de México.

Yamin, Alicia Ely, and María Pilar Noriega García. 1999. "The Absence of the Rule of Law in Mexico: Diagnosis and Implications for a Mexican Transition to Democracy." *Loyola Los Angeles International and Comparative Law Journal* 21:467–520.

Zamora, Stephen. 1993. "The Americanization of Mexican Law: Non-Trade Issues in the North American Free Trade Agreement." *Law and Politics in International Business* 24:391–459.

Zatz, Marjorie S. 1994. *Producing Legality: Law and Socialism in Cuba.* New York: Routledge.

Zavala, Silvio A. 1935. *La encomienda indiana.* Madrid: Centro de Estudios Históricos, 1935.

———. 1940. *De encomienda y propiedad territorial en algunas regiones de la América española.* México: Porrúa.

———. 1971. *Las instituciones jurídicas en la conquista de América.* México: Porrúa.

———. 1984–1987. *El servicio personal de los indios en la Nueva España.* 3 vols. México: Colegio de México, Centro de Estudios Históricos.

Zimmermann, Eduardo, ed. 1999a. *Judicial Institutions in Nineteenth-Century Latin America.* London: Institute of Latin American Studies.

———. 1999b. "Law, Justice, and State-Building in Nineteenth-Century Latin America." In Zimmermann (1999a), 1–7.

———. 1999c. "The Education of Lawyers and Judges in Argentina's *Organización Nacional* (1860–1880)." In Zimmermann (1999a), 104–123.

Zorraquín Becú, Ricardo. 1952. *La organización judicial argentina en el período hispánico.* Buenos Aires: Librería del Plata.

Bibliographies of Latin American Law and Legal History

American Association of Law Libraries. 1988. *Workshop on Latin American Law and Law-Related Reference Sources.* Conference director Daniel L. Wade. Atlanta, Ga., June 30, 1988.

Avalos, Francisco A. 2000. *The Mexican Legal System.* 2d ed. Littleton: Rothman.

Bayitch, S.A. 1967. *Latin America and the Caribbean; A Bibliographical Guide to Works in English.* Coral Gables: University of Miami Press.

Clagett, Helen L., and David M. Valderrama. 1973. *A Revised Guide to the Law and Legal Literature of Mexico.* Washington: Library of Congress.

Dagrossa, Norberto C. 2000. *Bibliografía de historia del derecho indiano.* In *Colección proyectos históricos tavera (I) nuevas aportaciones a la historia jurídica de Iberoamérica.* José Andrés-Gallego, ed., Madrid: Digibis.

Gilissen, John. 1963–1988. *Introduction bibliographique á l'histoire du droit et á l'ethnologie juridique.* Bruxelles: Editions de l'Institut de Sociologie, Université Libre de Bruxelles. (organized by country)

Snyder, Frederick E. 1985. *Latin American Society and Legal Culture: A Bibliography.* Westport, Conn.: Greenwood Press.

Trelles, Oscar M, II. 1981. *Spanish Law and Its Influence in the Americas: Bibliography to Accompany a Workshop Presentation.* Rare Law Book Conference, Austin, Texas. January 1981. Typescript.

Villalón-Galdames, Albert. 1969, 1985. *Bibliografía jurídica de América Latina (1810–1965).* 2 vols. Vol 1. Santiago de Chile: Editorial Jurídica de Chile. Vol. 2. Boston: G. K. Hall.

Widener, Mike. 1999. *Resources on Aztec and Mayan Law.* http://www.law.utexas.edu/rare/aztec.htm.

Useful Internet Sites

Catálogo bibliohemerográfico del Instituto de Investigaciones Jurídicas de la Universidad Nacional Autónoma de México: http://info4.juridicas.unam.mx/jusbiblio/

Índice de la *Revista de estudios histórico-jurídicos:* http://www.derecho.ucv.cl/

Justicia constitucional en Iberoamérica: http://www.uc3m.es/uc3m/inst/MGP/JCI/OO-portada.htm

LatCrit Homepage: http://personal.law.miami.edu/~fvaldes/latcrit/

Law and Justice in Latin America-LANIC: http://lanic.utexas.edu/la/region/law/

Law and Society Section of the Latin American Studies Association: http://darkwing.uoregon.edu/~caguirre/lawandsociety.htm

Mexican Law: http://www.mexlaw.com/

Ansotegui, Juan Crisótomo, 48
Antilles, 77
Antioquia, 156
antitrust, 212, 213
antivagrancy laws, 203
apoderados, 115
appeals, 179–180
apprenticeship, 37
aqueducts, 69
Aragon, 55
Aranda, Francisco, 114
Arbenz Guzmán, Jacobo, 206
arbitration: nineteenth-century, 109, 115;
    twentieth-century, 181, 182, 196, 215,
    233
arbitratores, 31
arbitrators, 31
arbitri, 31
Argentina: borrowing law in, 128; *cabildo*
    in, 107; *caudillos* of, 99; civil code of,
    123, 138–141, 194; commercial law of,
    157–158, 159, 160, 240; constitutions
    of, 272n1; courts of, 108, 109, 110, 174,
    176, 182, 273n45; decrees in, 195; feder-
    alism in, 102; and homosexuality, 201;
    Indians in, 146; inheritance in, 208;
    jurisprudence in, 198; legal education
    in, 190; marriage in, 148, 202; and
    Mercosur, 230; mining law in, 163,
    164, 213, 214; procedural law in, 130,
    142; property law in, 207, 223, 224,
    225; slavery in, 144; women in, 203
Armas, José, 134
Arnold, Linda, 108, 111
Arosemena, Justo, 130, 156, 157
Arras, 56, 149
Arrillaga, Basilio José, 130
Arrom, Silvia, 149
asesor, 29, 32, 43, 73
asientos, 78
Asociación Latinoamericana de Integra-
    ción, 230
Association for the Reform of Legal
    Education, 189
Asunción, Treaty of, 230
Aubry, Charles, 129, 138, 139, 140, 169,
    197
audiencias: as court, 22–24, 38, 105; juris-

diction of, 10, 22–23, 29, 33, 34, 47,
    107, 108, 111; officials of, 23–24, 32, 42,
    48, 73, 105; records of, 30
Audiencia y Real Chancillería de Valla-
    dolid, 23
Autos acordados, 18
Avendaño, Diego de, 52
Ávila Camacho, Manuel, 221
Ayala, Antonio de, 52
Ayala, Manuel José, 48, 51
ayllus, 6
Azon, 52
Aztec law, 1–6
Azúa, Tomás de, 48

bachiller, 35, 37, 117, 138
Balcarce, General, 110
Baldus, 17, 52
bancos de fideicomiso, 212
banking: and codification, 213; and com-
    merce, 161, 207, 212; and labor law,
    215; and land reform, 223; LL.M. in,
    191; regulation of, 231; U.S. influence
    on, 168, 170
Bank of Mexico, 160
bankruptcy: codes, 196, 213; and com-
    merce, 76, 155, 211, 212, 231; in com-
    mercial codes, 158, 160
Banrural, 223
barrio, 183
Bartholomeus Brixiensis, 35
Bartolus, 17, 36, 52
Bases Orgánicas (Mexico), 112, 136
Baudry-Lacantinerie, Gabriel, 169
beaterios, 148
Belgium, 140, 161, 197
Bellemare, Guret, 110
Bello, Andrés: and Chilean Civil Code,
    137–138; illustration of, *132;* influence
    of, on other countries, 136, 137, 140,
    156, 158; and *mayorazgos*, 152; and new
    nations, 100; and Ocampo, 159; and
    testamentary freedom, 154
Bellomo, Manlio, 98
Benitez, Rafael C., 188
Bentham, Jeremy, 104, 118, 119, 136, 137,
    138
Bentura Beleña, Eusebio, 252n17

Bern Convention, 211
bienes comunes, 201
bienes parafernales, 56
bigamy, 57. *See also* polygamy
Bilbao, 29, 51
Board of Trade: as colonial institution, 20, 21, 28, 32, *33;* and commerce, 70, 71; grants by, 14; and passage to the Indies, 55; in probate, 68; in the *Recopilación,* 48; and slavery, 78, 79
Bobadilla, 52
Bogotá. *See* Santa Fe de Bogotá
Bok, Derek, 189
Bolívar (Colombia), 157
Bolívar, Simón, 97-98, 107, 109, 119, 134, 137
Bolivia: *amparo* action in, 180; and Andean Common Market, 230; civil code of, 135, 160; colonial procedure in, 28; court procedure in, 109, 182; debt peonage in, 204; inheritance in, 208; judicial reform in, 175, 176, 177, 273n22; land reform in, 223, 224, 226; mining in, 213; slaves in, 79
Bologna, 16
Borah, Woodrow, 27, 93
Borchard, Edwin, 139
borrowing: as codification method, 135, 142, 156-157; and legal underdevelopment, 128, 156-157, 236, 239; of trust law, 167-168, 212
Bourbon reforms, 21, 45, 48
Boyacá, Colegio de, 120
Brazil: land reform in, 224; legal education in, 189; and Mercosur, 230; slavery in, 79, 144; source of law in, 139, 158, 224, 230, 240
British Council, 273n22
British Library, 137
Bucareli, Treaty of, 206
Buenos Aires: *Audiencia* of, 10, 23; *cabildo* of, 26, 27, 40, 109, 121; commercial code of, 157; *consulado* in, 29; and León Pinelo, 49; notary in, 123; procedural law in, 130; slavery in, 79, 143; tax tribunal of, 32; and trade, 99; University of, 118, 139, 141, 157, 158; and Vélez Sársfield, 138, 139

bufetes colectivos, 233-234
bulls, papal, 12
bureaucracy, colonial, 19-31, 33
Burgos, 29, 75
burial, 67
Busey, James L., 172
business associations, xi, 75-76, 155, 161, 210. *See also* corporations; partnerships
Bustamante, Antonio Sánchez de, 181, 198

Cabero y Salazar, José, 134
cabildo: abierto, 107, 247n77; ecclesiastical, 34; in granting and holding land, 62, 154; and independence, 121; Indian, 92; jurisdiction of, 26-27, 40, 47, 107, 108, 109; local officials of, 25-27, 30, 32, 33; and slavery, 78
Cabrera, Luis, 206
cacicazgo, 92
caciques, 85, 86, 90, 92
CACM. *See* Central American Common Market
Cadastres. *See* civil registries
Cádiz, 21, 71
Caja de Comunidad, 90
Caja de Consolidación, 32
Calles, Plutarco Elías, 214
calpulli, 2
Camagüey, 233
cámara de apelaciones, 108
cámara de comercio, 213
Canario, Antonio, 52
canon law: in ecclesiastical courts, 51, 139; and legal education, 35, 36, 117, 119, 120, 265n32; limited use of, 17; and marriage law, 148, 202; as supplemental source, 52, 53
capellanía, 66, 255n51
capitanes generales, 25
Capitant, Henri, 169
capitulación, 14, 24
Caracas: *barrios* of, 182; and Bello, 100, 137; city of, 10; Colegio de Abogados de, 38; colonial lawyers in, 40; slavery in, 79, 143; tax officials of, 32; University of, 35, 36

Cárdenas, Lázaro, 214, 221
Carleval, Tomás, 52
Carranza, Venustiano, 206, 220, 221
Cartagena: city of, 10, 120; *consulado* of, 29, 51, 113; Inquisition in, 28; legal education in, 117, 120; as official port, 70; slavery in, 80
Cartario, 52
cartas, 45
casación, 179–180, 197
Casa de Contratación. See Board of Trade
caso de corte, 33
castas, 145, 146. *See also* race
Castile: law of, 15–18, 45–46; lawyers in, 38–39, 42; litigation in, 11–12, 18, 27, 39
Castillo Armas, Carlos, 206
Castillo de Bobadilla, Jerónimo, 52
Castro, Fidel, 224, 232, 233
Castro, Manuel Antonio de, 108, 109, 118, 139
Cátedra de Clemetinas, 36
Cátedra de Decreto, 36
Cátedra de Prima de Cánones, 36
Cátedra de Sexto, 36
catedrático, 35
Cauca, 117
caudillo, 99, 100, 102, 105, 123, 150
Cedulario de Puga, 46
Cedulario índico, 48
cédulas, 45, 46, 52, 126, 127, 251n1
censo: and church, 256n51; *consignativo*, 74; *enfitéutico*, 74; on Indian lands, 91; *reservativo*, 74
Central America, 78, 144, 208, 273n22
Central American Common Market, 229
Centro de Estudios Judiciales, 177
Chabot, Georges Antoine, 140
Chamorro, Violeta, 226
Champeau, Edmond, 168
chanciller, 24
Chancillería de Valladolid. *See* Valladolid, Chancillería de
Charcas: *Audiencia* of, 10, 23, 50, 86, 108; legal education in, 36, 37
Charles II, 47
Charles III, 32, 48
Charles IV, 48

Charles V, 62, 78
Chávez, Hugo, 224
Chiapas, 146
Chihuahua, 186
children: assumed, 64, 68; colonial, 58–59, 67, 68, 256n62, 256n68; Indian, 85, 86; and *mayorazgos*, 64; nineteenth-century, 153–154; representation of, 27; slave, 81, 143, 144; twentieth-century, 200, 202, 208, 239. *See also* legitimacy
Chile: and Andean Common Market, 230; *Audiencia* of, 10, 23, 48; banks in, 231; codification in, 97, 99, 100, 137–138, 158–160, 164; contract in, 162; custom in, 198; *encomiendas* in, 89; and foreign sources, 110, 168; inheritance in, 208; judicial reform in, 175–178; land reform in, 223–226; Law Program, 189; legal education in, 37, 187, 189, 190, 265n32; marriage in, 148; *mayorazgos* in, 151; mining in, 72, 163, 213; securities regulation in, 211; slavery in, 77, 79, 143; trusts in, 212; twentieth-century, 195, 272n1; University of, 159, 186; women in, 203
Chilean National Institute, 159
China, 145
Chommie, John C., 188
Chuquisaca, 10, 36
Church. *See* Roman Catholic Church
cinco hermanas, 215
Citation, Rule of (1499), 17
citizens, 98, 145–146
city government, 26
civil code: and borrowing, 105; in building nations, 100; Colombian, 129, 197; and decree laws, 195; German, 207; and land, 206; of Louisiana, 140
Civil Code of 1804 (France): and case law, 197; in colonial law, 126; and *mayorazgos*, 151; as model, 98, 104, 135, 138, 140, 141; testamentary freedom in, 153; and women's property, 149
Civil Code of 1830 (Bolivia), 135, 267n12, 267n17
Civil Code of 1852 (Spanish draft), 136,

138, 140. *See also* García Goyena, Florencio
Civil Code of 1855 (Chile): and Bello, 137–138; and case law, 197; as model, 136, 137, 139, 140, 158; and Ocampo, 159; testamentary freedom in, 154
Civil Code of 1857 (Buenos Aires), 140
Civil Code of 1857 (Mexico), 136
Civil Code of 1868 (Veracruz), 137
Civil Code of 1870 (Mexico), 141, 149, 153, 162
Civil Code of 1871 (Argentina), 138–141, 147, 194
Civil Code of 1879 (Mexico), 137
Civil Code of 1884 (Mexico), 137, 148, 154, 162
Civil Code of 1889 (Argentina), 158
Civil Code of 1889 (Spain), 234, 268n73
Civil Code of 1926 (Argentina), 203
Civil Code of 1928 (Mexico), 195, 196, 197, 202
Civil Code of 1962 (Venezuela), 138
Civil Code of Teixeira de Freitas (Brazil), 139, 140
civil law (course), 119, 120, 184, 185
civil procedure: Aztec, 3; codification of, 138, 140, 141–142; colonial, 27–28, 49, 51; and Indian litigants, 93–94; in legal education, 120, 184; nineteenth-century, 114, 126, 140; orality in, 3, 27, 30, 179, 196, 197, 250n45, 274n57; twentieth-century, 179–181, 195, 196–197. *See also* Code of Civil Procedure
civil registries. *See* registries
Clark, Gerard, 233
Clark, Robert, 169
class actions, 181
Clement, Norris, 226
clergy, 12–13, 74. *See also* priests; Roman Catholic Church
coartación, 81, 144
coats of arms, 145
Code Napoléon. See Civil Code of 1804 (France)
Code Noir, 80, 258n22
Code of Civil Procedure: of Argentina, 141–142; of Chile, 114; of Colombia, 127; of Guanajuato, 196; of Mexico,

138, 141, 142, 179, 196–197; of Puebla, 142; of Spain, 138, 142; of Venezuela, 114
Codex, 36
codicilio, 67
codification: and borrowing, 128; impediments to, 135; and legal education, 118; of mining law; 163–164; and Napoleonic codes, 135, 138, 141; and nation building, 98–100, 105, 114, 126, 131; nineteenth-century, 133–142, 155–162, 167, 239
Código Barranda, 160
Código Béistegui, 142
Código civil nacional concordado (Colombia), 129
Código de Negros, 80
Código Lares, 160
Código Negro de Carolino, 80
cofradías, 31, 66
cohabitation, 57, 207
Colbert, Jean Baptiste, 75
Cold War, 187, 223, 228
Colegio de Abogados de Caracas, 40, 123
colegios, 117
colegios de abogados: colonial, 38, 40, 41; nineteenth-century, 123, 159; twentieth-century, 192
Colin, Ambroise, 169
Collegiate Tribunals of the Curcuit, 178
Colombia: and Andean Common Market, 230; arbitration in, 181; and Bolívar, 97; codification in, 137, 156–157, 160, 168, 213; *consulados* in, 113; corporate law in, 169–170; doctrine in, 130, 197; early national law of, 125, 126; foreign sources in, 168; illegitimacy in, 148; inheritance in, 208; international law in, 198; and Jesuits, 147; judicial reform in, 175, 176; land reform in, 223, 225; legal education in, 117, 119, 120, 186, 189, 191; legal practice in, 192, 240; and *mayorazgos* in, 151; and slavery, 78, 144; *tutela* action in, 180
Columbus, Christopher, 14, 39
comandantes generales, 24
comisario, 256n62

course in, 119, 184, 185; and forfeiture of property, 92; nineteenth-century, 127; orality in, 274n57; twentieth-century, 241

cronista mayor, 21

Crusades, 12

Cruzada, 23, 31

Cuba: and Bustamante, 181; codification in, 268n73; constitutional actions in, 180; Council of Ministers of, 233; Council of State of, 233; foreign investment in, 229, 234; foreign laborers in, 145; and land reform, 223, 224, 227; lawyers in, 39; National Assembly of, 233; refugee lawyers from, 188; revolutionary law and structures of, 232–234; slavery in, 79, 81, 144

Cuervo, José, 48

Cuervo, Rufino, 119

Cueto Rua, Julio, 190

Cujas, Jacques, 138

Cundinamarca, 156

Curia Filípica Mexicana, 126

Curia Philipica, 28, 37, 51, 75, 126

cursos simultáneos, 36, 119, 249n20

custom: preconquest, 6, 7; as source of law, 51, 93, 127, 197

customs (duties), 51, 71

Cutter, Charles, 11, 31, 53

Cuzco: *Audiencia* of, 23; city of, 6, 10

Dádivas, 42

Dalloz, Victor Alexis Désiré, 129

Dámaso Xigena, José, 119, 138

daños morales, 216

debt peonage, 82, 89, 91, 144–146, 203–204

debts: Aztec, 6; in colonial sources, 51; in commerce, 74, 211; of decedents, 88; imprisonment for, 74; Indian land as security for, 92; inheritability of, 89; interest on, 6, 74; on land, 152; national, 103, 128; of partnerships, 75

decodification, 194

decrees, 195, 199

Decretals, 35, 36, 50

Decretos, 45

Decretum, 36

degrees (law): colonial, 35, 37; nineteenth-century, 117, 119, 138; not needed for legal practice, 120; twentieth-century, 186

dehesas, 63, 152

De indiarum iure, 50

De la propiedad en la Nueva Granada, 130

demanda, 179

demandado, 179

Demante, Antoine Marie, 129

Demolombe, Charles, 129, 140, 169

derecho indiano, xii, 45, 243n1

Derecho mercantil mexicano, 130

development, 228–229. *See also* law and development

Diario del Imperio, 131

Díaz, Porfirio, 130, 147, 153, 163, 220, 221

Díaz de Montalvo, Alonso, 50

Diccionario de gobierno y legislación de Indias, 51

Diccionario razonado de la legislación, 127

Digest, 36

Diputación territorial, 72

divorce: Aztec, 3, 4; nineteenth-century, 148; twentieth-century, 200, 202–203, 239. *See also* marriage

doctor: as colonial title, 35, 37; as doctrinal authority, 53; as nineteenth-century title, 118, 119, 158; as twentieth-century title, 186

doctrina, 53

doctrinal sources, 129–130, 194, 197, 199

Domínguez, José Luis, 142

Dominican Republic: codification in, 135, 160; landholding by church in, 270n22; land reform in, 223–225, 281n35; land registration in, 207; marriage in, 201; Supreme Court of, 174; testamentary trusts in, 208

Dominicans, 36, 82, 85, 117

Dondé, Rafael, 136

Doroteo, 52

dowry, 41, 56, 59, 94, 149, 256n68

drug trafficking, 238

Dublán, Manuel, 131

dúplica, 179

Duranton, Alexandre, 129, 140

dyes, 74

Easterbrook, Frank, 169
ecclesiastical courts: colonial, 28, 29, 30, 33, 51, 54; nineteenth-century, 112, 113, 127, 148
ecclesiastical law. *See* canon law
Ecuador: alternative dispute resolution in, 181, 182; and Andean Common Market, 230; children in, 148; codification in, 134, 137, 160, 267n12; constitution of, 180; debt peonage in, 204; judicial reform in, 174, 176, 273n22; land reform in, 223, 225, 226; slavery in, 79
Eder, Phanor J., 139, 176, 181
Eguía Lis, 136
Eisenberg, Melvin, 169
Ejército Zapatista de Liberación Nacional, 222
ejido, 6, 221–222, 223, 226
Elements of Political Economy, 119
Eli Lilly Co., 188
El Salvador: alternative dispute resolution in, 182; antivagrancy laws in, 203; codification in, 137, 160; constitutional actions in, 180; judicial reform in, 175, 176, 177, 273n45; land reform in, 223, 224, 225
Encinas, Diego de, 47
encomenderos, 85, 86, 87
encomienda: abolition of, 85, 88–89, 152, 255n37, 260n27, 261n70; alienation of, 87; *audiencia* jurisdiction over, 33; Indian landholding in, 93; of Indians, 54, 83, 86, 87–89, 236; inheritability of, 14, 88, 260n35; in León Pinelo, 50; limitations on takers of, 88; marriage of holders of, 57; numbers of, 87; in *Recopilación,* 48
enfiteusis, 152, 159. See also *censo*
England: and Bello, 100, 137; and Protestants in Argentina, 147; and slavery, 71, 79, 143, 144; and testamentary freedom, 153
English language, 117, 168, 241, 266n29
entails. See *mayorazgos*
environmental law, 170, 175, 230
escribano: de cámara, 24; colonial, 21, 32, 40, 41–42, 68; Indian, 30; nineteenth-

century, 123, 124; *público de número,* 41. *See also* notary
Escriche, Joaquín de, 127
Escudero, 18
Escuela de práctica forense, 38
Escuela Judicial, 177
Escuela Libre de Derecho, 186
Escuela Nacional de Jurisprudencia, 117, 118
Escuela Nacional de Leyes, 184, 185
especialización, 191
espousals, 28
Esquirol, Jorge, 238
estancias, 63
Estatuto Provisional (1815), 109
estatutos, 75
Esteves Saguí, M., 130
Estudio sobre el derecho civil colombiano, 130
evidence, 3, 27
examinations, 35, 36, 38, 186
Executive, control of judiciary, 112, 174–175, 178, 193
executor. See *albacea*
exidos, 63. See also *ejidos*
expediente, 63

factor, 32
family: and church, 113–114, 147–148; colonial law of, 56–60, 125; Cuban, 233, 234; customary law of, 183; and inheritance, 153–154, 207–208; and landholding, 220; nineteenth-century, 143, 147–148; twentieth-century, 202, 220
Family Relations Law of 1917, 202
Febrero, José, 52, 126
federalism: and codification, 136–137, 156–158, 173; and courts, 111, 113, 173; and law, 102, 105
fees, court, 27, 58
feminism, 203
Ferdinand, 17
Ferdinand VII, 49, 107, 145
Fernández de Córdoba, Miguel Tadeo, 134
Ferreiro, María de la Mercedes, 59
fideicomisos. See trusts
fiel ejecutor, 26

Figuerola, Justo, 134
fiscal, 21, 46, 48, 50, 68, 86
Fiss, Owen, 190
"five sisters," 215
fleets: inspection of, 23; of trading ships, 70, 71; and slavery, 79
flotilla, 70, 71
Ford Foundation, 188, 189, 273n22
foreign investment: and alternative dispute resolution, 182; and commercial law, 210; in Cuba, 234; and Kemmerer, 168; and land reform, 219; and trade agreements, 170, 229–232
forensic medicine, 185
forfeiture, 32
Fox, Vicente, 222
Fragmento preliminar al estudio del derecho, 128
France: and alternative dispute resolution, 181; and Chile, 168; and codification, 97, 104, 110, 114, 129, 135, 139–141, 147, 158, 161, 194, 197, 239; and Colombia, 168; and constitutional thought, 103, 108, 167; and legal education, 168, 169, 187, 190, 194; and *mayorazgos*, 151; and Mexico, 128; and slavery, 79
Franciscans, 87, 138
Franco, Francisco, 168
Franco-Colombian Company, 161
Franks, 15
Free Trade Area of the Americas (FTAA), 229, 230
Frei, Eduardo, 224
Freitas, Augusto Teixeira de, 139
French Civil Code of 1804. *See* Civil Code of 1804 (France)
FTAA. *See* Free Trade Area of the Americas
fuero: as colonial jurisdiction and laws, 25, 28–31, 32, 46, 49, 52, 54; peninsular, 16, 17, 49, 52, 235; nineteenth-century, 103, 105, 111, 112, 113, 126, 145, 155
Fuero de Layrón, 18
Fuero Juzgo, 15, 16, 126
Fuero Real, 16, 49, 52, 126, 140
Fuero Viejo de Castilla, 16
Fujimori, Alberto, 195, 229, 230
future interests, 207, 208–209

Gaceta Judicial, 131
Gaius, 52
Galván Rivera, Mariano, 126
Gamboa, Marcelo, 140
gañanes, 55
gap: in colonial law, 46, 65, 235–236; as feature of Latin American law, xi, xiii, 235–238, 240, 241
García, Baldomero, 140
García de Hermosilla, Juan, 52
García Goyena, Florencio, 140
García Torres, Vicente, 130
Garro, Alejandro, 180, 198
GATT, 230
General Indian Court of New Spain, 30, 58, 93, 113
General Tribunal of Mining, 73
Genoa, 79
Germany, 167, 187, 207
Gibson, Charles, 237
Gide, Charles, 185
globalization, 229–232
glossators, 50
Gobierno de Perú, 50
Gómez, Antonio, 17, 52
González, Joaquín V., 214
Gorostiaga, José, 140, 157
Government of Peru, 50
governor, 25, 30, 33, 48
Gramática, 100
Granada, 43
Gran Colombia, 97, 100
Grange. *See Mesta*
Gratian, 36
Guadalajara: *Audiencia* of, 22, 23, 89; city of, 10; *consulado* of, 29; University of, 36, 186
Guadalupe Hidalgo, Treaty of, 266
Guanajuato, 10, 136, 185, 186, 196, 197
Guatemala: alternative dispute resolution in, 181, 182; antivagrancy laws in, 203; *Audiencia* of, 10, 23, 46; codification in, 137; constitutional actions in, 180; judicial reform in, 175, 176, 177; land reform in, 223, 224; marriage in, 201; mining in, 72; nineteenth-century, 129; and United Fruit Co., 206
Guayaquil, 113

163, 206, 207, 229; Inca, 6; Indian,
92–93; in large estates, 63, 150–153,
219–220, 255n37, 256n70; nineteenth-
century, 150–153; registries, 153, 206–
207; transfer of, 62–63, 73, 153, 222;
twentieth-century, 205–207; vacant,
62, 219, 220
land reform: and codes, 195; in Cuba,
232; and the gap, 237; and guerrilla
movements, 205, 222; institutes, 225;
and laborers, 151; in Mexico, 219–222;
procedures for, 178, 219–227; tribunals
of, 174
Langdell, Christopher Columbus, 169
La Paz, 204
Lara Bonilla, Rodrigo, 177
Lares, Teodosio, 160
Larombière, Léobon, 129
Larrea y Loredo, José de, 134
Las Casas, Bartolomé de, 13, 82, 85
Las Villas, 233
LatCrit, 241
Latifundios, 63, 150, 219
Latin American Free Trade Association,
230
Latin American Free Trade Zone, 230
Laurent, François, 197
Lavrin, Asunción, 59
law and development movement, 188–
190, 228, 231, 237, 238
law as written. *See* gap
Law Dividing National Property, 150
Laws of Burgos, 78, 85
Lawyer of the Americas, 188
Lawyers. See *Abogado*
leaseholds, 207
Lecciones de derecho civil, 130
legal clinics, 184, 187, 190
legal education: colonial, 34–38, 249n18;
in Cuba, 233; nineteenth-century,
116–121; twentieth-century, 184–191
legal history, 118, 185
legal periodicals, 131, 198, 199
legal philosophy, 118, 185
legal realism, 189
Legislación mexicana, 131
legítima: in colonial inheritance, 67, 68;
and *encomiendas,* 88; and *mayorazgos,*

65; nineteenth-century, 141, 153, 154;
twentieth-century, 208
legitimacy: church jurisdiction over,
28, 147, 148; and inheritance, 57, 67,
153, 256n65; through legal procedure,
59; and *mayorazgos,* 64; nineteenth-
century, 101, 103, 116, 141, 148; and
race, 55, 57–58; twentieth-century,
196, 201, 202, 239; and *vecino,* 55
León Pinelo, Antonio Rodríguez de, 21,
47, 49, 50
Lerminier, Eugène, 128
lese majesty, 65
lesión, 162, 163
Levene, Ricardo, 49, 85, 86, 118, 236
Lex Romana Visigothorum, 15
Lex Visigothorum, 15
*Ley de Administración de Justicia y Orgá-
nica de los Tribunales de la Federación,*
112
Ley de Desamortización, 152
Ley de Desamparo, 112
Ley de Enjuiciamiento Civil (Spain), 114
Leyes de Estilo, 51
Leyes de Layrón, 18
Leyes de Toro: in colonial law, 52, 59; and
inheritance, 17, 67; and legal authori-
ties, 49; and legal education, 37; and
mayorazgos, 17, 64; in peninsular law,
17; and prohibition of Roman law, 17;
and testaments, 256n62
Leyes hechas . . . por la brevedad, 51
Ley Juárez, 112
Ley Lerdo, 152
Ley Orgánica del Poder Judicial (Mexico),
173
Ley sobre Extranjería y Nacionalidad, 147
Ley Vallarta, 147
Lezica, Faustino, 157
liberalism: in commercial law, 155, 162,
164; in legal education, 116, 120;
nineteenth-century, 102; and property, 152, 154
Liber Judiciorum, 15
Libri feudorum, 50
licenciado, 35, 37, 86, 118, 186
Lima: *Audiencia* of, 10, 22, 23, 43, 49, 50;
cabildo in, 26; *consulado* in, 29; courts

of, 25, 33; Inquisition in, 28; inten-
dants of, 32; legal education in, 36;
tax tribunal in, 29, 32, 33; university
in, 36, 49, 50, 186
Limosna de la Santa Bula de Cruzada. See
Cruzada
limpieza de sangre, 34, 38, 58
Lira, Andrés, 93
L.L.C., 210
Llewellyn, Karl, 159
LL.M., 168, 188, 191
López, Gregorio, 13, 17, 21, 50, 52
López, Vicente Fidel, 141, 157
López de Alcocer, Pedro, 18, 38
López de Arrieta y Atienza, 18
López de Palacios Rubios, Juan, 13
López Mateos, Adolfo, 221
Louisiana State University, 190
Lozano, José María, 131
Lynch, Dennis, 168, 189

Machado, José Olegario, 123, 129
Madrid: city of, 129; Congregation of
Lawyers of, 38, 40, 49
maestrescuela, 34, 35
maestría, 191
Magdalena, 157
Maldonado, 46
Maldonado, Adolfo, 196
Manning, Bayless, 169
manumission, 42, 68, 80, 143–144
maquiladoras, 213
Maracaibo, 68
Marcadé, Victor, 129
Margadant S., Guillermo Floris, 46, 147,
152, 196, 215
marriage: Aztec, 4; colonial law of,
28, 49, 56, 57, 59–60, 68, 103; and
community property, 201; and contracts, 41; Inca, 6; of judges, 42;
nineteenth-century, 130, 136, 141,
147–148, 269n42; *Real Pragmática* of
1776, 57, 59–60; registers, 111, 114,
147, 200; secular, 148, 200–201, 239;
of slaves, 81
Martínez de Zamora, Fernando, 50
Matienzo, Juan de, 50, 52
Mateos Alarcón, Manuel, 130

Maximilian, 117, 128, 131, 136, 160, 220
Maynz, Charles Gustave, 140
mayorazgos (entails): abolition of, 103,
126, 151–152, 153, 154; and *cacicazgos,*
92; colonial law of, 64–65, 68, 69,
255n37, 255n45; and *encomiendas,* 88;
and large estates, 63; and *Leyes de
Toro,* 17; licenses for, 65; prohibition
of, 65; regular and irregular, 64; tax
on, 65
May Revolution of 1810, 107
Means, Robert Charles, 119, 120, 129,
135, 156, 213, 236
Mecham, J. Lloyd, 172
media anata, 31
mediation, 181, 182
mediators, 31
mejora, 67–68, 154, 208
memorias, 22
Menem, Carlos, 174, 178, 195
Menochio, Giacomo, 52
Mercado, Thomás de, 51
merced, 63, 92
Mercosur, 230
mercury, 74
Merlin, Phillipe Antoine, 129
mesada, 31
Mesta, 18, 30, 33, 73
mestizo, 55, 57, 59, 62
Mexico: alternative dispute resolution
in, 181, 182; *amparo* action in, 178;
Audiencia of, 10, 22, 23, 25, 43, 46,
94; *cabildo* of, 26; church in, 66, 152,
269n38, 270n47, 277n3; codification
in, 133, 134, 136–137, 148, 160, 162;
colegio de abogados, 40; condominium
in, 207; constitution of, 167, 206; *consulado* in, 29, 75; commercial law in,
160, 162, 163, 170, 210, 213; courts in,
25, 72, 108, 111–113, 173; divorce in,
148; doctrinal writings in, 130, 197;
encomiendas in, 88; foreigners in, 146–
147; foreign ownership in, 206, 207,
229; future interests in, 209; Indian
litigation in, 94; Inquisition in, 28;
intellectual property in, 211; *ius commune* in, 240; judicial decisions in,
131, 197–198; land reform in, 219–

taments, 208; twentieth-century, 186, 211–212. *See also* registries

Nóvisima Recopilación: as Castilian law, 47; inheritance law in, 67; and legal authorities, 49; use in colonial period, 18, 53; use in nineteenth century, 124, 126, 140

Nueva España. *See* New Spain

Nueva Galicia, 10, 90

Nueva Granada: *Audiencia* of, 52; doctrinal works in, 130; legal education in, 37, 117; mining in, 72; Viceroyalty of, 22, 23, 122. *See also* Colombia

Nueva Recopilación de Castilla: as colonial law, 18, 38, 47, 53; commentary on, 52; and legal authorities, 49; in legal education, 36, 37, 140; and mining, 72; and testaments, 67; use in nineteenth century, 126, 127, 140

nuns, 67

Oaxaca, 1, 66, 92, 93, 136

Obarrio, Manuel, 142

obligaciones extraconractuales, 216. *See also* torts

obligations. *See* contracts

obrajes, 48, 90

Obregón, Alvaro, 206

Ocampo, José Gabriel, 101, 141, 157, 158–159, 161, 162

oficial real, 29

offices, sale of, 32, 42

Offner, Jerome, 2, 5

O'Higgins, Bernardo, 97, 151

oidor: as judges, 23, 42–43, 49, 50, 86, 107; and legal education, 34, 36. *See also* judges

oil, 147, 163, 213–214, 225

Ojeada filosófica, 128

Ordenamiento de Alcalá de Henares, 17, 49, 126

Ordenanzas, 27, 45

Ordenanzas de Aranjuez, 72

Ordenanzas de Bilbao: in codification, 158, 159; and colonial commercial law, 51, 75; and nineteenth-century commercial law, 155, 156, 160

Ordenanzas de Burgos, 18

Ordenanzas de Encinas, 47

Ordenanzas del Antiguo Cuaderno, 72

Ordenanzas del Nuevo Cuaderno, 72

Ordenanzas del Patronazgo, 12

Ordenanzas de Minería de Nueva España, 72

Ordenanzas de Monzón, 24

Ordenanzas de Perú, 72

Ordenanzas de Poblaciones (1573), 26, 62, 64

Ordenanzas de Toledo, 71, 72, 90

Ordenanzas Reales de Castilla, 17, 18

órdenes, 45

Ordinances of Alfaro, 86, 88

Organization of American States, 187, 199, 229

Oriente, 233

Origen e historia ilustrada de las leyes de Indias, 51

Oro, Domingo, 163

orphans, 90

Ortíz, Venancio, 130

Ortíz de Ceballos, Ignacio, 134

Ortolán, Joseph Louis Elzéar, 169, 185

Oruro, 50

Ots Capdequí, José María, 46, 50, 64, 72, 73, 235, 236

Ovando, Juan de, 20, 46–47

"pacification," 13

Palacios, Prudencio Antonio de, 48

Palares, Jacinto, 130

Palermo, University of, 190

Palmiter, Alan, 169

Pan Am, 188

Panama: alternative dispute resolution in, 182; *Audiencia* of, 10, 23, 48; codification in, 156, 157, 162; condominiums in, 207; constitutional actions in, 180; courts in, 171; judicial reform in, 175, 176, 177; land reform in, 225; testaments in, 208; trusts in, 209, 212

Pan-American Congress of Law, 198

Pan-Americanism, 229

Panormitanus, 17, 52

Papinian, 52

parafernales, 56

Paraguay: alternative dispute resolution

in, 182; codification in, 137, 160; condominiums in, 207; constitutional
actions in, 180; *encomiendas* in, 88, 89;
and international law, 198; judicial
reform in, 175, 176, 177; land reform
in, 223; and Mercosur, 230; missions
in, 91; reductions in, 86; slavery in,
144; testaments in, 208
Paris: city of, 127, 130, 168; Convention,
161
Parladorio, Juan Yáñez, 52
partnerships, 29, 51, 59, 75–76, 161, 210
pasantía, 37
patents, 161, 162, 170, 211
patria potestad, 56, 141, 148, 149
Patronato Real, 12, 28, 49, 50, 66, 244n12
Paul, 52
Paul III, 85
PEMEX, 214
Pérez, José, 140
Perfecto de Salas, José, 48
Perón, Juan, 202, 214, 224
Perpetuities, 207, 209, 212
Peru: and Andean Common Market,
230; codification in, 134, 135, 160,
271n29; colonial law in, 46; corpora-
tions in, 271n34; decrees in, 195;
Indian litigation in, 93, 94; exclusion
of lawyers from, 39; foreign invest-
ment in, 229; judicial reform in, 174,
175, 176, 177, 273n22; labor in, 90,
94, 145; land reform in, 223, 224, 225;
legal education in, 189; marriage in,
147, 201, 269n38; mining in, 71, 72,
78, 90; slavery in, 77, 78, 79, 80, 144;
Viceroyalty of, 10, 22, 23; women in,
149, 203; *yanaconas* in, 86
"Peruvian Solon," 22
Petit, Eugène, 169
Phelan, John, 236, 237
Philip II: and commercial law, 75;
and laws for discovery, 62, 64; and
Ovando's compilation, 47; and sale of
lands, 61; and slavery, 79
Philip III, 86, 88
Philip V, 32, 75
Philippines, 145
Pico, Francisco, 157

pieza, 79
Pinochet, Augusto, 224
Pinzón, José Gabino, 213
piracy, slave trade as, 144
Plan de Ayala, 220, 281n10
Plan de Sierra Gorda, 219
Plan General de Organización Judicial,
110
Planiol, Marcel, 169, 185, 197
playing cards, 31
pliego de mortaja, 22
poblador principal, 64
Política indiana, 21, 50, 59
political economy, 119, 184, 185
Política para corregidores, 52
polygamy, 4, 6, 57, 94
Pombo, Lino de, 127
poor: colonial, 74, 90; and debt peonage,
203–204; and land reform, 219, 226;
nineteenth-century, 104; representation of, 38, 39, 40, 58, 192, 241 (*see
also* legal clinics); twentieth-century,
177–178, 180, 219, 226
Popayán, 10, 29, 117, 120
Portales, Diego: Chilean leader, 99, 101,
138; University of, 190
Portalis, Jean Etienne Marie, 154
Portobello, 70
Portugal, 12, 78, 79, 158
positivist, 116, 184
Pothier, Robert Joseph, 129, 140
Potosí, 10, 49, 50
powers of appointment, 42
Pradier Fodéré, Paul, 168, 169
prados, 63
pragmáticas, 45, 127
precedent. *See* jurisprudence
presidentes, 25
priests: in dispute settlement, 31, 40;
Indian, 87; as land owners, 66; as law
graduates, 37; and legal practice, 38,
250n43; and marriages, 201; positions held by, in colonies, 55; and
reductions, 90; status of, 104; and
testaments, 67
Prillaman, William, 174, 175, 178
prima de Cánones, 36, 249n17
prima de Leyes, 36, 249n17

primogeniture: Aztec, 243n22; and *ca-cicazgos*, 92; and *encomiendas*, 88, 255n37; and *mayorazgos*, 64, 153, 154
Principios de derecho civil mexicano, 130
prior, 29, 71
privatization, 175, 223–224, 227, 230, 231, 232
probate, 23, 28, 24, 48, 68
procesillo, 34
procurador: abolition of, 110; *cabildo*, 26; colonial, 40, 41, 94; *general*, 26; *de hecho*, 41; nineteenth-century, 123; *de número*, 41; *de pobres*, 21, 58; *síndico*, 109
Prontuario de práctica forense, 139
propiedad por piso. See condominiums
propios, 63
Protector of Indians, 30, 90
Protestants, 147
protocol. *See* civil registries
protomedicato, 30, 33
Provisional Constitution of 1815 (Río de la Plata), 109
prueba, 27
public service, 187, 233
Puebla (Mexico), 1, 29, 196
Pueblo Revolt, 88
Puerto Rico, 82, 144, 240, 268n73
Puga, Vasco de, 46
Punta del Este, Charter of, 223

"quasi-law," 99
Querétaro, 112
Quijano, Agustín, 134
quinta, 72
Quintana Roo, 207
quinto, 94
Quiroga, Vasco de, 91
Quiroga de la Rosa, Manuel J., 119
Quito, 10, 23, 29, 49, 89, 90

race: in colonial period, 54, 55–60, 80; in nineteenth century, 104, 116, 143–146; in twentieth century, 200, 204
railroads, 147, 151, 163, 212
Rau, Frédéric-Charles, 129, 138, 139, 140, 169, 197
RCA, 187

Real Academia Carolina de Leyes y Práctica Forense, 37
Real Caja de Amortización, 66
Real Cédula sobre la Educación, Trato y Ocupaciones de los Esclavos, 81–82
Real Chanillería de Granada, 33
realengo, 61, 63
rebeldía, 27
receptores, 24
recogimientos de mujeres, 148
"reconquest," 12, 16
reconvención, 27
Recopilación de las Indias (1680): on *cabildos*, 27; as colonial source, 21, 45, 50, 52, 53; content of, 47–48; and contracts, 73; *encomiendas* in, 88; and immigration law, 55; and Indians, 84, 86, 88, 90, 91; and legal authorities, 49; marriage in, 57; mining in, 72, 90; as nineteenth-century source, 126, 127; and probate procedure, 68; slavery in, 80; trade in, 71, 75
Recopilación de leyes de Nueva Granada, 127
Recopilación sumaria, 252n17
rector, 34
recurso de fuerza, 30, 110
recusación, 27
reductions, 48, 86, 90
regent, 24
regidor, 26, 30, 109
regidor perpetuo, 26
registries: commercial, 212; land, 206–207, 211, 225, 227; marriage, 110, 114, 136, 200–201, 211; mining, 212; of testaments, 208, 212
registros públicos, 206–207
Reglamento de Esclavos, 82
Reglamento de Institución y Administración de Justicia, 107
relator, 21, 24, 27, 32
rendición, 74
repartimiento, 20, 48, 50, 61, 89–90, 260n49
Repertorio de las cédulas, provisiones, y ordenanzas reales, 46
réplica, 179
republicanism, 102–103
requerimiento, 13, 244n17

Santo Tomás, University of, 36
Sastre, Marcos, 128
Savigny, Friedrich Carl von, 128, 138, 140
Scevola, 52
Schlesinger, Rudolf, 169
Schwartz, Audrey, 182
Schwartz, Murray, 182
scribe. See *escribano*
sealed paper, 31, 145
Secretarías de Despacho Universal, 32
secretaries, 32
secretario, 26
securities regulation, 169, 211, 232
Seminario judicial de la federación, 198
sentencia: as colonial judgment, 27; *fundada*, 53, 114
Seoane, Guillermo Alejandro, 140
separation of powers, 108, 112, 175–177
Sepúlveda, Juan Ginés de, 13
Serafino, 52
Serna, Pablo, 59
Serrador, Miguel José, 48
Serrigny, Denis, 140
servitudes, 69
Seville: Board of Trade in, 21, 28, 71;
    consulado in, 29, 71, 75; mentioned, 51;
    and slavery, 78, 79
sewers, 69
Sexto, 36
share companies, 75, 76, 161. *See also*
    corporations
Shell Co., 187
Sierra, Justo, 136, 138
Siete Partidas: and alternative dispute
    resolution, 31; colonial procedure of,
    27, 51; as colonial source, 49–50, 52,
    53; and colonial status, 54; and con-
    tracts, 73, 74; and inheritance, 59, 67;
    in legal education, 37; and López, 13,
    52; and *mayorazgos*, 64; as nineteenth-
    century source, 126, 127, 140; and
    peninsular law, 17; and slavery, 80;
    and testaments, 67; and trade, 75; and
    women, 59
Sigüenza, 49
slavery: abolition of, 101, 103, 126, 128,
    143–145, 269n14; Aztec, 4; in colonial
    law, 56, 77–83; justifications for, 78;

licenses for, 77, 78, 79, 80; mentioned,
    55; preconquest, 6; and purchase of
    freedom, 77, 81, 143, 144; and traders,
    78–79
slaves: Aztec, 2; branding of, 82; breed-
    ing of, 144; as children, 81; in colonial
    law, 54, 77–83; importation of, 71; as
    labor, 11, 91; limitations on conduct
    of, 80; in mining claims, 72; as part
    of estate, 63; as spouse, 94; and testa-
    mentary manumission, 68; as witness,
    82
smuggling slaves, 79, 144
socialism: in constitutions, 231; in Cuba,
    232, 233, 234; in land reform, 224; and
    Mexican legislation, 215; and private
    property, 205; and women, 203
sociedad conyugal, 201
sociedad cooperativa, 210
Sociedad de Estudios Sociales, 185
sociedades anónimas. See corporations
Sociedades mercantiles. See partnerships
Socratic method, 189
sodomy, 65
solar de casa, 62
soldiers, 2
solicitadores, 41
Soloman, Lewis, 169
Solórzano Pereira, Juan de, 21, 43, *44*, 49,
    50, 59
Somellera, Pedro, 118, 157
Somoza, Anastasio, 205, 224
Sonora, 196, 197
Soto, Domingo, 52
Southern Methodist University, 190
Soviet Union, 233, 234
Spanish College, Bologna, 16
Spanish Cortes, 23, 89, 111. *See also*
    Constitution of 1812 (Spain)
spices, 31, 74
Squibb Co., 187
Standard Oil Co., 187
Stanford Law School, 189
Statement of Principles on the Teaching
    of Law, 187
state of emergency, 195
state of siege, 195
steamboats, 161

Story, Joseph, 140
strikes. *See* labor law
Suárez, Francisco, 13
Sublimis Deus, 85
suerte, 62
suffrage, 146, 203
Summa de tratos y contratos, 51
summario, 47
supreme court: of Argentina, 131, 158, 174, 202; of Bolivia, 174; of Colombia, 131; of Costa Rica, 182; of Cuba, 232; of Dominican Republic, 174; of Ecuador, 174; of Mexico, 111–112, 131, 174, 178, 198, 213; of Peru, 174; and twentieth-century court structure, 173; of Uruguay, 177
Supreme Legal Council (Supreme Judicial Council), xvi, 2

Tamaulipas, 196
Tannenbaum, Frank, 203
tanteo, 74
Tapia, Eugenio de, 129
terrasguerros, 92
tasación, 86
tasador, 21, 24
Taulier, J. Frédéric, 129
tax: colonial; 23, 24, 31–32, 47, 48, 71, 89; and legal education, 191; payment of, for foreign ownership, 163; tribunals, 29, 32, 112, 174; twentieth-century, 240
Tejedor, Carlos, 139
Tellería, Manuel, 134
teniente, 27
teniente letrado, 32
Tenochtitlán, 1, 2
tesorero, 32
testaments: and capacity, 67; colonial law of, 67, 69, 256n62; Indian, 68, 93, 256n77; and intent of testator, 68; legitimization in, 59; of mission property, 91; nineteenth-century, 125, 126, 153–154; and scribes, 41; and *Siete Partidas*, 50; and testamentary freedom, 208
testimonio, 63
Texas, 40

Texas Company, 187
Texcoco, xvi, 1, 2
Theodosian Code, 15
Thome, Joseph, 231
Thompson, Robert, 169
tiempo compartido. *See* time sharing
tierras baldías, 63
tierras concegiles, 63
tierras realengas, 63
time sharing, 207
tithes, 12, 33
Tlacopan, 1
tla-qua, 3
Tlaxcala, 86, 196, 197
tobacco, 31
Toledo, Francisco de, 22, 46, 50, 71
Tolima, 157
Tordesillas, Treaty of, 12
Torrens system, 207
torts: and judicial decisions, 194; mentioned, xi, 240; twentieth-century, 196, 215–216, 280n37, 280n42
Toullier, Charles Bonaventure Marie, 129
trade (commerce, navigation): colonial, 47, 48, 49, 51, 70–71, 73; nineteenth-century, 103, 158, 160, 161, 239; regional agreements concerning, 229–232; twentieth-century, 239, 240
trademarks, 51, 76, 161, 162, 211
transplants. *See* borrowing
Tratado de confiraciones reales, 50
Tratado de jurisprudencia mercantil, 129
Tratado elemental de los procedimientos civiles, 130
travaux pratiques, 169
treasure trove, 31
Treasury, Council of (Texcoco), 2
Tribonian, 52
Tribunal de Alzadas, 29, 110
Tribunal de la Acordada, 30, 33
Tribunales Colegiados de Circuito, 178
tribunales de aguas, 29
tribunales de comercio, 29
tribunales de concordia, 109
tribunales de cuentas, 29, 32, 33
tribunales de justicia constitucionalista, 173
tribunales de minas, 29
tribunales de primera instancia, 158

tribunales indígenas, 29, 183
Tribunal Extraordinario, 109
Tribunal General de Minería, 73, 163, 257n28
tribute: abolition of, 145; in colonial sources, 48; crown revenue from, 31; and *encomiendas*, 87; and Indian litigation, 94; reduced by Indian property on death, 93; those assessed against, 86, 90, 91
Triple Alliance, 1
Troplong, Raymond Théodore, 140
trusts, 168, 206, 207, 208–209, 212
Tucumán, 10, 79, 86, 88
Tusco, Cardenal de, 52
tutela, 180

Ugarte, Marcelino, 140
UNAM, 186
UNCITRAL, 170, 182
UNDP. *See* United Nations Development Program
Uniform Commercial Code, 159
United Fruit Co., 187, 206
United Nations Development Program, 231, 273n21
United States Court of Private Land Claims, 266n29
United States of America: alternative dispute resolution in, 181, 182; as constitutional model, 97, 108, 167, 173; and depository receipts, 211; as foreign investor, 147, 213; as foreign source, 167–168, 228, 239; and intervention, 206; and land reform, 223, 227; and LatCrit, 241; and law and development, 188–191; and legal education, 118, 120, 168, 169, 170, 187, 188–191; mentioned, 237; occupation of Mexico by, 112; and private international law, 198; Supreme Court, 110; testamentary freedom in, 153
Universal Secretary of the Indies, 21
Universidad Central de Venezuela, 169, 186
Universidad de Cargadores de las Indias, 70
Universidad de los Andes, 189

Universidad de Mercadores, 28
Universidad Iberoamericana, 186
Universidad Javeriana, 36
Universidad Tomística, 36
university: colonial, 34; labor law, 215; tribunals, 29–30
University of Miami Inter-American Law Review, 188
Urbaneja, Luis Felipe, 169
Uribe-Uran, Victor, 121, 122
Urquiza, Justo José de, 140
Uruguay: and Acevedo, 157, 158; alternative dispute resolution in, 182; codification in, 137, 158; judicial reform in, 176, 177; land reform in, 223, 225; marriage in, 148; and Mercosur, 230; and Ocampo, 159; and private international law, 198; slavery in, 144
USAID, 176, 182, 188, 189, 231, 273n21
usury, 51, 217
Utopia, 91
Utrecht, Treat of, 71

Valdivieso, Francisco, 134
Valencia, 51
Valencia Zea, Arturo, 197
Valladolid: Audiencia y Real Chancillería de, 23, 245n9; mentioned, 85
Valle, fourth marqués del, 63
Vanderbilt, Arthur T., 187
Vargas, Getúlio, 224
Vargas, Jorge, 216
vecino, 26, 54
veedor, 32
vejamen, 35
Vélez, Bernardo, 157
Vélez, Fernando, 130, 197
Vélez Sársfield, Dalmacio: and civil codification, 123, 138–141, 194; and commercial codification, 100, 157; his *Instituciones*, 130; and marriage, 147
Venezuela: *Audiencia* of, 23; codification in, 114, 134, 137, 160; constitutional actions in, 180; future interests in, 209; judicial reform in, 175, 176, 177; labor law in, 203; land in, 150; land reform in, 222, 223, 225; lawyers in, 40; legal education in, 169, 186,

265n32; marriage in, 201; mining in, 72, 214; political views in, 102, 205; procedure in, 28, 114; slavery in, 78, 144

Veracruz, 1, 29, 70, 136, 186, 215

Verdugo, Agustín, 130

viceroy, 22

Vidal, Mateo, 157

Villa, Pancho, 220

Villadiego Vascuñana y Montoya, Alonso de, 52

vinculación. See *mayorazgos*

Vinnius, Arnold, 35, 36, 37, 138

Visigoths, 15, 16

visitadores, 86

Viso, Julián, 137

víspera de cánones, 36

Vitoria, Francisco de, 13

Voltaire (François-Marie Arouet), 103

War, Council of, 1

War of the Reform, 112

Washington, 98

widows, 90

wills. *see* testaments

"Wisconsin boys," 275n48

women: Aztec, 3–4, 5; in *beaterios,* 148; colonial, 56, 57, 59, 74, 256n61, 256n68; and commerce, 59, 141, 203, 278n31; and exemption from tribute, 86; Indian, 85; as judges, 273n22; as

law students, 184; as litigants, 94; nineteenth-century, 101, 104, 141, 148, 149; as property, 6; *recogimientos de,* 148; and slavery, 81; as takers under *cacicazgos,* 92; twentieth-century, 196, 200, 202–203, 226, 239; as viceroy, 14

World Bank, 176, 227, 231, 273n21

World War II: and foreign sources, 167, 168, 170; and land reform, 221; and legal education, 170, 184, 186, 187; mentioned, 205; and Organization of American States, 199; and U.S and Mexico, 214

WTO, 230

Wurtemberg, 158

Yale Law School, 189, 190

yanacona, 6, 86

yanaconazgo, 152

Yáñez, Mariano, 136

Yáñez Parladorio, Juan, 52

Yucatán, 89, 215, 219

Zacatecas, 136, 149, 196, 197

Zachariae, 140

Zapata, Emiliano, *218,* 220, 221

Zatz, Marjorie, 233

Zedillo, Ernesto, 174, 222

Zorilla, Diego de, 47, 49

Zorita, Alonso de, 43, 46

Zurita, Santiago, 48